CURIOSITY, IMAGINATION, AND PLAY

On the Development of Spontaneous Cognitive and Motivational Processes

CHILD PSYCHOLOGY

A series of books edited by **David S. Palermo**

CURIOSITY, IMAGINATION, AND PLAY

On the Development of Spontaneous Cognitive and Motivational Processes

Edited by

DIETMAR GÖRLITZ
Technical University of Berlin

JOACHIM F. WOHLWILL
The Pennsylvania State University

LEA LAWRENCE ERLBAUM ASSOCIATES, PUBLISHERS
1987   Hillsdale, New Jersey   London

Lawrence Erlbaum Associates, Inc., Publishers
365 Broadway
Hillsdale, New Jersey 07642

The cover of this book is a reproduction of the painting entitled *Children's Games* by Pieter
Breughel (1560, oil on oakwood, 46½″ × 63″; reproduced by courtesy of the Kunthistorisches
Museum, Vienna). Details of this painting introduce individual chapters in this book.

Library of Congress Cataloging-in-Publication Data

Curiosity, imagination, and play.

Revised, expanded, and updated papers presented at
a conference held September 1981 in West Berlin under
the auspices of the Technical University of Berlin
and the Deutsche Forschungsgemeinschaft.
Includes bibliographies and indexes.
1. Curiosity (Child psychology)—Congresses.
2. Imagination in children—Congresses.   3. Play—
Psychological aspects—Congresses.   4. Cognition in
children—Congresses.   5. Child psychology—Germany
(West)—Congresses.   I. Görlitz, Dietmar, 1937–
II. Wohlwill, Joachim F.   III. Technische
Universität Berlin.   IV. Deutsche Forschungsgemeinschaft.
BF723.C8C87 1986   155.4'13   86-6254

ISBN 0-89859-683-1

Printed in the United States of America
10 9 8 7 6 5 4 3 2 1

CONTENTS

PART TWO
EMPIRICAL RESEARCH AND
METHODOLOGICAL ISSUES: EXPLORATION

PREFACE

The present volume originated in a conference on curiosity, imagination, and play that was held in September 1981 under the auspices of the Technical University of Berlin and the *Deutsche Forschungsgemeinschaft* (German Research Association) in the State Library of the Prussian Cultural Foundation in Berlin (West). The president and the chancellor of the Technical University also provided much support for the resulting publication we now present. That conference brought together a group of about 15 developmental psychologists from Germany, England, and the United States who are active in research on diverse aspects of the three topics constituting the title of this book. Most of the contributors to the present volume were among the participants; additional contributors were enlisted for the purposes of this publication to provide fuller treatment of certain topics. The conference papers were revised, expanded, and updated by their authors for this edition.

The volume is intended to serve a dual purpose. On the one hand, it presents a cross section of current research and thinking on the topics of children's curiosity and exploratory activity, imaginative activity, and play and should thus serve to stimulate further work on issues that we consider to be centrally important to developmental psychology. To judge from the current ferment in this general area (notably as regards research on play), we are not alone in that judgment.

The second purpose of this book is to make readers in the English-speaking world aware of recent work done in this area by child and developmental psychologists in Germany, the hope being to promote collaboration and interchange between researchers in Germany, Great Britain, and the United States (as well as in other parts of the world). A comparison between the chapters by our German contributors and those by our British and American colleagues will reveal the many themes and perspectives they have in common, suggesting that we all have much to gain from continued contact and interaction with one another.

With that in mind, the second editor feels impelled to express his admiration for the willingness of our German-speaking contributors to submit their chapters in English and for the forebearance of the participants and audience alike regarding the decision to hold the conference in English—in deference to our guests from Great Britain and the United States. Inevitably, although the general command of the English language demonstrated by our contributors was of a high order indeed, some additional work was involved to turn our manuscript into fully publishable form. Here we find ourselves immeasurably in debt to David Antal for his valiant and painstaking editorial labors in converting these chapters into correct and, we feel, truly readable English. The assiduous and adept translation of the German editor's three chapters into English is owed completely to Mr. Antal's work.

The Museum of Art History in Vienna generously permitted the reproduction of *Children's Games*, the painting by Pieter Brueghel, the elder—at once an inexhaustible work and pictorial catalogue that we have chosen as the motto for our book. In deciding on the spelling of the artist's name, we have followed the *Art Index* currently edited by Dougan and Joel (New York: Wilson), the latest volumes of which (from No. 20, 1973, on) list him as Pieter (prior to that as Peeter) Brueghel, the elder. The use of detail reproductions of the painting, which serve in their own right to separate the various chapters of this book, goes back to the presentation of *Children's Games* in a Hungarian publication by János Kass and András Lukácsy. We are grateful to the German copyright holder, the Verlag Werner Dausien in Hanau, for allowing us to follow up this idea. Incidentally, *Children's Games* has only rarely been cited in the 31 volumes of the *Art Index* (extending from Vol. 1, 1933, to Vol. 31, 1984). By our own count, there are always entries under the name of the painter, but only four contributions devoted specifically to the painting accompanying our book. This is probably because the extensive monographs on Brueghel always treat it. The American reader will find anything of interest pertaining to this work in Grossmann,[1] who also furnishes information for decoding and identifying the games, as done by Victor de Meyere (*De Kinderspelen van Pieter Bruegel den Oude verklaard*, Antwerp, 1941) and Jeannette Hills (*Das Kinderspielbild von Pieter Bruegel d. Ä.*, Vienna, 1957). Mr. Helmut Langer (Cologne) made valuable suggestions for the design of our book's cover.

In addition to giving thanks for the receptive interest of his university and for access to the resources of his institute, the European editor is indebted to the *Deutsche Forschungsgemeinschaft* for the confidence that launched the work on this project, to his coeditor for stimulating, ever helpful collaboration, to Mr. Jack Burton of Lawrence Erlbaum Associates in Hillsdale, New Jersey, for his trusting patient cooperation and an unusual measure of support, and to Art Lizza and Jane Zalenski for their aid in preparing the manuscript. In leaving the reward servitude of a managing author, the German editor acts in the name of both in thanking Karin Albrodt-Pfeil, Daniela Birk, Martin Böcker, Brigitte Hartmann, Martina Heiche, Ralph Kroll, Beate Mutz Karin Scherrinsky, Christof Schleifer, and Elvira Valamanesh, without whose assistance this book could never have been published, and to each and every contributor for their patience and colleagiality.

Dietmar Görlitz
Joachim F. Wohlwill

[1]F. Grossmann (1973), *Pieter Bruegel: Complete Edition of the Paintings* (3rd ed.) (London: Phaidon). (Distributed in the United States by Praeger Publishers, New York).

CURIOSITY, IMAGINATION, AND PLAY

On the Development of Spontaneous Cognitive and Motivational Processes

CHAPTER ONE

INTRODUCTION

JOACHIM F. WOHLWILL
Pennsylvania State University

CURIOSITY, IMAGINATION, AND PLAY:
COMMUNALITY AND INTERRELATIONSHIPS

This volume is devoted to three interrelated concepts that are widely recognized as being of focal relevance for child and developmental psychology, and for anyone dealing with children, whether as researcher, teacher, or practitioner. Thus the question arises, what do these concepts—curiosity, imagination, and play—have in common? That question can be answered in several different ways.

Intrinsic Relevance for Child Behavior

If one were to judge from the recent and current research literature on child psychology, or from the contents of the two most recent editions of the major reference volumes covering the field (Mussen, 1970, 1983), one would come away with the impression that what children do mostly is to cognize, ad infinitum—that is, they conserve (or fail to do so), they make judgments about issues of moral conflict, they think about the behavior and motives of others, and so on. Yet, if one asks parents or teachers of preschool children what their children do most of the time, the activity most frequently mentioned would probably be "playing." Similarly, one suspects that if a mother, distraught at the behavior of her toddler in "getting into" every nook and cranny in the home, or worn out by the constant barrage of questions that her preschool child pesters her with, were asked to name her child's most conspicuous traits, the term *curious* would figure prominently among the responses.

Finally, as for imagination, even if the word itself might loom slightly less salient as a descriptor of children and their activity, the pertinence of the concept to highly diverse activities of infants and young children, from pretend play and role play to drawing and constructive play, and to the invention of imaginary companions, imaginary story characters, imaginary maps and locales, is apparent.

One answer, then, to the question posed at the outset, concerning the common theme shared by the three component topics of our volume, is that all three refer to aspects of children's behavior that are eminently "child-like." This is not to say, of course, that we do not find manifestations of play, of imagination, of curiosity, at all levels of the lifespan—as well as at subhuman levels, for that matter, at least as far as the first and last are concerned—but only that they appear with particular prominence in the behavior and activities of the

2

immature human being, from late infancy through early or perhaps middle childhood.

Neglect by Child and Developmental Psychology

The prominence of curiosity, imagination, and play in early child behavior and development is, as already intimated, sharply at variance with the relative amount of attention they have received from researchers in the field, at least until comparatively recently. To be sure, although a comprehensive history of work on these topics remains to be written, the topic of play, both in general and as an aspect of childhood, has for many years occupied the thinking of philosophers, educators, and others concerned with the development of the child. Indeed, a number of the most prominent theories of play, dating back to Darwin, were formulated in the 19th century. And throughout the early, observational phase of research on child development, descriptive accounts of both imaginative activity and play were quite common (e.g., Griffiths, 1935; Lehman & Witty, 1927; Markey, 1935). Yet one looks in vain for any comprehensive or systematic treatment of any of these three topics or of such related ones as exploratory activity, fantasy behavior, and pretend play in any of the first three editions of the *Manual of Child Psychology* (Carmichael, 1946, 1954; Mussen, 1970). Nor did they generally receive more than incidental coverage in the standard texts in the field that appeared in the 1950s and 1960s.

Fortunately, the situation has changed markedly over the past decade, especially in the United States. In the realm of curiosity and exploratory behavior, following up on the work of Hutt (e.g., Hutt, 1970) and the important theoretical analysis and review by Nunnally and Lemond (1973), we saw Keller and Voss's (1976) highly useful, comprehensive treatment of this topic. Although concerned with manifestations of curiosity and exploration in adults as well as children, it nevertheless occupies a central place in the developmental literature on the topic. The most recent translation of this volume into English (Voss & Keller, 1983) is thus all the more welcome.

With regard to imaginative and fantasy behavior, there was first of all the noteworthy publication of the work of Singer (1973) and his associates on *The Child's World of Make-Believe*, which has played a most significant role in bringing imaginative activity back into currency as a subject for empirical investigation on the part of child and developmental psychologists. This impact, and the extent of the rediscovery of this topic more generally, are given convincing testimony in Fein's (1981) most useful review of the literature on pretend play in childhood. And research on play has similarly flourished over the past 10 years, as reflected in the appearance of a number of volumes dealing with this topic (Garvey, 1977; Rubin, 1980; Yawkey & Pellegrini, 1984), as well as an admirably comprehensive review of the area in the most recent edition of the *Handbook of Child Psychology* (Rubin, Fein, & Vandenberg, 1983).

Given the central place of these three topics in the life of young children, it is hardly surprising that child and developmental psychologists would eventually find their way back to them and accord them the attention they merit. What is perhaps more surprising is the sharp decline in work on them that characterized the middle decades of this century. The answer for this seemingly anomalous situation probably lies in a feature shared by all these behaviors, one that underlies their character as "child-like"—namely, their essentially spontaneous nature. In an attempt to explain this point, we turn to a further, more substantive feature that our three topics have in common.

Motivational Basis

As just mentioned, exploration, imaginative activity, and play may all be considered as "spontaneous" forms of behavior, that is, behavior that occurs apparently in the absence of any external force or event instigating such behavior. The qualifier "apparently" is used advisedly, for in principle it is difficult to establish that such behavior is not at least partially under the control of some presently unknown set of stimuli, reward contingencies, or the like. Indeed, there are undoubtedly those who would assert that designating these kinds of activities as "spontaneous" represents no more than a cloak for our ignorance of the factors, and more especially the motivational mechanisms, that govern them. The fact remains, nevertheless, that most investigators of exploration, imaginative activity, and play, both at animal and human levels (e.g., Harlow, 1953; Singer, 1973; White, 1959) have stressed their independence from primary drive and secondary reward systems and have been inclined to consider them as "intrinsically" rather than "extrinsically" motivated.

Granting the validity of this point for a moment, if only for the sake of the argument, how might a recognition of the spontaneous or intrinsically motivated character of these activities help account for their relative neglect in the child psychology the 1950s and 1960s in the United States? The answer is not difficult to find: To the extent that the term *spontaneous* implies behavior that is not under external control, it means that it is not under the researcher's control—that is, that functional relationships between these forms of behavior and particularly independent variables manipulated by the investigator become difficult to specify and build into a research paradigm. But it is precisely during the 1950s and '60s that we found child and developmental psychologists in the United States becoming progressively more experimental in their approaches (see Wohlwill, 1973). It is thus not so surprising that they would have shied away from the study of such seemingly elusive phenomena that appeared to defy the canons of experimental methodology. Let us examine this point in more detail, as it applies to research on each of the three topics. It is readily illustrated, to begin with, in the realm of exploratory activity.

Note, first of all, that even when studied in animals, exploratory activity has generally proved a difficult phenomenon to pin down, both theoretically and methodologically. Although attempts to subsume such activity under the drive concept have not been lacking (see Fowler, 1965), they have generally remained unconvincing and far from generally accepted. It is furthermore significant that one of the primary paradigms for the study of free exploration in animals such as the rat has been via the study of "spontaneous alternation" in a maze (e.g., Glanzer, 1953)—a phrase itself suggesting a failure of effective control over the behavior on the part of the experimentalist. That feature emerges much more positively and forcefully from the accounts of animal-behavior investigators content to observe exploratory activity, such as Shillito (1963), who pointed to an animal's tendency to engage in exploration of an environment, whether familiar or unfamiliar, in the absence of any eliciting condition, given only a relative state of satiation of the primary drives.

In contrast to such instances of the recognition of the unprogrammed nature of exploration, we do find a large number of investigations that have attempted to study this topic while remaining faithful to experimental methodology, either in terms of a focus on exploration as a response to stimulus change—which is, of course, readily brought under an experimenter's control—or in terms of the manipulation of certain stimulus variables. Among the latter, particular attention has been directed at those of complexity and incongruity, which have been treated as determinants of the amount of exploration of a particular stimulus or object that an individual engages in, following the concept of "collative" properties of stimulation developed by Berlyne (1960) (see later).

These opposing tendencies have met head on in the more recent efforts to extend the methodological and theoretical conceptions of exploratory behavior to the level of child behavior. A prime example of this clash is to be found in the influential analysis of exploratory behavior by Nunnally and Lemond (1973). These writers offer a most suggestive model for conceptualizing the temporal course of a child's behavior when confronted with a novel object, starting from the initial exposure to the object and moving through exploration and manipulation to play. A further phase following the satiation of the play behavior is posited in which the child is presumed to be motivated by an arousal-enhancing need to seek out new stimuli or sources of stimulation. This analysis constitutes a most valuable extension of that which Hutt (1966, 1970) had previously presented to encompass the transition from exploration to play, although, as Josef Keller points out in the perceptive discussion in his chapter in this volume, the circumstances under which this temporal sequence can be expected to run its full course remain to be specified. Yet when Nunnally and Lemond proceed to review the literature on exploration, they confine themselves almost exclusively to research relating specific stimulus parameters such as complexity, novelty, and incongruity to the time a child spends in exploring a stimulus, or to responses of preference between alternative stimuli.

This curious discrepancy appears to reflect Nunnally and Lemond's predilection for the experimental method of research, in which given independent variables under the experimenter's control are related to dependent variables. In the process, the spontaneous, intrinsically motivated character of exploration and play is apt to become obscured, if not lost sight of altogether.

It is easy to appreciate, then, why so much of the research on exploratory activity should be confined to studies of "voluntary looking time" in response to stimuli presented to a subject whose only choice is to look at a stimulus or to refrain from doing so. A fortiori we find a ready explanation for the concomitant reluctance of experimentally minded child psychologists to undertake the study of imaginative activity and play, because these latter categories of behavior are even more difficult to subject to strict experimental control.

It is perhaps advisable at this point to note that the preceding account of the nature of exploratory activity, imagination, and play and its implications for the possible reasons for their relative neglect by researchers in the field of child psychology should not be read as an argument for rejecting the experimental method in a broader sense—far from it. Indeed, much of the most interesting recent work in this area is of an experimental nature, to the extent that the role of particular variables relevant for these forms of child behavior are systematically manipulated by the experimenter. These variables include, among others, the environmental conditions under which exploration is studied, the degree of structure of play materials, and the kind of experience provided to children in attempts to modify the amount and kind of their imaginative use of play materials. What is being argued is that the application of such experimental methodology must be reconciled with a recognition of the place of spontaneous, internally instigated behavior as central to these domains. To that extent it presupposes a willingness to study behavior whose manifestation, and the forms that it may take, cannot be completely subjected to the experimenter's control but must be given considerable opportunity to be "spontaneously" emitted. Fortunately, investigators dealing with all three of these topics have been willing to make this concession (if they experienced it as such at all) for the sake of the interest in the problem they wished to study. The result has been a mushrooming of activity on all three of these fronts, amounting to a virtual revolution in the field of developmental research and turning these topics into very live research areas indeed—as the present volume should help to demonstrate.

Interrelationships Among Curiosity, Imagination, and Play

The common bonds among the three processes that have been pointed out previously suggest that it should be possible to determine certain relationships among them in their mode of functioning in the child. Such relationships have indeed figured prominently in discussions of exploration and play, and these are examined in several different places in this volume, notably in the chapters by Schneider and by Voss, as well as this writer's (see also Wohlwill, 1984). To foreshadow the detailed discussions in these chapters to follow, it appears that exploration and play can be looked at across a dimension of time, in terms of a shift from one to the other as a child's familiarity with a stimulus object increases—though it turns out that this statement is a considerably oversimplified account of the interrelationship between them.

In the case of imaginative activity, the relationship to the remaining two is much less clear cut, in part because such activity has been in considerable measure looked at in the context of play itself, as representing one particular category of play, i.e., pretend play. The chapter by Greta Fein brings this point out most effectively. Some writers (e.g., Escalona, 1968; Singer, 1973) have, however, suggested that a child may be kept from engaging in imaginative elaboration of reality to the extent that he or she exhibits active exploratory activity. But convincing evidence for such an effect, or for the inverse correlation between these two activities that it presupposes, is difficult to come by. Furthermore, if we accept the proposition that imaginative activity is a manifestation of creativity, and if we combine that with the frequently voiced assumption that curiosity or exploration is prerequisite for creativity, we should expect rather to find a positive relationship between exploration and imaginative activity. Admittedly, the relationship between exploration and creativity itself is open to question (see Keller & Voss, 1975; Voss & Keller, 1977), but all in all it is probably unwarranted to propose too definitive a statement concerning the exploration–imagination relationship. Indeed, it may be that the two processes are fundamentally unrelated, representing, on the one hand, a process of extracting information about the environment and, on the other, a process of transcending the limits of reality as the child experiences it. Although it is of course possible that *individual differences* in the strength of these two processes are inversely correlated, there seems no apriori reason to suppose that that would be the case.

When we consider the exploration–imagination relationship developmentally, however, the picture may well be different: We may expect a shift to occur over the course of early development from exploration to imaginative elaboration of stimuli; that is, a young child or infant will be prone to explore stimuli (notably through manipulation) in order to obtain information about them, whereas older children, already more familiar with the stimuli in question, or similar ones, and better able to engage in the symbolic elaborations and transformations implied by imaginative activity, will tend to respond to these stimuli through pretend play. Precisely such a developmental sequence has indeed been demonstrated, notably by Belsky and Most (1981, see also Lowe, 1975).

If there is thus some basis for considering exploration and imaginative activity as successive phases along a developmental continuum, the issue of the developmental course of exploratory behavior remains at this point quite uncertain.

A number of the presentations in this volume provide evidence on this point. A usable—and valid—theory of exploration is perhaps one of the signal needs in this whole area and is surely deserving of attention on the part of developmental theorists. We can but hope that some of the analyses contained in various chapters in this volume may provide the impetus for such theoretical development.

RECENT AND CONTEMPORARY INFLUENCES

In spite of the commonalities and the manifold relationships among curiosity, imagination, and play, the theoretical influences and linkages to more general developments within psychology are not so readily formulated in terms of any single, cohesive set of forces or influences in the field. Rather, it seems appropriate to differentiate among at least three major directions from which researchers and theorists have come to this field, directions that have shaped the major thinking in the field discernible today.

The Influence of Berlyne

Without a doubt, the theory and research of Daniel Berlyne represents one of the salient influences on work in the area of curiosity and exploration today, and it is prominently acknowledged in a number of the chapters in the present volume. As will become apparent, however, this influence does not extend far into the realm of the other two topics of our volume, imagination and play. Note, furthermore, that Berlyne was not especially interested in child behavior and even less in developmental issues.

What, then, did Berlyne have to contribute to this area? First of all, a comprehensive, thorough, ongoing analysis of the problem of exploratory behavior as such, which he examined in part from an evolutionary perspective—that is, emphasizing the adaptive value of such activity—and in part from a functionalist standpoint, aimed at differentiating among diverse forms and components of exploration, such as observation, inspection, and manipulation. The focus is thus a strongly behaviorist one—a fact that is not surprising if we take into account Berlyne's early intellectual history, shaped as it was by the doctoral program at Yale University during the days of Hull, Miller, and their colleagues. Thus it is significant that, although *curiosity* appears in the title of Berlyne's first, and probably most influential, work—*Conflict, Arousal, and Curiosity* (Berlyne, 1960)—the term clearly takes a backseat to that of exploration and is in fact almost entirely reserved for the analysis of "epistemic behavior," that is, of search for knowledge, as exhibited by the mature human being. In any case, it is apparent that Berlyne was not interested in curiosity as a trait, or even a behavioral disposition characterizing the perpetually inquisitive toddler or young child, preferring to consider rather specific instances of investigatory and other forms of exploratory behavior.

At the same time, it is evident that Berlyne's model of exploratory activity proved to be a vigorous stimulus for research, including research on children. More than anything else, it was his concept of "collative properties" of stimuli that other researchers in the field found appealing and fruitful. In fact, although this concept was specifically intended to refer only to "specific" exploration, that is, observation or investigation of stimuli confronting an individual, and to the role of conflict and uncertainty in eliciting such activity, the very large bulk of research on children's exploration was based on this concept—probably because it permitted the investigator to study determinate functional relationships between given stimulus parameters and behavior (as pointed out previously).

As just indicated, Berlyne's contribution centered primarily on the first of our three topics, that of exploration. His attention to the subject of play was limited to a portion of a single chapter that he wrote for the second edition of the *Handbook of Social Psychology* (Berlyne, 1969), which, significantly, included the topics of laughter and humor along with that of play. It is not surprising that Berlyne should have been attracted to the problem of humor—indeed, he devoted a major part of a chapter to it in *Conflict, Arousal, and Curiosity* (Berlyne, 1960)—for humor responses have proved notably amenable to analysis in terms of one of Berlyne's central collative properties, that of incongruity (see McGhee, 1979). Play, on the other hand, was much less readily assimilated into his conceptual framework; thus it is understandable that one of his central conclusions is that psychologists would do better to dispense with the play concept altogether! That conclusion was, of course, in considerable measure based on the undeniable fact that the concept includes a great diversity of types of behavior, thus dooming from the start any attempt at formulating a single all-encompassing theory of play. At the same time one obtains the impression that Berlyne's heart was not really in even attempting a systematic analysis of play. Because he had never had occasion to examine children's spontaneous play activity, his seeming disinterest in this problem does not seem overly surprising.

There is, however, one aspect of Berlyne's theory that has proved to be of some influence for students of child play, notably through the work of Corinne Hutt (1966, 1970). It is his differentiation between "specific" and "diversive" exploration. The former consists of curiosity-instigated exploration directed at a specific stimulus or object confronting the individual, based on its collative properties. The latter, on the other hand, is primarily directed at ensuring a satisfying level of arousal for the person (e.g., to dispel boredom) and thus might be elicited by any stimulus that has that potential. It should be noted here, parenthetically, that the concept of optimal-arousal level maintenance, though not quite effectively integrated with his theory of curiosity, played a very prominent part in Berlyne's theorizing (e.g., Berlyne, 1967).

Hutt saw play as a manifestation of diversive exploration, and more particularly as a phase in a child's interaction with an originally unfamiliar object that followed upon an initial exploration phase. Once the child, by dint of manipulation, visual exploration, etc., had satisfied its curiosity about the object and its characteristics, it would, according to Hutt, shift to a play mode in interacting with the object, a shift that served the purpose of maintaining a satisfying arousal level for the child. Note that in this conception play serves little purpose in its own right, e.g., in terms of any involvement of symbolic activity, problem-solving, or other cognitive or social ends.

Be that as it may, it is proper that we acknowledge Hutt's signal contribution (partly with the collaboration of her associate, Miranda Hughes), which was to devise a conceptual as well as operationally feasible basis for differentiating between exploration and play—despite frequent assertions both before and since that these concepts cannot be consistently disentangled one from the other. It was in fact Hutt's identification of play with diversive exploration that permitted her to establish a basis for such a differentiation in terms of the overall level of arousal, tension, etc. displayed by the child in each of these activities (e.g., Hughes & Hutt, 1979; Hutt, 1966). Although one might argue that some forms of play, such as constructive play, do not conform to her characterization of play as devoid of tension or as lacking focus on the object, it is undeniable that Hutt and Hughes, following up on Berlyne's formulation, have made a promising start for others working in this field.

The Neopsychoanalytic Influence

One would have to go through the collected works of Freud (and those of his daughter, Anna, as well) with a very fine comb indeed to come across references to the topic of curiosity or exploration; it is difficult to reconcile with the libidinal model of behavior on which Freudian theory is based. As for imagination and play, the analysis of fantasy obviously plays a very central role in the theorizing, as well as the practice, of psychoanalytically oriented therapists; similarly, we can identify a psychoanalytic theory of play, building on the concept of projection and emphasizing the expression of sub or unconscious wishes, feelings, and thoughts. The field of play therapy is to a considerable extent based on such a view.

If that were all to the psychoanalytic approach to the topics of our volume, it would not need to detain us long, because it would not seem to have very much to offer in helping us to understand imagination and play as phenomena of normal child behavior in their own right, much less of their development in the normal child. But as it happens, neo-Freudian psychologists and psychoanalysts have been concerned with these phenomena, and with exploration and curiosity as well, in a much more intrinsically relevant way and have, in fact, occupied a position of considerable influence in the development of this field.

This is true in particular of Robert White (1959), whose article on competence motivation has surely been one of the most widely read and cited in child and developmental psychology. It was the particular merit of White's paper to have brought to the fore the very similar limitations of the experimentalist's views of the primacy of drive reduction in motivating behavior and those of the orthodox Freudians, committed to a libidinal energy view of motivation. He pointed quite specifically to children's play as a prime example of behavior that could not adequately be encompassed within the views of motivation current at that time and suggested his concept of "effectance motivation" as an alternative.

The work of Susan Harter (e.g., Harter, 1978) represents a prime example of a fruitful approach to research that has been built directly on White's analysis; in a larger sense, the recent work on intrinsic motivation (Deci, 1975; Lepper, 1980) has been carried out in the same framework. But White was by no means the only psychoanalytically oriented psychologist to have left a mark on this field. There are, first of all, the psychoanalysts with an ego-psychological orientation—of whom Hartmann was probably the most notable example—who emphasized motivation based on the development of competence and of mastery, though he did so motivated less by a particular interest in child behavior or its development than by clinical concerns.

In a rather different vein, we may point to the writings of Schachtel (1959)— unjustly neglected by developmental psychologists, in the mind of this writer— who out of an initial interest in childhood amnesia elaborated a developmental theory of the individual's response to stimulation in the different modalities, a theory that in many ways foreshadowed such formulations as Berlyne's distinction between specific and diversive exploration as well as this writer's own between inspective and affective exploration (Wohlwill, 1981). What makes Schachtel's contribution noteworthy, as argued more extensively in this writer's chapter in the present volume, is its developmental focus. He suggests a shift with age in the child's mode of engaging the world of environmental stimuli, from one centered on affective gratification to one with a primary informational (i.e., curiosity-based) aim. Related to that differentiation is one relating to the sensory modalities that are primary in the child's exploration of its world: At the youngest ages, that is, during the heyday of the "autocentric" mode, the senses of smell, taste, and touch are thought to be primary; subsequently, as the child shifts into the "allocentric" mode, the distance senses of vision and audition replace the former, in Schachtel's view. (Here, incidentally, is found the link to the phenomenon of childhood amnesia, which Schachtel traced back to this shift in the sensory modalities that are dominant at different stages of the child's development.)

In a broader sense, Schachtel's analysis, like White's, is predicated on a recognition of the inadequacy of a conflict or drive model of motivation such as that underlying orthodox Freudian psychology, and of the predominantly autonomous, conflict-free character of the small child's transactions with its environment. In Schachtel's writings, and in those of the other neo-Freudians, we find the concepts of libidinal energy, oedipal conflict, etc. being replaced by more cognitive-toned views of children's exploration and play, focused on a reality-oriented mode of relating to the environment, as well as on the construction of both a real and an imaginary world elaborated by the child.

A significant further direction in recent and current research on imagination and play, reflecting in some sense an extension of the neopsychoanalytic framework (albeit with a more strongly developed cognitive slant) is to be found in the work of Singer and his associates (Singer, 1973). Here we find a systematic account of pretend play from a functional perspective, emphasizing the positive value for the child's general development of such activities as daydreaming, pretend play, and other manifestations of the child's fantasy. However indebted to both the neo-Freudian and the Piagetian perspectives, Singer has taken aspects of both and succeeded in creating a synthesis that qualifies as a new and original formulation, one that has more recently been extended in several important directions. Thus, Singer and Singer (1976) have studied children's responses to fantasy material in the media, and on television in particular. A further important direction that the Singers and their associates (e.g., Freyberg, 1973) have taken in their research involves attempts to train children to play—that is, to improve the quality of the child's play through directed experience—a focus that has come to play a prominent part in much recent research on play (e.g., Dansky, 1980; Saltz, Dixon, & Johnson, 1977).

The Piagetian and Related Cognitive Influences

Piaget occupied himself but little with the kinds of problems that are the focus of our volume. To be sure, one of his early works touched incidentally on children's games, through his well-known work on the ontogenesis of the understanding of rules (Piaget, 1932), but it is fair to say that here the interest in play per se was subordinate to his interest in the development of the child's cognitive world. Even his much more influential volume, *Play, Dreams, and Imitation in Childhood* (Piaget, 1962), which, as the title suggests, is quite directly related to some of the themes of our book, proved to represent no more than a way station along the path of Piaget's formulation of the total course of cognitive development.

It seems particularly significant that the title of Piaget's book in the original was *La Formation du symbole chez l'enfant*. Nothing could establish more convincingly the strong cognitive, not to say ratiomorphic flavor characterizing Piaget's theory. This focus on symbolic activity represents a view of play that, although related to the neo-Freudian one, constitutes a separate approach in its own right. This focus had, indeed, proved a potent influence among contemporary researchers on play, as shown in the work of Fein, and of Gardner and his associates (see Chapters 14 and 15 in this volume), along with a substantial body of other work (e.g., Garvey, 1977; Hughes, Chapter 12, this volume; Nicolich, 1977; see also the reviews by Fein, 1981 and Rubin, Fein, & Vandenberg, 1983).

These various approaches to research on play go well beyond Piaget's assimilation-accommodation framework in important respects, and in their symbolism perspective they appear at times more akin to the structuralist view of language development. The emphasis here is on the child's transformation of reality through pretend activity and on the elaboration of roles and other play elements through symbolic processes, analyzed in a fashion akin to that of the structural linguistics approach.

This dominance of a cognitive orientation towards play and imaginative activity is hardly surprising if one considers the preeminent position of cognition in developmental psychology over the past two decades. It undoubtedly has made important contributions to our understanding of central aspects of play, particularly as regards the problem-solving side of play, the inferential aspect of sociodramatic and role play, and the role of symbolism and language in pretend play. Whether it has succeeded in doing full justice to all these phenomena is an open question. One suspects that there are some cognitive aspects to children's imaginative and creative activity (e.g., in the elaboration of an imaginary companion, in the invention of games and of imaginary physical and biological systems) that may require a model of cognitive activity even further removed from the logic-inspired one of Piaget, or from the models rooted in concrete social and linguistic experience that appear to dominate much of the work in this field. The previously mentioned work of Singer and his associates may point the way to the loosening of the theoretical structures that the somewhat elusive quality of children's imagination calls for.

Concluding Comment

It is important to recognize that the three aforementioned influences on current work and thinking on the three themes of our volume by no means exhaust the impressive range of work that is taking place. In the realm of exploratory activity, for instance, a flourishing approach quite divorced from the Berlyne-Hutt framework is that based on the work of Ainsworth and her colleagues (Ainsworth, Blehar, Waters, & Wall, 1978), which looks at relationships between exploratory activity and mother–child attachment, especially in infancy. It is significant that here the focus is more on exploration of the environment than on exploration of particular objects, and the processes involved are correspondingly different (see Wohlwill, 1981). It is also worth noting that exploration is considered here as a dimension of individual differences, i.e., in terms of the correlates of a given infant's disposition to engage in environmental exploration. We return to this aspect of our topics and its relevance for a full-fledged developmental analysis of them in the concluding section of this chapter.

In the realm of play we find an even greater diversity of directions beyond those noted earlier. Among approaches that have gained prominence in recent years are those derived from behavioral ecology (e.g., Smith & Connolly, 1980) and from an interest in environmental experience (Moore, in press). Nor should we slight approaches stressing the social-interaction side of play (e.g., Eifermann, 1971; Smith & Connolly, 1972) and sociocultural and anthropological views of the field (e.g., Schwartzman, 1978; Sutton-Smith, 1981). It is indeed a broad and diversified field, as well as currently a very vigorously evolving one, and thus one may look forward to new trends and influences that will undoubtedly further transform this field beyond its somewhat amorphous shape today.

THE PRESENT VOLUME IN CONTEXT

Historical Trends on the European Continent

The preceding overview of this volume's topic and its recent history makes no claim to presenting a comprehensive, thorough treatment of either the historical trends or the current themes in this area. It is primarily intended to provide some context for the material to follow. But even in that aim it is glaringly deficient in at least one major respect: It is clearly written from the perspective of an American psychologist most intimately familiar with the work that has been carried out in the United States and to a lesser extent in Great Britain. Yet the overwhelming majority of the chapters in this volume are written by European— and predominantly German—psychologists. Indeed, a major purpose that we hope this volume serves is to introduce the work of our German colleagues to English-speaking readers. We had hoped, in fact, to include a chapter presenting the historical evolution of the field as it has taken place in Europe, but we were unsuccessful. Under the circumstances, let it suffice to indicate very briefly some of the major theoretical and empirical trends at work in research on play and curiosity on the European continent and to place the contributions to this volume in the context of these trends, as well as those delineated in the preceding pages.

In contrast to the several editions of the Carmichael *Manual of Child Psychology*, the volume on developmental psychology of the *Handbuch der Psychologie* (Thomae, 1959) contains a chapter dealing with play by Rüssel (1959)— though it is surely significant that the chapter is entitled *Play and work in human development*. An examination of that chapter reveals that the early history of the study of play in Europe was in some ways similar to that in the United States— that is, it was predominantly atheoretical and descriptive, except for the purely theoretical and typically speculative accounts given of play by philosophers and some psychologists, accounts that have been frequently reviewed (e.g., Berlyne, 1969). Perhaps the dominant influence, at least in Germany and Austria, was the work of both Karl and Charlotte Bühler, the former through his functional exercise theory of play (K. Bühler, 1930), the latter through her more general work in child psychology (C. Bühler, 1931) in which the topic of play figures prominently, just as was true of the work of William Stern and his associates (see Stern, 1930). Thus, Charlotte Bühler, with her associate Hildegard Hetzer, undertook extensive surveys of time spent in play and of the relative incidence of play of different types—e.g., function, fantasy, and constructive play, and sociocultural games (see Bühler, 1931; Bühler & Hetzer, 1927; Hetzer, 1927). This account of the prewar state of research on play might well be extended to cover the rest of the European continent. In France, the only country on the continent that might have rivaled Germany for contributions to developmental psychology, it does not seem that play was a major research topic, though Claparède, Piaget's mentor, did make references to it, notably in conjunction with the theory of Groos (e.g., Claparède, 1934). As we have already seen, the appearance of Piaget's *La Formation du Symbole* did not essentially alter this situation.

Main Themes of the Present Volume

If we now examine the present volume, with its impressive cross section of German and other European contributions, it becomes apparent that the problems addressed and the methodologies employed derive in a number of instances from American psychology rather than from the earlier history of the field in European child psychology—a phenomenon that appears to characterize much of contemporary Germany psychology since its revival following the ravages of the Nazi era and World War II. Thus, we have a major focus on the problem of exploration as formulated by Berlyne and extended by Hutt, and its relationship to play (see the chapters by Josef Keller, Voss, and by Schneider).

In a rather different vein, the elegant experimental research reported by Papoušek and his associates on infants' physiological and behavioral responses in their exploration of stimuli while interacting with their mothers brings to mind some of the work conducted in the infant laboratories in the United States, particularly in regard to the methodological refinements exhibited, but it is apparent that the conceptualization of this work is wholly that of this major European investigator.

The chapter by Heidi Keller and her associates represents yet a different case. It combines a concern for the early manifestations of exploration as considered by infant and child psychologists in the United States with a more particular interest in the role of different sensory modalities in this realm. In this respect the chapter recalls the aforementioned work of Schachtel (1959), although for Keller et al. the major focus is more on individual differences in children's use of the various modalities than on developmental shifts in this regard.

A number of further chapters provide clearer exceptions to the predominance of themes taken over from American psychology. Moch's intriguing work on children's questions clearly gets at the heart of the problem of curiosity, but from an approach and a perspective differing markedly from the much more typical exploratory-activity approach with which we have become familiar. Indeed, there is very scant literature on this problem, though Tizard in England has recently begun systematic research on it (Tizard, Hughes, Carmichael, & Pinkerton, 1983). Similarly, Görlitz's attempt to interrelate attribution theory and curiosity and to investigate the latter under highly naturalistic conditions is a most original contribution, one that—though attribution theory itself has of course been developed in the Unites States—brings an entirely new and fresh perspective to the problem of curiosity. Another, quite different, view of play is to be found in Burtchen's contribution, with its action-theory framework, and its focus on children's understanding of the rules of a game, reminiscent of Piaget's (1932) early work. Finally, we have Heckhausen's essay on what we might call *intrinsic motivation* in children (though Heckhausen does not use the term) and on the role of achievement motivation in children's play activities. This is another contribution that certainly owes no debt to any non-European perspective or theory but rather serves to reveal the thinking of one of the major figures in psychology on the contemporary European scene and perhaps to introduce his ideas to some developmental psychologists from the English-speaking world who might not have been familiar with them.

In sum, this volume provides a sampling of current German work on curiosity and play along with a scattering of contributions on the same topics from other European countries and the United States. If it cannot lay much claim to unity and cohesiveness, it does at least concentrate on a delimited number of topics and issues in a way that makes at times for a welcome sense of interrelatedness among the individual contributions. For instance, Schneider's research ties in very clearly and directly with Voss's theoretical analysis of the interrelationships between exploration and play and indeed corroborates some of the latter's statements in this regard. Similarly, Heidi Keller's work on exploration in infancy and early childhood affords many points of contact with the theoretical analyses provided by Voss and Josef Keller. Yet her attention to the role of manipulative responses in exploration calls attention to a major category of exploratory behavior that has not always received its due in analyses of such behavior in childhood. Finally, it might be interesting to consider the principles of children's questions presented by Moch in the light of Görlitz's discussion of exploratory behavior and its kinship with attributional psychology.

TOWARDS A VIABLE DEVELOPMENTAL APPROACH TO THE STUDY OF EXPLORATION, IMAGINATIVE ACTIVITY, AND PLAY

A concluding comment is in order concerning both the state of research on these three topics generally and the work and thinking contained in the chapters of this volume. For all the significant advances we have seen in recent years and the evident vigor marking the field today, it appears to be characterized as a whole by two salient, closely interrelated characteristics that, taken together, may not be wholly favorable for arriving at a comprehensive theory of the development of any of these three forms of child behavior, and even less for a full understanding of their interdependence.

The field is dominated first of all by what Emmerich (1968) has called a *classical* developmental approach, as opposed to a differential one—that is, there has been a relative neglect and disregard of individual differences among children and of the correlates of those differences. Second, the behaviors have been studied as relatively specific types of overt behaviors exhibited in a particular situation rather than as a child's broader disposition to display a certain behavioral tendency or trait.

As already intimated, these two characteristics are in fact part and parcel of the same dominant approach to the field, which is more interested in children's behavior as manifestations of a particular phenomenon than in its generality or its significance as an attribute of a particular child. The difference is nicely illustrated in contrasting studies of children's exploratory activity, as represented in the work inspired by Berlyne (or, in the present volume, that reported by Schneider) with the research carried out by Maw and Maw (1978). These latter writers treat *curiosity* as a trait that different children possess to varying degrees and study its relationships to other aspects of the child's behavior and personality. A similar point could be made for the contrast between studies of sociodramatic or pretend play (such as Fein's) and Lieberman's (1977) work on "playfulness," considered as a dimension of individual differences among children, or Singer's (1973) similar work on the correlates of different degrees of "imaginativeness" in children.

These aspects of the field are discussed and elaborated more fully in the chapter by Josef Keller with particular reference to the topic of exploration. Let us consider here only the question of the relevance of these twin factors—i.e., attention to individual differences and the situational specificity or generality of the behaviors studied—for an understanding of the developmental significance of exploration, imaginative activity, and play. For there is a very real possibility that a comprehensive account of the developmental history of these forms of behavior will only come about once we examine interrelations among different but functionally related behaviors across development. It may prove inadequate to confine ourselves to examining changes with age (or, more typically, differences among age groups) with respect to a particular form of exploration, of pretend play, of constructive play, etc. Rather we may need to consider possible instances of "heterotypic continuity" (Kagan, 1971; Wohlwill, 1973) involving relationships between a variable X at one age and a *different* variable Y studied at a subsequent age. In fact, none of the behaviors that are the subject of this volume can be profitably studied across a significant segment of the age continuum—indeed, one of the supposed characteristics of imaginative and artistic activity is that it declines with age beyond the preschool year (e.g., Ames

& Learned, 1946; Gardner & Winner, 1982). But a broader conceptualization of our variables, based on closer attention to their developmental history might well disclose instances of heterotypic continuity, involving, for instance, a relationship between one mode of play at one age and a different mode of imaginative activity at a subsequent one. The only concrete example of this kind known to this writer is the tantalizing report by Hutt and Bhavnani (1972) that in a group of boys, but not of girls, amount of exploration of a novel object during the preschool years was predictive of creativity scores at age 9, based on the children's performance on one of Torrance's tests of creativity.

Additional research of this type, and especially more systematic, fine-grained analyses of the developmental course of the forms of expression of exploration, imagination, play, and creativity as children develop from preschool through adolescence will surely further our understanding of the significance of these forms of behavior from a developmental standpoint. Thus, manifestations of imaginative activity and pretend play in the preschool years may well be a more promising bet as possible precursors of later creative or artistic attainment; an examination of sociodramatic play in early childhood from the standpoint of its continuity with subsequent forms of social cognition and person perception would similarly appear worthwhile.

Given the vitality and ferment that characterizes this field of research today on both sides of the Atlantic, there is reason for optimism that significant advances in our understanding of our three topics and of their developmental significance will be forthcoming. We hope that the present volume conveys some of this sense of vitality and, above all, that it will promote more effective communication and interaction among American and European researchers in this field so as to stimulate new ideas and new advances.

REFERENCES

Ainsworth, M. D. S., Blehar, M. C., Waters, E., & Wall, S. (1978). *Patterns of attachment: A psychological study of the strange situation*. Hillsdale, NJ: Lawrence Erlbaum Associates.

Ames, L. B., & Learned, J. (1946). Imaginary companions and related phenomena. *Journal of Genetic Psychology, 69,* 147–167.

Belsky, J., & Most, R. (1981). From exploration to play: A cross-sectional study of infant free-play behavior. *Developmental Psychology, 17,* 630–639.

Berlyne, D. E. (1960). *Conflict, arousal, and curiosity*. New York: McGraw–Hill.

Berlyne, D. E. (1967). Arousal and reinforcement. In D. Levine (Ed.), *Nebraska Symposium on Motivation* (Vol. 15, pp. 1–110). Lincoln: University of Nebraska Press.

Berlyne, D. E. (1969). Laughter, humor, and play. In G. Lindzey & E. Aronson (Eds.), *The handbook of social psychology* (Vol. 3, 2nd ed., pp. 795–852). Reading, MA: Addison Wesley.

Bühler, C. (1931). *Kindheit und Jugend* (3rd ed.). Leipzig: Hirzel.

Bühler, C., & Hetzer, H. (1927). Inventar der Verhaltensweisen des ersten Lebensjahres. *Quellen und Studien zur Jugendkunde, 5,* 125–150.

Bühler, K. (1930). *The mental development of the child.* New York: Harcourt, Brace. (Original German edition published 1918)

Carmichael, L. (Ed.) (1946). *Manual of child psychology.* New York: Wiley.

Carmichael, L. (Ed.) (1954). *Manual of child psychology* (2nd ed.). New York: Wiley.

Claparède, E. (1934). Sur la nature et la function du jeu. *Archives de Psychologie* (Genève), *24,* 350–369.

Dansky, J. L. (1980). Cognitive consequences of sociodramatic play and exploration training for economically disadvantaged preschoolers. *Journal of Child Psychology and Psychiatry, 20,* 47–58.

Deci, E. L. (1975). *Intrinsic motivation.* New York: Plenum.

Eifermann, R. R. (1971). Social play in childhood. In R. E. Herron & B. Sutton-Smith (Eds.), *Child's play* (pp. 270–297). New York: Wiley.

Emmerich, W. (1968). Personality development and concepts of structure. *Child Development, 39,* 671–690.

Escalona, S. K. (1968). *The roots of individuality.* New York: Basic Books.

Fein, G. G. (1981). Pretend play in childhood: An integrative review. *Child Development, 52,* 1095–1118.

Fowler, H. F. (1965). *Curiosity and exploratory behavior.* New York: Macmillan.

Freyberg, J. T. (1973). Increasing the imaginative play of urban disadvantaged kindergarten children through systematic training. In J. Singer (Ed.), *The child's world of make-believe* (pp. 129–154). New York: Academic Press.

Gardner, H. E., & Winner, E. (1982). First imitations of artistry. In S. Strauss (Ed.), *U-shaped behavioral growth* (pp. 147–168). New York: Academic Press.

Garvey, C. (1977). *Play.* Cambridge, MA: Harvard University Press.

Glanzer, M. (1953). Stimulus satiation: An explanation of spontaneous alternation. *Psychological Review, 60,* 257–268.

Griffiths, R. (1935). *The study of imagination in early childhood and its function in mental development.* London: Routledge.

Harlow, H. F. (1953). Mice, monkeys, men, and motives. *Psychological Review, 60,* 23–32.

Harter, S. (1978). Effectance motivation reconsidered: Toward a developmental model. *Human Development, 21,* 34–64.

Hetzer, H. (1927). Das Volkstümliche Kinderspiel. *Wiener Arbeiten zur Pädagogischen Psychologie,* 6.

Hughes, M., & Hutt, C. (1979). Heart-rate correlates of childhood activities: Play, exploration, problem-solving and day-dreaming. *Biological Psychology, 8,* 253–263.

Hutt, C. (1966). Exploration and play in children. *Symposia of the Zoological Society,* London, *18,* 61–81.

Hutt, C. (1970). Specific and diversive exploration. In H. W. Reese & L. P. Lipsitt (Eds.), *Advances in child development and behavior* (Vol. 5, pp. 120–180). New York: Academic Press.

Hutt, C., & Bhavnani, R. (1972). Predictions from play. *Nature, 237,* 171–172.

Kagan, J. (1971). *Change and continuity in infancy.* New York: Wiley.

Keller, H., & Voss, H.-G. (1975). Neugier, Exploration und Kreativität. *Bericht über den 29. Kongress der Deutschen Gesellschaft für Psychologie,* 157–159.

Keller, H., & Voss, H.-G. (1976). *Neugier und Exploration.* Stuttgart: Kohlhammer.

Lehman, H. C., & Witty, P. Z. (1927). *The psychology of play activities.* New York: Barnes.

Lepper, M., R. (1980). Intrinsic and extrinsic motivation in children: Detrimental effects of superfluous social controls. In W. A. Collins (Ed.), *Minnesota symposium on child development* (Vol. 14, pp. 155–214). Hillsdale, NJ: Lawrence Erlbaum Associates.

Lieberman, J. N. (1977). *Playfulness: Its relationship to imagination and creativity.* New York: Academic Press.

Lowe, M. (1975). Trends in the development of representational play in infants from one to three years: An observational study. *Journal of Child Psychology and Psychiatry, 16,* 33–47.

Markey, F. (1935). Imaginative behavior of young children. *Child Development Monographs, 18.*

Maw, W. H., & Maw, E. W. (1978). Nature and assessment of human curiosity. In P. McReynolds (Ed.), *Advances in psychological assessment* (Vol. 4, pp. 526–571). San Francisco: Jossey–Bass.

McGhee, P. E. (1979). *Humor: Its origin and development.* San Francisco: Freeman.

Moore, G. T. (in press). The role of the socio-physical environment in cognitive development. In C. S. Weinstein & T. G. David (Eds.), *Spaces for children: The built environment and child development.* New York: Plenum.

Mussen, P. H. (Ed.). (1970). *Carmichael's manual of child psychology* (3rd ed., 2 vols.). New York: Wiley.

Mussen, P. H. (Ed.). (1983). *Handbook of child psychology* (4th ed., 4 vols.). New York: Wiley.

Nicolich, L. (1977). Beyond sensorimotor intelligence: Assessment of symbolic maturity through analysis of pretend play. *Merrill–Palmer Quarterly, 33,* 89–99.

Nunnally, J. C., & Lemond, C. (1973). Exploratory behavior and human development. In H. W. Reese (Ed.), *Child development and behavior* (Vol. 8, pp. 59–108). New York: Academic Press.

Piaget, J. (1932). *The moral judgment of the child.* New York: Harcourt, Brace. (Original French ed. published 1932)

Piaget, J. (1962). *Play, dreams and imitation in childhood.* New York: Norton. (Original French edition published as *La formation du symbole chez l'enfant,* Neuchâtel: Delachaux & Niestlé, 1946.)

Rubin, K. H. (Ed.). (1980). *Children's play.* San Francisco: Jossey–Bass. (*New directions for child development,* #9)

Rubin, K. H., Fein, G. G., & Vandenberg, B. (1983). Play. In P. H. Mussen (Ed.), *Handbook of child psychology* (4th ed., Vol. 4, pp. 693–774). New York: Wiley.

Rüssel, A. (1959). Spiel und Arbeit in der menschlichen Entwicklung. In H. Thomae (Ed.), *Entwicklungspsychologie.* (*Handbuch der Psychologie,* Vol. 3, pp. 50–534). Göttingen: Hogrefe.

Saltz, E., Dixon, D., & Johnson, J. (1977). Training disadvantaged preschoolers on various fantasy activities: Effects on cognitive functioning and impulse control. *Child Development, 48,* 367–380.

Schachtel, E. G. (1959). *Metamorphosis: On the development of affect, perception, attention and memory.* New York: Basic Books.

Schwartzman, H. B. (1978). *Transformations: The anthropology of children's play.* New York: Plenum.

Shillito, E. E. (1963). Exploratory behavior in the short-tailed vole, *Microtus agrestis. Behaviour, 21,* 145–154.

Singer, D. G., & Singer, J. L. (1976). Family television viewing habits and the spontaneous play of preschool children. *American Journal of Orthopsychiatry, 46,* 496–502.

Singer, J. L. (1973). *The child's world of make-believe: Experimental studies of imaginative play.* New York: Academic Press.

Smith, P. K., & Connolly, K. (1972). Patterns of play and social interaction in preschool children. In N. Blurton Jones (Ed.), *Ethological studies of child behavior* (pp. 65–96). Cambridge, England: Cambridge University Press.

Smith, P. K., & Connolly, K. J. (1980). *The ecology of preschool behaviour.* Cambridge, England: Cambridge University Press.

Stern, W. (1930). *Psychology of early childhood: Up to the sixth year of life* (2nd ed.). New York: Holt. (First German edition published 1914)

Sutton-Smith, B. (1981). *A history of children's play: The New Zealand playground, 1840–1950.* Philadelphia: University of Pennsylvania Press.

Thomae, H. (Ed.). (1959). *Entwicklungspsychologie.* (*Handbuch der Psychologie,* Vol. 3). Göttingen: Hogrefe.

Tizard, B., Hughes, M., Carmichael, H., & Pinkerton, G. (1983). Children's questions and adults' answers. *Journal of Child Psychology and Psychiatry, 24*, 269–281.

Voss, H.-G., & Keller, H. (1977). Critical evaluation of the obscure figures test as an instrument for measuring "cognitive innovation." *Perceptual and Motor Skills, 45*, 495–502.

Voss, H.-G., & Keller, H. (1983). *Curiosity and exploration: Theory and results.* New York: Academic Press.

White, R. W. (1959). Motivation reconsidered: The concept of competence. *Psychological Review, 66*, 297–323.

Wohlwill, J. F. (1973). *The study of behavioral development.* New York: Academic Press.

Wohlwill, J. F. (1981). A conceptual analysis of exploratory behavior: The "specific–diversive" distinction revisited. In H. I. Day (Ed.), *Advances in intrinsic motivation and aesthetics* (pp. 341–364). New York: Plenum.

Wohlwill, J. F. (1984). Relationships between exploration and play. In T. D. Yawkey & A. D. Pellegrini (Eds.), *Child's play: Developmental and applied* (pp. 143–170). Hillsdale, NJ: Lawrence Erlbaum Associates.

Yawkey, T. D., & Pellegrini, A. D. (Eds.). (1984). *Child's play: Developmental and applied.* Hillsdale, NJ: Lawrence Erlbaum Associates.

PART ONE
OVERVIEW OF THE PRESENT AND THEORETICAL PROBLEMS

CHAPTER TWO

MOTIVATIONAL ASPECTS OF EXPLORATORY BEHAVIOR

JOSEF A. KELLER
University of Würzburg

In a posthumous book fragment, Berlyne (1978) repeatedly and explicitly points out the importance and necessity of developing a theory of motivation for explaining human behavior. This can be thoroughly appreciated if it is realized that psychologists try to explain such important phenomena as activation, orientation or direction, persistence, and reinforcement of subjective experience and behavior by drawing on motivational theories (see Keller, 1981).

It is hardly surprising, then, that motivation psychologists view exploratory behavior in much the same way, asking about its activation, direction, persistence, and reinforcement. According to a new view, this catalogue should be expanded by adding the important question concerning the change from one activity to another (Atkinson & Birch, 1970, 1978). Except for the research of Hutt (1970) or Nunnally and Lemond (1973), this latter aspect has not yet found much consideration in the investigation of exploratory and curiosity behavior. Schneider, Moch, and Auerswald (1982) also demonstrated the transitions or changes between various forms of curiosity and exploratory behavior. The most systematic effort to give an answer to these "motivational questions" was presumably made by Hunt (1963a). Berlyne's theory (1960, 1963a, 1967)—certainly the most elaborate work to explain exploratory behavior—also offers a fairly extensive answer to the stated questions. Equally noteworthy is the attempt of McReynolds (1956, 1971) to offer suitable answers on the basis of his cognitive theory.

It would surely be profitable to draw a critical comparison between the answers that have been offered to these questions from different quarters. Hunt (1963a) has already done that for the classical drive theory, distinguishing it from a more cognitively oriented theory. Although many of these questions are touched upon, the primary concern in this chapter is to examine some other aspects of existing theories of exploratory behavior and to analyze some of their hypotheses and ideas for motivational facets in order to point out some deficiences and problems that could and should be tackled soon.

Several main problem areas that emerged from a careful review of the relevant literature, especially recent work, are discussed in detail under the following questions:

1. The basic question of the specificity or generality of the postulated motivational basis of exploratory behavior.

2. The question of the possible influence that differential or dispositional factors may have, e.g., that there may be motives that may vary from individual to individual—an aspect of exploratory behavior that has been almost forgotten because of emphasis on situational determinants.

3. The question of possible relationships between exploratory behavior and emotion.

4. The question of the intrinsic versus extrinsic character of exploratory behavior.

5. The question of the development of exploratory behavior and the motivational basis underlying this development.

Although the developmental significance of the fifth topic is obvious, it is rather questionable for the first four. In these topics, more general or basic problems are discussed, problems concerning questions that must be answered, as far as possible, before any fruitful motivational-developmental investigation can be conducted. To some extent, the first four topics also entail problems that are significant in the developmental sense, such as the question of the development and change of traits like curiosity, of emotional components of exploratory behavior, and of intrinsic versus extrinsic motivation of behavior.

SPECIFICITY VERSUS GENERALITY

To analyze the *specificity* or *generality* of the motivational basis for exploratory behavior, it is essential to define these terms clearly and to avoid their inaccurate, even contradictory, application. Often these terms seem to be interchangeable denotations for the same phenomenon. Therefore it is necessary to deal first with the tasks of disentangling the existing confusion of terms (see Keller, 1981, p. 239, for example) and of precisely defining terms like *exploration, manipulation, curiosity behavior, spontaneous activity, play, imagination, aesthetic behavior*, and *stimulation seeking*. Furthermore, one has to clarify the relation between the single kinds or tendencies of subjective experience and behavior. That means one must clarify whether, for example, curiosity is regarded as a motivational condition for exploratory behavior, whether "curiosity behavior" is a synonym for "exploration," whether manipulation or stimulation seeking are only components of exploratory behavior, or whether they represent separate and independent phenomena sui generis. After such classification the question of the motivational basis underlying the individual patterns of experience or behavior will be seen in a new and perhaps clearer light. Past attempts to shed light on the motivation of exploratory behavior can be regarded to some extent as a reaction to the existing variety of terms. Thus a number of authors postulated different "drives" or "motives," e.g., manipulation drive, boredom drive, manipulation motives, exploratory drive, sensory drive, and information drive. Apart from the fact that such attempts to postulate specific drives or motives for certain behavior patterns keep running the definite risk of circular definition, they do little more than merely describe the corresponding behavior. By contrast, some authors (e.g., White, 1959) have tried to assume a general motivational basis for all behavioral manifestations of personal or social competence. Although White's work is quite valuable—especially because of its integrative effect, which cannot and should not be denied—it must not be overlooked that such a general view more or less frustrates the necessary analysis that differentiates patterns of behavior and experience and that the frequent citation of White might rather indicate the psychologist's understandable preference for an economy of ideas and concepts.

There are many studies with different methodological approaches (observation, experiment, factor analysis) that show the complexity and heterogeneity of the different constructs and that suggest splitting them up into several subconstructs. Such further differentiation is, in my opinion, at present appropriate for an adequate scientific investigation of the motivational bases of exploratory behavior. From the studies cited previously, the following constructs or subconstructs resulted: curiosity, need for variety, need for novelty, sensation seeking, novelty experience, effectance and competence, exploration, spontaneous activity, and play.

Berlyne's distinction between specific and diversive exploration, which in the meantime has been empirically tested several times, can be regarded as an example of a differentiating approach, too. The activation of these different behavior patterns is explained in a highly speculative way by means of two different motivational processes, and their reinforcement is said to be caused by the function of two different mechanisms of reinforcement (see Berlyne, 1963b, 1971a, p. 100).

The question of the specificity or generality of exploratory behavior patterns and the related question of the underlying motivational basis also arises, especially if one considers the different efforts to show sequences or flows of exploratory behavior. Hutt (1970) speaks in a rather vague way of an irreversible sequence of specific exploration → diversive exploration. Vandenberg (1978) postulates a sequence of exploration—play—application to make clear the mediating role of play for the development of significant adaptive strategies that are ontogenetically and phylogenetically important. Nunnally and Lemond (1973, p. 63), Crozier (1974, p. 32), and Keller and Voss (1976, p. 50) offer more or less comprehensive flow diagrams of exploratory behavior. Crozier and Keller and Voss remain within Berlyne's terminology and merely illustrate brief cause–effect relationships for certain behavior patterns, whereas Nunnally and Lemond try to put different exploratory behavior patterns into an interrelated temporal sequence and to attach them to corresponding internal processes of the organism.

At first sight such an attempt at integration naturally meets general approval. But one must ask what is gained by these efforts, especially when one comes to know that the authors make the emergence of the total sequence dependent on the presence of suitably stimulating objects. The viability of such an integrated sequential view therefore remains limited to a few special situations, and no one of them can claim general validity for all situations and all types of exploratory behavior. Moreover, such a schema in my opinion suggests that behavior patterns, some of which are extremely dissimilar, result from one another, or at least follow one another, in some sort of orderly or regular way. Many authors, however, think that these diverse behavior patterns are based on different stimulus constellations and different motivational conditions and that they involve different innerorganismic physiological processes and affective states. Therefore, such a schema is rather questionable or even dangerous, at least in the view of motivational theory, because it may lead to the premature conclusion that there exists a uniform and homogeneous motivational cause or basis for these behavior patterns, some of which, according to all we presently know, are extremely heterogeneous.

It seems to be rather difficult to draw a final conclusion from the conceptual and definitional problems mentioned previously in the first section. From my point of view, it is first necessary to question the usefulness of subsuming all these terms and constructs under one heading. The various operationalizations of these constructs used in all the different studies are so distinct and specific that any precipitate attempt at a conceptual integration must fail from the start.

In my opinion there are at least two ways to overcome the existing conceptual chaos. First, any experimental study in this field should be planned and conducted within the stringent framework provided by some kind of paradigm. The implications for theory construction and research of such a paradigm—accepted by scientists working in one domain—are clearly described, for example, by Byrne (1971, pp. 3–22). Second, behaviors like exploration, manipulation, or play should first be thoroughly analyzed by means of a phenomenological descriptive approach as conducted, for example, by Csikszentmihalyi (1975). Such a procedure promises to some extent an absolutely new understanding of the phenomena in question.

THE INFLUENCE OF DISPOSITIONAL FACTORS

Recently, an interactionistic approach to the observation of exploratory phenomena has been taken more and more often (see, for example, Boyle, 1983; Zuckerman, 1976). In the past, the old research paradigm dominated, which restricted the scientific analysis of exploration to the experimental study of the effects certain perceptual stimuli had on the manifestation of certain reactions or behavioral patterns. The influences that individual factors might exert usually remained unconsidered. Nevertheless, such trait influences were hypothesized by several psychologists working in this field. In recent times this assumption led to the development of different tests of curiosity, need for variation, etc. In the view of a motivational psychologist, the traits measured with these tests are conceived as motives, as dispositions of persons or individuals, which are temporarily relatively stable and which, in addition to provoking corresponding stimulating cues, also provoke exploratory behavior or influence it in a certain way.

By contrast, the "states" view rests on the assumption that experience and behavior are determined by the actual and specific state of affairs in which the individual finds himself "here and now" (see Zuckerman, 1976). Working with this conception, Neary (1975) developed a scale for the measurement of state-sensation-seeking.

Meanwhile, a great many different psychological tests have been designed for the diagnosis of motivational traits (see the summary in Keller & Voss, 1976, and Krieger, 1976). According to their authors and to the definition of the construct underlying the single test, these diagnostic instruments make it possible to identify explicitly or implicitly the more or less active or passive, interoceptive or exteroceptive, sensitive or cognitive, experiential or behavioral manifestations of a need (or of several needs) for internal and/or external—but always variable—stimulus input.

Different investigations in which the tools used to measure a single trait were compared with each other (see e.g., Acker & McReynolds, 1967; Langevin, 1971; McCarroll, Mitchell, Carpenter, & Anderson, 1967; Pearson, 1970) generally yielded only moderate correlations between the empirical and behavioral characteristics measured by the different tests. These intercorrelational results once more raise the question of the uniformity of the personality trait measured by the single methods, a question that already arises when the different definitions of constructs and item contents of scales are inspected more closely. Possible answers to this question are that: (a) The tests measure single dimensions or subaspects of a unitary personality construct called "novelty preference" or "variation tendency"; (b) the tests measure different though interrelated characteristics or constructs of personality.

Even if the question of the correctness of (a) or (b) is not under discussion at the moment, it would be useful to avoid broad generalizations about the results of different tests concerning curiosity or variation seeking and instead define the measured construct as clearly as possible, that is, in close connection with the content of the item. The postulation of a detailed phenomenological analysis and description of exploratory behavior and its concise conceptual definition as stated in the preceding section is basic for the construction of measuring tools such as trait tests, too.

Tests that were originally developed to identify one trait in a comprehensive way and that repeatedly turned out to measure several dimensions—like the Sensation-Seeking Scale from Zuckerman, Kolin, Price, and Zoob (1964)—have required several theoretical and methodological revisions. It therefore seems to be appropriate to make use of a procedure recommended by Fiske (1966). Fiske suggests first analyzing a personality construct precisely and then subdividing it into different, conceptually homogeneous subconstructs. In a second step the measuring instrument is developed according to the definitions that have been formulated for the construct. Pearson's (1970) attempt to construct a measuring instrument for novelty seeking can be considered as a good example of the conceptually appropriate operational procedure. Nevertheless, even with the development of this test, the call for a comprehensive multidimensional curiosity test as expressed by Keller and Voss (1976, p. 82) has not been answered yet.

Finally, it deserves to be mentioned that the necessity of considering individual differences or dispositional factors in the study of exploratory behavior was accentuated by developmental psychology, too, primarily in research on the conditions in which children are reared. Studies have shown that animals or human beings explore much more if they were reared in a more complex home or environment with a greater degree of stimulus variation (see e.g., Collard, 1967, 1971; Rubenstein, 1967; Sackett, 1967, 1972). Whereas most studies on rearing conditions were conducted many years ago, Maddi and Kobasa (1981) recently proposed three personality variables that are especially relevant to the topic of exploratory behavior (and intrinsic motivation): (a) commitment, i.e., the predisposition to involve oneself in certain activities, (b) control, i.e., the belief that events are internally controlled, and (c) challenge, i.e., the positive anticipation of changes as a stimulus to development. The function of these variables according to Maddi, Hoover, and Kobasa (1982), can be seen as follows:

> The more a person is predisposed toward commitment, control, and challenge, the greater the likelihood that he or she will show such signs of intrinsic motivation as exploratory behavior. This is not to say that such considerations as task complexity and novelty are unimportant but rather that they are most effective in arousing the interest and curiosity marking intrinsic motivation in persons with these personality characteristics. (p. 885)

EXPLORATION AND EMOTION

Considerations about a possible relationship between exploratory behavior patterns and certain emotions concentrate almost exclusively on the subjects of exploration or curiosity and anxiety. The special interest in that subject is explicable by the rather paradoxical fact that novel and unknown objects or persons cause anxiety or fear on one hand and preference or exploratory behavior on the other. In the opinion of most psychologists, anxiety or fear are manifested in withdrawal or avoidance behavior; by contrast, curiosity or exploration are indicated by the occurrence of approach behavior.

The conditions that promote anxiety or fear are seen in detail as follows:

1. Anxiety develops if the degree of stimulus-complexity, -novelty, or -changes is too high (Berlyne, 1960).

2. Excessive frequency of unassimilated perceptual objects leads to anxiety (McReynolds, 1956).

3. Anxiety results when the incongruity between situation and standard becomes too great (Hunt, 1963a).

4. Certain preexperiences (kind of treatment or duration of isolation, for example) determine whether fear or exploration will arise (Glanzer, 1958).

5. Fear or anxiety less often originate from unknown stimuli alone than from an unusual combination of new and already familiar stimulus material (Hebb, 1946, 1949).

6. Fear drive and exploration drive are both simultaneously evoked by novel stimuli; the predominance of one of these antagonistic drives is determined by additional situational characteristics or experimental conditions (e.g., fear prevails when shock is applied or when "dangerous" [not enclosed and elevated] mazes are used) (Montgomery, 1955; Montgomery & Monkman, 1955).

7. Withdrawal results partly from the "newness" of objects, partly from the internal state of the exploring subject (Shillito, 1963).

8. Strangeness as such is a cause for the rise of fear (Bowlby, 1969).

9. Neophobic behavior (i.e., avoidance of unfamiliar objects in familiar surroundings) only occurs in wild but not in domesticated animals (Barnett, 1958b).

10. Fear (at least of a low or middle intensity) is the motivational basis of exploratory behavior (Halliday, 1966; Lester, 1967, 1968; Mowrer, 1960; Watson, 1961).

11. Fear leads to exploratory behavior for the purpose of finding a possibility to escape; i.e., it leads to a kind of "exploratory avoidance behavior" (Welker, 1957). Similar to Welker's assumption is the one Dember and Earl (1957) make, according to which a distinction between approach behavior (caused by curiosity) and avoidance behavior (caused by anxiety) is superfluous because both behaviors include exploratory attention.

12. Anxiety or fear develop when a situation's degree of novelty is too great, resulting in the expectation of higher risk (of harm or loss). Zuckerman (1976) states: "The risk expectation is the most crucial [factor] in the increase of fear drive" (p. 164).

These diverse hypotheses raise a number of questions, including the following: Above all it should have become clear that extensive uncertainty about the relationship between anxiety or fear and exploration still exists. A series of empirical investigations suggests that the inverse relationship (e.g., Hayes, 1960) often believed to exist between exploration and anxiety is rather questionable. Another consideration resulting from these hypotheses relates to the frequent practice, mentioned before, of equating exploration with appetitive behavior. Several investigations show that this practice is not really admissible (Welker, 1957) and suggest making a distinction between appetitive exploration and aversive exploration instead (the latter serving as a preparation for an eventually necessary escape). In a given situation it certainly might be quite difficult or even impossible to draw this distinction based on the observation of the actual behavior of an animal or a person. At the human level, however, one could get subjective reports from the subjects participating in the study. To avoid precipitate conclusions special caution seems to be required because, for instance, the nonoccurrence or the decrease of a certain kind of exploration does not necessarily have to do with possible anxiety or fear but might simply depend on the object of exploration at hand. For example, Eckerman and Rheingold (1974) found that children exhibited prompt approach behavior and a willingness for direct contact (touch and manipulation) with toys. Children seldom made physical contact with persons, however; they more often established visual contact and, especially with reactive subjects, smiled.

On the whole, several results support the assumption that anxiety or fear in novel situations not only depends on certain characteristics of the stimulus or the situation but also on such factors as individual disposition (anxiousness), the perception that the activity of exploring of novel subjects is accompanied by a special risk, the extent to which a subject has been deprived of a stimulus or a state of anxiety that may have been induced either shortly before or during the exploration phase.

Apart from fear and defense, certain stimulus characteristics that provoke exploratory behavior release "positive" emotions, too. One can assume that such emotions occur to a lesser extent in the specific exploration phase aimed at gaining information but that they occur more often in the diversive exploration phase. Wohlwill (1981) calls this kind of exploration "affective exploration," which in his opinion helps above all to maintain an optimal level of hedonic activity.

If one conceives of play and aesthetic experience as forms of exploratory activity, as frequently happens, then emotional relationships for these behaviors or experiences can be shown, too. As far as play is concerned, positive affection, relaxation, pleasure, and feelings of comfort and delight during the quick change between excitement and relaxation (the so-called activation circle) have been reported again and again (see e.g., Fein & Apfel, 1979; Heckhausen, 1964; Hutt, 1970; Weisler & McCall, 1976).

Aesthetic judgments are based on the perceived stimulus characteristics of art objects. Berlyne's collative variables (complexity and novelty, for example) represent some of those important stimulus characteristics. The degree of inner-organismic activation and, related to that, the positive or negative "hedonic value" of the stimuli or stimulus constellations that are to be judged depend on the intensity of such stimulus characters. But whereas Berlyne (1963a), Vitz (1966a, 1966b), and Wohlwill (1968) assume an inverted U-shaped relationship between the intensity of the collative variables and their attractiveness or preference, Birkhoff (1933) and Cantor (1968) favor an inverse relationship, Jones (1964) and Jones, Wilkinson, and Braden (1961) a linear relationship, and Terwilliger

(1963), Munsinger and Kessen (1964), and Day (1967) a bimodal M-shaped relationship. This enumeration of some relevant studies does not really contribute to a clarification of the relationship between collative variables and positive affection. This lack of consistency in the results may have resulted in part from different operationalizations of the independent variables (intensity of collative stimulus characteristics) and dependent variables (attractiveness or preference of the stimulus constellation) or from methodological deficiences (such as the inclusion of too few or too narrow segments of the spectrum of complexity rather than the entire, systematically varied continuum from very simple up to very complex stimuli). Basically this self-critical avowal, however, does not change our inability to throw light on the question of the relation between the experience of art and the experience of affection.

Because this chapter has so far dealt almost exclusively with the repulsive or attractive effects of collative stimulus characteristics, let us finally turn to the question of possible emotional or affective states that may induce or prevent exploratory behavior.

Shillito (1963) believes a kind of "exploratory mood" to be necessary in order to evoke exploratory behavior generally caused by appropriate novel objects. Berlyne (1971a, p. 94) presumes that sadness, depression, or frustration, from which resignation and apathy result, make an individual more or less unable to react to external stimulation and thus keep him or her from engaging in exploratory behavior. Maddi, Hoover, and Kobasa (1982, p. 885) suggest that "feelings of alienation" have inhibiting effects on exploratory behavior. In my view these feelings of alienation have much to do with other psychological constructs like "external locus of control" or "learned helplessness." Therefore, the results of the work from Maddi et al. may have many fruitful hypotheses for further research in the field of exploratory behavior. Shillito, Berlyne, and Maddi, Hoover, and Kobasa draw attention to affective states of the individual that possibly work like sensitizers or desensitizers for stimuli or objects that activate exploration. The role of these stimuli as the only activators of exploratory behavior is thus clearly weakened.

EXPLORATION: INTRINSIC OR EXTRINSIC?

According to Koch (1956, p. 72), the relationship between intrinsic and extrinsic determinants of behavior is perhaps the most difficult problem in formulating a metatheory of motivation. Exploration and curiosity behavior often are considered to be the paradigm of intrinsically motivated behavior. This view is based on a definition that denotes *intrinsically motivated* behavior as behavior that is performed for its own sake, that is, independently of any external reinforcement (see, for example, Condry, 1977; DeCharms, 1968; Deci, 1975; Hunt, 1965). By contrast, a behavior is labeled as *extrinsically motivated* if it is performed to receive external reinforcement that is attainable only through that behavior. Consequently the denomination *intrinsic* or *extrinsic* is closely connected with the question of the function, the purpose, and the aim of certain patterns of subjective experience and behavior. Intrinsically motivated behavior is functionally autonomous and has its intrinsic aim and purpose; it is, therefore, *autotelic*. Extrinsically motivated behavior is functionally heteronomous, leads to aims outside itself, is rather a means to an end, and is thus *exotelic*. In spite of the danger of being redundant concerning this point, I want to illustrate this with the following example. A student of psychology is intrinsically motivated if he were to go to the university solely out of interest in his field and bravely endure all the troubles and doubts connected with it. By contrast, he would be extrinsically motivated if he were to study psychology only because of the academic degree he would receive and the possibility he could anticipate for earning money. This example quite effectively demonstrates how problematic it is to discriminate between the two kinds of motivation and to determine their importance or influence on behavior, because the one obviously does not necessarily exclude the other. Exploration, curiosity, play, spontaneous activity, imaginative behavior, and the like obviously are regarded above all as intrinsically motivated because it has proved to be extremely difficult, even impossible, to subsume them into a general principle of survival, to attribute to them a particular adaptive function or an instrumental character of whatever kind, or to demonstrate their dependence on any external reinforcements. Just this apparent biological "senselessness and aimlessness" led to the common practice of ascribing to those phenomena their own, genuine, intrinsic, rather psychogenic, and nonhomeostatic motivational basis.

Berlyne (1971b) points out the problematic nature of this opinion when he writes that, strictly speaking, intrinsic behavior in fact cannot be "self-reinforcing" except by virtue of certain internal conditions of the organism that result from that behavior and that function as the real reinforcers. According to Berlyne, there is no reason why one should suppose that intrinsic motivation is less biological or less homeostatic than extrinsic motivation. With that criticism, the idea of regarding intrinsic and extrinsic motivation as distinct phenomena sui generis is questioned as a matter of principle, for the often loudly expressed absolute "either–or" becomes the relativizing "as-well-as."

Challenging the widely accepted assumption about the lack of any survival value aforementioned, Maddi, Hoover, and Kobasa (1982, p. 884) maintain that exploratory behavior, though intrinsically motivated, undoubtedly serves the survival of an individual, too, because it increases the organism's knowledge about its environment.

There are several theoretical explanations for intrinsic and extrinsic motivation. The most prominent ones, in my opinion, are an attributional or, more generally, a cognitive view—DeCharms' (1968) personal causation theory, Deci's (1975) cognitive evaluation theory, Kruglanski's (1975, 1978) distinction between endogenous and exogenous attribution, Lepper and Greene's (1978) means–end analysis of intrinsic and extrinsic motivation, Heckhausen's (1980) notion of endogeneity of an action and its goal, and Csikszentmihalyi's (1975, 1979) concept of "flow." This concept of flow seems to be a very useful and adequate explanation of intrinsically motivated exploratory behavior like play. On the basis of a holistic, systemic view that takes into account the organism's complexity and ability for self-reflexation—a kind of phenomenological approach— Csikszentmihalyi (1975) found the following elements or characteristics of flow experience: (a) merging of action and awareness, (b) centering of attention on a limited stimulus field, (c) self-forgetfulness or loss of self-consciousness, (d) control of actions and of the environment, (e) coherence and noncontradiction of demands for action and provision of clear, unambiguous feedback to a person's actions, and (f) "autotelic" nature, i.e., flow experience appears to need no goals or rewards external to itself.

Csikszentmihalyi (1979, p. 259) does not claim that his theoretical framework of intrinsic behavior offers the only possible explanation of play and similar phenomena, but he thinks that his model is complementary to arousal theories based on a different level of analysis and focused on physiological processes.

Csikszentmihalyi's phenomenological descriptive analysis is without doubt very interesting for the subject of exploration and intrinsic behavior. Nevertheless, this approach involves a remarkable lack of developmental reflections. By contrast, studies of the formation and organization of intrinsic or extrinsic motivations of behavior offering such a developmental reference are less clearly related to the area of exploratory behavior. Provided that one accepts the definition of *intrinsic* as "independent of any external reward," some investigations on the subject yield interesting results. Pittman, Emery, and Boggiano (1982) offer an example of such an investigation. The authors pointed out that changes in preference for complexity and, related to this, that an individual's more general intrinsic or extrinsic motivational orientation can be established by simple changes of certain reward or reinforcement patterns. In an empirical study the authors found that the no-reward or task-noncontingent reward condition engenders an intrinsic motivational orientation and a preference for an activity with greater complexity, whereas the introduction of task-contingent reward fosters an extrinsic motivational orientation, and this orientation may carry over into subsequent interactions with the activity, even when the conditions that originally fostered that orientation are no longer present.

DEVELOPMENT OF EXPLORATORY BEHAVIOR AND ITS MOTIVATION

A good deal of empirical research on exploratory behavior like curiosity, play, exploration, and imagination consists of developmental studies. However, studies that also deal explicitly and systematically with questions relevant to motivation theory are very rare. Similarly, there is a dearth of comprehensive theories in this field. The work of White (1960) and Hunt (1965, 1966) describing and explaining the development of exploratory behavior—with a more or less marked cognitive slant—may, however, with certain reservations be considered as explicitly motivational theories (see also Keller & Voss, 1976). Taking Freud's denotation of the psychosexual developmental stages as a formal basis, White tries to describe the process of development as a striving for and an increase of personal and social competence (see also White, 1959). In contrast, describing and explaining the child's development in terms of different phases of libido organization is not at all satisfying to White. In Hunt's reflections on developmental psychology, which led to a classification of three successive developmental stages, the influence of Piaget's theory of cognitive development is evident. Although Piaget's theory contains a series of interesting hypotheses on motivation, as Hunt (1963b) and Ulvund (1980) point out, it is not possible to discuss it here in detail.

Besides White and Hunt, Wright and Vlietstra (1975) also have dealt with the development of exploratory behavior, or, more exactly, with the development of selective attention, which, according to these authors, progresses "from perceptual exploration to logical search." Perceptual exploration is rather spontaneous and less systematic. It occurs in shorter sequences and shows less continuity from one sequence to another. It is more divergent and is more determined by external stimuli. As can be directly observed, it is rather playful, is instigated by curiosity or boredom, and is consummatory rather than instrumental in its information-producing function. By contrast, logical search seems to be rather systematic and planned. The controlling intentions can only be inferred indirectly from the continuity of behavior. It is more task and goal oriented and more convergent than exploratory behavior. It has the character of work, i.e., it is instrumental in the sense that the information acquired through it contributes to the control of the goal-oriented behavior and to ongoing decision making. The latter points to the fact that logical search is extrinsically motivated, whereas the motivation for exploratory behavior is rather intrinsic.

To support their theoretical assumptions, the authors cite a variety of empirical research. For the evaluation of Wright and Vlietstra's assumptions, the following can be said for the time being: Whereas the quite significant motivational implications of these assumptions deserve our full interest, the sequence postulated by the authors (exploration–logical search) appears to be inconsistent with common conceptions, according to which specific exploration generally appears before diversive exploration (see, for example, Hutt, 1970; Nunnally & Lemond, 1973). As already mentioned, White (1959) offered a relatively vague concept of "competence" and "effectance." His developmental model based on this concept and published 1 year later hardly gained in concreteness—thus indicating that empirical testing and development of this concept hardly took place. Several papers by Harter serve, however, to specify and extend White's conceptualization. Harter (1978) strives to split up the construct "effectance" (or "competence") motivation into several single components or dimensions, an effort consistent with her intention to extract testable hypotheses from the originally quite global concept. Harter and Zigler (1974) and Harter (1978) distinguish four researchable categories of behavior that suggest the existence of an underlying effectance or competence motivation, that is to say, (a) response variation, (b) curiosity for novel stimuli, (c) mastery for the sake of competence, and (d) preference for challenging or demanding tasks. Besides the quite plausible attempt to isolate dimensions of behavior, Harter (1978) arranges the construct of effectance or competence motivation in an integrative structure of components that might be interdependent. This effort deserves our special attention. The multiple relationships she presents can quite easily be translated into testable hypotheses. Initial empirical tests confirmed Harter's assumptions (see Harter's summary, 1978).

The approaches of Hunt, White, and Wright and Vlietstra discussed here leave much to be desired with regard to their theoretical elaboration and their empirical verification. If the fundamental task of a developmental approach is to consider changes in behavior over time (Wohlwill, 1973), then some further developmental tasks follow from this basic postulation. Considering Wohlwill's demands and comparing them with the actual state of developmental research on exploration, it is obvious that many questions still remain unanswered; the existing theories are rather fragmentary and incomplete, and adequate methods for conducting an empirical investigation into the main problems of the area are either insufficient or nonexistent.

CONCLUDING REMARKS

My aim in this chapter was to point out several motivational aspects of exploratory behavior and its development. Unfortunately, I was unable to deal further with certain problem areas although they contain many aspects relevant to motivation psychology, subjects like "exploration and psychophysical activation" or "exploration and reinforcement." However, these topics have already been discussed to some extent in previous treatments, particularly by Berlyne (e.g., 1963a, 1967).

In general the motivation psychologist can be rather satisfied because almost no paper concerning theory and research on curiosity and exploration neglects the subject of "motivation." Interesting hypotheses for motivation psychology can be found in most publications. The attempts to present comprehensive models or theories for the description or explanation of exploratory behavior are extraordinarily noteworthy.

Nevertheless, it seems to me that the research on exploration and motivation and its development is, to a great extent, still in a kind of preparadigm state. A few elaborated and commonly accepted paradigms would strengthen and improve the theoretical and empirical efforts in this area considerably. For the development of such paradigmatic approaches, an important leitmotiv may have been provided by Barnett (1958a), who saw that the subject of exploration "obviously demands a theory of motivation more subtle and complex than those which have prevailed hitherto" (p. 305).

SUMMARY

In a review of the relevant literature, the author attempts to point out psychologists' views on "exploratory behavior" (curiosity, play, exploration, spontaneous activity, and manipulation, for example) from the perspective of motivation theory.

The following motivation-related themes are discussed briefly: (a) the specificity or generality of the motivational basis for exploratory behavior patterns, (b) the influence of dispositional factors, (c) the possible relationships between exploratory behavior and emotion, (d) the intrinsic or extrinsic character of exploratory behavior, and (e) the development of exploratory behavior and its motivational basis. A consideration and discussion of these problem complexes results in a few general ideas and conclusions for theory and methods that could be formulated as a catalogue of relatively concrete suggestions for further exploration research.

A thorough and discriminating analysis should be a matter of course when investigating exploratory behavior patterns and their motivational basis. Hasty and inadequate generalizations will more likely be avoided with such an approach. A comprehensive search for possible determinants must be based on situational *and* individual factors; that is, the influence of possible dispositional factors is to be considered accordingly. Similarly, research on emotions and affects as concomitants, conditions, or consequences of exploratory behavior deserves special attention. Furthermore—although the definition of exploratory behavior as intrinsically motivated behavior can lead to fruitful and far-reaching empirical work—one would do best to avoid too strict (and artificial) a conceptual division between intrinsic and extrinsic motivation when studying exploratory behavior. Finally, the attempt should be made to elaborate a testable theory of development of exploratory behavior while explicitly including motivational aspects of development.

REFERENCES

Acker, M., & McReynolds, P. (1967). The "need for novelty": A comparison of six instruments. *Psychological Record, 17*, 177–182.
Atkinson, J. W., & Birch, D. (1970). *The dynamics of action.* New York: Wiley.
Atkinson, J. W., & Birch, D. (1978). *Introduction to motivation* (2nd ed.). New York: Van Nostrand.
Barnett, S. A. (1958a). Exploratory behaviour. *British Journal of Psychology, 49*, 289–310.

Barnett, S. A. (1958b). Experiments on "neophobia" in wild and laboratory rats. *British Journal of Psychology, 49*, 195–201.

Berlyne, D. E. (1960). *Conflict, arousal, and curiosity.* New York: McGraw–Hill.

Berlyne, D. E. (1963a). Exploratory and epistemic behavior. In S. Koch (Ed.), *Psychology: A study of a science* (Vol. 5, pp. 284–364). New York: McGraw–Hill.

Berlyne, D. E. (1963b). Complexity and incongruity variables as determinants of exploratory choice and evaluative ratings. *Canadian Journal of Psychology, 17*, 274–290.

Berlyne, D. E. (1967). Arousal and reinforcement. In D. Levine (Ed.), *Nebraska Symposium on Motivation* (pp. 1–110). Lincoln: University of Nebraska Press.

Berlyne, D. E. (1971a). *Aesthetics and psychobiology.* New York: Appleton–Century–Crofts.

Berlyne, D. E. (1971b). What next? Concluding summary. In H. I. Day, D. E. Berlyne, & D. E. Hunt (Eds.), *Intrinsic motivation: A new direction in education* (pp. 186–196). Toronto: Holt, Rinehart & Winston.

Berlyne, D. E. (1978). Curiosity and learning. *Motivation and Emotion, 2*, 97–175.

Birkhoff, G. (1933). *Aesthetic measure.* Cambridge, MA: Harvard University Press.

Bowlby, J. (1969). *Attachment and loss: Vol. 1. Attachment.* London: Hogarth Press.

Boyle, G. J. (1983). Critical review of state-trait curiosity test development. *Motivation and Emotion, 7*, 377–397.

Byrne, D. (1971). *The attraction paradigm.* New York: Academic Press.

Cantor, G. N. (1968). Children's "like–dislike" ratings of familiarized and nonfamiliarized visual stimuli. *Journal of Experimental Child Psychology, 6*, 651–657.

Collard, R. R. (1967). Fear of strangers and play in kittens with varied social experience. *Child Development, 38*, 877–891.

Collard, R. R. (1971). Exploratory and play behaviors of infants reared in an institution and in lower and middle-class homes. *Child Development, 42*, 1003–1015.

Condry, J. (1977). Enemies of exploration: Self-initiated versus other-initiated learning. *Journal of Personality and Social Psychology, 35*, 459–477.

Crozier, J. B. (1974). Verbal and exploratory responses to sound sequences varying in uncertainty level. In D. E. Berlyne (Ed.), *Studies in the new experimental aesthetics* (pp. 27–90). Washington: Hemisphere.

Csikszentmihalyi, M. (1975). *Beyond boredom and anxiety.* San Francisco: Jossey–Bass.

Csikszentmihalyi, M. (1979). The concept of flow. In B. Sutton-Smith (Ed.), *Play and learning* (pp. 257–274). New York: Gardner Press.

Day, H. (1967). Evaluations of subjective complexity, pleasingness and interestingness for a series of random polygons varying in complexity. *Perception and Psychophysics, 2*, 281–286.

DeCharms, R. (1968). *Personal causation.* New York: Academic Press.

Deci, E. L. (1975). *Intrinsic motivation.* New York: Plenum Press.

Dember, W. N., & Earl, R. W. (1957). Analysis of exploratory, manipulatory, and curiosity behaviors. *Psychological Review, 64*, 91–96.

Eckerman, C. O., & Rheingold, H. L. (1974). Infants' exploratory responses to toys and people. *Developmental Psychology, 10*, 255–259.

Fein, G. G., & Apfel, N. (1979). The development of play: Style, structure, and situations. *Genetic Psychology Monographs, 99*, 231–250.

Fiske, D. W. (1966). On the coordination of personality concepts and their measurement. *Human Development, 9*, 74–83.

Glanzer, M. (1958). Curiosity, exploratory drive, and stimulus satiation. *Psychological Bulletin, 55*, 302–315.

Halliday, M. S. (1966). Exploration and fear in the rat. *Symposium of the Zoological Society, London, 18*, 45–59.

Harter, S. (1978). Effectance motivation reconsidered: Toward a developmental model. *Human Development, 21*, 34–64.

Harter, S., & Zigler, E. (1974). The assessment of effectance motivation in normal and retarded children. *Developmental Psychology, 10*, 169–180.

Hayes, K. J. (1960). Exploration and fear. *Psychological Reports, 6*, 91–93.

Hebb, D. O. (1946). On the nature of fear. *Psychological Review, 53*, 259–276.

Hebb, D. O. (1949). *The organization of behavior*. New York: Wiley.

Heckhausen, H. (1964). Entwurf einer Psychologie des Spielens. *Psychologische Forschung, 27*, 225–243.

Heckhausen, H. (1980). *Motivation und Handeln*. Berlin: Springer.

Hunt, J. McV. (1963a). Motivation inherent in information processing and action. In O. J. Harvey (Ed.), *Motivation and social interaction: Cognitive determinants* (pp. 35–94). New York: Ronald Press.

Hunt, J. McV. (1963b). Piaget's observations as a source of hypotheses concerning motivation. *Merrill–Palmer Quarterly, 9*, 263–275.

Hunt, J. McV. (1965). Intrinsic motivation and its role in psychological development. In D. Levine (Ed.), *Nebraska Symposium on Motivation* (pp. 189–282). Lincoln: University of Nebraska Press.

Hunt, J. McV. (1966). The epigenesis of intrinsic motivation and early cognitive learning. In R. H. Haber (Ed.), *Current research in motivation* (pp. 355–370). New York: Holt, Rinehart & Winston.

Hutt, C. (1970). Specific and diversive exploration. In H. W. Reese & L. P. Lipsitt (Eds.), *Advances in child development and behavior* (Vol. 5, pp. 119–180). New York: Academic Press.

Jones, A. (1964). Drive and the incentive variables associated with the statistical properties of sequences of stimuli. *Journal of Experimental Psychology, 67*, 423–431.

Jones, A., Wilkinson, H., & Braden, I. (1961). Information deprivation as a motivational variable. *Journal of Experimental Psychology, 62*, 126–137.

Keller, H., & Voss, H.-G. (1976). *Neugier und Exploration*. Stuttgart: Kohlhammer.

Keller, J. A. (1981). *Grundlagen der Motivation*. München: Urban & Schwarzenberg.

Koch, S. (1956). Behavior as "intrinsically" regulated: Work notes towards a pre-theory of phenomena called "motivational." In M. R. Jones (Ed.), *Nebraska Symposium on Motivation* (pp. 42–87). Lincoln: University of Nebraska Press.

Krieger, R. (1976). *Determinanten der Wißbegier. Untersuchungen zur Theorie der intrinsischen Motivation*. Bern: Huber.

Kruglanski, A. W. (1975). The endogenous–exogenous partition in attribution theory. *Psychological Review, 82*, 387–406.

Kruglanski, A. W. (1978). Endogenous attribution and intrinsic motivation. In M. R. Lepper & D. Greene (Eds.), *The hidden costs of reward* (pp. 85–107). Hillsdale, NJ: Lawrence Erlbaum Associates.

Langevin, R. (1971). Is curiosity a unitary construct? *Canadian Journal of Psychology, 25*, 360–374.

Lepper, M. R., & Greene, D. (1978). Overjustification research and beyond: Toward a means–ends analysis of intrinsic and extrinsic motivation. In M. R. Lepper & D. Greene (Eds.), *The hidden costs of reward* (pp. 109–148). Hillsdale, NJ: Lawrence Erlbaum Associates.

Lester, D. (1967). Sex differences in exploration: Toward a theory of exploration. *Psychological Record, 17*, 55–62.

Lester, D. (1968). Two tests of a fear-motivated theory of exploration. *Psychonomic Science, 10*, 385–386.

Maddi, S. R., Hoover, M., & Kobasa, S. C. (1982). Alienation and exploratory behavior. *Journal of Personality and Social Psychology, 42*, 884–890.

Maddi, S. R., & Kobasa, S. C. (1981). Intrinsic motivation and health. In H. I. Day (Ed.), *Advances in intrinsic motivation and aesthetics* (pp. 299–321). New York: Plenum Press.

McCarroll, J. E., Mitchell, K. M., Carpenter, R. J., & Anderson, J. P. (1967). Analysis of three stimulation-seeking scales. *Psychological Reports, 21*, 853–856.

McReynolds, P. (1956). A restricted conceptualization of human anxiety and motivation. *Psychological Reports, 2,* 293–312.

McReynolds, P. (1971). The three faces of cognitive motivation. In H. I. Day, D. E. Berlyne, & D. E. Hunt (Eds.), *Intrinsic motivation: A new direction in education* (pp. 33–45). Toronto: Holt, Rinehart & Winston.

Montgomery, K. C. (1955). The relation between fear induced by novel stimulation and exploratory behavior. *Journal of Comparative and Physiological Psychology, 48,* 254–260.

Montgomery, K. C., & Monkman, J. A. (1955). The relation between fear and exploratory behavior. *Journal of Comparative and Physiological Psychology, 48,* 132–136.

Mowrer, O. H. (1960). *Learning theory and behavior.* New York: Wiley.

Munsinger, H., & Kessen, W. (1964). Uncertainty, structure, and preference. *Psychological Monographs, 78*(9), (Whole No. 586).

Neary, R. S. (1975). *The development and validation of a state measure of sensation seeking.* Unpublished doctoral dissertation, University of Delaware.

Nunnally, J. C., & Lemond, L. C. (1973). Exploratory behavior and human development. In H. W. Reese (Ed.), *Advances in child development and behavior* (Vol. 8, pp. 59–109). New York: Academic Press.

Pearson, P. H. (1970). Relationships between global and specified measures of novelty seeking. *Journal of Consulting and Clinical Psychology, 34,* 199–204.

Pittman, T. S., Emery, J., & Boggiano, A. K. (1982). Intrinsic and extrinsic motivational orientations: Reward-induced changes in preference for complexity. *Journal of Personality and Social Psychology, 42,* 789–797.

Rubenstein, J. (1967). Maternal attentiveness and subsequent exploratory behavior in the infant. *Child Development, 38,* 1089–1100.

Sackett, G. P. (1967). Response to novelty and complexity as a function of rats' early rearing experiences. *Journal of Comparative and Physiological Psychology, 63,* 369–375.

Sackett, G. P. (1972). Exploratory behavior of rhesus monkeys as a function of rearing experiences and sex. *Developmental Psychology, 6,* 260–270.

Schneider, K., Moch, M., & Auerswald, M. (1982). Neugierverhalten bei Vorschulkindern: Ein Querschnittvergleich. In R. Oerter (Ed.), *Berichtüber die 5. Tagung Entwicklungspsychologie* (Vol. 1, pp. 219–222). Augsburg: Universität Augsburg.

Shillito, E. E. (1963). Exploratory behaviour in the short-tailed vole microtus agrestis. *Behaviour, 21,* 145–154.

Terwilliger, R. F. (1963). Pattern complexity and affective arousal. *Perceptual and Motor Skills, 17,* 387–395.

Ulvund, S. E. (1980). Cognition and motivation in early infancy. An interactionistic approach. *Human Development, 23,* 17–32.

Vandenberg, B. (1978). Play and development from an ethological perspective. *American Psychologist, 33,* 724–738.

Vitz, P. C. (1966a). Affect as a function of stimulus variation. *Journal of Experimental Psychology, 71,* 74–79.

Vitz, P. C. (1966b). Preference for different amount of visual complexity. *Behavioral Science, 11,* 105–114.

Watson, A. J. (1961). The place of reinforcement in the explanation of behavior. In W. H. Thorpe & O. L. Zangwill (Eds.), *Current problems in animal behavior.* Cambridge: Cambridge University Press.

Weisler, A., & McCall, R. B. (1976). Exploration and play. *American Psychologist, 31,* 492–508.

Welker, W. I. (1957). "Free" versus "forced" exploration of a novel situation by rats. *Psychological Reports, 3,* 95–108.

White, R. W. (1959). Motivation reconsidered: The concept of competence. *Psychological Review, 66,* 297–333.

White, R. W. (1960). Competence and the psychosexual stages of development. In M. R. Jones (Ed.), *Nebraska Symposium on Motivation* (pp. 97–141). Lincoln: University of Nebraska Press.

Wohlwill, J. F. (1968). Amount of stimulus exploration and preference as differential functions of stimulus complexity. *Perception and Psychophysics, 4*, 307–312.

Wohlwill, J. F. (1973). *The study of behavioral development*. New York: Academic Press.

Wohlwill, J. F. (1981). A conceptual analysis of exploratory behavior: The "specific–diversive" distinction revisited. In H. I. Day (Ed.), *Advances in intrinsic motivation and aesthetics* (pp. 341–364). New York: Plenum Press.

Wright, J. C., & Vlietstra, A. G. (1975). The development of selective attention: From perceptual exploration to logical search. In H. W. Reese (Ed.), *Advances in child development and behavior* (Vol. 10, pp. 195–239). New York: Academic Press.

Zuckerman, M. (1976). Sensation seeking and anxiety, traits and states, as determinants of behavior in novel situations. In I. G. Sarason & C. D. Spielberger (Eds.), *Stress and anxiety* (Vol. 3, pp. 141–170). Washington: Hemisphere.

Zuckerman, M., Kolin, E. A., Price, L., & Zoob, I. (1964). Development of a sensation-seeking scale. *Journal of Consulting Psychology, 28*, 477–482.

CHAPTER THREE

EXPLORATION AND PLAY:
RESEARCH AND
PERSPECTIVES IN
DEVELOPMENTAL PSYCHOLOGY

HANS-GEORG VOSS
Technische Hochschule Darmstadt

POSSIBLE DISTINCTIONS BETWEEN EXPLORATION AND PLAY

At first glance, *exploration* and *play* are obviously distinct classes of behavior in everyday language, but, if asked, one may have trouble providing a clear definition of both behavioral systems in terms of observable, discriminating features. Several authors have therefore found it more comfortable to accept the definition of Weisler and McCall (1976), who "consider the distinction between exploration and play as only a verbal convenience whose major point is to punctuate the fact that exploratory play behaviors are incredibly diverse and occur under a wide variety of circumstances" (p. 497). Most reviews on exploration *and* play as well as the bulk of empirical studies are concerned about differences on empirical and hypothetical levels but seldom discuss the *relationship* between them (e.g., Collard, 1979; McCall, 1974; Nunnally & Lemond, 1973; Weisler & McCall, 1976).

We also find both terms treated synonymously in studies belonging to the area of animal experimentation or animal ethology (Baldwin & Baldwin, 1977, 1978). The main line of thinking is expressed by Welker (1961), who states that "the term play is often used in conjunction with, or in place of, the term exploration. In other instances play is used as the generic term, exploration being only one type of play" (p. 222). Play is considered here as the more global, multidimensional concept that is superordinated to exploration and that cannot be explained in terms of a single theory (Reilly, 1974).

The large variety of behaviors subsumed under the concept of play may be a part of the difficulty in clarifying it. Moreover, such concepts have largely excluded phenomena of curiosity. Curiosity research deals more with the connection between exploration and play (e.g., Berlyne, 1960; Hughes, 1978; Hutt, 1966, 1970; Voss, 1981a).

On the other hand, several investigators in the area of curiosity and exploration have felt it necessary and valuable to deal with both a conceptual as well as an empirical distinction between play and exploration (e.g., Hughes, 1978; Hutt, 1966, 1970; Nunnally & Lemond, 1973; Voss, 1981a). One general assumption implicitly mentioned in the work of these authors would be that the two behavioral systems can best be understood in terms of a process model, linking exploration and play together in a given situation. In research of this kind, the focus is on an inspection of exploration and play *in statu nascendi*, or on the temporal sequencing of both behavioral systems. Referring to play as a *follower* of exploratory activities, the main methodological orientation of these authors is on a *microanalytical* level, meaning the breaking down of the postulated behavioral sequence into smaller parts or "entities" such as gazing, locomotor approach

44

towards the novel object, touching, manipulating, and combining with other objects. The microanalytical research strategy can be put into the neighborhood of *microgenesis* (*Aktualgenese*, Sander, 1928) in the sense that the sequence under consideration refers to observable events that extend from the presentation of a stimulus to the formation of a stable response. On a hypothetical level, microanalysis represents a heuristic activity (Linschoten, 1959) of the organism that corresponds to a series of experiences that "proceed discontinuously and in a succession of readily discernible stages" (Draguns, 1984, p. 4). Originally developed in an experimental laboratory setting, the microgenetical approach has also been demonstrated in instances of naturalistic observation of real-life situations; for example, Csikszentmihalyi and Getzels (1971) studied the actual process of artistic creation while "looking over the shoulders."

To make sure that the microgenetic perspective applies to a developmental analysis of exploration and play, one may remember Werner's (1957) application of the orthogenetic principle to microgenesis: As is true for other developmental sequences, the stages of diffusion and fragmentation are traversed, only to give way to a state of increasing differentiation, articulation, and integration. Informal observations of many investigators in the field of exploration and play have facilitated the interpretation of exploration–play sequences in terms of a progression of stimuli from maximal or pronounced informational uncertainty to the formation of a pattern of meaning that allows for a stable response. Throughout this chapter, exploration is defined in terms of the activity the child engages in to gain cognitive clarity over a somehow diffuse and fragmental stimulus, that activity set up at the very beginning of the behavioral sequence and proceeding through stages of confusion upon accumulation of discrepant and incongruous details, to the formation of a preliminary gestalt and, finally, of a complete and stabilized image. Play refers to the use of preexisting knowledge in manipulating the object. In this case, behavioral sequences become organism dominated rather than stimulus dominated (Weisler & McCall, 1976). Thus, as Belsky and Most (1981) have noted, by providing " a forum for the development and practice of behavioral subroutines that are subsequently integrated into more complex behavioral sequences" (p. 630), both exploration and play serve the function of acquiring skills and strategies that are later used in more goal-directed activities.

The latter sentence points in the direction of a more common perspective of developmental research—the investigation of ontogenetic changes and discontinuities across the several stages of the individual's lifespan. Based on the ontogenetic point of view in research on exploration and play, several investigators (e.g., Belsky & Most, 1981; Fein & Apfel, 1979; Fenson & Ramsay, 1980; McCall, 1974) have focused on infant exploratory and play activities as an area of inquiry in its own right and have tried to determine the validity of a developmental progression from undifferentiated exploration of the infant (e.g., simple manipulation, mouthing) to the more advanced forms of play (e.g., decontextualized play, pretense play).

Readdressing the formal parallels between microgeneses, ontogenesis, and phylogenesis that Sander (1928), Werner (1948), and other theoreticians speculated about, the next two parts of this chapter deal with (a) an inspection of the temporal sequencing of exploration and play in actual situations and (b) the ontogenetic course of both behavioral systems taken together. (Although very attractive, the phylogenetic point of view has to be neglected here, except for very tentative mention in a few instances.) The result of this venture then leads to some comments and conclusions concerning further research.

DEVELOPMENT OF EXPLORATION AND PLAY IN A MICROGENETIC PERSPECTIVE

The most common model of the relationship between exploration and play is based on the concept of process or temporal sequence. One of its earlier proponents was Corinne Hutt (1967) and, more explicitly, Nunnally and Lemond (1973). They considered several steps in the information processing of a novel or complex stimulus: orienting, perceptual investigation, manipulation, play, and search for a novel object or stimulus.

The behavioral subsystems of exploration and play may be paralleled by covert hypothetical motivational processes. In the terminology used by Berlyne (1960) and others, one of these processes is specific perceptual curiosity, which, on a behavioral level, includes an orienting response followed by active visual scanning. It should be mentioned that, according to Kreitler and Kreitler (1976), this early phase of orienting already includes cognitive processes that are instrumental on a level below that of conditioned responses. In exploration the result of this early stage of processing points to the role of specific stimulus properties such as novelty, complexity, uncertainty, and ambiguity. Specific curiosity means a motivational tendency to reduce subjective uncertainty by generating meaning. Another behavioral system referred to by Berlyne is the individual's manipulation of the object in order to reach the goal of generating meaning. According to Piaget (1936), the behavior of the child can be characterized in terms of an "active experimentation" or in terms of the attempt to overcome the "resistance of the object." We may also speak of this process as the generation and testing of hypothesis concerning the object's meaning and potential use. Indeed, the former process resembles problem solving in which no solution is presently available; the latter, problem solving in which there is a mental block. At the observational level, this part of the sequence has often been described in terms of facial expression, indicating tension or arousal, for example, and in terms of stereotyped actions (Hughes, 1978). One possible result of the aforementioned stage is the termination of the activity due to the individual's inability to reduce uncertainty further. In this case, the accompanying affects become increasingly unpleasant and may even shift to anger or rage. Exploration may begin again after a regeneration of the organism.

We assume that it may be of importance for the following activity, whether or not exploratory behavior has been terminated before leading to a meaningful interpretation of the stimulus. Hunter, Ross, and Ames (1982) demonstrated that 1-year-old children who were not allowed to finish habituation to an array of novel stimuli then preferred a familiar stimulus and that children who underwent full habituation to a novel stimulus then showed the tendency to select a novel object. However, it would be questionable to conclude that the same would be true under natural conditions (in the study by Hunter et al., children were not allowed to keep manipulating the same object after habituation). Exploratory behavior is followed by playful manipulation. At this point in the sequence, one may infer a transition from exploration to play and at the same time a change in the corresponding motivational processes: Tension and curiosity are replaced by joy and the pleasure of creating effects in the environment. Hutt (1966) referred to this point by posing the questions "what does this object do?" (exploration), followed by "what can I do with this object?" (play). With the latter question, some authors mention practice and repetition of manipulative acts in play (Bruner, 1973; Weisler & McCall, 1976). Playful manipulation is often elaborated on the plane of symbolic activities such as fantasy, imagination, or pretense play and also bears common features with creative thinking (Lieberman, 1965). Play activities can lead to diversive exploration (Berlyne, 1960). With the decrease of play activities, a negatively tuned feeling comes up. According to the model by Nunnally and Lemond (1973), boredom provides the motivational basis for a "search for new stimulation or change."

In an elegant critique of Berlyne's conceptual distinctions, Wohlwill (1981) suggests a third type of exploratory activity (in addition to specific, or inspective, and diversive exploration), one that he calls *affective exploration*. Whereas the functions of inspective and diversive exploration are uncertainty reduction and stimulus/sensation seeking, respectively, affective exploration is directed to the maintenance of an optimal hedonic tone. For example, affective exploration is mainly involved in aesthetic experiences and thus represents a "second force" besides the cognitive processing of a given object of art. One may also relate the affective mode to so-called nonpurposive activities where the consummatory act lies in the behavior itself, as it does in many playful activities such as sports— mountain climbing, scuba diving, or chess playing, for instance. In an original approach to this kind of activity, Csikszentmihalyi (1977) speaks of *flow states*. Whether affective exploration can be subsumed under these headings remains to be tested empirically; we think that this term refers to a specific quality of playful activity that corresponds to an individual's unique hedonic tone.

In the preceding paragraphs, we have given an outline of the temporal pattern that relates exploratory and play activities to each other. This view is compatible with the bulk of empirical studies dealing with stimulus conditions, types of responses, as well as context influences (for a review see Voss & Keller, 1981, 1983; Weisler & McCall, 1976). There remain, however, several unsolved problems. For example, how can the parts of the sequence be expressed on a behavioral level? Where are the transition points from one part to another? Which conditions lead to a complete or abridged sequence? What are the accompanying cognitive and affective processes? With respect to the first point, Weisler and McCall (1976) have pointed out that play may also be accompanied by negative affects related to danger—fear and mild distress, for instance. At the same time this would limit the validity of positive emotions as indicators of play. These authors mention activities such as climbing a tree, teasing, or riding a roller coaster, which may, however, be subsumed under the label of diversive exploration, representing thrill and adventure-seeking activities and not belonging to a true concept of play. We therefore do not agree with the skepticism of Weisler and McCall (1976) and instead emphasize the findings reported by Hughes (1978), who has empirically demonstrated the qualitative distinction between exploration and play for children from 3 to 5 years of age. Hughes described differences in the structural organization of both behavioral systems: In comparison with play, exploratory activities proved to be more uniform, and interindividual variation was smaller (Hutt, 1970). With respect to an empirical test of the total temporal pattern, Switzky, Ludwig, and Haywood (1979) found a decrease in the amount of exploratory behaviors along the time dimension, paralleled by an increase in play activities for both normal as well as moderately retarded preschool children.

Basing their work on an ethological point of view and learning theory, especially the type of learning that is shaped by the reinforcers of sensory stimulation, Baldwin and Baldwin (1978) offered a sequential model in which exploration and play are organized into six phases, beginning with "early exploration" and ending with late play and "end of play." This is compatible with the model proposed by Nunnally and Lemond (1973). It comprises two factors, exploration and play, which extend over the time span differently; the peak of the exploration gradient (inverse U-curve) precedes the one of play. Maximum overlap occurs in the middle part of the temporal sequence. This may explain why individuals sometimes tend to oscillate between exploration and play responses.

DEVELOPMENT OF EXPLORATION AND PLAY IN AN ONTOGENETIC PERSPECTIVE

There are only a few studies that deal explicitly with the development of the exploration–play sequence. Based on cross-sectional comparisons, work by Schneider, Moch, Sandfort, Auerswald, and Walther-Weckman (1983) showed that the expected behavioral pattern was exhibited in 3, 4, and 5-year-olds whose behaviors were observed during a 10-minute time interval. There was visual inspecting and question asking followed by touching and manipulating the object and playful manipulating. There was only one significant developmental trend— an increase in the rate of manipulation with age. In a longitudinal study on the development of exploratory behavior, the author (Darmstadt Longitudinal Study, 1979–1983) has demonstrated that there was an increase in the proportion of complete exploration–play sequences shown by children from 13 to 19 months (Voss, 1981b). Whereas the 13-month-old children more often showed periods of exploring an object without proceeding to play manipulations—repetitions and positive affects, for instance—there was found a higher degree of balance between periods of exploration and play by 19-month-old children, even a dominance of play over exploration. Two conclusions concerning the ontogenetic perspective can be drawn from these results: (a) With increasing age, there is more differentiation into different parts of the temporal sequence as well as a higher level of integration in the sense that the complete sequence represents a behavioral unit; (b) the temporal extension of specific parts of the sequence may change with increasing age.

The first notion reflects principles of cognitive development in general, principles such as differentiation and integration. According to the second assumption, Wohlwill (1984) has postulated that exploratory activities of the inspective type will follow a negatively accelerated curve, becoming asymptotic in children older than 8 years, whereas play follows an inverted U-curve, reaching its highest point when the child is 5 or 6 years old. One possible explanation would be that with increasing age an information-extracting attitude towards environmental stimuli becomes more important, repressing play activities at the same time.

When discussing general models of this kind, one has to take into account a high degree of individual differences in the relative importance of the different components of the temporal pattern and the specific kind of functional relationships with age. Here again, the inverse U-function seems to be appropriate for a description of age-dependent effects. Belsky and Most (1981), for example, revealed a quadratic trend of transitional play, that is, relational and functional-relational play as well as enactive naming, from 7½ to 21 months of age. Undifferentiated exploration (mouthing, simple manipulative acts) declined linearly across age groups, whereas contextualized pretend play increased in a linear fashion.

Whether a quadratic trend can be demonstrated may be primarily a matter of the design of the study, especially the age range under consideration. If one accepts the assumption that the result reported by Belsky and Most (1981) generally fits the inverted U-model, it becomes clear that linear trends would represent the descending or ascending branches of the curve, and one would expect, for example, that there is a maximum of simple exploration, in the sense

Belsky and Most used this term, prior to 7 months. It should be mentioned, however, that the question of whether such a distinction is useful is not answered by those results. Keller (personal communication, May 1984) has emphasized the developmental significance of the so-called simple as well as complex forms of exploration when considering a certain age level. We thus do not know whether the strength or quality of a behavior changes. Children use their behavioral potential, which, of course, changes over time. If an 8-year-old child generally explores by means of mouthing, we should not classify this as being a "simple form" of behavior but instead recognize a developmental delay.

The kind of research reported previously is aimed at identifying *dominant* types of exploration and play and their location on the age scale. From a developmental point of view, one may also describe these ontogenetical changes in terms of cumulation and hierarchization. Belsky and Most (1981) have accounted for these principles when conceptualizing the exploration–play sequence in terms of a one-dimensional and cumulative (Guttman) scale. This makes sense because it reflects a general trend, namely, that "higher" forms of exploration–play are superimposed upon simple forms in the course of development. This also includes the possibility that remote behavioral systems can be reactivated in later stages when needed.

One conclusion is that the special properties of a stimulus ("collative" variables, for example) determine whether the complete behavioral sequence will be exhibited at a given age level. This raises the question of what the "optimal" stimuli or objects for the instigation of play are when considering children at different ages. This problem has not yet been systematically investigated.

The general assumption that the kind of stimuli as well as the type of exploration and play determine the nature of age trends has also been stressed by Wohlwill (1984). He considered age levels ranging from 2 to 8 years and postulated an inverted U-function for play.

Keeping in mind that the concept of development also involves a concern for discontinuities and instability as aspects of developmental change (e.g., Wohlwill, 1973), one has to ask whether the methodological features of the studies carried out thus far are consonant with such concerns. A claim is made here for the longitudinal research design. In our longitudinal study on the development of exploratory behavior in early childhood (Darmstadt Longitudinal Study, 1979–1983), 44 children ranging in age from 1 to 4 years were observed in their homes as well as in the laboratory. The time interval of observations was 6 months. Preliminary results point to changes in the hierarchical organization of behavioral subsystems across age levels. With increasing age, sequences of exploration–play become more systematically related to each other in terms of both the probability of each step in the sequence being initiated on termination of a preceding step and in terms of the flexibility or reversibility of the sequence. This allows a higher rate of information processing (Voss, 1981a) at the expense of the empirical separation of the subsystems under consideration.

There may be a similar interpretation based on McCall's (1974) proposed model of qualitative developmental transitions in the first 2 years of life. He described five stages or "transitions" for cognitive development, and there is a similarity with Piaget's (1936) concept of early sensorimotor development. Exploratory behavior in the model is first mentioned by McCall when referring to stage 2 (2 to 7 months); here, exploration means contingent visual responses and simple, undifferentiated acts. Play is explicitly mentioned when discussing stage 4 (13 to 21 months), which refers to an ability to relate at least two external events or objects to each other correctly. Although McCall (1974) does not deal with conceptual or empirical distinctions of exploration and play, one can interpret his assumptions as supporting the ontogenetic view of a progression from simple forms of exploration to the first appearance of symbolic play. Special weight is put on the empirical manifestation of the child's tendency to exert an impact on the environment, which implies that the child would already be able to distinguish between "means" and "ends." This view is consistent with our opinion that goal-oriented behavior or the anticipation of effects is the main characteristic of play.

Because there is only a small number of longitudinal studies on the development of exploration and play in humans, we may direct our attention to related animal studies. In these studies exploration, which mainly occurs in species with "leisure time," is generally considered to be a subsystem of play (see, for example, the studies on the play of rhesus monkeys by Harlow and Harlow, 1965). Baldwin (1969) described the following stages in the play of squirrel monkeys: object exploration, early social exploration, contact play and wrestling, distance play or chasing, fight play or aggressive play, as well as "end of play." Here, again, one may be reminded of the parallel between ontogenesis and microgenesis, for which a progression from exploration to "higher" forms of social play is postulated for the juvenile and adult members of a species. Baldwin and Baldwin (1977) analyzed the development of exploration and play in terms of learning theory. In their view, the fact of a decrease in play activities through childhood is caused by a parallel decline of arousal level, the relatively rare occurrences of specific reinforcers, and the decrease of reinforcement potential. Exploration and play may expose the individual to new and dangerous situations (in free-field exploration, for instance). Activities of this kind are thought to lead to changes in the surroundings or even in the "cultural traditions" of a given society. In this respect it may be biologically important that there is a decline in exploration and play with increasing age (Kummer, 1971; Rowell, 1972).

However, comparability of animal and human development is rather restricted. This statement also can be extended to the comparison of different animal species. In her observational studies with chimpanzees, Lawick-Goodall (1968) has described the enormous behavioral complexity and idiosyncrasy of development that limit the identification of developmental stages. Thus, only general trends of maturation and learning processes can be indicated.

CONCLUSIONS

In this section we comment and elaborate on some of the critical points mentioned earlier.

Scientists Disagree about the Conceptual Status of Exploration and Play. Given the general premise that exploration and play represent "interlocked behaviors that are embedded in conditionally related processes" (Weick, 1969), the question is whether both behavioral systems can be separated empirically. This question has been answered—at least for the moment—in favor of a *process model*. This model postulates that exploratory behavior precedes play, which then leads to activities that the organism engages in to increase stimulation. The main theoretical assumption is that specific exploration operates in order to reduce stimulation or cognitive uncertainty; play is aimed at sustaining certain tolerable limits (this is similar to the "activation cycle" [Heckhausen, 1964]). When play is terminated, exploratory stimulus seeking will increase the activation level of the organism in order to avoid or reduce boredom.

We regard the model of a temporal sequence of exploration and play as a *research paradigm* that allows one to differentiate three domains in the structural and functional aspects of both systems: the internal cognitive and affective components and processes, the observable indicators for different behavioral states and segments, and the physical and social setting, i.e., ecological factors that influence the organism at a given moment.

A Sequential Point of View Includes the Problem of Segmentation. The question is how exploration and play can be empirically separated from each other and what determines the length of the segments. Evidence on that point is admittedly very limited. Collard (1962) attempted to define exploration and play empirically for children aged 8 to 12 months. There is also Collard's (1979) observation that less vocalizing occurred during a phase of exploration than during a phase of play. This result, which the author (Voss, 1981b, see also Chapter 8 this volume) was able to confirm, might be regarded as providing a basis for discriminating between exploration and play. With respect to *affective* behavioral correlates, there is evidence reported by Hutt (1966) and Hughes (1978) on facial expressions signaling different states of tension. We think the problem of segmentation in part reflects the difficulties in determining an adequate *level of analysis* for the micro–macro dimension (see later).

In General, Overall Exploratory Activity Seems to Decline with Increasing Age. This trend also includes an increase in play activities as the individual progresses through childhood. As a general explanation one may refer to a decline in "collative" variability such as novelty, ambiguity, complexity, and surprise

(Berlyne, 1960). Contextual influences like the social or cultural setting also may determine the direction of the developmental course. One hypothesis would be that the impact of educational institutions and other socializing agents will inhibit curiosity and play and successively replace them with "ritualized" forms of excitement and play such as sports, movies, and art.

Exploration and Play Must Be Considered in Relation to Qualitative Changes in Cognitive Development.   This statement calls for an inspection of the developmental patterns of a larger variety of cognitive abilities over the given age span. The transformational point of view implies that a behavioral system I can be transformed into a behavioral system II, indicating a change in the functional level of cognitive development. Bruner's (1968) concept of enactive, iconic, and symbolic stages and Piaget's (1936) stages of cognitive development may be examples for this view. It is fruitful and meaningful to look for the developmental sequels of the "simpler" forms of exploration and play. We would like to name potential candidates: epistemic behavior, directed thinking and problem solving (Berlyne, 1965), creativity and divergent thinking, imagination, daydreaming, and fantasy. Singer and Singer (1979) have postulated a strong relationship between imaginative play and exploratory behavior "in the sense that in many ways the child [and also adult, we would like to add] continues to be interested, and persists in exploring words and phrases and notions that are not clear" (p. 196). If one accepts the notion that cognitive change refers to a lifelong developmental process, the questions posed by Hutt (1966)—"What does this object do to me?" and "What can I do with this object?"—may be also involved in adult thinking and imagining. Examples may be the playful "inner" manipulation of thoughts and feelings, which is intimately related to daydreaming and creative production or scientific inquiry. It thus can be asked whether exploration and special forms of play, in the sense just described, are developmental phenomena per se, limited to infancy and childhood and then being replaced by other forms of mental activities.

Action Theory May Provide a Conceptual Framework for Systematic Research on Exploration and Play.   In the preceding paragraph we have reflected on the question of whether there are transitions or stages in the lifelong development of exploration and play. In terms of a metatheoretical point of view, the author's inclination is towards *General Systems Theory* (von Bertalanffy, 1968; Boulding, 1956; Weiss, 1971) and related biological concepts such as organization (Lorenz, 1978). This approach includes not only the analysis of the interactions of the elements or subsystems but also the analysis of the context (Weick, 1969). One requirement would be to consider both the macroproperties of the environment along with the microproperties of the behavioral system. Reilly (1974) defines organization theory as follows:

Organization theory defines a hierarchy as composed of stages or domains distinguished in terms of time sequences in which older, simpler forms of behavior are
transformed to newer and more complex forms. The functions of the hierarchy is
to process change quantitatively from small to large, from simple to complex, and
qualitatively from lower to higher forms of behavior. (p. 124)

This view is compatible with a conceptualization in terms of *action theory*, and
we discuss this point for the remainder of this chapter.

We (Voss & Keller, 1983) speak of exploratory action as a "goal-directed
activity of an organism that involves an active dealing with objects or events of
the environment aimed at building up new structures of knowledge and that can
be conceptionalized in terms of a process model of exploration" (p. 159). Actions
represent organized sequences of ongoing behavior that may be mirrored by
observational data and that correspond to "inner" cognitive processes and entities
such as percepts, goals, values, and knowledge. In this formulation, sequences
of behavior refer to the temporal organization of actions and at the same time
to the hierarchical patterning of subsystems. If one adopts the notion of action
or act (Harré & Secord, 1972) as a basic unit of analysis, it would be the task
of further research to gain knowledge about the organizational structure in terms
of temporal and hierarchical aspects of exploration–play phenomena. The empirical description and analysis of exploration–play actions proceed through several
stages of breaking down the action unit into smaller parts or subsystems, namely,
exploratory and play behavior and more fine-grained elements such as perceptual
responses, manipulations, and vocalization.

With respect to the hypothetical level, exploration–play in Piaget's terms
refers to the process of equilibration involving assimilatory and accommodatory
efforts of the individual at the level of (a) subject–object relationships, (b) cognitive
subsystems of the person ("reciprocal" assimilation and accommodation), and
(c) relationships within these subsystems. One proposition would be to use the
term *play* to describe the process by which structural change on these latter levels
is guided. The main reason for this is that playful activities are organism dominated in the sense that, after exploration has come to an end, the newly formed
cognitive scheme has to be integrated into or balanced against preexisting cognitive structures of the individual. Whereas exploration refers to the subject–
object relationship, that is, accommodatory efforts are made by the individual
in order to "overcome the resistance of the object" (Piaget), play can be seen to
be based upon the "inner" experience of manipulating the cognitive scheme that
corresponds to the physical properties of the object. This would include attempts
of the organism to make use of other cognitive schemes or subsystems that might
lead to alterations or even to a falsification of the object's original meaning.
First, for example, exploring the so-called Hutt-box (Hutt, 1967) may result in
a clear image of a box equipped with a lever that can be used in order to produce

sounds and flashing lights. Second, there is something like "going beyond the information given" when the child wants to find out what other familiar action schemes can be successfully applied—sitting on top of the box and imitating a train conductor, for instance. Play, therefore, can lead to a reinterpretation or reconstruction of a familiar object and thus may represent a further attempt of the individual to increase or at least to maintain the "rate of cognitive structuring" (Voss & Keller, 1983) after a preceding phase of extensive exploration. This fits Hutt's (1967) notion that play may represent the time-out phase in the service of consolidating the information acquired during an epistemic activity.

The question of how to operationalize exploratory and play subsystems still remains. As we have discussed elsewhere, action theory provides a modest approach (Voss, 1983). It depends largely on the level of analysis, a problem that can be traced back to the molar–molecular distinction made by Tolman (1926). It is the question of whether one would be able to separate play from exploration empirically. In most laboratory and home settings in which a child is exposed to novel objects and behavior is videotaped, we found it most appropriate to work on a *microanalytical* level, analyzing or segmenting the ongoing stream of behavior by viewing them in slow motion. The work presented in Chapter 8 of this volume demonstrates the usefulness of this approach and shows that exploratory behavior can be understood as an activity aimed at the formation of a *behavioral intent* or the anticipation of a behavioral result that, in turn, signals the onset of playful activity.

We support the so-called microgenetic approach (Draguns, 1981; Graumann, 1959; Sander, 1928). In his review on microgenesis, Draguns (1984) explicitly points to the exploratory nature of any kind of heuristic activity that "involves progressions of stimuli from maximal or pronounced information deprivation to the presentation of adequate or optimal amounts of information for the response or decision at hand" (p. 5). Far from being able to provide a conceptual framework for research on exploration–play at the present time, we are concerned with the natural observation of the patterning of behavioral subsystems such as perceptual investigation, approach behavior, touching and manipulation, verbal communication about these actions, repetitions in handling the object, and more systematic experiments with the object.

Readdressing Werner's (1948) statement on the macro–micro correspondence mentioned in the opening paragraph of this chapter, and after having summarized the research evidence, we must still answer the question about whether the analysis of brief behavioral sequences adds to our knowledge of ontogenetic developments of the same behavioral systems and vice versa. The main reason sounds trivial: There is simply no direct test of this assumption, and there are practically no relevant studies. If one uses the micro–macro parallel as a working hypothesis, it may well serve as a reference point for the investigation of the development of exploration and play in the near future.

SUMMARY

There are two approaches to the study of exploration–play from a developmental perspective. First, the focus may be on an inspection of exploration and play *in statu nascendi*, or on the temporal sequencing of both behavioral systems. Second, both behavioral systems may be investigated for ontogenetic changes across the several stages of the individual's lifespan.

Common models of exploration–play involve the concept of process or temporal sequence, linking several stages or segments of exploration such as orienting, visual inspection, and manipulating and playful activities such as practice and repetition of manipulative acts, symbolic activities like fantasy and imagination, or pretense play. Ontogenetic changes can be related to principles of cognitive development in general, like those of differentiation and integration. Several investigators have focused on identifying dominant types of exploration and play and their location on the age scale. Most of these studies are based on the cross-sectional research paradigm, and there is a lack of longitudinal studies devoted to the description of both continuities and discontinuities in developmental patterns of exploration–play sequences.

The following topics for further research on exploration–play emerge after a discussion of the preceding approaches: the conceptual and empirical status of both behavioral systems, that is, the question of whether they can be separated in terms of conceptual properties and observable segments of the behavioral stream (this also includes the problem of segmentation); the description of both quantitative and qualitative changes and how these relate to cognitive development in general; and the specification of a theoretical framework (which might be action theory) for systematic research on exploration–play.

REFERENCES

Baldwin, J. D. (1969). The ontogeny of social behavior of squirrel monkeys (*Saimiri sciureus*) in a seminatural environment. *Folia primatologica, 11*, 35–97.

Baldwin, J. D., & Baldwin, J. I. (1977). The role of learning phenomena in the ontogeny of exploration and play. In S. Chevalier-Skolnikoff and F. Poirier (Eds.), *Primate socialization* (pp. 104–161). New York: Garland.

Baldwin, J. D., & Baldwin, J. I. (1978). Reinforcement theories of exploration, play, creativity, and psychological growth. In E. O. Smith (Ed.), *Primate play* (pp. 52–70). New York: Academic Press.

Belsky, J., & Most, R. K. (1981). From exploration to play: A cross-sectional study of infant free play behavior. *Developmental Psychology, 17*, 630–639.

Berlyne, D. E. (1960). *Conflict, arousal, and curiosity.* New York: McGraw–Hill.

Berlyne, D. E. (1965). *Structure and direction in thinking.* New York: Wiley.

Bertalanffy, L. von. (1968). *General systems theory. Foundations, development, application.* New York: Braziller.

Boulding, K. (1956). General systems theory—The skeleton of science. *Management Science* (Whole no. 2).

Bruner, J. S. (1968). *Processes of cognitive growth: Infancy.* Worcester, MA: Clark University Press.

Bruner, J. S. (1973). Organization of early skilled action. *Child Development, 44*, 1–11.

Collard, R. R. (1962). *A study of curiosity in infants.* Unpublished doctoral dissertation, University of Chicago.

Collard, R. R. (1979). Exploration and play responses of eight- to twelve-month-old infants in different environments. Discussion. In B. Sutton-Smith (Ed.), *Play and learning* (pp. 45–68). New York: Gardner Press.

Csikszentmihalyi, M. (1977). *Beyond boredom and anxiety.* San Francisco: Jossey-Bass.

Csikszentmihalyi, M., & Getzels, J. W. (1971). Discovery-oriented behavior and the originality of creative products: A study with artists. *Journal of Personality and Social Psychology, 19*, 47–52.

The Darmstadt Longitudinal Study on the Development of Exploratory Behavior from 1 to 4 Years. (1979–1983). Funded by the Volkswagen Foundation.

Draguns, J. G. (1981). Why microgenesis? An inquiry into the motivational sources of going beyond the information given. *Psychological Research Bulletin* (Lund University, Sweden), *21*, pp. 11–12.

Draguns, J. G. (1984). Microgenesis by any other name . . . In W. D. Froehlich, G. Smith, J. G. Draguns, & U. Hentschel (Eds.), *Psychological processes in cognition and personality* (pp. 3–17). Washington: Hemisphere.

Fein, G. G., & Apfel, N. (1979). The development of play: Style, structure, and situations. *Genetic Psychology Monographs, 99*, 231–250.

Fenson, L., & Ramsay, D. S. (1980). Decentration and integration of the child's play in the second year. *Child Development, 51*, 171–178.

Graumann, C. F. (1959). Aktualgenese: Die deskriptiven Grundlagen und theoretischen Wandlungen des aktualgenetischen Forschungsansatzes. *Zeitschrift für experimentelle und angewandte Psychologie, 6*, 410–448.

Harlow, H. F., & Harlow, M. K. (1965). The affectional systems. In A. M. Schrier, H. F. Harlow, & F. Stollnitz (Eds.), *Behavior of nonhuman primates* (Vol. 2, pp. 287–334). New York: Academic Press.

Harré, R., & Secord, P. F. (1972). *The explanation of social behavior.* Oxford: Oxford University Press.

Heckhausen, H. (1964). Entwurf einer Psychologie des Spielens. *Psychologische Forschung, 27*, 225–243.

Hughes, M. (1978). Sequential analysis of exploration and play. *International Journal of Behavioral Development, 1*, 83–97.

Hunter, M. A., Ross, H. S., & Ames, E. W. (1982). Preferences of familiar or novel toys: Effect of familiarization time in 1-year-olds. *Developmental Psychology, 18*, 519–529.

Hutt, C. (1966). Exploration and play in children. In *Play, exploration and territory in mammals. Symposia of the Zoological Society, London, 18*, 61–81.

Hutt, C. (1967). Temporal effects on responses decrement and stimulus satiation in exploration. *British Journal of Psychology, 58*, 365–373.

Hutt, C. (1970). Specific and diversive exploration. In H. Reese & L. P. Lipsitt (Eds.), *Advances in child development and behavior* (Vol. 5, pp. 119–180). London: Academic Press.

Kreitler, H., & Kreitler, S. (1976). *Cognitive orientation and behavior.* New York: Springer.

Kummer, H. (1971). *Primate societies.* Chicago: Aldine-Atherton.

Lawick-Goodall, J. van (1968). The behavior of free-living chimpanzees in the Gombe Stream area. *Animal Behavior Monographs, 1*, 161–311.

Lieberman, J. N. (1965). Playfulness and divergent thinking: An investigation of their relationship at the kindergarten level. *Journal of Genetic Psychology, 107,* 219–224.

Linschoten, J. (1959). Aktualgenese und heuristisches Prinzip. *Zeitschrift für experimentelle und angewandte Psychologie, 6,* 449–473.

Lorenz, K. (1978). *Vergleichende Verhaltensforschung.* Wien: Deuticke.

McCall, R. B. (1974). Exploratory manipulation and play in the human infant. *Monographs of the Society for Research in Child Development, 39,* (Serial # 155).

Nunnally, J. C., & Lemond, L. C. (1973). Exploratory behavior and human development. In H. W. Reese (Ed.), *Advances in child development and behavior* (Vol. 8, pp. 59–108). New York: Academic Press.

Piaget, J. (1936). *La naissance de l'intelligence chez l'enfant.* Neuchâtel: Delachaux & Niestlé.

Reilly, M. (1974). An explanation of play. In M. Reilly (Ed.), *Play as exploratory learning* (pp. 117–149). Beverly Hills, CA: Sage.

Rowell, T. E. (1972). *The social behavior of monkeys.* Baltimore: Penguin.

Sander, F. (1928, September). Experimentelle Ergebnisse der Gestaltpsychologie. In F. Sander (Ed.), *Bericht über den 10. Kongress für experimentelle Psychologie* (pp. 23–88). Jena.

Schneider, K., Moch, M., Sandfort, R., Auerswald, M., & Walther-Weckman, K. (1983). Exploring a novel object by preschool children: A sequential analysis of perceptual, manipulating and verbal exploration. *International Journal of Behavioral Development, 6,* 477–496.

Singer, J., & Singer, D. (1979). The values of imagination. In B. Sutton-Smith (Ed.), *Play and learning* (pp. 195–218). New York: Gardner Press.

Switzky, H. N., Ludwig, L., & Haywood, H. C. (1979). Exploration and play in retarded and nonretarded preschool children: Effects of object complexity and age. *American Journal of Mental Deficiency, 83,* 637–644.

Tolman, E. C. (1926). A behavioristic theory of ideas. *Psychological Review, 33,* 352–369.

Voss, H.-G. (1981a). Kognition und exploratives Handeln. In H.-G. Voss & H. Keller (Eds.), *Neugierforschung: Grundlagen—Theorien—Anwendungen* (pp. 175–196). Weinheim: Beltz.

Voss, H.-G. (1981b). A longitudinal study of exploratory behavior and meaning acquisition: *Research display.* Congress of the International Society for the Study of Behavioral Development, Toronto.

Voss, H.-G. (1983). Neugier und Exploration. In H. A. Euler & H. Mandl (Eds.), *Emotionspsychologie: Ein Handbuch in Schlüsselbegriffen* (pp. 220–226). München: Urban & Schwarzenberg.

Voss, H.-G., & Keller, H. (Eds.), (1981). *Neugierforschung: Grundlagen—Theorien—Anwendungen.* Weinheim: Beltz.

Voss, H.-G., & Keller, H. (1983). *Curiosity and exploration. Theories and results.* New York: Academic Press.

Weick, C. (1969). *The social psychology of organization.* Reading, MA: Addison-Wesley.

Weisler, A., & McCall, R. B. (1976). Exploration and play. *American Psychologist, 31,* 492–508.

Weiss, P. (Ed.). (1971). *Hierarchically organized systems in theory and practice.* New York: Wiley.

Welker, W. I. (1961). An analysis of exploratory and play behavior in animals. In D. W. Fiske & S. R. Maddi (Eds.), *Functions of varied experience* (pp. 175–226). Homewood, IL: Dorsey.

Werner, H. (1948). *Comparative psychology of mental development.* New York: International Universities.

Werner, H. (1957). The concept of development from a comparative and organismic point of view. In D. B. Harris (Ed.), *The concept of development* (pp. 125–148). Minneapolis: University of Minnesota Press.

Wohlwill, J. F. (1973). *The study of behavioral development.* New York: Academic Press.

Wohlwill, J. F. (1981). A conceptual analysis of exploratory behavior: The "specific–diversive" distinction revisited. In H. I. Day (Ed.), *Advances in intrinsic motivation and aesthetics* (pp. 341–364). New York: Plenum Press.

Wohlwill, J. F. (1984). *Research Proposal on the Development of Children's Exploratory Activity.* The Pennsylvania State University, Manuscript.

CHAPTER FOUR

VARIETIES OF
EXPLORATORY ACTIVITY
IN EARLY CHILDHOOD

JOACHIM F. WOHLWILL
Pennsylvania State University

As has been true in many areas of psychology, progress in the field of exploratory activity appears to have been hampered by a failure to make some important differentiations between types of behaviors that share little more in common than their designation by the same name—i.e., *exploratory*. Consider the following two examples:

1. An infant—let us say, aged 12 months—is brought to a child development "lab" with its mother. It is "set loose" at the entrance to a large, empty room, into which it enters, on all fours, of course, and which it thoroughly "explores" by moving through this environment to its heart's content, returning periodically to its mother for reassurance, or simply glancing in her direction to satisfy itself that she is still there.

2. A child—let us say, 4-years-old—is shown a picture of a creature containing features of a bird, a dog, and a man and told to look at it for as long as it would like. It scans the picture for a certain period of time—12 seconds, maybe—and then indicates that it would like to see the next one. The figure of 12 seconds is recorded as a measure of its "voluntary exploration time."

It would be difficult to think of two kinds of behaviors more disparate than these—taken, respectively, from the research of Rheingold and Eckerman (1970) and of Nunnally, Faw, and Bashford (1969). Yet both are not only designated by the same term, *exploration*, but are left undifferentiated in many accounts and interpretations of exploration, such as Nunnally and Lemond's (1973), Weisler and McCall's (1976), and, to a degree, even in that of Berlyne (1960). Most pernicious of all, in research at the human level the second of the previously cited cases is generally taken as prototypic of exploratory activity, to the general neglect of the first.[1]

EXPLORATION AS SEARCH FOR
AND AS EXAMINATION OF STIMULI

If we consider the two senses of exploration just referred to, the reason for the tendency of psychologists to study exploration in the second sense rather than the first is not difficult to find. The second case is initiated by the subject's

---

[1]This statement is intended to refer to the literature on exploration at the human level. The study of exploratory activity at the animal level has been much more prone to focus on free exploration of the environment by an animal, in part because of its relevance to certain theoretical issues derived from the field of animal learning (see Fowler, 1965). A particularly insightful analysis of such exploratory behavior has been provided by Shillito (1963).

encounter with a stimulus; the subject is assumed to be stationary and attending only to that stimulus, through his or her visual, auditory, and/or tactual sense organs. The situation is thus very much under the investigator's control, notwithstanding the supposedly voluntary character of the behavior, and accordingly systematic relationships between variable attributes of the stimulus that the investigator can manipulate experimentally and the measure of exploratory activity (typically amount of time spent attending to the stimulus) can be determined. This feature undoubtedly loomed important for such experimentally oriented psychologists as Berlyne and Nunnally, and many others who have conducted research within this paradigm (see Hutt, 1970, and Nunnally & Lemond, 1973, for reviews). But at the same time it has greatly restricted the conception of exploratory activity and its development that has evolved.

Indeed, it has led to a paradoxically passive picture of exploratory activity, according to which the organism, though engaging in purely voluntary behavior, seems to have its eyes "glued" as it were to a screen through the sheer force exerted by certain stimulus characteristics such as incongruity and complexity. Fortunately, the increasing resort to three-dimensional objects in studies of exploration of this type, and to the examination of children's manipulative behavior in exploring such objects (Belsky & Most, 1981; Henderson, Charlesworth, & Gamradt, 1982; Lowe, 1975; Switzky, Haywood, & Isett, 1974; Wohlwill, 1983) is serving to counteract such a view.

Yet, even when treated with due regard to the activity invested by the individual in the exploration of some stimulus or object, this type of exploration still represents behavior of a very different kind and reveals phenomena differing from those entailed in exploration of the first type, i.e., free exploration of an environment.

This point is readily documented by referring to one of the rare examples of research on exploration of this type, viz. the work of Rheingold and Eckerman cited previously. These investigators did not study an infant's or child's response to a particular stimulus; rather, they were interested in the infant's increasing tendency to move away from the safety and security afforded by its mother and to explore and thus learn about its environment. In the course of the research conducted from this vantage point, they were able to document the steadily increasing range within which infants explored their environment, i.e., progressively further away from their mother, corroborating findings previously obtained with subhuman primate infants. The role of the sheer number of toys distributed through the environment, varying from none to three, in promoting exploration could likewise be determined. In a subsequent study, furthermore, Eckerman and Rheingold (1974) were able to compare the relative potency of social versus nonsocial stimuli (the former being represented by an unfamiliar person sitting in the exploration room).

A further study, by Henderson, Charlesworth, and Gamradt (1982), is deserving of mention in this same context, as it investigated free exploration of an environment in much the same sense, but with older children. These researchers observed children, divided into a preschool and a grade school group, as they moved through the displays of a natural history museum that permitted direct touching and handling of the objects. One of the authors' prime findings related to the role of the parents, just as was true for Rheingold and Eckerman's work, but in a very different sense. It turns out that children who visited the museum accompanied by their parents experienced some constraints on their movement as a result of the presence of the parents in comparison with those who visited with their peers and who displayed a considerably higher level of activity. Henderson et al.'s focus on the amount and pattern of movement in the children's exploration of this museum is a good example of the different perspective animating such research as compared to that which focuses on response to stimuli that are exposed to the child.

Here, then, we see the essential difference between the two prototypes of research on exploratory activity that we have contrasted. One involves a search for stimuli, or for stimulation, whereas the other involves inspection of a stimulus, once it is encountered. This difference, some might argue, amounts to the differentiation between diversive and specific exploration, proposed by Berlyne as early as his 1960 book and considered by most of the major contributors to this literature, including Hutt (1970) and Nunnally and Lemond (1973). As is well known, Berlyne distinguished between a "diversive" mode of exploration directed at producing a certain level of arousal, and a "specific" one aimed at reducing uncertainty produced by the complexity, novelty, incongruity, or surprisingness of some particular stimulus encountered. Yet neither Berlyne nor Hutt or Nunnally and Lemond came to grips with the very different approach to research required by a conception of exploration as search behavior as opposed to inspection of a stimulus. Indeed, in his own research Berlyne assimilated diversive exploration to the paradigm utilized for the study of specific exploration; both entailed presentation of predetermined stimuli, with only a different response demanded of the subject, i.e., ratings of liking or preference for diversive, as opposed to ratings of interestingness, or free looking time, for specific. As for the reviews by Hutt and by Nunnally and Lemond, although both likewise emphasized the diversive–specific distinction, these writers similarly failed to concern themselves with its implication for research, much less conduct studies of search behavior to investigate diversive exploration. Thus their respective literature reviews were confined almost exclusively to studies of voluntary exploration of particular stimuli, relying on the use of exploration time for their dependent variable.[2]

---

[2]Significantly, Rheingold's work is not mentioned by Nunnally and Lemond; Hutt did refer to an early report of it, but again in such a way as to assimilate exploration of an environment in search of stimuli to exploration of stimuli or objects.

One of the reasons why the confusion over this differentiation has persisted is that those who have addressed themselves to this topic have failed to conceive of it as structured along a temporal dimension. Doing so would reveal that inspective exploration resulting upon encounter with a stimulus may, and frequently does, represent a second phase in the total exploratory process, that process being initiated through free exploration of the environment, in search of stimuli, or stimulation. Interestingly enough, Nunnally and Lemond give implicit recognition to this point in their model of exploratory behavior, which presents a temporal series of phases. Their sequence begins, however, with a stimulus–encounter episode, and ends with a phase of search for a new stimulus. Clearly, this last phase properly belongs at the head of the sequence, even if it is undoubtedly true that exploration frequently is set off by some incidental encounter with a stimulus, thus short-circuiting the initial phase. But perhaps more important is that we recognize some significant differences in the approach that is most appropriate to the study of each phase and in the major behavioral variables that are relevant to each.

If we start out, as do Rheingold et al. and Henderson et al., by setting an infant or child loose in an unfamiliar environment, the primary object of interest would seem to relate to the extent and pattern of movement engaged in by the child during the course of its exploration of that environment. Such indices as time spent exploring, distance traveled, degree of systematization in the pattern of movement through the environment from one locale, stimulus, or object to the next (e.g., to what extent does the child return to a given object that it has encountered previously), and other qualitative aspects of the child's behavior (signs of anxiety or fear, returns to or glances in the direction of the mother, or a security object, pace of movement, etc.) are of greatest relevance to this phase of environmental exploration. In contrast, study of the stimulus–encounter phase calls for recording behaviors specifically directed at the inspection and investigation of the stimulus. Even here we may expand our approach beyond the single measure that has been utilized in virtually all previous research on this topic: the amount of time spent looking at or listening to a stimulus. Qualitative aspects of exploration style could profitably be introduced to broaden the scope of the information about the process of exploration obtained, as this writer has in fact done for haptic exploration of stimuli (Wohlwill, 1975). And, to the extent that three-dimensional objects are employed, the mode of exploration can be studied—though this has all too rarely been done—in terms of the pattern of manipulation of the object. (For instance, given blocks featuring different pictorial material and/or material for haptic exploration on their six sides, to what extent does the child systematically turn a given block to expose each face in turn?) In short, what is being proposed is a more functionally oriented approach to the study of exploration, covering each of its successive phases.

DIFFERENT MODES OF RESPONSE
TO STIMULI DURING EXPLORATION

One reason for suggesting such a functional approach is that as the writer has previously proposed (Wohlwill, 1981), it is useful to differentiate between two different orientations that individuals may display in their exploration of a stimulus; it is worth restating that differentiation and to some extent expanding on it.

Let us consider an individual engaging in genuine diversive exploration, i.e., activity in search of stimulation, designed to relieve boredom, raise arousal, or the like. Although this behavior can be readily illustrated at any level of phylo or ontogenetic development, let us do so with reference to a child on a trip to the beach. The child goes "exploring" along the water's edge—beachcombing, as we generally call it—and at some point, comes across a large seashell. At this encounter "specific" exploration—or what I should prefer to call "inspective" exploration—ensues. The shell is picked up, visually examined, turned in the child's hand, perhaps tactually explored as well, and, last but not least, held against the ear. This complex of behavior conforms to the classical paradigm described by Berlyne, Hutt, Nunnally and Lemond, and others, of behavior directed at obtaining information about the object, i.e., at reducing uncertainty and possible conflict about its nature, its form, its characteristics. This is behavior that Hutt and Hughes (Hughes & Hutt, 1979; Hutt, 1966) have described as marked by a state of tension, reflecting the heightening of attention, the marshalling of orienting responses, the state of "intentness" to obtain information that characterizes the child during such behavior. But, lo and behold, we see the child's face break out into a broad smile as it listens to the sounds of the sea captured in the shell. Fascinated, but clearly delighted at the same time, the child keeps its ear against the shell, soaking in the sound.

Such a reaction is surely a common one in an encounter with many stimuli; indeed, it could be argued that any aesthetic experience (e.g., from a visit to a museum) is predicated on the occurrence of a similar response. Yet, although both temporally and functionally intertwined with exploratory activity of the inspective type, this response deviates sufficiently from inspective exploration in major respects to deserve a different designation. I have chosen the term *affective* to signify this type of exploration, that is, a response to a stimulus primarily oriented towards the elicitation of affective arousal, i.e., pleasure or enjoyment. It is to be contrasted to an *inspective* mode corresponding to "specific" exploration in Berlyne's sense, i.e., directed at information extraction.

As already noted, it is to be expected that exploratory activity that is instigated by an encounter with a stimulus will be a composite of both inspective and affective exploration taking place concurrently, raising the question of how they are to be separated. Before attempting to provide an answer, I should point out that this very fact, i.e., that exploration of a stimulus may (and generally does) serve both an information-extraction and an affect-producing function, means that the typical measure of exploratory activity, i.e., amount of time spent looking at (or in some cases listening to, or feeling) a stimulus, is at best a confounded measure of "specific" exploration as that term has been commonly used. Indeed, there is good evidence (e.g., Berlyne & Crozier, 1971; Wohlwill & Harris, 1980) to suggest that for some stimuli or under some conditions—e.g., where stimuli have already become familiar—looking time bears little relationship to information value but may reflect primarily the potential of the stimulus for affective arousal.

But how to separate the two in the context of an empirical study? Several possibilities may be entertained. First, if specific exploration and inspective exploration serve different functions, one might look for corresponding differences in the style of exploration characteristic of each, i.e., more active and complete for the inspective, in comparison with the affective. The difference may be illustrated by comparing the pattern of eye movements to be expected from the scanning of a complex stimulus configuration, such as a work of cubist art, with that which a simple but strongly affect-arousing scene, such as a sunset at sea, would elicit. (Note that the total amount of time spent in eye contact with each might be approximately the same or might even favor the sunset.) The difference can probably be most effectively studied in the domain of touch, as in comparing the movements involved in feeling a pleasing texture of cloth, such as a piece of fur, with those entailed in palpating a shape while blindfolded in order to determine its identity.

At the other extreme, in the case of audition it would be virtually impossible to differentiate patterns of exploratory movement that might correspond to these two different attitudes. Yet, it might still be possible to differentiate the two modes in terms of the state of relative tension or relaxation characterizing the individual. For instance, consider the contrasting ways in which people listen to a piece of music, one with body taut, highly attentive, aimed at detecting patterns of counterpoint or subtle rhythms, etc., the other in a state of complete relaxation, perhaps with lights dimmed or out, the listener simply absorbing the sound emanating from a record player.

It is noteworthy that it is precisely in these terms that Hutt (1966) differentiated *exploration* from *play* in young children. The point I want to make is that a state of relaxation, smiling, etc. may be equally characteristic of this alternate mode of exploration that I am calling affective, which is to be set off against inspective exploration just as much as play is. If so, we clearly need to be concerned about a differentiation between affective exploration and play. But that would not seem to pose a very difficult problem, because they can be distinguished in terms of the individual's mode of interaction with the stimulus. In the case of affective exploration, the diversity of response emphasized by Hutt (1966) and Hughes (1978) as characterizing play would be absent, as would be attempts to transform or in some way act on the stimulus material.

Some very provisional and tentative support for the potential viability of this approach to differentiating the two modes of exploration comes from a recent study by the writer in which videotapes were taken of preschool children's facial expressions in exploring a novel stimulus, i.e., a mobile. The mobile was suspended from the ceiling via an elastic band that would send it into motion through a very light yank on the string, or alternatively through a swipe at one of the component parts, which were thin stone slabs in the shape of cats (with appropriate internal detail); a faint tinkling noise was produced whenever one of the slabs touched another. Thirteen children aged 3 and 4 years were brought into the room one at a time, blindfolded; upon opening their eyes their attention was called to the mobile hanging down directly in front of them. They were simply asked to look at it and shown how they could set it into motion. The session was terminated when the child gave evidence of becoming bored or moved off target for more than a brief moment. (Before terminating the session, the experimenter asked the child whether it still wanted to play with the mobile. In a few cases the child did resume its response to the mobile.)

Our approach was to treat inspective versus affective exploration as representing opposite poles on certain dimensions susceptible to measurement via ratings based on direct observation, notably the dimension of tension. Accordingly, for every 15-second period a rating of the average degree of tension manifested by the child was taken from the videotape. These ratings reflected a composite of such signs as tenseness of expression (note that the picture on the videotape was largely limited to the head and shoulders; thus body posture did not enter into the judgments), smiling and laughing, fidgeting, and glances away from the target. The overall judgment (representing the average for the 15-second period) thus indicated the degree of tension, attentiveness, and target-centered exploration at one pole, as opposed to relaxation, positive affect, and target-removed exploration at the other. The ratings thus far have proved reasonably reliable in terms of agreement between two raters (for 40 observations, the mean absolute discrepancy was 0.78, on this seven-step scale). Efforts are being made to codify them so as to improve further on this aspect of these measures.

Of the 13 children, one failed to explore for at least 1½ minutes and was thus discarded for the purposes of the present analysis. Of the 12 remaining children, eight showed a decrease in mean degree of tension from the first to the second minute (no analysis beyond that minute was made because too few children explored for more than 2¼ minutes), with a significant mean drop in the means, from 4.14 to 3.31. This result is at least in agreement with our prediction, though it is obviously in need of verification through observation of further subjects. It is to be noted also that, apart from this overall decrease in mean tension ratings from the first to the second minute, there were considerable differences among the children in their average levels. Whether this means that the inspective-affective differentiation will itself turn out to be a dimension of individual differences cannot be answered with confidence at this point, but it is a possibility that must be considered, and we return to it at the end of this chapter.

In regard to the pertinence of the tenseness ratings to the inspective-affective differentiation, it should be noted that the latter entails more than simply a difference on the tense-relaxed dimension; in particular, the affective-exploration concept presupposes the expression of positive affect. We are currently working on the development of an index of this particular form of expression by adapting the scoring schema devised by Blurton Jones (1971) for the measurement of affective state from facial expression. Suffice it to note that such obvious indications of positive affect as smiling (varying all the way from a momentary, barely perceptible smile to a pronounced grin maintained over several seconds) as well as outright bursts of laughter were quite common, though only for some of the children. Anyone who has watched young children in similar situations (e.g., looking through a kaleidoscope) will be able to confirm the common occurrence of such responses.

A DEVELOPMENTAL PERSPECTIVE

Thus far little has been said about the developmental aspects of these issues— the age changes to be expected and the significance of the differentiations being suggested for a developmental model of exploratory activity. Directly relevant in this context is the theory of Ernest Schachtel (1959), outlined in his book, *Metamorphosis*.

In this volume Schachtel proposes a distinction between two modes of perception, which seems directly translatable into exploration terms. He believed that over the course of development one could observe a progressive shift from a predominant autocentric to a predominantly allocentric mode of responding to stimulus and objects, the former representing an orientation towards stimuli directed at affect and arousal, whereas the latter is directed at the extraction of information about the stimuli. The two different modes of perception were at the same time thought to be differentially related to the various stimulus modalities; whereas audition and vision are primarily used in an allocentric fashion, touch, and especially taste and smell are typically responded to in an autocentric manner, even by adults. Schachtel observed further that the two allocentrically directed modalities, audition and vision, gradually come to dominate over the other three, which gradually lose in importance after the infancy period, thus reinforcing the relationship between development and the perceptual mode.

Schachtel emphasized that this differentiation is far from an absolute one. On the developmental side adults certainly are able to respond autocentrically and do so in particular contexts, such as in their response to a sexual partner or to stimuli of aesthetic significance. Similarly, as regards the differentiations among the sense modalities, the sense of touch can be used for informational purposes, as it is by the blind, whereas people's responses to musical or landscape stimuli give testimony to the common occurrence of autocentrically based responses to auditory and visual stimuli, even in the adult.

A dissertation by Klein (1964) provides some empirical support for the kind of developmental shift from auto to allocentric response that Schachtel postulated. Klein found a progressive change from texture dominance to form dominance in a tactual matching-from-sample task modeled on the color-form dominance work in vision (i.e., the child is given a particular combination of shape and texture and asked to pick from a pair of choice stimuli the one that is "like" the sample, where one choice stimulus matches the sample according to form, and the other according to texture). Although it might seem questionable to equate response to texture with autocentric responding and response to form with allo-centric, such an identification could be justified in terms of the considerably greater information content of the shape aspect of these stimuli as compared to the homogeneous patches of texture, and the propensity, particularly of children, to respond to haptically experienced textures in evaluative or affective terms. This tendency was indeed supported by the children's spontaneous verbalizations in this situation.

All of which suggests an approach that might profitably be applied in an attempt to substantiate both the validity of the differentiation between affective and inspective exploration and the differentiability of either of these from play. The relationship between exploration and play has become a focus of interest for developmental psychologists, both at a theoretical level (Nunnally & Lemond, 1973; Weisler & McCall, 1976) and in empirical research (Hughes, 1978, 1979; Hutt, 1966; Schneider, Moch, Sandfort, Auerswald, & Walther-Weckman, 1983; Switzky, Haywood, & Isett, 1974; Switzky, Ludwig, & Haywood, 1979; see review by Wohlwill, 1984). In particular, Hutt and Hughes, via the use of their exploration box, have provided some most important and impressive documen-tation of these two as differentiable forms of behavior and of the temporal succession of exploration coming before play. Yet, to my mind, even these investigators have not fully resolved the problem of devising materials that would allow both of these forms of behavior to reveal themselves on equal terms.

The approach I suggest is via the use of blocks—the kind children have been playing with for many, many years, though surprisingly few child psychologists have deigned such play worthy of their attention (cf. Guanella, 1934, and—from a very different perspective—Erikson, 1951, for some rare exceptions). Blocks such as those given to children in nursery schools and in their own homes tend to be plain with unadorned faces of wood (or, in earlier days, particularly in Europe, of stone). Sometimes one finds blocks with brightly colored letters on them, presumably to entice children to form simple words, or at least to familiarize themselves with the shapes of letters, but apart from this rather special case blocks do not typically provide much occasion for active exploration. But there is nothing to keep one from turning them into objects that will elicit quite active exploration, and even exploration of both an inspective and an affective sort—simply by pasting pictorial material, as well as simple textures such as cloth, onto the faces of the blocks. This feature should induce the children to spend some time upon initial confrontation with the blocks in manipulating, visually examining, and feeling them (i.e., their textures). Following such initial exploration, one may predict that the information to be extracted from the blocks will have been exhausted—i.e., the child's curiosity has been satisfied—and that the child will start to play with them, constructing objects of one sort or another. Occasionally the child may return to further exploration, again both inspective and affective—the latter perhaps more than the former—but by and large one may predict a shift from either of these modes of exploration to play, insofar as the predominant activity with blocks over time is concerned. Such a shift would, of course, be in line with similar shifts observed by Hutt (1966), Hughes (1978), and Switzky et al. (1979), and its reality has indeed been shown in a recent study I have carried out (see Wohlwill, 1984). But what about the developmental picture?

It is not at all clear that any consistent age change would be expected in the amount of time spent in exploration, at least of the inspective variety, but according to Schachtel one would look for an increasing proportion of the exploration occurring to be of the inspective rather than affective variety—e.g., responding to the pictorial as opposed to the tactual stimulation derived from the faces of the blocks. The proportion of either of these kinds of exploration to play, on the other hand, might be expected to decrease progressively, at least up to a certain age, as the possibilities for constructive play are increasingly realized, in accordance both with the child's motor skills and its imagination.

Of particular interest developmentally would be evidence of children's attempts to relate the concrete pictorial material (and possibly the textures as well) to their constructive play, as by allowing some of these materials to suggest an object to construct with the blocks (e.g., a train, if a locomotive appears on one of the blocks). Perhaps developmentally more advanced would be evidence of the child's integrating the pictorial material into its constructive play—e.g., building a house for an animal or person depicted on the blocks.

At the preschool level, only very limited evidence for such integrative play appeared in the aforementioned study of the author's (Wohlwill, 1984). On the other hand, a rather different form of behavior with these materials appeared, one that seems also significant in a developmental sense. This is the tendency of many children to spontaneously arrange the blocks in certain patterns based on the colors or objects (and, less frequently, patches of texture) appearing on the various faces. Thus a child might form a 3 × 4 matrix with the blocks, laid out along the floor, such that in the first row all blocks were of the same color, the second row featured pictures of birds, the third row another set of objects, and the last row another color, for instance. The extent to which such orderly arrangements were carried through differed, of course, among the various children, but this clearly represents a type of behavior not readily subsumable under either exploration or play; rather it reflects an attempt by children to assimilate the content of the blocks into their activity with them and to set themselves problems to solve with them, as it were. For that reason, one would expect this form of behavior to reveal significant developmental changes, although this was not demonstrable within the very limited age span of the sample used for this study.

THE SIGNIFICANCE OF EXPLORATORY ACTIVITY: TOWARDS A BROADER PERSPECTIVE

Thus far in this chapter we have considered two major differentiations that need to be observed in analyzing exploratory behavior at both an empirical and a theoretical level. The first was the distinction between exploration in the environment in search of a stimulus or stimulation, and exploration directed at a stimulus object that the individual encounters or confronts. A second distinction was that between different modes of responding to a stimulus object during the course of exploring it. Although these differentiations need to be kept apart, as they concern rather different aspects of the problem of exploration, they are related to the extent that both concern the function served by exploration. In the first case, environmental exploration serves the purpose of either creating a suitable level of arousal or of providing knowledge about the content of the environment if not already known (it may frequently serve both of these at once), whereas object exploration serves the function of reducing the uncertainty aroused by a given object or stimulus when encountered (i.e., of reducing curiosity). In the second case, the differentiation is between the latter function of object exploration (curiosity reduction), and affective arousal or satisfaction derived from an already somewhat familiar object.

Not only are these two differentiations interrelated, but the various forms of activity to which they refer may in many situations conform to a three-phase process, starting with exploration in search of a stimulus, proceeding to inspective exploration to reduce curiosity, and culminating in affective exploration of the stimulus beyond the point of familiarization. The particular situation will determine whether all three of these phases will occur. First of all, stimuli often confront an individual without prior environmental exploration and can thus elicit inspective exploration directly. Furthermore, a given stimulus may or may not evoke positive affect, depending on its structural makeup, the associations it evokes, etc. The precise properties of stimuli that are associated with positive affect remain to be specified. It is thus apparent that affective exploration cannot be expected to occur invariably, whether accompanying or following inspective exploration.

Admittedly, the preceding account of exploration in its various forms is formulated at a fairly molecular level of behavioral analysis. Yet, considering the emphasis on function underlying the proposed distinctions, the possibility suggests itself of viewing exploration in a broader context by examining its place in the child's overall behavior and development. Because inspective exploration—i.e., curiosity—is central to both of the distinctions just reviewed, and because our knowledge concerning it is most extensive, we focus on this aspect of exploration in the following brief attempt to broaden the base of our discussion.

Exploration and curiosity have typically been considered to be positive factors enhancing the child's cognitive development that should be encouraged and facilitated. To the extent that such behavioral modes or traits serve to expose the child to information concerning the world around it and thus to enlarge its storehouse of knowledge, there can be little doubt about their place as a positive force in cognitive development. Empirical support for this proposition might be seen, furthermore, in the results of a study by Hutt and Bhavnani (1972) indicating that for boys—though curiously enough not for girls—amount of responsiveness to novel stimuli in the preschool years was associated with higher scores on a creativity test at age 9.

The relationship between exploration or curiosity and creativity has, however, been thrown into question by the work of Keller and Voss (1975), who have found a consistent pattern of negative relationships between contemporaneous measures of visual exploration (i.e., amount of voluntary looking time spent in exploring stimuli high in "collative" properties such as complexity or novelty) and diverse measures of creativity. A further study (Voss & Keller, 1977) showed no correlation between measures of visual exploration (based on collative properties of the stimuli presented) and another measure of creativity, the "Obscure Figures" test. In explaining these findings, Keller and Voss consider visual exploration to demand an intermediate level of arousal, which may not be compatible with maximization of exploratory activity, whereas creative activity was thought to be facilitated by either very low levels of arousal or, in certain situations, by high levels (see Keller & Voss, 1976; Voss, 1977). This is an interesting notion and deserves to be more fully investigated, in my view, especially given the all too pervasive assumptions concerning the positive value of exploration.

There may be another way of looking at the matter, however. Is it not conceivable that curiosity, though surely no more harmful to children than to cats, may yet have a negative side to it, one that would be particularly in evidence in the context of creative activity? For the latter demands concentration on a particular task or problem, focusing on the materials required or helpful for the successful execution of the task or solution to the problem, to the exclusion of extraneous stimuli. Curiosity, on the other hand, may take the form of distracting the child from some activity in order to investigate some stimulus that happened to attract its attention. Of course, we do not ordinarily investigate exploratory activity directed at stimuli that are extraneous or incidental to some other activity; rather, the stimuli we present to a subject are assumed to be the focal ones and the only ones attended to. But it may be that for a younger child the same tendency that would promote active exploration of a novel stimulus, for instance, would also dispose it to be prone to distraction from extraneous stimuli while engaged in some task. Relevant in this context is the finding by Turnure (1970) that visual distractors inhibit performance of kindergarten-age children more than for early primary grade children, whereas no such age decrement is to be found in the case of auditory distractors. Apparently, in the visual case the older children are more readily able to resist the distractor simply by keeping their eyes focused on the relevant aspect of the stimulus situation and thus avoiding visual contact with extraneous stimuli.

The hypothesis being suggested is, however, of greatest relevance to the examination of individual differences in curiosity and their possible meaning. It would suggest that children who score high on measures of visual exploration may, at least in part, be those who are highly distractible, i.e., prone to turn their attention in whatever direction some stimulus happens to appear—to the obvious detriment of their performance on a creative task. To the extent that this is the case, it could provide an alternate explanation for the negative findings of Voss and Keller concerning the relationship between exploratory activity and creativity.

What this suggests is a much more intensive concern for individual differences in exploration, possibly by correlating it with measures of cognitive style, notably the flexible-restricted control dimension (Gardner et al., 1959; Klein, 1954; see also Schlesinger, 1954), which has been elaborated by Santostefano and Paley (1964) for work with children. In fact, the test of this cognitive control devised by these investigators is a very direct measure of a child's tendency to explore a stimulus array so as to interfere with a focus on the information relevant to a task.

THE NEED FOR AN INDIVIDUAL-DIFFERENCE FOCUS

The point just made leads to a much more general one. It may appear rather trite to exhort investigators to pay greater heed to individual differences so as to complement both a focus on the role of particular experimental variables and a concern with general developmental change. Yet a concern for individual differences in exploratory activity, as well as in such related areas as play, imaginative behavior, and the like, is even more essential than it is in many other realms of behavior for a very simple reason: We are dealing here with voluntary, spontaneous activity on the part of a child, ideally instigated by the child itself with a minimum of situational constraints or externally based demands.

Given this relative relaxation of externally imposed demands, it is to be expected that individual differences among children would become particularly prominent—differences that are most likely independent of level of maturity or development, reflecting rather temperamental differences (possibly related to anxiety level and other personality variables) that govern readiness for free exploration of an environment, or of investigatory responses to unfamiliar stimuli. Preliminary results from the pilot study of children's exploration of novel stimuli, referred to earlier, provide some support for this assertion, at least to the extent that the interindividual variation in mean tension ratings appeared to outweigh by far the shift observed within any given child from the first to the second minute. That is to say, although there was some overall change towards a less intent, or tension-laden demeanor as the child's exploration of the mobile proceeded, this shift has to be placed in the context of the substantial differences among the children in their modal level of tension. Thus some children started their exploration in the high-tension range of the rating scale (mean values of 5.0 and 6.0, for instance), whereas others started in the low-tension range (mean values of 3.0 and 3.25). (A value of 4.0 represents the neutral point on this 7-point scale, though obviously not too much can be assumed about the equal-interval character of this frankly impressionistic measure.)

The pervasiveness of individual differences in stimulus exploration and related activities was even more in evidence in the author's previously mentioned study of the transition from exploration to play, where different children showed rather diverse patterns of change among the three major categories of exploration, play, and spontaneous ordering (see the preceding presentation), even though overall there was a definite downward trend with time in exploration and an upward trend in play.

Unfortunately, we know very little as yet about the correlates of differences in exploratory tendencies such as those just described. Certain aspects of stimulus exploration have been investigated with regard to such correlates, as in Mendel's (1965) study of response to novelty in preschoolers, which was found to be inversely related to anxiety level (there was, in addition, a marked sex difference, boys showing a greater preference for novelty than girls). Kagan's (1982) observations concerning temperamental differences in young children's responsivity to stimuli likewise point to some possible origins of individual differences in exploration that are related to variations in the strength of inhibitory tendencies provoked by strange or novel objects and situations.[3]

The preceding discussion of exploratory activity should, however, alert us to avoid the all-too-facile assumption that exploration is a unitary trait. Indeed, in a factor analytic study of diverse measures of exploration and curiosity in preschool and second-grade children, Henderson and Moore (1979) found that response to novelty was but one of three main factors derived from these measures—albeit the one accounting for the greatest amount of variance. Two

---

[3]Perhaps relevant in this context is the work of Yarczower (e.g., Yarczower & Daruns, 1982), which has pointed to a social inhibition effect in the display of emotion through facial expression in the presence of others.

other factors, breadth and depth of exploration, emerged; significantly enough, they were defined exclusively by items derived from a "Curiosity drawer box" and involved such aspects of the children's behavior as amount of manipulation of different parts of the box, number of toys removed from the drawers after they had been pulled open, and a measure of the orderliness of the children's response to the diverse drawers—18 in number—in terms of the sequence in which they were opened. The latter measure, in particular, recalls the behavior pattern observed in our block study involving the arrangement of blocks according to some pattern of the colors or designs on their faces. It should be noted, however, that here we are dealing with the creation of order, whereas in Henderson and Moore's curiosity box, the measure is one of orderly search for stimulus objects that might be contained in the drawers.

The preceding considerations are relevant to the evaluation of work on curiosity in school-age children, and particularly on individual differences in curiosity. In principle, curiosity would seem to be a behavioral variable closely akin to, if not identical with, exploration, and the two have in fact been used almost interchangeably by some writers. Yet the typical measures of curiosity in the research that has treated this variable as a trait, i.e., a dimension of individual differences (e.g., Maw, 1971; see also Vidler, 1977, for references to other similar work), generally has relied on paper-and-pencil tests or teacher ratings, which implicitly assume a unitary dimension of curiosity. It seems much more likely that there are rather diverse manifestations of curiosity in children, differentiated both in terms of the object of attention, i.e., the stimulus materials involved, and the nature of the behavior (e.g., directed at information, at stimulation, or at problem solution). Thus a much more fine-grained analysis of this topic is called for, and one perhaps more directed at a behavioral level. Such an approach promises to bring together these two lines of research, which have tended thus far to remain largely separated from one another.

CONCLUSION

Much of the research on exploratory behavior carried out to date with children has been cast in a rather narrow mold, taken over from the experimentalist's view of the world of research, with its insistence on rigorous control over all stimuli and conditions that may affect behavior. Whereas this work has contributed an impressive body of knowledge on stimulus determinants of attention, looking behavior and preference, and on developmental changes in this area, it can be argued that this has been at the expense of a more comprehensive view of exploratory activity, one that does justice to the spontaneous nature of such behavior. Perhaps investigators themselves could profit from a more exploratory attitude toward methodologies and approaches to research in this area that will succeed in retaining the baby while letting the bathwater go down the drain.

There are, fortunately, indications of precisely this kind of broadening of our methodological vistas, notably in the work relating exploration to play that was reviewed earlier (particularly that of Hutt and Hughes), which manages to capture at least some of the essence of this kind of activity. The same may be said of the pioneering work with infants carried out by Rheingold and Eckerman. But much remains to be done. Above all it would be invaluable to have an overarching framework that would allow us to relate exploration not only to play but to other, in part quite different, forms of internally instigated behavior, such as imaginative activity and creative and artistic activity. This is an ambitious goal, perhaps, but one that surely seems worth striving for.

SUMMARY

Exploratory activity typically has been treated as a type of behavior directed at information extraction for the sake of satisfying curiosity, a conception that has governed the selection of behavioral indices measuring this form of behavior. Certain distinctions between different forms as well as functions of exploratory activity are suggested to enlarge our picture of such behavior. One such differentiation important at the outset is that between exploration involving a search for an object or for stimulation and exploration involving an examination of a stimulus confronting the individual. With regard to the latter (which constitutes the bulk of the research on exploration) a further distinction between two modes of exploration is suggested, one concerning information extraction ("inspective" exploration), the other, affective arousal or gratification ("affective" exploration). Some preliminary empirical evidence in support of the latter distinction is offered and the problem analyzed in terms of a suggested developmental perspective. The role of individual differences in modes of exploration is emphasized, and the need for a broadening of current methodology in the study of these forms of behavior is noted.

REFERENCES

Belsky, J., & Most, R. K. (1981). From exploration to play: A cross-sectional study of infant free-play behavior. *Developmental Psychology, 17*, 630–639.

Berlyne, D. E. (1960). *Conflict, arousal, and curiosity.* New York: McGraw-Hill.

Berlyne, D. E., & Crozier, J. B. (1971). Effects of complexity and prechoice stimulation on exploratory choice. *Perception and Psychophysics, 10*, 242–246.

Blurton Jones, N. G. (1971). Criteria for use in describing facial expressions of children. *Human Biology, 43*, 365–413.

Eckerman, C. O., & Rheingold, H. L. (1974). Infants' exploratory responses to toys and people. *Developmental Psychology, 10*, 255–259.

Erikson, E. H. (1951). Sex differences in the play configurations of pre-adolescents. *American Journal of Orthopsychiatry, 21*, 667–692.

Fowler, H. F. (1965). *Curiosity and exploratory behavior.* New York: Macmillan.

Gardner, R. W., Holtzman, P. S., Klein, G. S., Linton, H. B., & Spence, D. P. (1959). Cognitive control: A study of individual consistencies in cognitive behavior. *Psychological Issues, 1*, No. 4, (Whole No. 4).

Guanella, F. M. (1934). Block building activities of young children. *Archives of Psychology, 174*, 1–92.

Henderson, B. B., Charlesworth, W. R., & Gamradt, J. (1982). Children's exploratory behavior in a novel field setting. *Ethology and Sociobiology, 3*, 93–99.

Henderson, B., & Moore, S. G. (1979). Measuring exploratory behavior in young children: A factor-analytic study. *Developmental Psychology, 15*, 113–119.

Hughes, M. (1978). Sequential analysis of exploration and play. *International Journal of Behavioral Development, 1*, 83–97.

Hughes, M. M. (1979). Exploration and play re-visited: A hierarchical analysis. *International Journal of Behavioral Development, 2*, 215–224.

Hughes, M., & Hutt, C. (1979). Heart-rate correlates of childhood activities: Play, exploration, problem-solving and day-dreaming. *Biological Psychology, 8*, 253–263.

Hutt, C. (1966). Exploration and play in children. *Symposia of the Zoological Society*, London, *18*, 61–81.

Hutt, C. (1970). Specific and diversive exploration. In H. W. Reese & L. P. Lipsitt (Eds.), *Advances in child development and behavior* (Vol. 5, pp. 120–180). New York: Academic Press.

Hutt, C., & Bhavnani, R. (1972). Predictions from play. *Nature, 237*, 171–172.

Kagan, J. (1982, January). *Continuity and change in behavioral inhibition.* Paper presented at symposium on "Enduring and reversible effects of early experience," held at meetings of American Association for the Advancement of Science, Washington, DC.

Keller, H., & Voss, H.-G. (1975). Neugier, Exploration und Kreativität. *Bericht über den 29. Kongress der Deutschen Gesellschaft für Psychologie*, 157–159.

Keller, H., & Voss, H.-G. (1976). *Neugier und exploration.* Stuttgart: Kohlhammer.

Klein, G. S. (1954). Need and regulation. *Nebraska symposia on motivation* (Vol. 2, pp. 224–274). Lincoln: University of Nebraska Press.

Klein, S. D. (1964). A developmental study of tactual perception. (Unpublished doctoral dissertation, Clark University, 1963). *Dissertation Abstracts, 24*, 1977.

Lowe, M. (1975). Trends in the development of representational play in infants from one to three years: An observational study. *Journal of Child Psychology and Psychiatry, 16*, 33–47.

Maw, W. H. (1971). Differences in the personalities of children differing in curiosity. In H. Day, D. E. Berlyne, & D. Hunt (Eds.), *Intrinsic motivation: A new direction in motivation* (pp. 91–98). Toronto: Holt, Reinhart & Winston.

Mendel, G. (1965). Children's preferences for differing degrees of novelty. *Child Development, 36*, 453–465.

Nunnally, J. C., Faw, T. T., & Bashford, M. B. (1969). Effect of degrees of incongruity on visual fixations in children and adults. *Journal of Experimental Psychology, 81*, 360–364.

Nunnally, J. C., & Lemond, C. (1973). Exploratory behavior and human development. In H. W. Reese (Ed.), *Child development and behavior* (Vol. 8, pp. 59–108). New York: Academic Press.

Rheingold, H. L., & Eckerman, C. O. (1970). The infant separates himself from his mother. *Science, 168*, 78–83.

Santostefano, S., & Paley, E. (1964). Development of cognitive controls in children. *Child Development, 35*, 939–949.

Schachtel, E. G. (1959). *Metamorphosis: On the development of affect, perception, attention and memory.* New York: Basic Books.

Schlesinger, H. J. (1954). Cognitive attitudes in relation to susceptibility to interference. *Journal of Personality, 22,* 354–374.

Schneider, K., Moch, M., Sandfort, R., Auerswald, M., & Walther-Weckman, H. (1983). Exploring a novel object by preschool children: A sequential analysis of perceptual, manipulating, and verbal exploration. *International Journal of Behavioral Development, 6,* 477–496.

Shillito, E. E. (1963). Exploratory behavior in the short-tailed vole, *Microtus agrestis. Behaviour, 21,* 145–154.

Switzky, H. N., Haywood, H. C., & Isett, R. (1974). Exploration, curiosity and play in young children: Effects of stimulus complexity. *Developmental Psychology, 10,* 321–329.

Switzky, H. N., Ludwig, L., & Haywood, H. C. (1979). Exploration and play in retarded and nonretarded preschool children: Effects of object complexity and age. *American Journal of Mental Deficiency, 83,* 637–644.

Turnure, J. E. (1970). Children's reactions to distractors in a learning situation. *Developmental Psychology, 2,* 115–122.

Vidler, D. C. (1977). Curiosity. In S. Ball (Ed.), *Motivation in education* (pp. 17–43). New York: Academic Press.

Voss, H.-G. (1977). The effect of experimentally induced activation on creativity. *Journal of Psychology, 96,* 3–9.

Voss, H.-G., & Keller, H. (1977). Critical evaluation of the obscure figures test as an instrument for measuring "cognitive innovation." *Perceptual and Motor Skills, 45,* 495–502.

Weisler, A., & McCall, R. B. (1976). Exploration and play: Résumé and redirection. *American Psychologist, 31,* 492–508.

Wohlwill, J. F. (1975). Children's voluntary exploration and preference for tactually presented nonsense shapes differing in complexity. *Journal of Experimental Child Psychology, 20,* 159–167.

Wohlwill, J. F. (1981). A conceptual analysis of exploratory behavior: The "specific–diversive" distinction revisited. In H. J. Day (Ed.), *Advances in intrinsic motivation and aesthetics* (pp. 341–364). New York: Plenum.

Wohlwill, J. F. (1984). Relationships between exploration and play. In T. D. Yawkey & A. D. Pellegrini (Eds.), *Child's play: Developmental and applied* (pp. 143–170). Hillsdale, NJ: Lawrence Erlbaum Association.

Wohlwill, J. F., & Harris, G. (1980). Responses to congruity or contrast for man-made features in natural-recreation settings. *Leisure Sciences, 3,* 349–365.

Yarczower, M., & Daruns, L. (1982). Social inhibition of spontaneous facial expressions in children. *Journal of Personality and Social Psychology, 43,* 831–837.

CHAPTER FIVE

EXPLORATION AND
ATTRIBUTION IN A
DEVELOPMENTAL CONTEXT

DIETMAR GÖRLITZ
Technische Universität Berlin (West)

CURIOSITY AND THE STATE
OF KNOWLEDGE: A COLLAGE

Drawing on the latest discoveries in the field of astrophysics, Steven Weinberg (1981) reconstructs the first 3 minutes in the creation of our universe and reflects the disconsolate search for meaning in the comprehensible history of the universe:

> But if there is no solace in the fruits of our research, there is at least some consolation in the research itself. Men and women are not content to comfort themselves with tales of gods and giants, or to confine their thoughts to the daily affairs of life; they also build telescopes and satellites and accelerators, and sit at their desks for endless hours working out the meaning of the data they gather.

And he writes that:

> the effort to understand the universe is one of the very few things that lifts human life a little above the level of farce, and gives it some of the grace of tragedy. (p. 149)

Stimulation, consolation, and encouragement from the unconfined inquiry of epistemological curiosity?

In the age of space probes that investigate our planetary system, we are vicarious explorers on voyages of unimaginable dimensions. As stated in *Spiegel* (1981): "According to flight plan, on September 28, 1981[1] the 'encounter of an extraordinary kind' . . . between Voyager II and Saturn will be over. Then 'myth will be disclosed, curiosity satisfied.' " Or our curiosity will be extended further to curiosity without feedback for him who asks: "The journey of Voyager II then continues in the direction of the 'white dwarf' AC + 793888. Expected date of arrival: in 40,000 years" (p. 163).

That our epistemological curiosity exceeds the horizon of our own life is something we experience in two ways—as interested observers and readers and as developmental psychologists conducting research on the course of human life.

Almost two hundred years ago an anonymous writer lamented in the *Magasin Encyclopédique* about a session of the "Société des Observateurs de l'Homme," which was a society of scholars in postrevolutionary Paris at the end of the 18th century whose efforts to establish a positive science of man based on "facts of observation" led to the founding of cultural anthropology and ethnology. Using a surprisingly modern interdisciplinary approach (Moravia, 1977), the writer explained that:

---

[1]The date was altered in *Spiegel, 36* (1981), 207.

man has nearly always directed his curious gaze into the distance, almost never on himself. . . . Man is as great a puzzle to himself now as ever, and anyone wanting to contemplate his own capabilities at once plunges deeply into uncertainty and error. There have been researchers who spent years observing the habits and activities of an insect or who tirelessly and patiently awaited the blooming of a plant. But no one has yet attentively turned his eyes to the cradle of a child and kept a detailed diary on the progress of his intelligence and the development of his faculty of perception. (p. 18)

So many fruits of human curiosity, yet so little curiosity about curiosity behavior itself? Or as Kagan (1984) writes:

It has always struck me as odd that we come to understand an exotic phenomenon, like the eclipse of the sun, before so many commonplace events, like the beginning of the baby's birth. Although children have been scurrying under the watchful eyes of interested and intelligent adults for a very long time, we have a less satisfying explanation of human psychological development than of the life cycle of the fruit fly . . . (p. XI)

Is it that one should heed Voltaire's suggestion of proceeding in the investigations of humans "as in astronomy" (after Moravia, 1977, p. 19)? Admittedly, it would not only *privilege observation and experimentation as methods* but would also encourage one to demote the human being to no more than a "mere phenomenon of nature." Rather, we should observe humans in their natural context as actors and inquirers, in life contexts that change and develop with them and in which humans also change and develop themselves.

INTRODUCTION AND OVERVIEW

My interest in curiosity and exploration grew out of my work in developmental psychology within the context of attribution research (Görlitz, 1978, 1983a), specifically my work on the processes that are found when observing actual interpersonal behavior among children. That was a period so short that I still cannot contribute more than preliminary comments to the actual topic of curiosity and exploration.[2]

Our working group approached this topic—nevertheless a promising one— more practically and not overanxiously by staging a presumably curiosity-related situation in a biotic context. We set up a small cage containing semiautomatic

[2]The author is grateful to Professor Joachim Wohlwill for many insights gained through joint discussions during a sabbatical research semester spent at the Berlin Technical University in the summer of 1981.

stuffed toys (dogs) in front of Berlin's main train and subway station, Zoologischer Garten, and in other places around the city, observed the behavior of the passersby, and recorded it on video film.[3] In a separate chapter I report those experiences, embedded in an initial attempt at shaping the topic, that occasioned these as yet uncontrolled observations. In terms of developmental psychology, the present approach is genetic—and for this we are indebted to Heinz Werner— in that it clarifies diverse genetic extensions, by which I mean the microgenetics of a course of events in a situation (the behavior of passersby), the ontogenetics as the participation of passersby of different ages (as well), and the historiogenetics and sociogenetics as the frame of reference within which all of us move in this epoch.

It will prove fruitful for this approach to keep the links to attribution in mind, so in this chapter I embark on the topic by establishing the relation between exploration research and attribution research. The introduction does not fulfill the desire for a more historical and biographical legitimation for the author; rather, it helps to illustrate relations that will be useful in our future work. We first conduct a formal and systematic discussion of ways to coordinate different areas of research, namely, attribution and exploration. We suggest a loosely sequential model of order with which perspectives useful in developmental psychology are presented. The question of the course and consequence of both activities are then reformulated, this time in terms more commensurate to the observed behavior.

The second, and main, part of our exposé is limited to curiosity and exploration. It cites first a few of the dilemmas and problems of researching curiosity (in developmental psychology) that seem to us to be worth pointing out in the beginning. We are not able to present solutions to these problems yet, and for some we will in principle perhaps never be able to present any, as is documented by the reference to diverging organismic conceptions or pictures of the human being pieced together by research in developmental psychology.

We go on to sketch a *basic model* of situations involving aspects of curiosity in which we differentiate historic-epochal,[4] ontogenetic, and actual situational, conditional factors and separate the positions of the partners participating in the action. Using our design for a basic model, we then try to derive a set of research topics or initial perspectives to order the field of work on curiosity and exploration. They have arisen from our practical preliminary soundings. They are not treated in more detail here but rather are only introduced for now and commented on with examples. Only one topic on this list of criteria is the focus of a more

---

[3]Special thanks go to four of many students—Mr. Bott, Mr. Röhrig, Mr. Sunderhauf, and Mr. Wellmann—for their valuable assistance with the project's technical aspects.

[4]Discussed more generally in the concluding chapter of this book. History as the basis of what we actually do is not only an important marginal condition, as life-span-oriented developmental psychology teaches with the demonstration of cohort effects. It is an independent dimension of the temporal extension of everything and, hence, of our topic in developmental psychology.

in-depth discussion: exploration as activity in its procedural or temporal exten-sion, a description of that which our passers-by actually did when confronted with an event they had not been expecting, how they behaved, what they did and said in the few minutes that many of them stopped.

In their well-researched, somewhat dry overview of the data on the charac-teristics of the methods used in research on curiosity and exploration, Nunnally and Lemond (1973) conclude that "many of the methods have a laboratory-like flavor, which in conjunction with one of the types of instructions employed, may have been artifically induced by their 'demand characteristics' " (p. 104). With the strategy of taking a "fresh look" at "old things," we try to design a process model of exploration on the behavioral level and relate it more directly to everyday situations. It was stimulated by empirical observations in a little-controlled, everyday situation and is put forward in its first draft form for dis-cussion. Only later work with the statements that several observers made about various materials will show if and how the subphases of this microgenetic model of exploration can be identified and supported and which ontogenetic extrapo-lations it allows for developmental psychology.

I am not sure how much curiosity and anticipation a pile of promises instills in the reader, so I now get quickly to the heart of the matter.

EXPLORATION AND ATTRIBUTION AS AN AREA FOR DEVELOPMENTAL PSYCHOLOGY

Possible and Necessary Linkages

Which links are possible and necessary? We do not want to justify Nunnally and Lemond's reproach (1973, pp. 60–61) that it is only beating a dead horse to state that research ignored the topic of curiosity and exploration until the early 1970s, which might be true for Anglo–American psychology (see Fowler, 1965, for a thorough review; Nunnally revised his opinion in 1981). It is a situation that has changed radically in the last 10 years, and it is described by Keller and Voss in their well-formulated introduction to the topic in German (1976, p. 23) as a change of interest during the second half of the 1960s. The horse is perhaps not "so dead," though, if we consider that this burgeoning interest in curiosity and exploration has not been balanced by an equally great effort to establish conceptual order and precise definitions. It could be argued that that imbalance is a guarantee of freshness and vitality in the work conducted during the initial phases of research in a particular area (just as Flavell, 1977, p. 1, has argued in citing such ambiguity as an advantage for the concept of cognition in devel-opmental psychology). According to Hunt (1965), studies on curiosity and explo-ration probably focus with less controversy on that phenomenon or realm of behavior "when painful stimulation, homoestatic needs, and sex are absent and

when any acquired drives based upon them are minimized so that play, exploration, manipulation, and curiosity behaviors are most likely to occur" (p. 194)—
a realm that is characterized more by the absence of positive features such as
urgent demands of preserving life. Corinne Hutt (1970, p. 159) was of the opinion
that curiosity research began at a stage when exploration was "the behavior
without a definition," a stage that—if we take the relevant chapter in Keller and
Voss (1976, pp. 23–36)—is continuing at least insofar as no broadly accepted
operational concept can yet be cited for the phenomena in question on the plane
of either behavior or constructs.

Our introductory attempt at going through both areas of work represented by
exploration research and attribution research and looking for possible linkages
between them thus cannot start with stable definitions of curiosity and exploration. Perhaps it is thanks to its deliberate adherence to the ordinary and its
commitment to common sense that attribution research is more comprehensible
(Görlitz, 1980b). With comparable diversity among leading theoretical models,
the matters of interest to attribution researchers can be listed quite concretely:
explanation in common, everyday terms by lay observers; the conditions and
the consequences of explanations already formulated. But there is diversity here,
too. Kelley (1977) states: "there is no single theory, hypothesis, or method on
which researchers in this field are emotionally fixated" (p. 3). At the same time,
it means that this field is more programmatic, less encumbered, for attribution
research did not find itself "struggling" to establish the existence of controversial
phenomena but proceeded—perhaps making too much a point of using ordinary
language to talk about ordinary things—from the simple fact of their existence.
This reflects an optimism that became uncommonly fruitful heuristically and that
is making attribution research the possible core of "social cognition," which is
a significant area within social psychology (for a more detailed outline, see
Weiner, Graham, Taylor, & Meyer, 1983).

If research on curiosity and attribution is linked, there are a number of often
provisional theories to be reckoned with. Kelley and Michela (1980) assert:
"[There] is not one but many attribution 'theories'" (p. 458). And, according to
Keller and Voss (1976), "Only very isolated attempts have been made so far to
integrate statements about exploratory phenomena into patterns that could be
taken as a consistent theoretical system" (p. 35; from the German original).
These theories do not always characterize phenomena of human behavior and
judgment clearly and without exception. "[The] term refers to several different
kinds of problem" (Kelley & Michela, 1980, p. 458), and Voss produces examples for a "confusing . . . number of concepts in the surrounding field of curiosity
and exploration" (Keller & Voss, 1976, p. 23), whereby the divergence between
the terminological and the objective is felt to be smaller in attribution research.
Still, there seems to be something of a "phenomenal plausibility" inherent in
both curiosity and attribution, which reduces the number of competing interpretations. Kelley and Michela (1980) stress the joint idea that "people interpret

behavior in terms of its causes and that these interpretations play an important role in determining reactions to the behavior" (p. 458). And Voss praises "that quality of 'being curious' which anybody can easily understand" as justification for the independence of this research area (Voss in Keller & Voss, 1976, p. 36; from the German original). Basic focal activities seem to be closely attached to both. In the attribution process according to Görlitz (1980a, 1983b) in an outline for an action or behavior oriented program, there is causal, medial, and final linking. In the curiosity context there is stimulus selection and conflict exhibited by the perceiving actor (see Hutt, 1970, p. 138: "Exploratory behavior is essentially stimulus selection behavior"; on both characteristics, see Berlyne, 1960, pp. 1–17).

Hence, many different types of solutions seem possible in these daring undertakings. It is to be expected that there are many—and more controversially establishable—"junctions" between attribution and exploration.

Linkages in the Microgenetics of Situations

Are such linkages not only possible but also necessary after they have already been linked by the developmental and pedagogical theories of everyday life in a formulation of the "questioning age of the child"? Do we have here two expanded research areas sharing the noteworthy distinction of not having been "discovered" by developmental psychology (the more recent type, at least) in order now to be made fruitful for developmental psychology's concerns?

It seems to us that attribution research and investigations of exploration and curiosity—defining with comparable imprecision the boundaries of the areas they cover—can be related to each other in more than just the thematic sense. They— or better, the activities they investigate—are necessarily connected with each other in a very precise sense of "genetics" as well (necessarily connected for a prescriptive model and no doubt frequently connected in real life). And they are connected in several ways. Here, genetics means, first, the micro or actual genetics of concrete actions and reactions. In more programmatic formulations of the motivational psychology in everyday common sense (see Görlitz, 1974), this author has tried to show that the questions about motivation in everyday life have many different facets and that there is, therefore, a set of distinct investigative tasks. At that time the aim was to familiarize German-speaking psychologists more with attribution research, but the intention also was to show that such research can contribute to only one part of the topic area. Attribution theory typically concerns itself with the everyday observer's often causal explanations of matters that have provoked questions. That is the first point. In addition, this theory investigates actualizing processes, strategies, and rules, and it highlights the information used and the consequences that given explanations may have for subsequent action or judgment (see the model by Weiner, 1980a), supplemented, for instance, by the consequences for the ongoing interaction between people, their interactive arrangement. To do this, attribution researchers design rational models, those by Kelley (1967, 1972a, 1972b) and Jones and Davis (1965) having become particularly effective.

Attribution theory pertains to only one subarea of the research on everyday issues and explanations of motivation. Before, during, and after attributing activities, a great deal more occurs that is relevant to our investigations. The many facets of this research field were summarized formally by the author elsewhere in the basic question: When does someone ask why about what, and in which manner and for which purpose does he ask? Which consequences can his answers be shown to have? And how did he come to his answers? This part about "how he came to his answers" and "what their consequences are" comprises most of the attribution work published so far. As the basic question shows, however, this work must necessarily (or usually) be based on proleptic decisions: decisions about the external situation in which the questions arise (this corresponds to the "when" part of our basic question, aforementioned). In other words, what distinguishes the question-provoking element of a situation from the self-evident truths with which we live? I refer also to decisions concerning a certain operation that is presented here concretely—yet no doubt onesidedly—as people's verbal questioning (that is, the "in which manner" part of our basic question).

In attribution studies, and not only there (experimental work in general contains the arbitrariness of the person planning the experiment), the subjects involved usually do not ask anything themselves. The experimenter anticipates their questioning, formulates questions himself, and either encourages or pressures his subjects to answer them. The focus is not on the spontaneous desire to know, by which is meant here that desire to explain that humans have in the everyday context. Thus it is that we now often know nothing about a subject's own spontaneous desire to know. Human-oriented psychology often shapes a situation similar to that shaped by animal psychology, of which Berlyne (1960) writes: "Until recently, rather little has been done to find out how animals behave, whether in the wild or in captivity, when they have nothing particular to do" (p. 1). This deferred interest of the attribution researcher can make curiosity research attractive for him, too, and that would bring about an important shift or broadening of attribution work. The review by Kelley and Michela (1980) touches on one of the essential characteristics of attribution research: "The investigator has a conception of the alternative explanations the naive subject may entertain for a given kind of event. The investigator also has an hypothesis about the antecedents of causal attribution . . . [and] a hypothesis about the consequences of the subject's making a particular attribution" (p. 459). That undoubtedly characterizes earlier empirical attribution research correctly, but this asymmetry in the desire to know that exists between the researcher and the subject becomes at least more balanced in recent attribution work when Weiner, Graham, Taylor, and Meyer (1983) write: "Rather than passively observing what goes on around us, we extract meaning from behavior, make attributions for events that have occurred, infer characteristics of people associated with those events and, more generally, construct social reality" (p. 110). Research on curiosity and exploration has investigated many operations or activities (see the list in Keller & Voss, 1976, pp. 23–36; pp. 63–82) of the sort that occurs when exploring is taking place. Admittedly, verbally formulated questioning represents only an especially convincing and common example.

Proleptic decisions can be made about the actor, the "who" in our basic question who asks questions and who tries to get explanations and answers. Here, we developmental psychologists see our interests documented with particular clarity—a research topic that was the concern of some frequently more programmatic contributions (Görlitz, 1980a, 1983b; Weiner, 1980a). At first, attribution researchers handled this as more of a postulate and wanted to start with the layperson and everyday observer. It was not until later that the ontogenetic part of the subject became as interesting (see Heckhausen, 1983; Meyer, 1984; Weiner & Kun, 1977; Weiner & Peter, 1973). What remains is the "about what," "in which manner," and the "for which purpose" of the why questioning, which should highlight the object of the questioning and investigating (with other, perhaps fruitful subspecifications that are not repeated here, see Görlitz, 1974, p. 545).

If we shorten our preceding basic question to "When does what lead whom to start questioning?" it becomes clear that curiosity and exploration constitute, at least formally, the "procedural forefield" of attribution, that attributive linking (as it is called in an earlier work by the author, see Görlitz, 1983b) is dependent on the emergence of elements to be linked, on the degree to which they become conspicuous. By the "in which manner" and "for which purpose" parts of why questioning—to end the self-quotation—is meant elements that are processed in a certain way, with a certain goal, and under a certain operational theme. (For recent attribution research this theme was often that of explaining the causes for an event in question.) This basic formula illustrates nothing more than that exploration and attribution research are closely linked by virtue of the processes they investigate. That is a practical and not purely impression-based linkage as a coupling of two modes with which, say, promotion effects can be exploited. Determining just how fruitful this link is for developmental psychology as well may be one outcome of further research.

Activities preceding and concurrent with the act of attributing were not neglected in later attribution theory. According to Weiner (1980a), it was customary to characterize them partly as antecedent conditions in the attributional area of work. Among them, the spontaneous, active search for information was, in fact, not especially emphasized. For Kelley and Michela (1980) the differentiation between antecedent and consequent phenomena of attribution was reason to differentiate between attribution theories and attributional theories within the context of a general model of the attribution concept (Kelley & Michela, 1980): "[It] is possible to draw a rough distinction between what might be called 'attribution' and 'attributional' research. The first involves sytematic assessment or manipulation of antecedents. . . . 'Attributional' research concerns the consequences of attributions" (p. 460). Attribution theory would then be capable of integrating curiosity and exploration topics, which admittedly would not enhance the work in either field of the theory because it "freezes" exploratory behavior at a specific point in the sequence—namely, at the antecedents—while masking such behavior's inherent value to do more than merely prepare attribution. Besides, such general solutions have not particularly interested attribution researchers.

In the realm of preceding activities, it was the situation or the inducement of causal attributions in particular that captured much more special attention under the term *when question* (Görlitz, 1974; Kelley, 1977). Kelley cited expectancy and disappointment for this when he explained[5] that the attribution models he and others conceived were to be understood as foils that needed to be corrected by at least five critical questions. Of these the first one for Kelley was the "when" question ("When do people make causal inferences?" "Are they always going around asking why things occur?" Kelley, 1977, Mimeographed, p. 5). It was also a topic that had received very little attention: "One of my disappointments with attribution research thus far is that this question of *when*, the conditions under which attributions are made, has not been addressed. . . . If we know when the process occurs, both what initiates it and what terminates it, we will be better able to understand its functions, the various forms it may take, and its limits" (pp. 5–6 and 19). And he pointed out, together with the ensuing questions (here the second and third in particular), the errors that the everyday judger (for us he is also an *exploring* everyday judger) makes in receiving and processing information, to what extent he lets himself be guided by his expectations, and how often he refrains from making new observations (Kelley's questions of "information bias" and "expectations"): "A great deal of attribution is based on preconceptions rather than on information processing" (Kelley, personal communication, May 2, 1974).

Suppose that the objective connection between exploring and attributing as just described is valid, that is, that exploring is in fact frequently an antecedent activity to subsequent attributions, as in curiosity-related situations. It then becomes important to specify in the ontogenetic context the conditions under which this coupling dissolves or changes until one of the complexes of activities involved is diminished, that is, the conditions under which attributing occurs with proportionately less exploring and vice versa.

Evidence from Curiosity Research for the Sequence of Exploration and Attribution

But that is a suggestion for future work and is still a premature attempt to define the relationship between attribution and exploration. In the present investigations on the development of curiosity and exploration, the comments on attribution

---

[5]Upon the occasion of an invitation to the Technical University Berlin in 1977.

are of a more incidental nature and allow for differing definitions of the relationship. Kelley himself has pursued his own "when question" in a study with Cunningham, restricting the parameters to the provocation of specific causal schemata evoked by unusual situations (Cunningham & Kelley, 1975). Even in view of these diverse definitions of the relationship, it does not seem wise to set up a rigid sequence model of "first this happens, then that," or to make one-way statements of conditions. The cognition-emotion discussion opened by Weiner (at the 1977 Bielefeld Symposium on Attribution) has taught us how short-lived such delimitations can be in view of recent empirical findings (see Weiner, Russell, & Lerman, 1979) and more precise analyses (Weiner, 1980b; Weiner & Graham, 1984). And whatever might later occur in the temporal sequence of a specific action or judgment, it need not be any less important or any less autonomous. As anticipated goals of action, subsequent attributions, too, can steer antecedent explorations and the contents studied thereby.

Now that we have covered the sequence thesis (or better, a thesis providing the possibility of ordering these activities sequentially), let us pursue our task of looking for a linkage in a second direction by supplementing the topic with somewhat incidental, inconclusive evidence to be found in the curiosity and exploration literature concerning attribution. A rich source here is Nunnally and Lemond's review (1973) of the developmental psychologist's view of exploratory behavior stressing the behavior in question on the visual level. According to the authors, one could substantiate a sequence thesis for any coupling (which naturally is not the purpose in the empirical literature they report on). With this approach, Nunnally and Lemond (1973) start from an attributional concept that is also current in the "social judgment" literature. This attribution concept deals with the meaning of the stimuli in question or the decision between competing meanings. For such concepts of attribution, antecedent exploratory activities have, first of all, an assisting function: "Because novel objects present a distinct challenge for attribution of meaning, novelty is thought to be a potent instigator of exploratory behavior" (pp. 66–67). This is a function that the authors believe exploration must doubtless fulfill, for the appropriate attribution of significance is important to existence and survival: "An organism must attribute meaning to a stimulus in order to respond appropriately; and the organism's survival frequently is contingent upon the responses that are made" (p. 69). That, of course, restricts explorations and attributions (or their sequence) to those situations in which the importance of stimuli are open or debatable, which according to face evidence meanwhile conforms to our understanding of curiosity-related situations.

Yet Nunnally and Lemond's emphasis on attribution of significance also documents precisely the other consequence of the sequence of exploration and attribution by which exploratory activities follow conflicting attributions. The authors maintain (pp. 66–70) that the conflict of information, which they consider central for the novelty of stimuli, is reduced to competing attributions of significance that contradict each other—as in figures of the Berlyne type. They thus constitute subsequent explorations as well. If the conflict of information is a universal characteristic of stimulus novelty, which means that "there are two or more strongly competing cues for attributing meaning" (p. 67), then subsequent exploratory activities contribute to a clarification and decision.

This second version of a sequence is more easily covered by the incidental comments Nunnally and Lemond make. Attributional conflicts initiate and constitute, exploratory activities follow. Be that as it may, however, comparing the "names" (attribution and exploration) on a more conceptual, analytical plane, which we could prudently do without, would get us no further right now than deciding the temporal, objective, or logical priority of either of the activities being discussed.

Instead, let us extract from this discussion further support for our loosely formulated thesis for the link between and sequence of exploration and attribution. That piece of evidence, however, must be adapted to the narrower version of attribution research, which holds that events are not in general ambiguous or question provoking and that attribution does not contribute to each and every reduction of this ambiguity (reduction such as naming and characterizing previously unfamiliar events). Attribution is a linking activity with causes (and perhaps means and ends), and the explored events would have to be involved in this linking in one way or another. That points to a more clearly definable line between the domains of exploration and attribution.

In seeking evidence for sequence formulations, one could, of course, also begin with attribution research instead of exploration research. We reap the benefits from attribution research in later, more detailed theses and refer at this point only to Duval's "focus of attention" hypothesis (1971), which contends that one ascribes the greatest degree of causal effect to those events that inherently— Berlyne would say "in their collative dimensions"—attract attention. That could be their novelty, too, which, in turn, would ascribe exploration the priority in the sequence (see Arkin & Duval, 1975; Duval & Hensley, 1976; Herkner, 1980, pp. 27–29).

Not all exploring serves subsequent (causal) attributions. And not every conflict of meaning is resolved through attributions. Attribution is only a part of what is involved in reducing that which provokes questions, with exploratory activities helping. But explorations do not begin only when competing causes (or reasons) and goals arise in events that have been experienced and observed. And not all attributions are based on perceived and explored series of events. Thus the two activities presumably have a relationship whereby linkage is determined on a case-by-case basis and where they alternately follow each other.

Aside from such formal outlooks (which, of course, tend to relate to the microgenetics of situations), it is more appropriate for developmental psychologists to ask whether the development, the ontogenetics, of both activity domains provides support for making sequence formulations. This would permit us to extend the main subject of this chapter in a third direction. Errors and weaknesses on the cross-sectional level of general and social psychology will become very painfully obvious if topics are pursued from an ontogenetic approach because the developmental psychologist is concerned longitudinally with the change of topics and constructs, which themselves should be stabilized, at least for the most part. That this is not the case in either of the work areas we are involved in has already been mentioned here.

Evidence from Developmental Psychology for the Sequence of Exploration and Attribution

The Question of Genetic Invariants.   Perhaps we can get further along this path by scrutinizing the question of the basic activities occurring in exploration and attribution. If basic themes or basic activities in both fields can be more or less concordantly identified, they could form the ontogenetic invariants for research that then seeks out the life-span developmental changes in the reification of these invariant themes taken from exploration and attribution. This road has not yet been travelled, let alone charted.

As a first step in this direction we have already tried elsewhere (see Görlitz, 1980a) to show that the causal (medial and final) linking of separate moments on the basis of perceived and actual unit formations is a key element in all attributions. Which corresponding characteristics can be identified for exploration and curiosity? Berlyne and his followers believe that all curiosity-related exploratory behavior is a matter of comparing (see Berlyne's "collative variables") on the basis of stimulus selection (as Hutt and others have stressed). But is that a sufficient and specific labeling of the activity in question?

Not all comparing is exploring. The comparative structure of our social judging also seems more comprehensive than explorations would have us believe— take valuations and judgments, for instance. Often it may only be a matter of the temporally prolonged, exacting categorization of an object, an event, or a person that is the focus of the entire exploratory act. If comparing is the basic activity of exploring, then other specifying characteristics of this activity must be added. If it is not the basic activity but is to be equated with other "basic activities" of mental operating like identifying and memorizing, then the basic activity of exploring is perhaps composed of other more important activities that make up the core of all exploring behavior. On the basis of unit forming based on a series of events that has been observed or experienced, one example of such an important activity might be the singling out, an accentuation (forming figures on the ground) either linked with concurrent comparisons or unrelated to them. This is one suggestion that adheres closely to Hutt (for whom, as quoted, exploratory behavior was essentially stimulus selection behavior).

Charlotte Bühler's Basic Types of Life Processes.   We have opened our sequence question in the ontogenetic direction with the presentation of a task that is not yet solvable. Quite apart from this task, we now discuss in a more cursory fashion the developmental literature about the relationship between exploration and attributions. We turn for this to Charlotte Bühler (here, 1928) as one of many possible representative sources from classical continental European developmental psychology and to Jean Piaget, who until his recent death was the most effective teacher of developmental psychology. Charlotte Bühler presents two versions of this relationship, both of which substantiate a more ontogenetic preordering of exploratory activities before attributing activities even though Bühler's model, inconsistent with itself, does not expressly mention both (it does cite curiosity, boredom, interest, and attending to familiar and unfamiliar stimuli, but not attribution). According to her, exploration precedes attribution as long as one does not speculate that attribution is the basic mechanism that brings about habit formation and changes in affect.

Exploration and Curiosity Concepts of Piaget.   The situation is different with Jean Piaget. Taking Piaget's early work for our purposes (*The Origins of Intelligence in Children*, the first French edition of which [1936] is contemporary with Bühler), we find that Piaget uses *three concepts of exploration* for this early period of human life, as much as it can be recognized. They only partly correspond to J. McV. Hunt's three levels in the development of intrinsic motivation— change, the familiar, the new (see J. McV. Hunt, 1965, pp. 231–260). For one, Piaget uses a general concept of exploration in many statements intended in a general sense, particularly when referring to the functioning of the assimilation tendency (Piaget, 1936, Part I). He also uses an everyday, trivial concept of exploration in an incidental manner in many recorded observations (especially in Part I: Op. 18, Op. 28–31, Op. 33–36, Op. 52–54, Op. 82). And in the second part of Piaget's early work that we already have cited, he draws on a special concept of exploration that he links with the introduction of more explicit intentionality and sees it documented in a broad range of phenomena. These include "letting interesting phenomena continue," "secondary circular reactions," "the study of novel objects and phenomena," and "tertiary circular reactions and phenomena." Secondary literature like Ginsburg and Opper (1979) cite him only when discussing tertiary circular reactions and when introducing the principle of moderate novelty (pp. 56–58, pp. 67–68).

How is one to proceed if one wishes to have more ontogenetic details and to seek a connection to attribution? Various sources of support are possible. One realizes that Piaget's special, explicit exploration concept is introduced in the context of a matter that is highly significant for attribution, in the context of explicit intentionality, and the attribution researcher will feel himself reminded of the many studies on other's premeditated action and behavior. We do not dwell on this point further here (for instance, by postulating a genetic priority placing intentional action before exploratory action or by asserting the existence of certain conditions). If instead we link both Piaget's general and his special application of the exploration concept or let them hold equally, we would expand the preceding list of relevant phenomena as follows: The exploring schemata of the very earliest sensory–motor period are functionally independent at first. Their manifestation results from self-actuation (that is, functional assimilation). The coordination with other schemata and mechanisms of generalizing assimilations in the domain of sucking, seeing, hearing, and grasping extend the objects acted upon.

If in seeking genetic antecedents of exploration and attribution one proceeds from this general understanding of the concepts and in so doing consults the second chapter in Piaget's early work cited earlier, it will seem that curiosity and exploration have their place essentially in the assimilations of primary circular reactions (specifically in functional and, especially, in generalizing assimilations). As an essentially linking activity, however, attribution finds its basic patterns in the coordination of schemata specific to and transcending the modes of the senses.

These interpretations of Piaget's general concept of exploration and attribution (Piaget himself never used the latter term, at least not as far as can be discerned in the extensive index by Gruber and Vonèche, 1977) do not indicate what sequence exists for the first weeks and months of life. Nor is the answer to this question any clearer if we look to special finite phenomena on the basis of explicit, genetically early intentionality of action and behavior in the third stage of sensory–motor development in infants. This unanswered question, however, has in fact a slight overtone favoring attribution, attribution to oneself as an action center, however it may be experienced, that seems to present a stimulating condition for subsequent behavior.

Causality Pleasure and "Funktionslust."   Then there is some evidence— even if little of it is experimental at this point—from research with infants that the distinction between these two different sources of action (oneself and other people or other things) emerges surprisingly early. J. McV. Hunt (1965, pp. 264– 65) reports on experiments with Ina Užgiris from the same year in which the attention of 2-month-old infants (measured by length of visual fixation) was examined to discover which factors were decisive for the attractiveness of persons and objects (here, mobiles). Amount of movement and familiarity of the objects or persons were the experimenters' relevant variables. The findings with these children support the familiarity hypothesis more clearly than the variable of movement because Užgiris and Hunt inadvertently confounded two levels of movement—first, that the mobile was moving at all, and second, that it was the child's own movements that set the crib, and thus the mobile, in motion. This failure to discriminate the two levels of movement seems to obscure significant components that have to be separated (motion per se and motion caused by others vs. motion caused by self).

Recent studies of adults by Weiner and his colleagues (see Weiner, 1980b; Weiner, Russell, & Lerman, 1979) were able to show that causal attributions of a desired result to the actor himself (his effort or ability) increase certain positive affects (like pride, self-confidence) and presumably increase the probability of future activities—in their study, mastery behavior. Using a procedure by Nuttin (1973), Weiner wanted to verify these findings with younger age groups (preschool youngsters and elementary school pupils) in concrete action situations (see Kun, Garfield, & Sipowicz,   ; Weiner, Kun, & Benesh-Weiner, 1980). He also refers to, though does not replicate, Watson's work (1966, 1967) with infants 9–14 weeks old in the Merrill–Palmer Infant Laboratory. Watson studied and documented the extent to which contingency manipulations (especially in the presentation and coupling of acoustical and optical stimuli) become effective in the learning process in these early weeks of life. (A contributor to this volume, Professor Papoušek from Munich, has made important contributions to this subject.) That does not, however, represent key evidence for the differentiability and prevalence of self-attributions and causality pleasure at this early age, although Weiner et al. (1980) interpret Watson's findings in this sense. Consider in this context the following quotation from Weiner (1980a):

> It may seem far-fetched to draw the inference that eight-week-olds have the cognitive capacities to make causal deductions. However, it also may be that a differentiation between the self and the environment has developed by that age, and that primitive inferences about locus and control can be made using proprioceptive feedback information. If this interpretation has any validity, then Watson perhaps has identified the existence of attempts at mastery among very young infants. (p. 69)

Broader empirical data are needed for this period of life. The review of past studies presented by Heckhausen (1983) is encouraging in this regard: "One can say not only that experiencing contingency in the sense of one's own effectiveness is an innate capability but also that it simultaneously possesses a motivating character as well" (p. 52; from the German original). Heckhausen proposes a sequence of development that begins with the experience of contingency centered on activity which takes place in the first few weeks of life and that proceeds to the experience of contingency centered on effects of action, with the concomitant experience of the self in the first encounter with success and failure and the experience of skill (*Tüchtigkeit*) in the third year of life. The attributional processing of events in the environment is thereby differentiated from the attribution of one's own activity, and the development in the organization of activity and action is differentiated from the development in the experience of the self, at least in a thematic sense, for the first 2 years of life. Microanalyses of children's expression (emotions have an indicative function in Weiner's orientation as well) and the potential of video technology, so ingeniously exploited by Lewis and Brooks-Gunn (1979), will help make it possible to describe with increasing clarity the localization of the causality experience in early childhood.

Summary. To summarize, recourse to work in developmental psychology on attribution (in the context of mastery, too) and exploration produced no convincing evidence for an ontogenetically determined order in the sequence of these two activities. A linking of the two seemed possible only from the attributional point of view, if at all, and even that only by virtue of studies on mastery, according to Weiner et al. (1980),—itself an "impoverished research area within developmental psychology . . . in which our thinking has been little advanced in recent years" (pp. 104, 109). We return to this point later. If developmental psychology's attribution researchers wish to expand the relatively rigid and still-frame approach to their investigations of achievement and other situations—and there are good reasons, like the representativeness of everyday situations, for doing so—then coalitions between the attribution and exploration research fields would be especially expedient and fruitful. This is because of the fundamental treatment of uncertainty and conflict, of explanation of the environment and the accessibility of information common to both subject areas, whereby exploration focuses more on the aspect of comparative selection and attribution more on the aspect of causal, goal, and means-centered linkages. It is also because of the somewhat similar functions that attribution and exploration have. To cite one outstanding example, they both contribute to satisfying the human urge to establish solid moorings in a controllable environment—the basic anthropological concept of attribution theory, as it was labeled by Heider (1958) in particular and by Kelley (1967). More recent work (Weiner et al., 1980) has formulated it more generally as "the desire to understand and to affect the environment" (p. 105). Exploration and attribution also contribute, but certainly not as the only activities. And perhaps not as the exclusive urge, either, for imagination and play, as an oft-noted subsequent phase of exploratory activity (see Nunnally & Lemond, for example), seem to lack this function of achieving control over the environment in a positive and productive way. Attributive activities allow for fanciful linking, too. Even with difficult tasks fairy tales are not the only places where there is the good fairy or the magic lamp to help fulfill impossible demands.

TYPES OF INVESTIGATIONS AND PARADIGMS: EVIDENCE FROM WHITE'S AND HARTER'S CONCEPT OF COMPETENCE

With the present state of knowledge and with comparable operationalization of concepts, it does not seem so important for developmental psychology to be certain of the sequential patterning between attribution and exploration. In the light of White's (1959) provocative work, which sees exploration, curiosity, mastery, play, and competence as expressions of one and the same basic tendency—the urge toward competence or effectance—the significance of such sequence questions is enhanced, well beyond the typically uncertain status of sequential patterning in developmental studies. That is also true for the extension of this sketchy concept and its reorientation within developmental psychology by Susan Harter (1978). If we are correct, Harter expands White's summary construct of competence by adding decisive components (like the absence of reinforcement when failure occurs, the experience of failure in general, the experience of success commensurate with the demands of the task, and the significance of the socializing environment). Terminologically, she places the construct more graphically and clearly on "effectance motivation." The aspects of observable and, for example, exploratory action only seem to get short shrift. True, "mastery attempts" in the cognitive, social, and physical domain are only one of 12 stations in Harter's developmental model. But her earliest attempt at operationalizing components of "effectance motivation" (in 1972) is in keeping with the phenomena of curiosity and attribution when she cites four components of these aspects (Harter, 1978): "response variation," "curiosity for novel stimuli," "mastery for the sake of competence," and "preference for challenging tasks" (p. 39).

In view of this analysis it seems at present more reasonable to highlight the manifestation and developmental change of certain successions (sequences) of attributive and exploratory activities and to derive from them testable hypotheses so that one can—just like Harter (1978) in a comparable situation—"translate theoretical concepts into researchable formulations which can be empirically tested within a developmental context" (p. 34). This is precisely the service for which we have Wohlwill (1973) to thank in particular, for developmental psychology's treatment of whatever question is at hand has not been solely preoccupied with comparing children of different ages but has rather gone beyond comparisons of age groups to investigate the developmental functions and their longitudinal changes throughout the subjects' lifespan, especially those in the early periods.

Illustrations of Certain Sequence Versions: Kelley's ANOVA Model

But which of these functions and how? For reasons of time and preparation we illustrate the possibilities more thoroughly for that sequence version in which exploratory behavior forms antecedent activity for subsequent attributions. To simplify, we proceed first from temporally longer situations that may be repeated several times (as in Kelley's ANOVA case). For attribution theory, covariation information in the localization and the explanation of events is the basis for and fundamental datum of the attribution process. Heider (1958) states: "[It is assumed] that condition will be held responsible for an effect which is present when the effect is present and which is absent when the effect is absent" (p. 152). When events repeat themselves several times, covariation information leads to the attributions to entities, situations, and persons in Kelley's basic case of causal attribution ("that is because"). They steer the attribution of achievement effects (Weiner, 1974) and the formation of self concepts (Meyer, 1981). They also form, as suggested by more recent arguments and evidence (Weiner et al., 1980), the basis for feelings of mastery: "covariation of perceived effort expenditure with a desired outcome provides sufficient evidence of personal control. That is, perceived effort-outcome covariation produces *feelings of mastery*" (p. 105).

Perhaps, however, the utilization of covariation information is only one exemplary case of rule learning in the receiving and processing of information. Moreover, this case is conceived for ideal types of situations. More precisely, it allows clear-cut attributions in only a very specific range of situations. For the numerous ambiguous cases with "hovering localizations," i.e., with various different moorings and placements of the events in question, equally unequivocal attributions are not possible. Exploratory activities can have a central function in contributing to clarification of "hovering" localizations by both generating more covariation information and by considering it more closely. For Kelley's ANOVA situations this means that combining his three criteria (distinctiveness, consensus, and consistency) each in two versions (high vs. low or plural vs. singular) results in eight basic situations of alternately unambiguous information clusters. Only three of them are important insofar as the effect (the event) varies only with one of the three components. They are the cases of clear-cut person attribution, entity attribution, and situation attribution focused on by Kelley and graphically illustrated by Meyer and Schmalt (1978), but these cases are only an excerpt from a total of 26 information patterns that Orvis, Cunningham, and Kelley (1975; see especially p. 610) have distinguished.

In the clear-cut case of *person attribution*, the event varies across the persons of the actors (the consensus is minimal), but not across the situations and the objects of the action (consistency is high, distinctiveness is minimal).

In the clear-cut case of *entity attribution*, the event varies across the object of the action (distinctiveness is high), but not across the situations and the persons of the actors (consistency and consensus are high).

In the clear-cut case of *situation attribution* (which has been treated in different ways in the literature), the event varies across the situations (consistency is minimal), but not across the persons and the entities (consensus is high and distinctiveness is low).

If it is a basic characteristic of everyday psychological thinking to prefer *uni*factorial explanations of effects whenever possible (Baldwin, 1967, p. 73; also Dörner, Kreuzig, Reither, & Stäudel, 1983), then only three of the eight combinations of possible criteria cited here offer this favorable case—that is, that the effect in question varies with only one of the three components (in three other cases, the event varies with two components, in one case it varies with all three, and in one case, with none at all).

I take this particularly intelligible model from the field of attribution theory, make it more concrete, and complete it formally in order to illustrate the ideal typology of the three aforementioned cases. It would be helpful to recall the everyday example by Meyer and Schmalt (1978, pp. 110–111), in which it is assumed or observed that a particular pupil A (one among "all" persons) hits another pupil B (one among "all" entities). It is also known that A always does this (always out of "all" points in time) to others as well (all among "all" entities) and that the other pupils in the class do not hit B. The consensus in this case is minimal (only one person is hitting another), consistency is high (he does this often), and the distinctiveness is low (he hits others as well). In this example the event varies across the person component only, and one would tend to attribute it to the person of this particular pupil A. Let us symbolize high and low consensus with K ↑ and K ↓ (verbally as "all" and "he alone"),[6] high and low consistency as C ↑ and C ↓ (verbally as "always" and "once"), and high and low distinctiveness as D ↑ and D ↓ (verbally as "only him" and "everyone").[7] We can thus formalize these eight cases of combining information:

As Table 5.1 shows, there remain four cases of "hovering localizations" in which the event varies across two of three components; there is one case without variation of any of the three components.

The first deduction is that the extent of exploratory activities preceding attributions will be higher in situations where the event varies across several components than in situations where the effect/event varies across a single component only. The former situations will be more significant to exploration than the latter insofar as persons in their everyday judgments tend toward clarification through the use of unifactorial explanations. These situations are entered in Table 5.1

TABLE 5.1
Cases of Clear-Cut and "Hovering" Localizations after Kelley's
ANOVA Model (1967)

Consensus (K) →	K ↑	"All	K ↓	"He alone"
Consistency (C) → Distinctiveness (D) ↓	C ↑ "Always"	C ↓ "Once"	C ↑	C ↓
D ↑ "Only him"	Entity Attribution	EXP	EXP	Situation Attribution*
D ↓ "Everyone; others as well"		EXP*	Person Attribution	EXP

Note: In the cells: Entry of the clear-cut cases of the variations of the event one component only.
EXP = Situation significant for exploration.
*Placement in this cell deviates from my text and agrees with Kelley's more familiar notation.

---

[6]The symbols in the original German text are retained here to preserve the clear differentiation between consensus (*Konsens*) and consistency (*Konsistenz*).

[7]It must be noted that the attribute "high" when used with "distinctiveness" is opposite in meaning from its use with "consensus" and "consistency."

as "EXP" according to the hypothesis that they are "significant to exploration," foregoing at present more explicit predictions for the initial heuristics.

Extensions and Additions, Particularly to the Concept of Causal Schemata

Other additions are just as important. By citing such studies as McArthur (1972) or Feldman, Higgins, Karlovac, and Ruble (1976), Meyer and Schmalt emphasize the accepted significance of this ideal information pattern. But Meyer and Schmalt (1978, p. 112) also concede that the attribution process based on the model of analysis of variance is certainly not characteristic for most everyday situations, for the individual doing the explaining usually lacks the opportunity, time, and motivation to make the repeated observations necessary to gather the information for an "ideal" analysis. That is where the configuration concept of causal schemata comes in that Kelley designed to supplement the covariation concept (see Kelley, 1973, for an instructive treatment) and to cover the typology of judgment and the attribution process in unique, one-time-only situations.

So much for surmisable linkages between exploratory activities and certain basic situations significant for attribution. We are still at the level of analyzing models, leaving the matter at an initial testable deduction and combining an as-yet vague concept of exploration with attributional "folklore," i.e., the very first and familiar systematizations of this field. This would be for future empirical research to elaborate, and such research could certainly be broadened through the express treatment of exploratory activities as a consequence of precursory attributions, an area opened up by Weiner's work in particular.

The real significance of this still stylized linkage between the topics of attribution and exploration is that it sets up a completely ideal situation in both the covariative and the configurative cases to which not only everyday deviations (in the sense of judgment bias) but especially variations and changes of development can be tailored. Indeed, that is only now being worked out. Heckhausen's article (1983) has compiled the findings central to this subject and organized them ontogenetically. The development of causal schemata he discusses such as the 11 steps of development that he elaborates in the causal attribution of the results of action are decisive aids in specifying ontogentically the linkage between exploration and attribution.

Illustration of Other Sequence Versions—Exploration As a Consequence According to Weiner

However, we are touching upon the version mentioned previously. The developmental relationships to attribution theory are less clear when exploratory activity is a consequence-variable of precursory attributions. The reasons for this are not principally systematic but rather more historical. Weiner's classifications, which are influential in this regard, more recently listed (see Weiner in Görlitz, 1980b, pp. 65–66) three independent causal dimensions: stability (as unstable–stable), locus (as internal–external), and the newly included dimension of control or controllability (as uncontrollable–controllable). The subsequent "primary effects" and "other consequences" of these causal dimensions (see Fig. 5.1) are based in particular on Weiner's own contributions, which concentrated mostly on the achievement context. Effects and consequences are not confined to achievement. And it has more than face validity to assume that exploratory activities are to be linked with these three dimensions in different ways—more with unstable, controllable combinations, for example, than with stable, uncontrollable combinations derived from the dimensions cited. Weiner's new dimension of controllability seems to have special significance for exploratory activities. In Weiner it is the only piece of evidence for exploration as a behaviorally effective consequence, restricted to the self-perception of control. But there is another reason why the chances for treating exploration in the context of the control dimension are difficult to gauge at present. Weiner's findings, obtained by using Nuttin's method, have shown (see Weiner et al., 1980, p. 108) that the actor's certainty of control can itself be an ontogenetically changing phenomenon (see the findings on erroneous "contingency awareness"). The concepts of covariance and those of configuration will undoubtedly have different consequences, too. And the three dimensions of controllability, stability, and locus can each determine different precursory exploratory activities: What amount of precursory exploration leads one, for example, to classify a result of action as stable, controllable, and internal (to the actor himself)?

In addition to these links of exploration in the antecedent and consequence positions, the developmental psychologist also sees exploration's varied role in attributional activity as significant. When is explaining and giving reasons so obvious or so resistant to experience that children of a specific age ignore precursory, accompanying, or subsequent explorations? And which other strategies

FIG. 5.1 Partial representation of Weiner's attributional theory of motivation.

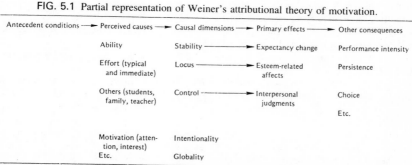

Antecedent conditions →	Perceived causes →	Causal dimensions →	Primary effects →	Other consequences
	Ability	Stability ————→	Expectancy change	Performance intensity
	Effort (typical and immediate)	Locus ————→	Esteem-related affects	Persistence
	Others (students, family, teacher)	Control - - - →	Interpersonal judgments	Choice
				Etc.
	Motivation (attention, interest)	Intentionality		
	Etc.	Globality		

for information gathering take over? Or do only those areas change in which these strategies are used?

SUMMARY

On the basis of preliminary experience and data gathered in an experiment on the behavior of passersby in a curiosity-related situation, the four sections of this contribution discuss exploration essentially as an activity of comparing and highlighting in relation to attribution essentially as an activity of causal analysis and what place this relation has in the development of sociocognitive action and behavior. This relation is taken as a possible and necessary linkage between both domains and is illustrated with the microgenetics of questioning and explaining. Additional evidence from other research areas involved—especially from developmental psychology—show that certain sequential consequences of exploration and attribution or genetic priorities cannot at present be proven conclusively. It seems more fruitful heuristically, too, for empirical work to forego a rigid coupling in sequence models of exploration and attribution in favor of discussing certain sequences that have a basis in theory and to study their changes in development. Initial inferences drawn from Kelley's and Weiner's models from the realm of attribution theory exemplify this approach.

REFERENCES

Arkin, R. M., & Duval, S. (1975). Focus of attention and causal attribution of actors and observers. *Journal of Experimental Social Psychology, 11,* 427–438.

Baldwin, A. L. (1967). *Theories of child development.* New York: Wiley.

Berlyne, D. E. (1960). *Conflict, arousal, and curiosity.* New York: McGraw-Hill.

Bühler, C. (1928). Zwei Grundtypen von Lebensprozessen. *Zeitschrift für Psychologie, 108,* 222–239.

Cunningham, J. D., & Kelley, H. H. (1975). Causal attributions for interpersonal events of varying magnitude. *Journal of Personality, 43,* 74–93.

Dörner, D., Kreuzig, H. W., Reither, F., & Stäudel, T. (Eds.). (1983). *Lohhausen. Vom Umgang mit Unbestimmtheit und Komplexität.* Bern: Huber.

Duval, S. (1971). *Causal attribution as a function of focus of attention.* Unpublished manuscript, University of Texas.

Duval, S., & Hensley, V. (1976). Extensions of objective self-awareness theory: The focus of attention-causal attribution hypothesis. In J. H. Harvey, W. J. Ickes, & R. F. Kidd (Eds.), *New directions in attribution research* (Vol. 1, pp. 165–198). Hillsdale, NJ: Lawrence Erlbaum Associates.

Feldman, N. S., Higgins, E. T., Karlovac, M., & Ruble, D. N. (1976). Use of consensus information in causal attributions as a function of temporal presentation and availability of direct information. *Journal of Personality and Social Psychology, 34,* 694–698.

Flavell, J. H. (1977). *Cognitive development.* Englewood Cliffs, NJ: Prentice-Hall.

Fowler, H.: *Curiosity and exploratory behavior.* New York: Macmillan, 1985.

Ginsburg, H., & Opper, S. (1979). *Piaget's theory of intellectual development* (2nd ed.). Englewood Cliffs, NJ: Prentice-Hall.

Görlitz, D. (1974). Motivationshypothesen in der Alltagskommunikation. *Kölner Zeitschrift für Soziologie und Sozialpsychologie, 26*, 538–567.

Görlitz, D. (1978). Nachwort. In D. Görlitz, W.-U. Meyer, & B. Weiner (Eds.), *Bielefelder Symposium über Attribution* (pp. 245–255). Stuttgart: Klett–Cotta. (Translated in D. Görlitz [Ed.], *Perspectives on attribution research and theory. The Bielefeld symposium* [pp. 219–230]. Cambridge, MA: Ballinger, 1980.)

Görlitz, D. (1980a, July). *Perception and attribution: On the development of unit formation strategies.* XXIInd International Congress of Psychology, Leipzig, GDR. Abstract Guide (Vol. 2, p. 619).

Görlitz, D. (Ed.). (1980b). *Perspectives on attribution research and theory. The Bielefeld symposium.* Cambridge, MA: Ballinger.

Görlitz, D. (Ed.). (1983a). *Kindliche Erklärungsmuster. Entwicklungspsychologische Beiträge zur Attributionsforschung* (Vol. 1). Weinheim: Beltz.

Görlitz, D. (1983b). Entwicklungsmuster attributionaler Handlungsanalyse. In D. Görlitz (Ed.), *Kindliche Erklärungsmuster. Entwicklungspsychologische Beiträge zur Attributionsforschung* (Vol. 1, pp. 146–179). Weinheim: Beltz.

Gruber, H. E., & Vonèche, J. J. (Eds.). (1977). *The essential Piaget. An interpretive reference and guide.* London: Routledge & Kegan Paul.

Harter, S. (1972). *A manual of tasks constructed to measure effectance motivation.* Unpublished manuscript, Yale University.

Harter, S. (1978). Effectance motivation reconsidered. Toward a developmental model. *Human Development, 21*, 34–64.

Heckhausen, H. (1983). Entwicklungsschritte in der Kausalattribution von Handlungsergebnissen. In D. Görlitz (Ed.), *Kindliche Erklärungsmuster. Entwicklungspsychologische Beiträge zur Attributionsforschung* (Vol. 1, pp. 49–85). Weinheim: Beltz.

Heider, F. (1958). *The psychology of interpersonal relations.* New York: Wiley.

Herkner, W. (Ed.). (1980). *Attribution—Psychologie der Kausalität.* Bern: Huber.

Hunt, J. McV. (1965). Intrinsic motivation and its role in psychological development. In D. Levine (Ed.), *Nebraska Symposium on Motivation* (pp. 189–282). Lincoln: University of Nebraska Press.

Hutt, C. (1970). Specific and diversive exploration. In H. W. Reese & L. P. Lipsitt (Eds.), *Advances in child development and behavior* (Vol. 5, pp. 120–180).

Jones, E. E., & Davis, K. E. (1965). From acts to dispositions. The attribution process in person perception. In L. Berkowitz (Ed.), *Advances in experimental social psychology* (Vol. 2, pp. 220–266). New York: Academic Press.

Kagan, J. (1984). *The nature of the child.* New York: Basic Books.

Keller, H., & Voss, H.-G. (Eds.). (1976). *Neugier und Exploration. Theorien und Ergebnisse.* Stuttgart: Kohlhammer. (Translated as H.-G. Voss & H. Keller [Eds.], *Curiosity and exploration. Theories and results.* New York: Academic Press, 1983.)

Kelley, H. H. (1967). Attribution theory in social psychology. In D. Levine (Ed.), *Nebraska Symposium on Motivation* (pp. 192–240). Lincoln: University of Nebraska Press.

Kelley, H. H. (1972a). Attribution in social interaction. In E. E. Jones, D. E. Kanouse, H. H. Kelley, R. E. Nisbett, S. Valins, & B. Weiner (Eds.), *Attribution—Perceiving the causes of behavior* (pp. 1–26). Morristown, NJ: General Learning Press.

Kelley, H. H. (1972b). Causal schemata and the attribution process. In E. E. Jones, D. E. Kanouse, H. H. Kelley, R. E. Nisbett, S. Valins, & B. Weiner (Eds.), *Attribution—Perceiving the causes of behavior* (pp. 151–174). Morristown, NJ: General Learning Press.

Kelley, H. H. (1973). The processes of causal attribution. *American Psychologist, 28*, 107–128.

Kelley, H. H. (1977, June). *Recent research in causal attribution.* Paper presented at the Department of Psychology of the Technische Universität Berlin, FRG.

Kelley, H. H., & Michela, J. L. (1980). Attribution theory and research. *Annual Review of Psychology, 31*, 457–501.

Kun, A., Garfield, T., & Sipowicz, C. (   ). *Causal pleasure in young children: An experimental study of effectance motivation.* Unpublished manuscript.

Lewis, M., & Brooks-Gunn, J. (1979). *Social cognition and the acquisition of self.* New York: Plenum.

McArthur, L. A. (1972). The how and what of why: Some determinants and consequences of causal attribution. *Journal of Personality and Social Psychology, 22*, 171–193.

Meyer, W.-U. (1981, April). *Processes of self-assessment: The case of perceived ability.* Paper presented at the meeting of the U.S.A. Social Science Research Council's "Committee of Life-Course Perspectives on Middle and Old Age," Heidelberg, FRG.

Meyer, W.-U. (1984). *Das Konzept von der eigenen Begabung.* Bern: Huber.

Meyer, W.-U., & Schmalt, H.-D. (1978). Die Attributions theorie. In D. Frey (Ed.), *Kognitive Theorien der Sozialpsychologie* (pp. 98–136). Bern: Huber.

Moravia, S. (1977). *Beobachtende Vernunft. Philosophie und Anthropologie in der Aufklärung.* Frankfurt/M: Ullstein.

Nunnally, J. C. (1981). Explorations of exploration. In H. I. Day (Ed.), *Advances in intrinsic motivation and aesthetics* (pp. 87–129). New York: Plenum.

Nunnally, J. C., & Lemond, L. C. (1973). Exploratory behavior and human development. In H. W. Reese (Ed.), *Advances in child development and behavior* (Vol. 8, pp. 60–109). New York: Academic Press.

Nuttin, J. R. (1973). Pleasure and reward in human motivation and learning. In D. E. Berlyne & K. B. Madsen (Eds.), *Pleasure, reward, preference. Their nature, determinants, and role in behavior* (pp. 243–274). New York: Academic Press.

Orvis, B. R., Cunningham, J. D., & Kelley, H. H. (1975). A closer examination of causal inference: The roles of consensus, distinctiveness, and consistency information. *Journal of Personality and Social Psychology, 32*, 605–616.

Piaget, J. (1936). *La naissance de l'intelligence chez l'enfant.* Neuchâtel: Delachaux & Niestlé. (*The origins of intelligence in children.* Trans. by M. Cook. New York: International Universities Press, 1952.)

Voss, H.-G., & Keller, H. (Eds.). (1983). *Curiosity and exploration. Theories and results.* New York: Academic Press. (Original work published 1976)

Watson, J. S. (1966). The development and generalization of "contingency awareness" in early infancy: Some hypotheses. *Merrill–Palmer Quarterly, 12*, 123–135.

Watson, J. S. (1967). Memory and "contingency analysis" in infant learning. *Merrill–Palmer Quarterly, 13*, 55–76.

Weinberg, S. (1981). *The first three minutes. A modern view of the origin of the universe.* Glasgow: Collins.

Weiner, B. (Ed.). (1974). *Achievement motivation and attribution theory.* Morristown, NJ: General Learning Press.

Weiner, B. (1980a). A theory of motivation for some classroom experiences. In D. Görlitz (Ed.), *Perspectives on attribution research and theory. The Bielefeld Symposium* (pp. 39–74). Cambridge, MA: Ballinger.

Weiner, B. (1980b). The role of affect in rational (attributional) approaches to human motivation. *Educational Researcher*, July–August, 4–11.

Weiner, B. (1984). Principles for a theory of student motivation and their application within an attributional framework. In R. Ames & C. Ames (Eds.), *Research on motivation in education: Student motivation* (Vol. 1, pp. 15–38). New York: Academic Press.

Weiner, B., & Graham, S. (1984). An attributional approach to emotional development. In C. Izard, J. Kagan, & R. Zajonc (Eds.), *Emotion, cognition, and behavior* (pp. 167–191). Cambridge, MA: Cambridge University Press.

Weiner, B., Graham, S., Taylor, S. E., & Meyer, W.-U. (1983). Social cognition in the classroom. *Educational Psychologist, 18,* 109–124.

Weiner, B., & Kun, A. (1977). *The development of causal attributions and the growth of achievement and social motivation.* Unpublished manuscript.

Weiner, B., Kun, A., & Benesh-Weiner, M. (1980). The development of mastery, emotions, and morality from an attributional perspective. In W. A. Collins (Ed.), *Development of cognition, affect, and social relations. The Minnesota Symposia on Child Psychology* (Vol. 13, pp. 103–129). Hillsdale, NJ: Lawrence Erlbaum Associates.

Weiner, B., & Peter, N. (1973). A cognitive-developmental analysis of achievement and moral judgments. *Developmental Psychology, 9,* 290–309.

Weiner, B., Russell, D., & Lerman, D. (1979). The cognition–emotion process in achievement-related contexts. *Journal of Personality and Social Psychology, 37,* 211–220.

White, R. W. (1959). Motivation reconsidered: The concept of competence. *Psychological Review, 66,* 297–333.

Wohlwill, J. F. (1973). *The study of behavioral development.* New York: Academic Press.

PART TWO
EMPIRICAL RESEARCH AND METHODOLOGICAL ISSUES: EXPLORATION

CHAPTER SIX

EXPLORATION IN AN EVERYDAY
CONTEXT: SITUATIONAL
COMPONENTS AND PROCESSES
IN CHILDREN AND ADULTS

DIETMAR GÖRLITZ
Technische Universität Berlin (West)

PROCESS ORIENTATION AND RESEARCH DILEMMAS

Processes of Action

We have tried to show in another chapter of this book how developmental studies on attribution and exploration can interact. The appropriate definitions of attribution were thereby found to be clearer and more comprehensible than those of the often general label *exploratory activities*. This task should be reserved for thorough treatment in its own right so as not to compete with questions of cooperation and agreement as we have pursued them thus far. Efforts to respond to this task have meanwhile become indispensable, for otherwise we would continue with an approach about which Nunnally and Lemond (1973) have already expressed regret. They point out that exploratory behavior lacks a comprehensive scheme for classifying the subprocesses involved, that instead many different types of behavior are lumped together in a single term and treated uniformly—behavior patterns that should be distinguished from one another ontogenetically, too (pp. 62–63). This call from Nunnally and Lemond to developmental psychologists—a call echoed by Papoušek et al. in this volume for the phenomenon of play—should be taken more seriously than has hitherto usually been the case. What they ask for would have been understood earlier by psychologists as the study of phenomena through the observation of behavior and action in order to prepare a conceptual analysis and a definition of curiosity and exploration. For some present-day developmental psychologists this plea also contains the call to concentrate on studying the observable temporal extension, the overt process characteristics of the behavioral phenomena in question (Görlitz, 1983). Projected on a lifelong continuum, then, these brief segments of time, the thematically specific behavior in a concrete situation, are the core of developmental psychology in addition to products or effects of action.

Such a process-oriented approach can be traced clear back to Heinz Werner (1937) but has never really achieved popularity among developmental psychologists.[1] Nevertheless, this approach is promising for curiosity and exploration in particular. Most phenomena that are otherwise difficult to specify assume their individuality only when they are seen as manifested in a concrete situation over an identifiable stretch of time. That is the case for their "overt" as well as their inferable "covert" characteristics. Accordingly, Nunnally and Lemond (1973) emphasize that "[what] has been lacking in the efforts to subdivide all of explanatory behavior into meaningful categories is a temporal scheme that articulates the various processes in relation to one another" (p. 63). To do this they outline

---

[1]On the significance of this approach in today's psychology, see Draguns (1984), especially also Kaye (1982); on the consideration of microsocial variables in analyzing processes of exchange within a family, see, for example, Patterson (1984, p. 46).

an exploration cycle that, formulated at the observational level, is supposed to contain overt and covert components of the process in a single temporal sequence, whereby some components of the two sets are not aligned.

It can be shown that both subjects referred to in this chapter—exploration and attribution—would profit from this developmental orientation to microprocesses. Developmental psychology and developmental psychologists in particular will not be content with merely registering effects (their standardization as test scores, for example) and their repeated investigation in longitudinal research in order to provide evidence of change. In addition to an orientation to effects or products, this field should be broadened to include a process orientation that takes changes in the microgenetic findings gathered in concrete situations and interprets them at the ontogenetic and historiogenetic level, too. To complete the argument, a developmental psychology in this extended sense is concerned with courses of change of different temporal spans, ranging from microgenesis to onto- and phylogenesis, and with the change of products and processes, states, and traits at these different levels.

Our own contact with the everyday behavior of passersby who find themselves in a curiosity situation, which is briefly described later, was established with this call in mind. In the list of criteria recording the distinguishing features of this field, the viewpoint known as "the process and the means and levels of exploration," mentioned later, refers to this program. But in this initial introduction to the spontaneity of curiosity and exploration, more fundamental problems also became relevant, problems that are briefly treated under four subtitles. They seem to be particularly central to research on curiosity. Thereafter, our attempt to become acquainted with exploratory activity in terms of its course and the structure of its components are presented without the results. The main focus is more on a presentation of components that can be differentiated according to situation and action. The process orientation of developmental psychology, referred to earlier, certainly provides especially important components. Although this is a system whose rules of linkage have yet to be worked out, these components are nevertheless partial determinants and are descriptive aids by which sequences of action and types of situations can be more reliably identified and differentiated in the future. The detailed analysis of the findings will be conducted elsewhere. If we present such a basic concept and a process model of exploratory activity whose individual microgenetic components of observable behavior may be new but whose basic thesis is already familiar, then we are presupposing some decisions that are the source of many conflicts within the research on exploration and curiosity carried out in developmental psychology.

Dilemmas of the Research Approach

We list some dilemmas prosaically and in unrefined terms in order to stimulate discussion about them. Introducing them briefly—and not necessarily in order of their importance—they are the problems of spontaneity, individuality, labeling (specificity), and functionality (open functions). (For further treatment of these aspects, see Joseph A. Keller's contribution to this volume.)

The Problem of Spontaneity.   For many people curiosity is the hallmark of spontaneity. However, important reviews of this field of work (such as those by Nunnally & Lemond, 1973; and Hutt, 1970) present accounts of systematic and controlled experiments that center on stimulus or reaction, with the experimenter presenting materials to cooperating subjects for their optical inspection and then recording their various strategies for dealing with these materials.

Earlier in this volume we explained that, under these circumstances, curiosity is no longer of interest if it is also a spontaneous activity of the subject who is engaged in seeking information or generating dissonance. With the subject's questioning excluded, the setting for the experimental partner's activity is already prescribed. By contrast, Berlyne's psychological experiments (in Hutt, 1970) with animals do not ask what induces this stimulus, but rather "which stimulus this animal will respond [to] and [Hutt] why?" (p. 139). The differentiation between "diversive and specific exploration" (Berlyne, 1960; Wohlwill, 1981) can be subsumed under this problem, too. The terminological variations that Keller and Voss (1976, pp. 32–33) bring into the global concept of the search for stimulus or information concentrate on this issue (particularly Livson's concept of "productive curiosity"). Curiosity often tends to be experienced by the researcher testing his hypotheses, but not by the experimental subject doing what he is told to do.

That, more than other dissonances, tempts one to get reacquainted with the topic in situations more representative of everyday life, though admittedly this would not resolve the conflict. If in our experiment we ask what unfamiliar passersby do in a largely unfamiliar, curiosity-arousing situation that at least causes these people to pause without their having planned to do so—and the external observer is able to ascertain that beyond the shadow of a doubt—then we may be a bit closer to the spontaneity of the behavior being studied than if we were to invite our subjects to the institute to look at pictures. Still, both situations are contrived, differing only in the degree to which each can be controlled. Where does the spontaneity of the participating passersby come in? Without dwelling on this point further now—spontaneous and reactive behavior and action in the context of curiosity research—it is nevertheless clear that the difference between anthropological positions is reflected here, as Reese and Overton have shown for developmental psychology (see Reese and Overton's discrimination between mechanistic and organismic concepts in 1970, 1973). Where is the spontaneity in these studies on reacting, experimental subjects? Could it be documented in the very changes of stimuli they actively seek? On what basis can well-founded statements be made about the spontaneity of the behavior, which the experimenter has not only observed but also provoked?

More important still, how much stimulation and control come from the "third parties involved," who, in the monologic models (like the process model of

Nunnally and Lemond) normally used at present are not included at all, even though their presence may have an active role in the definition, support, modulation, and solution of curiosity situations that arise in everyday life? (See the criterion of exploration control and effectance strategies, page 123, and the behaviors associated with "dialogic modulation.") To deal with the problem of spontaneity, we need to develop such diverse models instead of simply abandoning experimental situations that limit the reactions of the experimental subjects. We faced this problem in our exploratory study (described more fully following), in which a "curiosity cage" was placed in a public place (at the central train and subway station in Berlin). Here we left a broad spectrum of behavior open to the passersby entering the square from the subway exit, a spectrum that ranged from initial orientation to disregard or surreptitious viewing.

The Problem of Individuality.   Curiosity has a very individual side. In studies of curiosity and exploration, the researcher is dependent in a special way on a knowledge of the experimental subject's past confrontations or encounters with the object in question. Only with this knowledge can the observer say that he is viewing behavior toward an object that is to a definable extent "new" to the actor. Such in-depth knowledge can be expected—if at all—only from close social contact in which, for example, an older partner is familiar enough with the significant facts of the child's everyday experiences to be able to gauge the novelty of objects that have just been introduced. One will want to rely on the accuracy of the information provided by the accompanying parents and on their willingness to volunteer it, but this certainly does not eliminate the difficulty of standardizing individual learning histories about different subjects to the point that the researcher can compare them. The value of differentiating degrees of novelty according to how recent or remote the experience in question was for the individual, as Berlyne has done, is more apparent than real, for such a differentiation itself requires knowledge of an individual's history even if the time spans involved are reduced from the macrohistory of weeks and years to the microhistory of hours.

The problem of individuality has yet another aspect, however. For it is worth pondering whether an object of the animate and inanimate (or inactive) environment can be confined in this way to a stable dimension of measurable novelty and whether that object can retain this label over long periods of confrontation. Does not a good deal of productivity and creativity consist of seeing a totally new side of things that are already familiar and well known in some respects? This could mean that features of the object that were not noticed earlier are now perceived or that new ways of using an object become apparent in a particular context. Presumably, one characteristic of something that is new in too many respects is precisely and paradoxically that it does not induce exploratory behavior (in terms of Berlyne, see Berlyne, 1960, p. 21; see also Piaget's "principle of moderate novelty"). Imagination is always likely to allow the mere existence of long-known objects to be transcended.

Our solution to the problem of individuality—the "curiosity cage" containing stuffed animals that move and make noises semiautomatically—draws more on the contextual aspects of curiosity; this scene, in front of the central subway and train station or across from the Memorial Church, is (very probably) novel to the passersby without the animals or cage necessarily being a new experience for most of them. Still, curiosity always has a different history for every person, and we knew less than anyone about those individual backgrounds.

The Problem of Labeling (Specificity). Exploration and curiosity have a graphic plausibility. But what is it about another person's action or behavior that allows an observer to state reliably that exploratory activities are involved and not consumatory terminal action or activities in a different context? Exploratory behavior is manifested in the range of behaviors that an active individual exhibits—his locomotion, manipulation, gestures, and facial expressions, in his verbal and perceptual behavior, his gross and fine movements (ranging from turns of the head to changes in the position of the entire body or its parts). And it is often expressed simultaneously in these behaviors—unlike the frequently isolating concentration on eye movement that typifies current research practice, for example—with interesting links between and consequences of the exhibited actions. Although the findings are still controversial, exploration can also be coupled with other activities, as Berlyne (1960, pp. 119–128) believes. Berlyne had considered his differentiations between such forms of exploratory behavior, which were so influential, to be only preliminary.

Only future experimentation, on both behavioral and physiological levels, can tell us where the natural affinities and oppositions within exploratory behavior lie (Berlyne, 1960, p. 79).

But if, as the problem of individuality shows, the novelty of an exploration-related object is a difficult attribute to define—a feature that that attribute shares with some of the object's other dimensions such as complexity (see Kreitler, Zigler, & Kreitler, 1974)—if novelty is thus not a quality that can be "assigned" unambiguously to objects, might it then be specific object–action intertwinements and their temporal structure that define exploratory behavior as a class of action and behavior in its own right? The microgenetic process model we suggest tries to develop criteria in this direction. But remember that there are criteria referenced more to the actor himself: To what extent can one avoid inferences to one's intentions, and how desirable and helpful are they? Inferences, that is, to the actor's defining activities of the "what-is-that?" or the "what-could-that-be?" type. Piaget, for example, saw himself compelled, as explained earlier to place explicit intentionality ontogenetically before the express introduction of exploration (that is, in the third developmental stage of sensomotory intelligence). And regardless of whether it is necessary to make inferences or exclude them, how often does the everyday and scientific observer in fact succumb to such inferences? Jones and Davis (1965) in particular provided testable rules for them in attribution research. A more exacting analysis could shed light on the matter of whether there are certain object–action intertwinements that foster such inferences of intentionality (as with the observation of another person's actions) and whether these then facilitate the labeling of the behavior as "inquisitive," as "exploratory."

In our curiosity situation, the entire burden of determining (and making mistakes in determining) the definition and description of the observed behavior depended on the optical appeal of the "curiosity cage," an approach acceptable only in the preliminary stages of pilot projects. We close here with the problem of functionality.

The Problem of Functionality (Open Functions).   In the eyes of adults, curiosity and exploration have the connotation of excess and superfluity if nothing much urgently needs to be fulfilled. This also means, however, that the discernable goal relatedness or goal determination (functionality) in other people's curiosity behavior seen by an external observer is less evident than in actions terminated by clearly defined effects—as in achievement tasks, which often result in concrete products. Thus—coming back to the problem of specificity or labelling—one cannot try to derive a positive criterion for definition from sharply delineated, specific functions, unless one were to accept the lack of specific goals as a positive criterion (which would, in effect, make exploration a catchall category for all borderline cases of unclear actions, too). This indefinite functionality is complicated by the fact that exploratory behavior itself can be autonomous in different ways. Berlyne called attention to this difference without, as we believe, utilizing it empirically (see Berlyne, 1960, pp. 79 and 137).

Whereas there is an actual product or a termination of an action to which achievement activity is anchored, indeterminate functionality makes it more difficult to say when exploratory behavior begins and ends. To formulate it a bit one-sidedly, the effect of exploratory activity is not a tangible product. The effect of exploratory activity involving a search for stimuli is an encounter with a stimulus; and for curiosity research, pinpointing the beginning and end of exploratory activity is a dilemma in itself. We already have discussed links between developmental psychology and attribution research and suggest that the anchoring of "hovering localizations" treated at that point and the clarification of other still indeterminate attributions be regarded as a possible termination of exploratory behavior.

The behavior of the passersby in front of the "curiosity cage" in our experiment offered some help in solving the dilemma. In approaching the cage, these individuals altered their original path considerably and clearly terminated their contact with the cage—both visually and spatially—when they turned to go. That delimits the overall time span in which the sequences of behavior we are interested in are to be sought, yet does not necessarily define all behavior within that span as exploratory behavior.

PILOT STUDY OF EXPLORATION IN AN EVERYDAY CONTEXT

Design

The problems sketched previously became clear during an introductory practical example in which the author, aided by four student assistants,[2] tried to record random samples of behavior exhibited by passersby who were unexpectedly confronted with a peculiar situation. This "peculiar situation" was a small cage of the type available in toy shops, into which five stuffed toys had been placed. Three of them were battery-powered, semiautomatic animals (a monkey and two dogs) capable of performing a limited series of movements. The monkey beat a drum while changing from a sitting to a lying position and back again, and the dogs made small movements and little whimpering sounds as they opened and closed their snouts. The two other, equally large, animals in the cage were immobile stuffed toys like those found in nearly all stores. This cage was set up at various well-frequented places in Berlin (such as Bahnhof Zoo, the sidewalk of Tauentzienstrasse opposite the Kaiser Wilhelm Memorial Church, and in front of the supermarket next to the Institute of Psychology at the Berlin Technical University on Dovestrasse). We chose different hours on days when the weather was not causing the passersby to be in a particular hurry (often on sunny days, for example; never in the rain). After placing the cage in the desired position, the semiautomatic stuffed animals were activated, the small door to the cage was closed, and the cage left to itself. Without discussion of filming or editing techniques, the student assistants then used an unhidden video camera to record what the adults and children passing by did when they spotted the cage. It is important to stress that the author did participate in preparing the first phase of the pilot study, but not in the actual filming of the action and that the students did not film continuously but rather in segments and from different focal distances without, however, reducing the possibility of recording entire behavioral sequences of individual passersby from the time they first came up to the cage to the time they left.

Thus, several curiosity situations were superimposed upon one another: passersby, like the mother directing her child in the baby buggy on her way to the cage—a student letting the camera begin to film and changing the focal length, pausing occasionally, then continuing to film—the university professor who deals

[2]The author cordially thanks Werner Bott, Manfred Röhrig, Manfred Sunderhauf, and Bernhard Wellmann for all the work they invested in the preparation and actual filming of this part of the study.

with the video tape in the laboratory in a certain way, repeatedly inspecting and analyzing it at different playback speeds.

In the second part of the pilot study, we made one of these three situations (one frame of reference) stable—that of the students. It was arranged that they would use two cameras and would film the situations without stopping, with one camera recording the entire scene while the other would isolate certain aspects of interest to us by taking close-ups. The "peculiar situation," the cage, was systematically varied according to two criteria—the animation of the stuffed animals (the cage contained either the immobile stuffed toys or the semiautomatic toys, but not both) and the extent to which they were enclosed (the toys were placed either in the cage or on the open street). We felt that this manipulated the situation substantially enough to produce sharply defined initial experiences under sufficiently contrastive circumstances. The analysis of the extensive observational data gathered in the second part of the pilot study has not yet been completed. All the findings reported here relate to the first part. Still lacking data, they are nothing more than impressions and a preliminary extraction of increasingly important components and processes stemming from everyday observation.

To give a more detailed description of the observational situation, the systematic analysis and its application to a conceptual framework in developmental psychology is preceded by a record of the events as recalled by Manfred Röhrig, one of the participating students.

A Record of the Study

In the following paragraphs I report the impressions I formed [during the observational part of the study]. In so doing, it seems useful to distinguish between children, adults, and elderly persons:

The Children.   The children, particularly the younger ones, were the actors who stood out the most. They walked directly to the cage and touched the animals, unless they were restrained by their parents. The amount of time spent was very great, and [the activity] was usually interrupted by the parents. The interest was focused primarily on the animated animals making noises. The somewhat older children (from about 10 years on) showed interest in the video equipment. [Compared to other age groups,] on the whole, children attended to the object of their curiosity the most, and the exploration was correspondingly intensive.

The Adults.   The adults (ranging from approximately 20 to 50 years of age) were reserved for the most part. They rarely came up to the cage to remain there. Their typical curiosity behavior consisted primarily of establishing eye contact with the cage, often fixing their gaze [upon it] (with a turn of the head) while walking by. All assumptions about this curiosity behavior (for example, that working people have less time; that they would not exhibit a great deal of curiosity so as not to be labeled "childish"; that they were censuring themselves for other reasons; or that [the situation] was simply too uninteresting to them) remain speculation. Questions, asked primarily by people from this age group, occasionally surfaced and indicated more interest in the idea and purpose behind our undertaking.

The Elderly.   In everyday language, words associated with curiosity are often used in negative contexts ["Curiosity killed the cat"]. [Exhibiting] curiosity is punished verbally or in other ways ("You're nosy!"). The elderly were very curious for the most part. They often remained standing at the cage, stepped over to it, and even bent down, but touching it directly was rare. They often remained standing for a long time and not uncommonly communicated with each other about what they were observing. We were often asked by the elderly how much the animals cost and where they were to be purchased. One scene that impressed me was that of an elderly woman who spoke kindly to the animals. She seemed delighted and had no reservations about talking in front of quite a big crowd. All in all the willingness to exhibit curiosity was greater among the elderly than among adults of other groups. Unlike the children, however, the elderly avoided touching the objects.

Foreigners.   I often noticed foreigners who stood quite uninhibited and simply watched. One scene, which unfortunately was not recorded, involved about 10 young foreign men who, to avoid interfering with the "filming," observed the happenings from a distance of about 10 meters for a long time (about 10 minutes). Standing and looking was not unusual for foreigners.

THE CONCEPTUAL FRAMEWORK OF COMPONENTS AND PROCESSES

The scene is perhaps familiar enough that one can easily afford the loss of atmosphere caused by analyzing concrete reality more formally for its essential components. These are then integrated within a conceptual framework, discussed individually, and documented. A qualification to be noted is that the case dealt with in this pilot study conveys only one of many basic types of constellations that can be involved in curiosity situations: It was contrived situations that allowed for an impromptu encounter with a potentially interesting event (case D, after Wohlwill, 1981). Just how much the points of view elaborated here could be generally valid for exploration and curiosity is not being considered at present.

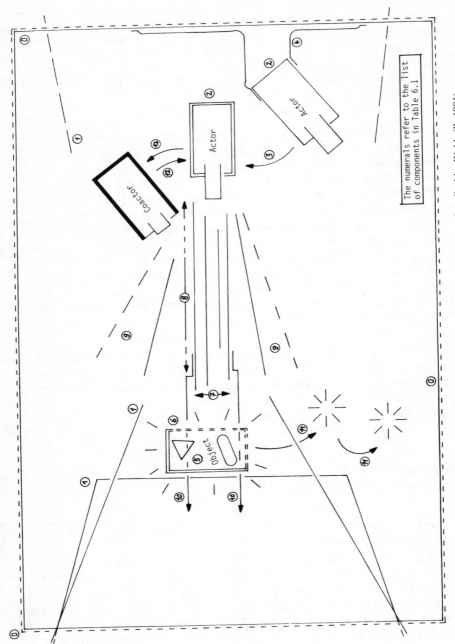

The numerals refer to the list
of components in Table 6.1

FIG. 6.1 A basic concept of curiosity-related situations (pertaining to case D described by Wohlwill, 1981).

Components (Criteria)

These components or criteria of a curiosity situation are a byproduct of intensive observational analysis of the video sequences taped during the pilot study. They are reported in this chapter, with the results to be published elsewhere, for, as future discussion may show, they have heuristic value for analyses of phenomena and for theoretical positions in curiosity research. If the list of them is relatively complete, they help one to figure out which parameters (those controlled in an experiment, for instance) are involved in a particular study of curiosity, and this makes it possible to provide a taxonomy of available studies on curiosity. Moreover, they are to allow one to pinpoint microgenetic processes in a given situation, with the process-like nature of exploratory action itself being one of these components or criteria. And beyond this cross-sectional perspective, they are also to identify the "vertices" marking the point at which ontogenetic development, too, begins and making it possible to describe this development. Of the many different purposes to pursue, this seems to be the most important one at present.

At the outset of this study was, as usual, the decision about where—in which situation—the phenomenon of "exploratory behavior and curiosity" was to be investigated and which pretense of control was to be linked with the choice and design of the situation. With due consideration of the author's own still limited scope of specific experience with such situations, a preliminary inquiry was selected as a framework for investigation, with random samples of everyday situations and behavior being taken, each lasting only a short time. This criterion, common to every experiment, heads the list of criteria and is called, in view of the topic, the frame of exploration, differentiating between laboratory, studio, and field study—distinctions that are important for standards of empirical verification (criterion 0).

In the framework selected for the investigation, there were various competing observer perspectives and positions from which the phenomenon of "curiosity and exploration" considered here arose as a topic of discussion. As mentioned earlier, these positions were (and will be) the exploratory interest of the present scientist in and during the investigation itself; the exploratory behavior of the student assistants, whose documenting of some of the events affected the investigative situation in a very real way; and the behaviors and actions of a wide variety of passersby, which differed in form and type from those of either of the former. Justification for establishing this criterion is not only formal; ever since Jones and Nisbett at least, social psychology has documented how great an effect "actor–observer" differences can have.[3] The differences in the mother–child position—the most important dyad—are known to developmental psychology. And we have already pointed out Berlyne's distinction between perceptive and epistemological curiosity, which can covary with such differences

---

[3]For information on the actor–observer difference, see Jones and Nisbett (1972); for a critical commentary and delimitation, see Effler (1983), for example.

in position. Dissimilar positions and perspectives of exploration (criterion 1 in our terms) overlap at this point not only in terms of a unidirectional propagation of effect (what one "does" affects others in a particular direction). Whether staggered in time (field study—laboratory analysis) or simultaneous, many different patterns of feedback are possible, too.

In connection with the differentiation between the preceding three perspectives of exploration, the scientist frequently defines who will be the actor, or the *thematic subject* as we call it. At a busy public place it is often not predetermined who is going to become the object of close analysis with his behavior or who is going to be the instigator of interactions in which several people then try to determine the event in question—one person, for example, through diverse exploration followed by others involved in specific exploration. Criterion 2 refers to this point of view in the analysis of components—the person who is exploring or, for short, the actor. Only in regard to the actor and his initial situation can the reason for his action—the inducement to exploration (criterion 3)—be decided; that is, only if one is observing a specific actor can it be determined if that actor—and this approximates what has been established about the spontaneity or reactivity of his behavior—generated the inducement himself or if it was presented to him, with him either taking the opportunity or rejecting it, or not taking notice of it at all.

The inducement to exploration is reified in a localized total situation (criterion 4), which must have a certain stability before it triggers exploratory behavior instead of defense, fear, and flight reactions. In the light of studies on early childhood (such as Cox & Campbell, 1968, and, more generally, the fear of strangers and fear of separation exhibited by young children), the stabilization of the total situation seems to be especially fruitful as a criterion. The inducement to exploration is manifested in a "thematic object" as the focus of exploratory action and behavior, which is listed under criterion 5 as the object. Current research on this component is not usually centered on particular types of objects of exploration, which may range from persons and things to the paths that connect them and the events that link them (all of which may be tangible or symbolically represented). What is interesting are those qualities of the objects relevant for curiosity and exploration that can be made to stand out or through which the objects and, hence, curiosity and exploration can be varied. These are always dependent, related features that are anchored to at least two points: to the actor's state of motivation and knowledge and to the perceptive-actional surrounding field of the object that becomes relevant for exploration. The traditional variables of curiosity research like novelty and complexity are a part of this criterion. Because of their dependency, we call these features related qualities of the object from among which a precise, stimulus-oriented analysis would isolate collative variables in the strict sense of Berlyne and which would have the remaining intensive and affective variables of "arousal potential" to redefine and probably expand on. To allow for a detailed discussion, we put these qualities of the object into a group of their own, criterion 6 in the analysis of curiosity situations.

Induced by and/or focused on these related aspects of particular objects, the subject acts or behaves on various action levels, which may be synchronically or asynchronically linked during action (with other special cases as discussed in the section on labeling). At the behavioral level, this involves expressive behavior, eye and head movement, locomotion, and other modes of regulating distance (like turning toward or away from an object), manipulation, and verbal activities. It also comprises smelling, sniffing, licking, and tasting (which, except for the last activity, were exhibited by the dachshunds that participated in our pilot study). Included, too, though not directly accessible to the observer, are operations on the mental-cognitive level that take place when, for example, the subject plays through and tries out a series of planned actions or when he enriches the restrictive qualities of the object through his imagination. Operations on the mental-cognitive level pose difficult problems of accessibility that modern research has been addressing more and more, as illustrated by detailed methodological proposals about "data-gathering for covert exploration" offered in Nunnally (1981, pp. 123–126). Domains and levels are brought together under criterion 7 as means and levels of exploration.

Processes of Exploration

Exploratory behavior—if it is clearly definable at all—is a determinable process; it lasts for a certain amount of time as a segment in the microgenesis of a concrete situation. This aspect has long been neglected, and the advances in testing illustrative initial concepts are few and far between, as is shown by the fact that the model Nunnally presented in 1981 is identical to the one he presented in 1973, the two being separated by what in all other respects are 8 years of research progress. We call special attention to the process of exploration (criterion 8) because it is a decisive breakthrough for process analyses in developmental psychology. As there may be more than one set of activities involved in exploratory action, we attempt here to conceptualize a model of phases based on the material from our own analysis. It is supposed to order the segments that occur, beginning with the entrance to the situation, then continuing with orientation, distal contact, social reference to exploration, inspection, verification, and solution, and ending with the actor's separation from the situation. Forms of operating other than exploratory behavior—playing and imitating, for example— must be discussed here.

Our diagram of phases in exploratory action illustrates four synchronic strands of action broken down according to time (phases, for example). The use of different levels of contact and action in general seems to be less characteristic of exploration than the specific content and the sequence of these phases, even

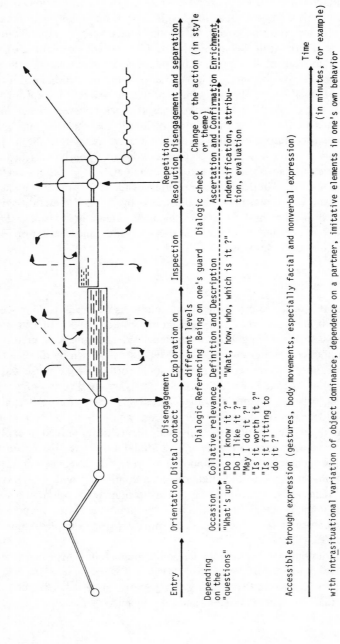

FIG. 6.2 Sequence of phases of exploratory action in an unprepared encounter with a potentially interesting event (corresponding to case D in Wohlwill, 1981, p. 346).

though close analysis may show that diachronic patterns of process as well as synchronic patterns of structure both contribute to specifying the particular phenomenon in question.

The first strand of action in our diagram (see Fig. 6.2), beginning with the entry and ending with the disengagement and separation, orders functions of action, whatever their nature, into a sequence. The first strand involves, say, distal contact or inspection. This ordering is anchored in the components of a situation that are felt to need clarification. After repeated inspection (labeled *repetition* in the diagram and illustrated with arrows pointing back to earlier phases in the sequence), one separates oneself from the situation. This can occur on a strictly local level or can involve merely a change of the preferred style of action, or better, the preferred theme of action, the transition to, say, play and other types of activity.

The points of transition (symbolized as circles), at which a function serving as the topic of the action is supplanted by another, simultaneously designate points at which general choices or decisions significant to the situation are made by the actor (at least implicitly). Figure 6.2 highlights only two, indeed especially important, alternatives—the decision to separate oneself from the situation, that is, to leave after fleeting distal contact has been made (separation), the decision to repeat phases of exploratory action after remote, then proximal, occupation with the object and, for example, a resolution considered to be inadequate (repetition).

The second strand of action in the diagram, represented in Fig. 6.2 as a vertical, curved arrow, goes into the ever-present social dimensions in exploratory action. It is the dialogic dimension of the model, with dialogue not being restricted to explicitly verbal exchange. Nevertheless, one can distinguish verbal types of dialogue and less verbal types of dialogue, and this also goes for actions and the behavior of the passersby we observed. Dialogic referencing like being on one's guard might thus go no further than glancing around and looking, whereas the dialogic check, say, to see whether uncertainties about the object in question or other matters have been sufficiently clarified will rely more heavily on the verbal exchange of questions and answers, supported by gesticulations (like pointing to something or describing circles around one's ear to express a certain opinion of someone).

Our model's third synchronic strand of action deals with the actor's overt and covert processes. If the first strand of action was ordered according to the functions fulfilled by, say, distinguishable phases of action, this strand involves a succession of action themes. Although everything "that the fellow over there is doing" may in fact be exploration in the broader or narrower sense, his exploring of what at first piques his curiosity might follow discernible themes. For purposes of illustration, among others, we have formulated these themes in our figure as verbal questions as if action were a sequence of different questions. (We do not wish to claim that one's exploration is always clearly motivated by or articulated through questions. We at least want to leave this issue open.)

The fourth and most fertile strand of action that can be matched to the microgenetic time axis, expression, receives notably brief mention in our diagram. It is still open for all the wealth of ordered entries according to which phases of action can be reliably distinguished—stably or, in a certain way, variably in the course of ontogenetic development—according to guiding phenomena of expression.

The unit of measure of the time axis to which all four strands of action are referenced can be minutes in order to describe what occurs in a specific situation. Two phases of exploration depicted in Fig. 6.2 are differentiated in a special fashion with an internal graduation to symbolize synchronic and asynchronic structures of the action levels. That contrasts decisive shifts of one's own proximity to the object in question, which one walks around, so to speak, and examines "from a different side." The diagram concludes by noting possible variations that go beyond intrasituational variability.

Further Components

Then follow the styles and strategies of exploration (criterion 9), which hark back to a familiar distinction drawn in curiosity research between specific and diversive exploration, forms that, like the goals of exploration in criterion 10, are associated with specific features of concrete action. If action in general is primarily "doing something intentionally in a certain way to achieve a particular purpose," then a variety of goals can probably be discerned in exploratory action and behavior. One could, for example, arrange these goals according to the customary interrogatives (who, what, when, where, why, and how) and then test to see if different goals of exploration correspond to different behavioral strategies—if such a clear goal profile does not "overdraw the account" of the customary explorations/inquiries (which are still characterized more by their indefinite functionality; see p. 112).

The two parts of criterion 11, the theme of exploration and the consistency of exploration, merely comprise other sides of the same complex behavior, not necessarily independent dimensions. The criterion concerns continuance or change in the theme and object of exploration, such as when the actor shifts from exploring the objects and persons of the situation being observed to exploring other parts of the external situation. It also concerns the homogeneity of the action, which proceeds continuously for long periods or in which the actor switches the theme of his action to pursuing achievement activity, playing with the given object, or engaging in imaginative production.

This list has so far seemed more "monologic" than would do the overall situation justice; that is, the subject seems to act more in isolation than is actually the case, even if only one person is in fact doing the exploring. Initiatives to establish social references (dialogic references) are a decisive characteristic of the process phases of exploratory action (see pp. 109–110). The social setting takes on an especially palpable form in the two parts of criterion 12, the control of exploration and strategies for inducement. Whoever begins exploring in a particular situation can do so independently or can be induced to do so by others exercising various degrees of control. The mothers holding their children's hands or pushing their children in the baby carriage are especially impressive examples of this in our films. Forms of controlling exploration can be found in the series of "self—agreed upon with another—consulting—supported—brought about— steered," forms of control that for the moment are only descriptive subcategories. The control exercised by the "important other" can go so far that he determines the beginning and the end of the exploratory activity or allows certain activities while forbidding others—a situation subsumed here by the term *strategies for inducement*. That can also imply that the other person decides on the admittance to and control of the situation, as did boys who, during our pilot study, placed themselves in front of the cage and blocked other children's access to it. The inducement strategies of the accompanying parents provide especially graphic documentation of pedagogical concepts relevant to everyday life and of the historical shift in our concept of how much spontaneity is permissible for children.

Our list of 12 criteria caps this rough analysis of curiosity situations as far as our experience in the matter is concerned. Table 6.1 summarizes them schematically. So much for analysis of components and processes of curiosity situations, conducted in this chapter for case D as described by Wohlwill (1981). Findings from our pilot study have yet to be added in order to make initial inferences for developmental psychology more specific, a step that must be reserved for a separate publication.

SUMMARY

After pointing out some general problems for empirical work in the fields of curiosity and attribution, the author posits some essential components and determinants of a conceptual framework limited initially to the analysis of a specific type of curiosity situation (case D described in Wohlwill, 1981). These components and determinants are illustrated by preliminary empirical findings. The sequence of phases in exploratory action and behavior in the microgenetics of specific situations is emphasized in the succession of the chapter's 12 points. The author also stresses the principle of exploration's dialogue-like character, which is evident at different levels of exploration (like motor behavior, gestures, facial expression, eye movement, and verbal activity). These references to dialogue range from incidental synchronization to restrictive and regulative control in which sociohistorical determinants of curiosity and exploration are apparent.

TABLE 6.1
A Conceptual Framework for Curiosity Situations

---

(0) Frame of exploration
for example: laboratory, studio, and field study

(1) Positions and perspectives of exploration
for example: scientist, student, passer-by

(2) Actor (the "thematic subject")
for example: mother and child, individual passers-by, several persons in direct
interaction, too

(3) Inducement to exploration
for example: self-generated, opportunity presented and taken, opportunity presented but
no notice taken of it, opportunity presented and rejected

(4) Total situation
particularly as regards its stabilization, followed by attending behavior or defense, fear,
or flight reactions

(5) Object (the "thematic object")
as focus of exploratory action and behavior
for example: the type, reality, or medium in which the object is represented

(6) Qualities of the object
for example: certain related qualities of the object (see "collative variables")

(7) Means and levels of exploration
for example: eye and head movement, locomotion, other modes of regulating distance,
manipulation, and verbal activities, smelling, licking, mental-cognitive
operations

(8) Process of exploration
for example: models of phases according, for example, to entrance, orientation, distal
contact, social reference, exploration, inspection, verification, solution,
separation, imitation, and play

(9) Styles of exploration and strategies of exploration
for example: specific versus diversive exploration

(10) Goals of exploration
for example: according to the customary interrogatives (Who, What, When, Where,
Why, How)

(11) Theme of exploration and consistency of exploration as continuance or change in the
theme and object of exploration and as consistency versus change in the type of action
for example: change from exploration of objects and persons to other parts of the
external situation—change from exploring to playing

(12) Control of exploration and strategies for inducement
for example: one's own exploring versus exploring brought about and controlled by
others, self, agreed upon with another, consulting, supported, brought
about, steered.
The determination by others of commencement and termination of the
possibility of exploring (control access)

REFERENCES

Berlyne, D. E. (1960). *Conflict, arousal, and curiosity*. New York: McGraw–Hill.

Cox, F. N., & Campbell, D. (1968). Young children in a new situation with and without their
mothers. *Child Development, 39*, 123–131.

Draguns, J. G. (1984). Microgenesis by any other name . . . In W. D. Froehlich, G. Smith, J. G.

Draguns, & U. Hentschel (Eds.), *Psychological processes in cognition and personality* (pp. 3–17). Washington: Hemisphere.

Effler, M. (1983). Unterschiede in den Kausalerklärungen von Akteuren und Beobachtern–Zum Geltungsbereich der JONES–NISBETT–Hypothese. *Zeitschrift für Sozialpsychologie, 14*, 229–240.

Görlitz, D. (1983). Exploration und Attribution im Entwicklungskontext. Bericht über den 33. *Kongreß der Deutschen Gesellschaft für Psychologie in Mainz 1982* (Vol. 1, pp. 440–443). Göttingen: Hogrefe.

Hutt, C. (1970). Specific and diversive exploration. In H. W. Reese & L. P. Lippsitt (Eds.), *Advances in child development and behavior* (Vol. 5, pp. 120–180). New York: Academic Press.

Jones, E. E., & Davis, K. E. (1965). From acts to dispositions. The attribution process in person perception. In L. Berkowitz (Ed.), *Advances in experimental social psychology* (Vol. 2, pp. 220–266). New York: Academic Press.

Jones, E. E., & Nisbett, R. E. (1972). The actor and the observer: Divergent perceptions of the causes of behavior. In E. E. Jones, D. Kanouse, H. H. Kelley, R. E. Nisbett, S. Valins, & B. Weiner (Eds.), *Attribution: Perceiving the causes of behavior* (pp. 79–94). Morristown, NJ: General Learning Press.

Kaye, K. (1982). The moral philosophy of microanalysis. In T. Field & A. Fogel (Eds.), *Emotion and early interaction* (pp. 237–251). Hillsdale, NJ: Lawrence Erlbaum Associates.

Keller, H., & Voss, H.-G. (1976). *Neugier und Exploration. Theorien und Ergebnisse*. Stuttgart: Kohlhammer. (Translated as Voss, H.-G., & Keller, H. [1983]. Curiosity and exploration. Theories and results. New York: Academic Press.)

Kreitler, S., Zigler, E., & Kreitler, H. (1974). The complexity of complexity. *Human Development, 17*, 54–73.

Nunnally, J. C. (1981). Explorations of exploration. In H. I. Day (Ed.), *Advances in intrinsic motivation and aesthetics* (pp. 87–129). New York: Plenum.

Nunnally, J. C., & Lemond, L. C. (1973). Exploratory behavior and human development. In H. W. Reese (Ed.), *Advances in child development and behavior* (Vol. 8, pp. 60–109). New York: Academic Press.

Overton, W. F., & Reese, H. W. (1973). Models of development: Methodological implications. In J. R. Nesselroade & H. W. Reese (Eds.), *Life-span developmental psychology: Methodological issues* (pp. 65–86). New York: Academic Press.

Patterson, G. R. (1984). Microsocial process: A view from the boundary. In J. C. Masters & K. Yarkin-Levin (Eds.), *Boundary areas in social and developmental psychology* (pp. 43–66). Orlando: Academic Press.

Reese, H. W., & Overton, W. F. (1970). Models of development and theories of development. In L. R. Goulet & P. B. Baltes (Eds.), *Life-span developmental psychology: Research and theory* (pp. 115–145). New York: Academic Press.

Werner, H. (1937). Process and achievement—A basic problem of education and developmental psychology. *Harvard Educational Review, 7*, 353–368.

Wohlwill, J. F. (1981). A conceptual analysis of exploratory behavior: The "specific–diversive" distinction revisited. In H. I. Day (Ed.), *Advances in intrinsic motivation and aesthetics* (pp. 341–364). New York: Plenum.

CHAPTER SEVEN

THE DEVELOPMENT OF
EXPLORATORY BEHAVIOR
IN THE FIRST FOUR
YEARS OF LIFE

HEIDI KELLER
University of Osnabrück

AXEL SCHÖLMERICH, DELIA MIRANDA, and GUDRUN GAUDA
Universität Osnabrück

EXPLORATORY BEHAVIOR DEVELOPMENT
IN THE FIRST FOUR YEARS

The importance of exploratory behavior for early childhood development is commonly stressed. Piaget (1952) understood the individual way and mode of exploration as a window to cognitive development. Fein and Apfel (1979) emphasize the relationship of exploratory behavior and virtual intelligence. Besides the general link between exploration and cognitive development (e.g., Fenson, Kagan, Kearsley, & Zelazo, 1976; Fenson & Ramey, 1980; McCall, 1974), exploratory behavior has been introduced as a diagnostic tool for general developmental delays as well as specific learning disabilities (e.g., Bruner, 1973; Millar, 1968; Piaget, 1951; 1952; Sutton-Smith, 1968; Voss & Keller, 1981).

Despite the conceptual importance of the problem and the research effort dedicated to it, Weisler and McCall (1976) feel that the basis of knowledge about that area of behavior is rather small. Belsky and Most (1981) aim in the same direction with their statement that exploration was used as an epiphenomenon for attention processes on the one hand and for the genesis of attachment on the other, and was no so much examined in its own right.

Exploration can be defined as a descriptive construct that includes molar behavior on different functional levels, e.g., locomotion, manipulation, visual perception, and verbal (question-asking) utterances. The outcome of exploratory behavior enables the individual to adapt to changing situations in the environment, to initiate changes in the environment in order to establish new concepts, and so to develop differentiated patterns of interaction and more efficient problem-solving strategies (Voss & Keller, 1983).

Depending on the theoretical orientation, exploration is described as drive (arousal theory, Berlyne, 1960, 1970), motive (e.g., Allport, 1955; Harlow, 1953), concept (e.g., concept of competence, Harter, 1978; Hunt, 1965; White, 1959), or behavioral system (in the ethological sense, e.g., Ainsworth, Blehar, Waters, & Wall, 1978; for summaries see Krieger, 1976; Voss, 1983; Voss & Keller, 1983). All the different theoretical positions agree that the exploratory system is operating at the time of birth as an inborn system. Because the assumptions of behavioral regulations on the basis of drive reduction were to a large extent not consistent enough to withstand empirical testing, discussion today centers mainly on two different theoretical positions concerning the development of the behavioral system: One is cognitive, the other ethological.

The Cognitive Position.   Different authors (e.g., Cohen, 1972; Hunt, 1965; Lewis, 1969; White, 1959) share the assumption that the regulation of behavior has to be conceived as intrinsic, i.e., based on processes that are integrated in the system of perception, information processing, storage, and attention. As an example we look at Kagan's (1978) hypothesis of discrepancy. This hypothesis assumes that schemata of objects and occurrences are formed during development on the basis of experience. The actual attention to a stimulus (which is synonymous with the exploratory reaction) is determined by the discrepancy of the stimulus to an existing schema. Stimuli that differ to a medium extent provoke longer attention periods than only minimally discrepant (i.e., well-known) stimuli, or maximally discrepant (i.e., those that have no resemblance to existing schemata). The hypothesis of discrepancy predicts a curvilinear relationship between the extent of discrepancy and attention. Despite extensive critiques (e.g., Haith & Campos, 1977; Pick, Frankel, & Hess, 1975), this approach is still the framework for numerous studies dealing with visual attention (fixation time) as the operationalization of exploratory behavior in the first year of life. The reactions to auditory stimuli are conceptualized on the same basis.

The Ethological Position.   This position incorporates the ATTACHMENT–EXPLORATION balance (see Ainsworth, 1967; Bowlby, 1969) as formulated in the theory of attachment. According to this position, the exploratory behavioral system can only be activated if the system of attachment is inactivated. In other words, if the child–mother relationship is secure (secure base), the child will explore the surroundings; according to this concept, exploration simply means being busy with something other than the mother or the relationship. If the child feels insecure, exploration stops, and the child aims to restore the physical relationship (proximity seeking). This concept is subject to two main restrictions:

1. The age range, or, better, the developmental level that is covered by the concept, is too narrow (generally between 6 months and 2 years) for a general model.
2. The definition of exploratory behavior is inadequate: Every behavioral outcome that is not in the service of attachment is in the service of exploration without specifying this process any further.

Both approaches are to be understood as research paradigms as we see later.

From empirical findings we understand that exploratory behavior develops on the basis of selective attention processes, first of all in the visual and auditory channels. The newborn is equipped with skills that allow exploratory contact with the environment and the processing of the information so acquired (Haith & Campos, 1977; Osofsky, 1979).

The majority of studies deal with general and specific characteristics of stimulus patterns determining selective attention, assuming a "steady increase in fixation on visual events between 3½ and 13½ months of age" (Zelazo & Kearsley, 1980), or postulating a curvilinear relationship (Sigman & Beckwith, 1980), because the fixation time increases first on the basis of an improved control of the state of the child (Stechler & Latz, 1966) but then decreases on the basis of repeated presentations of the same stimuli (e.g., Fantz, 1965; Wetherford & Cohen, 1973). The first part of this statement considers the total fixation time reflecting exploratory behavior and the second part reports reactions to habituation situations; thus, neither is comparable. With the general functional improvement, the isolated visual or auditory exploration loses significance; it is replaced by perceptual motor coordination, which is supposed to be functioning at about 6 months of age (Field, 1977). In our report, we concentrate on manipulation and neglect locomotion, which has been studied almost exclusively in the context of attachment (operationalized as the distance to the mother). The conceptual differences between exploration and play are discussed in more detail in Chapter 8). We limit ourselves to the exploratory behavior specified in the preceding definition: Exploratory behavior is an organized system of behaviors consisting of reactions to stimulus situations characterized by novelty, incongruence, and complexity. The confrontation, with a medium discrepancy to existing schemata, induces a cognitive–emotional situation in the individual (e.g., subjective uncertainty, Berlyne, 1962) accompanied by specific psychophysiological reactions. This specific situation is expressed in mimics, gestures, and body tension, and later verbal comments and questions. We can only speculate about the development of this behavioral system because the data base is too narrow. McCall (1979) assumes a "certain continuity" in the data from a study by Cox and Campbell (1968) that observed 14-month-old children over a period of 3 weeks and resulted in correlations sufficiently large to suggest stability over this period. The reported measurements are mainly quantitative (duration of behavior). Weisler and McCall (1976) ask for a more detailed inspection of qualitative parameters, a call that can still be emphasized 10 years later. It has to be noted that the explicit study of exploratory behavior has decreased during the last years. Moreover, it appears that the mode and intensity of tactile behaviors constituting exploration is widely ignored along with some molar distinctions like touching and manipulating (Hutt, 1967) or active and passive touching (e.g., Gibson, 1962).

Generally there is little information in the literature concerning the development of exploration and exploratory behaviors:

1. We have contradictory information about the course of development of visual exploratory behavior during the first year of life (linear or curvilinear).

2. There is almost no information on the development of exploratory behavior concerning auditory stimuli.

3. We have very little information on the course of development of manipulatory exploration after the first year of life.

4. We know nothing about the relationship between these different functional areas of exploration.

5. There are no data available on the basis of which to decide whether exploration is a unitary concept (Langevin, 1971)—that is a trait—or an organized pattern of functionally independent behavioral systems as suggested by a study by Kreitler, Zigler, and Kreitler (1974) using a cross-sectional sample of school children.

We do not attempt to answer all these questions in a single study. But we do try to show the structural relationships in a small sample with a longitudinal design.

At this point we do not subscribe to either of the theoretical positions outlined previously; we see our own theoretical perspective in the combination of both paradigms; the ethological approach tells us when there is exploratory behavior, and the cognitive approach tells us how exploratory behavior is used for the integration of information. In this respect we deal with general behavioral development and not with interindividual differences which will be analyzed in a future step of our research program.

METHOD AND RESULTS

All reported data are from a longitudinal study covering the first 6 years of life. All parents who volunteered to participate were contacted during the last trimester of pregnancy. If no complications were reported during pregnancy and birth, the subjects were included in the study. Of the total of 20 final participants, 10 babies were male and 10 female. The time schedule of the study is shown in Table 7.1.

During time 0 the parents were informed about the general guidelines of the project, and several questionaires were administered. At all other times different tasks for exploratory behavior were administered and recorded on video, as were free-play situations with mother and father; other parameters that had developmental significance at the specific times (e.g., physiological and mental status of the child, gender identity, measures of self-concept, and parental attitudes) were also recorded but are not reported here.

The data reported here cover exploratory tasks between 14 days and 4 years of age. For more details about the other parameters, see Keller (1982). Because it is not efficient to interrelate all parameters analyzed over the age levels, we extract only a few for each exploration task that represent maximal interindividual variability and that is comparable over time. The exploration was tested with exploratory tasks that were constructed according to the developmental status of the age groups.

TABLE 7.1
Observation Times and Places of the Longitudinal Study

Number T^a	Age	Home/Laboratory
0	3rd trimester of pregnancy	Home
1	14 days	Home
2	6 weeks	Home
3	10 weeks	Home
4	14 weeks	Home
5	18 weeks	Home
6	22 weeks	Home
7	8½ months	Home
8	11½ months	Home
9	2 years	Laboratory
10	3 years	Home
11	4 years	Home
12	5 years	Laboratory
13	6 years	Home

^{a}Time.

Visual Exploration

Six black and white stimuli varying in novelty and complexity, similar to those of Kagan (1970), were presented in an 18×18 cm display of a 100×77 cm large gray screen. The child was seated in a reclining chair such that the distance between the child's eye and the display was 20 to 30 cm. The stimuli were presented in a fixed trial, fixed-interval design with 10 seconds presenting time and 10 seconds intertrial interval. Each stimulus was presented four times in the same random order for each child. The whole sequence was recorded on a split-screen videorecorder. The experimenter observed the child's corneal reflection of the stimulus through a hole above the display and dictated the fixation times on a cassette recorder. This procedure made it possible to check the fixation time observed from the videotapes. The whole exploration task was repeated at every home visit from T1 to T8. Because an isolated testing of looking behavior is impossible when seeing and grasping are coordinated, the analysis of this behavioral mode only covers the first half year of life. The following parameters, that represent all possible looking responses were selected for further analysis:

(TFT) Total fixation time = Sum of all fixations in all four runs (maximally 40 seconds) per stimulus.
(DFF) Duration of first fixation = Sum of all first fixations in four runs per stimulus.

(DOF) Duration of all other fixations = Sum of all fixations minus first fixation per stimulus.

(DLF) Duration of longest fixation, no matter when it occurred.

(NF)   Number of fixations in all four runs per stimulus.

All reported measures[1] are based on an interrater reliability of over 90%. The analysis of these data shows that it is meaningless to record visual fixation times in the second half of the first year as an isolated variable because the functional pleasure in the use of motor and locomotor schemata cannot and should not be suppressed. For that reason we do not use the data of the last two sessions (T7 and T8). The variable DFF showed the most differentiated distribution over the age of the children (Keller, 1982). DFF increases to reach a maximum between the ages of 14 and 18 weeks and decreases then, thus indicating a curvilinear relationship. The greatest differences among the various stimulus patterns is at 18 weeks of age also as could have been expected from the literature (e.g., Kagan, 1978), i.e., highest fixation to the human face (distortion), and lowest fixation to the simple black and white pattern. According to these results, the DFF at 18 weeks (total score over all stimuli) is used as the parameter indicating visual fixation for further analysis (see Fig. 7.1a and 7.1b).

Auditory Exploration

According to existing studies (e.g., Papoušek, 1978; Simner, 1971) and with regard to the dimension of complexity, the following four stimuli were selected: *sinewave with 400 hz, weeping of a 5-year-old boy, singing of a 5-year-old boy,* and *instrumental music.* The stimuli were presented with a cassette recorder in a fixed trial, fixed-interval order of 5 seconds each with four repetitions in the same random order for each child. The whole sequence was videotaped; additionally a stimulus-free baseline and postline were recorded to separate stimulus-specific reactions from random ones. All coded behaviors were related to the child's individual baseline. This procedure was administered from T1 to T8. The analysis of reactions to auditory stimuli after the first year of life—when children have developed full locomotor capabilities—is not useful, because it is impossible to prevent distractions while the stimuli are being presented. On the basis of control experiments with 2½-months-old children, the following variables were reliably observed: laughing; smiling; mock surprise expression; crying; fussing; moving arms; kicking with legs; positive-, neutral-, negative vocalizations; facial distractions; motility stop; and startle.[2]

---

[1]Besides fixation measures, different mimical, gestural, and affective behaviors were coded but cannot be reported here. For further information, see Keller, 1982.

[2]*Startle* is defined as a sudden total body movement.

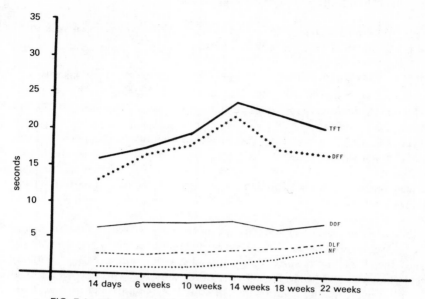

FIG. 7.1a The different fixation variables over the first 6 months of age.

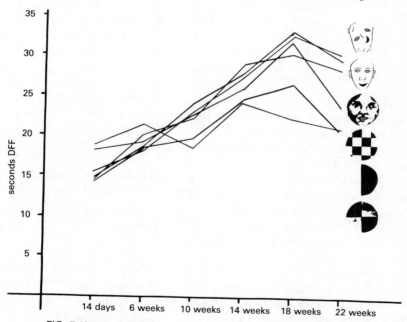

FIG. 7.1b Duration of the first fixation (DFF) toward the stimulus patterns over the first 6 months of age.

133

From these specific behaviors we combined the following percentages from the total presentation time for each stimulus and each T:

Type I: *Reaction of unpleasure*: Percentage of negative vocalizations, fussing, crying, and expression of distraction at the time the stimulus was presented.

Type II: *Assimilation reaction*: Percentage of smiling; laughing; neutral and positive vocalizations.

Type III: *Attention reaction*: Percentage of motility stop, mock surprise expression and startle.

The reactions were combined in this way so that the results could be compared to those in reported studies.

Results.   The analysis of stimulus-specific responses over the first five examinations revealed no differentiation. The maximum differentiation is at 8½ months of age. The attention reaction is the most intense type of reaction, increasing up to that point and decreasing thereafter. Assimilation reactions and reactions of displeasure approach the level of the stimulus-free baseline and then decrease below baseline level.

Because startles and mock surprise expression rarely occur attention is mostly defined by motility stop. For further analysis, the parameter of auditive exploration is thus attention (motility stop) at T7 (see Fig. 7.2a and 7.2b).

Manipulatory Exploration

The examination of manipulatory exploration requires multidimensional and multifunctional objects that are attractive enough visually to cause the children to explore the toy without specific instructions. We used unstructured situations (see also Belsky & Most, 1981) to have the child define the situations in order to sustain an optimal level of attention.

On the basis of pretests we decided to start the evaluation of manipulatory exploration at 8½ months of age. McCall (1979) did not find differences in the quality of exploration between 8½ and 11½ months, so the manipulatory potential of this age range should be covered. Manipulatory exploration was then assessed under comparable but not identical conditions each year.

General Procedure.   The children were confronted with the object to explore and their behavior was videotaped during the first 5 minutes of confrontation if not otherwise announced; if a child did not explore the toy for a full 5 minutes, the trial ended earlier. The child's mother and/or father and one or two camera assistants were present during the session.

On the basis of the videotapes of control children, behavioral categories for each object were defined covering the following areas:

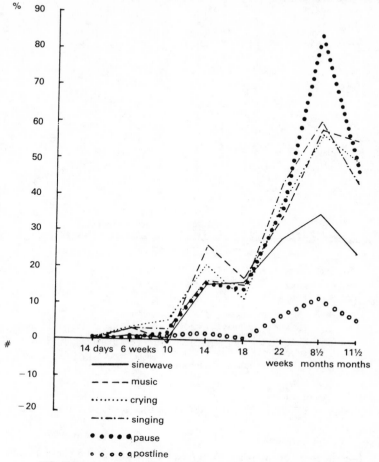

FIG. 7.2a Attention reactions to different auditory stimuli over the first year of life.

1. Mode of exploration

- *visual exploration*: the child tries to get information by looking at the object intensively; tactile or manipulatory actions are subordinated to the visual process.

- *tactile exploration*: the child gets information about the object's surface, texture, or form by touching it; the activity can be accompanied by visual contact with the object.

- *manipulative exploration*: the child gets information about the functional possibilities of the object by handling it; this process can be accompanied by visual contact with the object.

- *verbal exploration*: the child asks questions about the object.

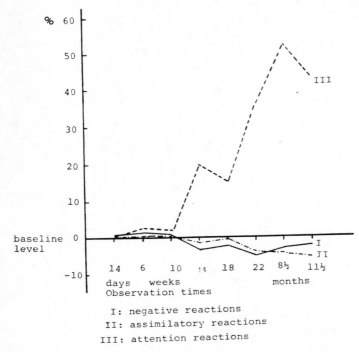

FIG. 7.2b Reaction patterns to auditory stimuli over the first year of life.

2. Variability of exploration
    - number and kind of differing actions in the tactile and manipulative mode.
3. Intensity of exploration
    - three degrees of intensity were rated according to the pressure and vigor the child employed in tactile and manipulative actions; 1 = low intensity; 2 = medium intensity; 3 = high intensity; an intensity score was calculated by summing intensities of all individually rated actions.
4. Range of exploration
    - number of different objects or parts of objects explored in the different modes.
5. Tempo of exploration
    - mean duration of a single action in the different modes.
6. Affective exploration[3]
    - smiling, laughing, vocalizing, singing, and tension rebuff (= reduction of motor tension by hitting the object, kicking with legs, rhythmic body movements, etc. during the exploration period).

---

[3]The term *affective exploration* is used here descriptively and not in the sense of Wohlwill, 1981.

For each exploratory situation the six areas (plus a protocol of special events) were operationalized into behavioral categories that were coded polygraphically from the videotapes on a real time basis by pressing buttons connected to a computer whenever the behavior was visible. Combinations of the categories could then be defined (e.g., child vocalizes while manipulating) to describe more molar behavioral units. The frequency, mean duration, total duration, and percentage of total exploration time were printed out.

For the different exploratory situations different numbers of categories were used to account for different degrees of complexity and to adapt to the changing variety of the child's behavior.[4]

In the result section following, the terms *parameters* or *variables* are used to refer to the categories or logical combination of categories. The time a certain category was coded is expressed as the percentage of the total time of a sequence (e.g., 5 minutes) so that the codes could be compared. For each session, correlations are computed among the occurring variables; the coefficients are reported in the result section following.

First-Year Task

We used a toy that was recently introduced on the German market and thus unfamiliar to the children. The Fisher Price Activity Center (AC) offered contingent feedback on the visual and/or auditory channel to the infants' manipulation.

FIG. 7.3 Activity Center (AC).

---

[4]The system of categories cannot be presented here in full detail; catalogues are available from the authors.

Results.   A total of 49 parameters were coded and analyzed in a correlational analysis across all children. It can be demonstrated that different kinds of tactile contact are performed with different intensities; in the following paragraph we report the significant correlations. The frequency of actions with medium intensities correlates with the action repetition score ($r = .67$), whereas the frequency of actions with high intensity correlates with variability (different actions) and range (different possibilities, objects) ($r = .619$ and $.656$, respectively); the amount of positive vocalizations is related to the variability score ($r = .373$). The most interesting result is the high negative relationship between tactile and visual exploration ($r = -.639$). High scores on visual exploration are related to high speed in tactile exploration concerning the single action ($r = .762$), as well as the single object ($r = .664$) with an overall low variability; the reverse is true for high scores of tactile exploration where many different actions ($r = .723$) are performed with low speed ($r = -.359$ to $-.367$). These results suggest that children use either the visual or the tactile channel of exploration, each reflecting, moreover, a specific style of duration, variability, and intensity.

For further analysis, the amount of tactile and visual exploratory behavior thus represents the exploratory behavior of the first year of life.

Second-Year Task

The second-year examination was recorded in the laboratory.

Task.   A two-toy, free-play situation, with one toy being familiar and one novel, was introduced after ½ hour of interaction with the parents.

Material.   A toy cash register served as familiar toy; a box constructed according to Hutt (1966) with modifications was the novel toy. The modified box was made of wood and covered with colored washable plastic material.

A gearshift with a red handle was on top of the box. By pushing the handle in different directions, the subject could switch buzzing or bell ringing on or off; colored lights also blinked. There was a large toy watch mounted on one side of the box. If the subject pressed a button on the side of the box, small pearls fell into a container below. On the front side was another small wooden box containing a plastic bear. (HB)

Procedure.   The two objects were located at fixed places on the floor of the playroom; from the time the child entered the room, the first 10 minutes were videotaped.

Results.   Reactions to the cash register are not reported here. From a total of 230 categories concerning the Hutt box, 7 parameters were defined. Due to the presentation of two different objects, the time a child spent exploring the

FIG. 7.4 Hutt-box (HB).

box varied considerably, from 9.2 to 262 seconds. One child did not explore the box at all.

Visual exploration correlated positively with verbal exploration, but this is based on a few cases of verbal exploration only ($r = .81$), and negatively with smile ($r = -.442$). The relationship between manipulative exploration and smile was medium positive ($r = .442$). Low intensity of manipulatory behavior and verbal behavior were positively related ($r = .446$). In other words, children who explored more visually also asked more questions and smiled less. Children who had high scores on manipulative exploration also used high intensities of manipulation and touched more often and smiled more, whereas children with high scores on tactile exploration touched objects frequently with low intensities. Range of exploration was not related to the different modes. The relationship between visual and manipulative exploration was close to zero ($r = -.177$); a slight but positive relationship was found between visual and tactile exploration ($r = .315$). Here different styles of exploration seem to emerge in parallel: The first style might be called the *distal* mode consisting of visual and verbal exploration; if children who perform this style do perform tactile or—even less—

manipulatory exploration, then they perform low intensity behaviors. The second style can be tentatively called *motor* exploration; children who exhibit this style of behavior manipulate with high intensities instead of tactile or visual information intake, and they smile while manipulating, thus possibly showing more *Funktionslust*. From case descriptions we can say that the distal explorers show more tense, stony faces whereas the children exhibiting intensive manipulations express a richer mimical variability. Both types appear to be independent.

For further analysis we use the percentages of visual, tactile, and manipulatory behavior; because verbal exploration is based on a few cases only, we did not analyze it further.

Third-Year Task

Material.   The exploration object was a modified Banta-box (Banta, 1970); the modifications were added to offer a broader range of possibilities, e.g., the touching quality. (BB)

Procedure.   The object was presented either in the living room or in the children's room due to the family's choice. Mother and/or father were present, but not younger siblings. The child could "play" as long as he or she wanted; the whole sequence was videotaped.

Analysis.   Based on the past examination and a control group of 3-year-old children, 48 categories were defined and coded in the way just described. These categories were combined into 18 parameters characterizing each child. Because the examination took place at home, the situations in the different families were held to be comparable, but not identical; some parents gave comments on the child's activities, which might have affected the child's behavior.

Results.   Eighteen parameters were defined; the correlations between the different modes of exploration (visual, tactile, manipulative, and verbal) were close to zero (between $-.2$ and $.205$). A negative relationship was found between visual exploration and moving the object ($r = -.435$). There was a slight tendency indicating that high rates of visual exploration are related to a small range of tactile and/or manipulatory actions ($r = -.273$); high rates of manipulatory exploration on the other side correlated with a wide range. Affective exploration in the sense described earlier did not seem to play a role at that age level; in other words, children who spent more time looking at the object and touching it did so in long durations ($r = .685$ and $.678$) and also asked more questions about it; children who manipulated less than others tended to move around more in order to get information about the object.

FIG. 7.5 Banta-box (BB).

For further analysis we use the amount of exploration in the different modes (visual, tactile, manipulative, and verbal).

Fourth-Year Task

Material.   For that age we constructed a box with different possibilities of exploration; the box consisted of wood and was covered with washable, colored plastic material; at one side pictures varying in complexity (number of elements) could be moved into a looking frame by pulling a string at the other side. A small box was attached with a smaller container filled with candies; another box containing a kaleidoscope, was fixed at the front side. On the top of the box, a toy music instrument was attached. (4 YB)

Procedure.   The procedure was the same as in the third-year task.

Analysis.   A total of 49 categories was defined and coded according to the procedure described previously. The coded categories were combined into 20 parameters describing each child. Correlations were computed.

FIG. 7.6 Four-year box (4YB).

Results. Visual exploration showed a positive relationship to tactile exploration ($r = .58$) and to verbal exploration ($r = .489$), a negative relationship to laughing ($r = -.41$), and no relationship to manipulatory exploration ($r = -.025$). Verbal exploration showed a positive relationship to tactile exploration ($r = .624$) and manipulative exploration ($r = .41$) as well as to moving subject ($r = .425$, i.e., walking around the object in order to explore it). In other words, children who tend to spend more time with visual exploration also ask more questions and have more tactile contact with the object, but laugh less. This is consistent with the findings for the second-year task and represents the "distal type" of exploration. Unrelated is the "motor type" of subject, who preferred manipulating, but who at that age also asks questions. The behaviors in the different modes were performed frequently and in long durations (correlations between $r = .53$ and $.748$). Range of exploration was not correlated with the other parameters. An interesting pattern was the parents' behavior. Comments from the parents that helped their child to continue the exploration came more often when the child was moving around the object and laughing. Interesting was the similarity between laughing and more disruptive events, which may mean that laughing —unlike smiling—is an indicator of or a reaction to stress and embarassment. For further analysis we use the amount of exploration in the different modes (visual, tactile, manipulative, and verbal).

Summary

We can summarize the results so far as follows:

1. Visual exploration as expressed in fixation times towards two-dimensional stimuli followed a curvilinear course with a maximum between 14 and 18 weeks.

2. Reactions to auditory stimuli, mostly consisting of attention reactions, while present from the beginning, reached maximum differentiation at 8½ months.

3. Exploratory behavior towards a novel object in the first year was characterized by two mutually exclusive reaction types: (a) Some children exhibited tactile behaviors exclusively (manipulations in the strict sense did not occur with the type of stimulus presented) with many different low speed actions of high intensity; (b) Some children engaged predominantly in visual behavior; they repeated their tactile actions many times at low intensity.

4. Exploratory behavior in the second year was characterized by the differentiation between tactile and manipulative behaviors; visual and tactile behaviors were interrelated, visual and manipulative behaviors were not. Manipulations were performed with high intensity; children who explored a great deal visually also asked more questions, but smiled less.

5. The different modes of exploration were not interrelated in the third year; the other parameters did not relate to the different modes and characterized them as in the years before.

6. The exploratory behavior at 4 years of age also showed two different qualities: One was manipulation that had no relations to the other modes except question asking; the second type was a combination of visual, verbal, and tactile behaviors; the other parameters had lost their significance.

THE DEVELOPMENT OF EXPLORATION

In this last section we discuss the relationship between different parameters reflecting exploratory behavior over the first 4 years. It has to be mentioned here that, on the basis of our data, no really high correlations can be expected because conditions and material are not consistent over the years. Nevertheless, some relationships appear to show a meaningful trend over time. For this reason and because of the high number of correlations, we did not test them against chance.

Fixation time towards black and white patterns of varying novelty and complexity in the first year of life reveals positive relationships with visual exploration at 2 years ($r = .477$) and 3 years ($r = .376$); it is negatively correlated with attention to auditory stimuli in the first year ($r = -.433$) and manipulatory exploration at 2 years ($r = -.509$); all other relationships are close to zero.

Attentive reactions to auditory stimuli during the first year are related negatively to visual behaviors towards two- and three-dimensional stimuli in the first year ($r = -.433$ and $-.497$); they correlate positively with manipulatory reactions at 2 years. The few remarkable correlations indicate that this mode of behavior is less interwoven in the net of exploratory responses (see Table 7.2).

Regarding the different modes of behavior, there are no clear-cut simple relationships over the first 4 years. Most of the correlation coefficients are close to zero; but the intramodal relationships have to be taken into consideration.

The meaningful correlations ($r > .4$) between the different modes of exploration and the task are exemplified in Fig. 7.7.

The trends could be summarized as follows: Children start with an exclusive reliance on a particular sensory channel in order to gather information in the first year of life (high negative correlations between visual and auditory and visual and tactile behaviors). The next developmental pattern that can be observed at 2 and 3 years of age seems to consist in the parallel usage of different information channels (zero or close to zero correlations between the modes); at 4 years, however, an integrated pattern has evolved, representing two types of exploration: a more distal one (with visual, verbal, and tactile behaviors of low intensity) and a more motor one based on more vigorous interactions with the material; question-asking behavior seems to be a more universal characteristic at that age. The differentiation into these types also becomes evident in the cross-age correlations. Thus, a trend that was initially discernible at 2 years becomes evident at age 4. It is thus apparent that manipulations seem to develop in contrast to all other exploratory behaviors (predominantly, negative correlations to the other modes), whereas visual and tactile exploration seems to develop into one type. In order to test for peson specifity of these types, we compared the mean scores of children ranging high versus low in manipulatory exploration at 4 years.

Children differing in the degree of manipulatory exploration at 4 years differ in their amount of visual exploration in all possible measures; i.e., children with low manipulation scores have higher visual exploration scores than children with high manipulation scores (except for visual exploration of the AC). They differ in the amount of tactile exploration with the exception of the first year: Children with low manipulation scores have lower tactile scores than children with high manipulation scores. They also differ in the amount of manipulatory exploration: Children with high manipulation scores in the fourth year have high manipulation scores at 3 years as well, whereas children with low manipulation scores at 4 years have low ones with 3 years, too. The 2-year scores are very similar in that respect (see Table 7.3). This comparison indicates that the different modes of exploration seem to develop in different children, each child developing his or her own characteristic mode of exploration.

TABLE 7.2
Correlations Between Different Measures of Exploration over the Years

		DFF	Attention to audit. stimuli	AC visual	AC tactile	HB visual	HB tactile	HB manip.	BB visual	BB tactile	BB manip.	BB verbal	4YB visual	4YB tactile	4YB manip.	4YB verbal
1st year	DFF	1	-.43	.09	.25	.48	.12	-.51	.38	-.29	.16	.33	-.11	.24	.09	.25
1st year	Attention to audit. stimuli		1	-.50	.06	-.28	.14	.42	-.00	.15	.30	-.32	.31	-.13	-.22	-.06
1st year	AC visual			1	-.64	.15	-.04	.02	-.33	-.16	.18	.34	-.10	-.05	.02	.05
1st year	AC tactile				1	-.26	.14	.02	.29	.20	-.04	-.14	.09	.13	.07	.01
2nd year	HB visual					1	.31	-.18	.14	-.23	.17	.18	-.26	.09	.07	.07
2nd year	HB tactile						1	.15	-.22	.22	.35	.21	.42	.37	.38	.60
2nd year	HB manip.							1	-.32	-.14	-.23	-.41	.06	-.51	.08	-.10
3rd year	BB visual								1	.05	.20	-.2	-.12	-.05	-.23	-.36
3rd year	BB tactile									1	.20	.13	.22	.36	.12	.12
3rd year	BB manip.										1	.20	.00	.21	.47	.27
3rd year	BB verbal											1	-.07	.18	.20	.22
4th year	4 YB visual												1	.58	-.02	.49
4th year	4 YB tactile													1	.32	.62
4th year	4 YB manip.														1	.41
4th year	4 YB verbal															1

Note: DFF = Duration of first fixation. AC = Activity center. HB = Hutt box. BB = Banta box. 4 YB = 4 year box.

145

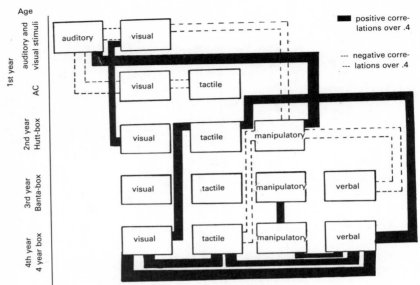

FIG. 7.7 The relationships between the different modes of exploration over the 4 years.

Conclusions

As we have shown, exploratory behavior seems to be a complex pattern of interrelated behaviors in different functional modes that occur exclusively in the first year, parallel in the next 2 years, and intramodally in the fourth year. From the beginning a differentiation into the visual mode—first occurring singularly and becoming more and more integrated with verbal and tactile behaviors—and manipulation can be noticed. The preference for one or the other mode develops as a person-specific characteristic. With the preference, specific behavioral qualities are expressed in the first 2 years, later disappearing. If children prefer the distal mode (visual/tactile/verbal), their manipulatory and tactile actions are stereotypical, of low intensity, and of short duration; they explore fewer objects than the manipulators, who on the other hand exhibit great variability, high intensity, and longer duration. As the most consistently affective expression in our sample, smiling is part of the manipulatory type in the first 2 years, then being replaced by laughing, which could indicate a developmental change as well because smiling has been interpreted as an indicator of mastered assimilatory and laughing processes and because laughing seems to be more closely related to tension. These expressions are related to parental comments.

In this respect, our study seems to be an example for the study of continuity/discontinuity following the paradigm of correlational analysis over different times (see Wohlwill, 1980). We did not address that question initially. As we have outlined elsewhere in more detail (Keller, 1983), the problem of continuity/

TABLE 7.3
Differences in Mean Values Between Children with High and Low Manipulation Scores at 4 Years of Age (t-Test)

		High manipulators		Low manipulators		
		X̄	STD	X̄	STD	t
1st year	DFF	142.68	49.14	145.94	45.58	.13
	AC visual	26.74	11.66	23.61	14.7	.46
	AC tactile	78.22	11.37	79.57	13.11	.21
2nd year	HB visual	11.34	12.37	14.36	20.34	.35
	HB tactile	35.71	30.05	22.18	21.15	-.99
	HB manip.	20.87	19.54	20.32	14.19	.04
3rd year	BB visual	31.04	9.63	40.09	9.56	1.82[+]
	BB tactile	8.21	5.96	5.43	5.18	-.96
	BB manip.	12.30	8.37	7.07	7.37	1.27

[+]significant at the 5% level.

Note: DFF = Duration of first fixation. AC = Activity center. HB = Hutt box. BB = Banta box.

discontinuity cannot be treated adequately by operationalizing behavioral concepts in different ways at different times and then correlating them. To do so, we should analyze and regard them individually in the context of meaningful, i.e., theoretically based interpatternings of developmental units. Exploratory behavior, thus, should be analyzed in relation to the developmental tasks of the specific age levels. Expanding the attachment theory to include a broader view of exploration could establish such a framework for research. In our study we assessed data on parent–infant interaction over the years so that we can address these relationships in further analyses.

We can venture preliminary answers to the introductory questions, concluding carefully that exploratory behavior is a behavioral system developing either toward integration of more distal behaviors or towards a rougher motor interaction with the material. The analysis of the exploratory behavior exhibited by children of the next age bracket (5 and 6 years) will show whether this developmental pattern continues or changes.

As the data on the fourth-year task indicate, changes have to be expected in the verbal mode because question asking is used by both types of children, but more by the distal explorers. In further analyses we will study the exploratory strategies used with the different objects over the years and the process characteristics of the exploratory action before turning to the interindividual differences and their conceptual significance.

SUMMARY

The development of exploratory behavior in children ranging in age from 2 weeks to 4 years is studied. Visual, auditory, and manipulatory exploration tasks were given. Visual exploration involving two-dimensional stimuli followed a curvilinear course, reaching a maximum between 14 and 18 weeks, whereas reactions to auditory stimuli peaked at 8½ months. In the first year of life of the subjects, exploratory behavior involving a novel object was characterized either by tactile or predominantly visual behavior. In the second year of life it was characterized by the differentiation between tactile and manipulative behaviors. The development of exploratory behavior through the first 4 years of life thus began with the children's exclusive reliance on a particular sensory channel. Among 2- and 3-year-olds there seemed to be a parallel use of different information channels, and at 4 years an integrated pattern of exploratory behavior had evolved.

ACKNOWLEDGMENTS

The study was supported by a grant from the German Research Council (DFG). We are grateful to Beate Benterbusch, Katharina Hanel, and Sigrid Rosskopf for their help in analyzing the data.

REFERENCES

Ainsworth, M. D. S. (1967). *Infancy in Uganda: Infant care and the growth of love*. Baltimore: The John Hopkins University Press.

Ainsworth, M. D. S., Blehar, M. C., Waters, E., & Wall, S. (1978). *Patterns of attachment: A psychological study of the strange situation*. Hillsdale, NJ: Lawrence Erlbaum Associates.

Allport, G. W. (1955). *Becoming: Basic considerations for a psychology of personality*. New Haven: Yale University Press.

Banta, T. J. (1970). Tests for the evaluation of early childhood education. The Cincinnati Autonomy Test Pattern. In J. Hellmuth (Ed.), *Cognitive studies* (Vol. 1, pp. 424–490). New York: Bruner & Mazel.

Belsky, J., & Most, R. (1981). From exploration to play: A cross-sectional study of infant free play behavior. *Developmental Psychology, 17*, 630–639.

Berlyne, D. E. (1960). *Conflict, arousal, and curiosity*. New York: McGraw-Hill.

Berlyne, D. E. (1962). Uncertainty and epistemic curiosity. *British Journal of Psychology, 53*, 27–34.

Berlyne, D. E. (1967). Arousal and reinforcement. In D. Levine (Ed.), *Nebraska Symposium on Motivation* (pp. 1–110). Lincoln: University of Nebraska Press.

Berlyne, D. E. (1970). Children's reasoning and thinking. In P. H. Mussen (Ed.), *Carmichael's manual of child psychology* (Vol. 1, pp. 939–975). New York: Wiley.

Bowlby, J. (1969). *Attachment and loss: Vol. 1. Attachment*. New York: Basic Books.

Bruner, J. S. (1973). *The relevance of education*. New York: Norton.

Cohen, L. B. (1972). Attention-getting and attention-holding processes of infant visual preferences. *Child Development, 43*, 869–879.

Cox, F. N., & Campbell, D. (1968). Young children in a new situation with and without their mothers. *Child Development, 39*, 123–131.

Fantz, R. L. (1965). Visual perception from birth as shown by pattern selectivity. *Annals of the New York Academy of Science, 118*, 793–814.

Fein, G. G., & Apfel, N. H. (1979). The development of play: Style, structure and situations. *Genetic Psychology Monographs, 99*, 231–250.

Fenson, L., Kagan, J., Kearsley, R. B., & Zelazo, P. R. (1976). The developmental progression of manipulative play in the first two years. *Child Development, 47*, 232–236.

Fenson, L., & Ramsay, D. S. (1980). Decentration and integration of the child's play in the second year. *Child Development, 51*, 171–178.

Field, J. (1977). Coordination of vision and prehension in young infants. *Child Development, 48*, 97–103.

Gibson, J. J. (1962). Observations on active touch. *Psychological Review, 69*, 477–490.

Haith, M., & Campos, J. J. (1977). Human infancy. *Annual Review of Psychology, 28*, 251–293.

Harlow, H. F. (1953). Motivation as a factor in new responses. In J. S. Brown, H. S. Harlow, L. G. Postman, U. Nowlis, Th. M. Newcomb, & O. H. Mowrer (Eds.), *Current theory and research in motivation* (pp. 24–49). Lincoln: University of Nebraska Press.

Harter, S. (1978). Effectance motivation reconsidered: Toward a developmental model. *Human Development, 21*, 34–64.

Hunt, J. McV. (1965). Intrinsic motivation and its role in psychological development. In D. Levine (Ed.), *Nebraska Symposium on Motivation* (pp. 189–282). Lincoln: University of Nebraska Press.

Hutt, C. (1966). Exploration and play in children. *Symposia of the Zoological Society*, London, *18*, 61–81.

Hutt, C. (1967). Effects of stimulus novelty on manipulatory exploration in an infant. *Journal of Child Psychology and Psychiatry, 8*, 241–247.

Kagan, J. (1970). The determinants of attention in the infant. *American Scientist, 58*, 289–306.

Kagan, J. (1978). *Infancy: Its place in human development*. Cambridge, MA: Harvard University Press.

Keller, H. (1982). *Die Entwicklung des Explorationsverhaltens in den ersten 3 Lebensjahren*. Zwischenbericht für die Deutsche Forschungsgemeinschaft.

Keller, H. (1983). Die Einschätzung der Früherfahrung für den weiteren Entwicklungsverlauf. In G. Lüer (Ed.), *Bericht über den 33. Kongreß der Deutschen Gesellschaft für Psychologie in Mainz, 1982* (Vol. 2, pp. 556–563).

Kreitler, S., Zigler, E., & Kreitler, H. (1974). The complexity of complexity. *Human Development, 17*, 54–73.

Krieger, R. (1976). *Determinanten der Wißbegier. Untersuchungen zur Theorie der intrinsischen Motivation*. Bern: Huber.

Langevin, R. (1971). Is curiosity a unitary construct? *Canadian Journal of Psychology, 25*, 361–374.

Lewis, M. (1969). Infant's responses to facial stimuli during the first year of life. *Developmental Psychology, 1*, 75–86.

McCall, R. B. (1979). Individual differences in the pattern of habituation at 5 and 10 months of age. *Developmental Psychology, 15*, 559–569.

Millar, S. (1968). *The psychology of play*. London: Penguin Books.

Osofsky, I. D. (Ed.). (1979). *Handbook of infant development*. New York: Wiley.

Papoušek, H. (1978, January). *Lernfähigkeit im Säuglingsalter*. Lecture delivered at the University of Kaiserslautern, FRG.

Piaget, J. (1951). *Play, dreams and imitation in childhood*. London: Heinemann.

Piaget, J. (1952). *The origins of intelligence in children*. New York: Rutledge & Kegan Paul.

Pick, A. D., Frankel, D. G., & Hess, V. L. (1975). Children's attention. The development of selectivity. In E. M. Hetherington (Ed.), *Review of child development research* (Vol. 5, pp. 325–385). Chicago: The University of Chicago Press.

Sigman, M., & Beckwith, L. (1980). Infant visual attentiveness in relation to caregiver–infant interaction and developmental outcome. *Infant Behavior and Development, 3*, 141–154.

Simner, M. L. (1971). Newborn's response to the cry of another infant. *Developmental Psychology, 5*, 136–150.

Stechler, G., & Latz, E. (1966). Some observations on attention and arousal in the human infant. *Journal of the American Academy of Child Psychiatry, 5*, 517–525.

Sutton-Smith, B. (1968). Novel responses to toys. *Merrill–Palmer Quarterly, 14*, 151–158.

Voss, H.-G. (1983). Überraschung and Interesse. In H. A. Euler & H. Mandl (Eds.), *Emotionspsychologie: Ein Handbuch in Schlüsselbegriffen* (pp. 177–183). München: Urban & Schwarzenberg.

Voss, H.-G., & Keller, H. (Eds.). (1981). *Neugierforschung: Grundlagen, Theorien, Anwendungen*. Weinheim: Beltz.

Voss, H.-G., & Keller, H. (1983). *Curiosity and exploration: Theories and results*. New York: Academic Press.

Weisler, A., & McCall, R. B. (1976). Exploration and play. Résumé and redirection. *American Psychologist, 31*, 492–508.

Wetherford, M. J., & Cohen, L. B. (1973). Developmental changes in infant visual preferences for novelty and familiarity. *Child Development, 44*, 416–424.

White, R. W. (1959). Motivation reconsidered: The concept of competence. *Psychological Review, 66*, 297–333.

Wohlwill, J. F. (1980). Cognitive development in childhood. In O. G. Brim & J. Kagan (Eds.), *Constancy and change in human development* (pp. 359–445). Cambridge, MA: Harvard University Press.

Wohlwill, J. F. (1981). A conceptual analysis of exploratory behavior: The "specific–diversive" distinction revisited. In H. I. Day (Ed.), *Advances in intrinsic motivation and aesthetics* (pp. 341–364). New York: Plenum.

Zelazo, P. R., & Kearsley, R. B. (1980). The emergence of functional play in infants: Evidence for a major cognitive transition. *Journal of Applied Developmental Psychology, 1*, 95–117.

CHAPTER EIGHT

AN EMPIRICAL STUDY OF EXPLORATION–PLAY SEQUENCES IN EARLY CHILDHOOD

HANS-GEORG VOSS
Technische Hochschule Darmstadt

DIFFERENCES BETWEEN EXPLORATION AND PLAY
IN TERMS OF ACTION THEORY

This chapter is aimed at providing a modest approach to an empirical study of exploration–play in ongoing behavior. In Chapter 3 of this volume, I gave a rough outline of a theory of exploration–play in terms of action theory. The term *action*, rather than behavior, refers to an active, goal-oriented, and purposive way in which the activity of an organism is organized in time and space. The concept of action includes several hypothetical constructs such as orientation, incentive, intention, the formation of a goal or task, the choice between alternative plans for reaching the goal, the expectancy with respect to the behavioral outcome, and the reevaluation of the situation after an action has been performed. Whether an action will be realized or not is a function of both the availability of a behavioral program or "plan" (Miller, Galanter, & Pribram, 1960) and the expectancy that the specific goal will be reached. Cognitive theories of behavior stress the view that there is a basic striving of the organism "to attain, preserve, and widen external and internal orientation on a cognitive level" (Kreitler & Kreitler, 1976). Exploratory action, in this sense, may be considered to represent that kind of activity that is instrumental to an innate tendency of the organism to acquire knowledge and to gain control over the environment (Voss, 1984a). This view is compatible with cognitive theories that postulate an optimal "rate of cognitive change," referring to the amount of change, elaboration, and consolidation of cognitive structures on an individually defined level (Piaget, 1936; Voss, 1981).

Our main concern throughout this chapter is with the qualitative changes associated with sequences of exploration–play. Action theory provides a conceptual framework, and the question arises how exploration and play can be subsumed under this heading.

One of the most relevant concepts is the goal-orientedness of behavior, a concept including the notion that action is intentional and that certain behavioral outcomes are expected. A full discussion of these terms is not possible here, so a few statements must suffice in order to demonstrate the utility of using terms from action theory when describing the patterning of ongoing exploratory and play behavior.

In a patterned sequence of behavior, goals represent endpoints (i.e., objects, events, experiences) that the individual seeks to obtain or achieve. In a recent review on goal theory, Pervin (1983) suggested that goals have cognitive, affective, and behavioral (motor) properties associated with them. Cognition refers to both the mental representation or image of the goal as well as to the construction of a plan in order to reach the goal. The affective component involves the association of the goal with positive or negative feelings such as pleasure and fear, as well as other emotional and affective states (interest, pride, guilt, for example). Action is to be taken by the individual when there is a plan for goal acquisition, and overt behavior is shown when the referent is a physical or social object. What is meant by goal-orientedness was described by McDougall (1930) more than 50 years ago: "We foresee a particular event as a possibility; we desire to see this possibility realized; we take action in accordance with our desire, and we seem to guide the course of events in such a way that the foreseen and desired event results" (p. 5).

How does this formulation apply to sequences of exploration–play? One assumption would be that qualitative changes in these sequences reflect different levels of clarity (intensity) and that there is variation in relative significance of the three components mentioned by Pervin (1983). Thus, exploration and play vary according to (a) the level of (cognitive) clarity with which a goal or an event is imaged or foreseen, (b) the sign (positive or negative), duration, and intensity (Young, 1961) of accompanying motivational and affective processes, and (c) the temporal patterning of behavioral movements associated with goal acquisition.

Cognitive clarity about a behavioral outcome or goal can also be described in terms of an *anticipation* of the result, a phenomenon that indicates the organism's ability to make use of stored images as well as plans or behavioral strategies available in a given situation.

According to Piaget (1959), play is an instance of the assimilatory process by which the object or the environment is adapted to preexisting cognitive structures or schemes and thus represents a "pleasurable" practice of familiar action sequences. In this respect, the object would not represent a "problem" in the sense that the individual has to overcome a barrier, or what Piaget called *resistance of the object*, but instead represents an opportunity to act in a familiar way. There may be affective correlates of this kind of playful activity such as joy, or pleasurable feelings of competence and efficacy (White, 1959).

Playful behavior is guided by the presence of a clear mental image of the behavioral outcome or by a goal that is expected to be reached by acting upon it (e.g., I want to build a tower with these blocks) and includes positive affects of pleasure and joy that last longer than exploratory acts. The notion that there is goal-orientedness in play behavior does not contradict the widely held view that play is performed "for its own sake" and therefore might be called *non-purposive* (e.g., McDougall, 1908). Whereas it is true that play behavior is not principally governed by appetitive drives or extrinsic goals (Weisler & McCall, 1976), there is also White's (1959) notion that it might serve the goal of "effect-ance" or control over objects and events. Bruner (1973) stressed the importance of play in exercising and developing behavioral subroutines that the child will later integrate into larger and more task-oriented sequences. With respect to the motor component of goal-oriented behavior, play is more open to spontaneous alterations in the sense that the sequence of behavioral elements will be less stereotyped and will include elements whose duration is shorter (Hutt, 1970) than those of exploration.

Exploratory action, on the other hand, corresponding as it does with subjective uncertainty, is more often associated with feelings of tension or apprehension. One central assumption that action theory makes about exploration is that some unresolved ambiguity or incongruity remains after an attempt to match the object against cognitive representations of a related stimulus array, with the result that the formation of a behavioral goal that is dominant among other goals would be inhibited or blocked (Voss, 1984a). Both exploration and play involve an active altering of the actual, sensorily defined "field of events" that corresponds to an "inner-organismic field of events" (Klix, 1971). The main difference between exploration and play, according to this concept, lies in the absence or presence, respectively, of a clear image of the result of the activity. Thus, exploratory action is instrumental for the formation of cognitive clarity about a forthcoming event in the environment or a certain state of the organism.

An act may be called intentional when it represents one of several alternative acts and when the expected outcome of that act is preferred over alternative outcomes (Irwin, 1971). Exploration, according to this definition, would imply a low-level hierarchy among alternative acts and therefore act-outcome expectancy would be low.

In the first study reported here I demonstrate how qualitative changes in the patterning of exploration–play sequences can be subjected to an empirical test. More concretely, facial movements of children are recorded while manipulating a problem box and are analyzed in terms of the anticipation of the behavioral result. Anticipatory responses (for a definition see p. 155) are considered to represent the formation of a behavioral intent as they become more frequent in the course of ongoing behavior.

The second part of this chapter is devoted to an examination of both how exploration and play are embedded in the sociocommunicative context (by thus describing qualitative changes on a larger scale) and how the structure of the exploration–play action system changes developmentally across the age levels of 13 and 19 months. The latter question refers to the process of how verbal and vocal exchanges between child and mother become more flexible and integrated in the first half of the second year through the exploratory and playful manipulation of an object.[1]

---

[1]The investigations reported here are part of a larger research project on the "Development of exploratory behavior in early childhood (ages 2 through 4) and the ontogenesis of the curiosity motive," which has been supported by the Volkswagen Foundation. Forty-four healthy, firstborn children, together with their parents, were observed every 6 months in quasiexperimental situations at home and in the laboratory. The longitudinal study started in 1979 when the children were 13 months old. Data to be reported here are based on observations of 13-month-olds and 19-month-olds.

STUDY I: THE ANTICIPATION OF A BEHAVIORAL RESULT
A MICROANALYTICAL APPROACH TO
EXPLORATION–PLAY SEQUENCES

As has been mentioned previously, the central assumption is that the occurrence of anticipatory responses indicates the onset of the formation of a behavioral goal that is being given higher priority than alternative goals. It also signifies the formation of a behavioral intent in the sense that the specific act leading to this goal is likely to become more frequent or preferable to others and that a stronger expectancy concerning the behavioral result is built up.

How would it be possible to gain knowledge about the covert processes that may indicate anticipation? One widely accepted approach involves observation of facial movements thought to represent expressions of the organism's affective or emotional states. This view is held, for example, in Differential Emotion Theory (Izard, 1977; Tomkins, 1962), which states that facial muscular inner-vations or *action units* are both results as well as amplifiers (via feedback mechanisms) of discrete emotions. Apart from the question of what the special action units are that may indicate the different affective states of the individual while that person is performing a specific activity, the overall assumption would be that changes in the temporal patterning of action units as well as the location of units in the face signify the formation of a behavioral intent and thus represent empirical indicators for qualitative changes in sequences of exploration–play.

Anticipatory responses can be defined in terms of behavioral outlets that signal a forthcoming event. If action is implied, the event equals any actual change in the stimulus field that is experienced by the actor to be self-initiated or personally caused (Görlitz, 1983; Heider, 1958).

Another operationalization of anticipation refers to the lowering of the response threshold. This is indicated by a shorter time interval between stimulus and response or a decrease in response latency.

In the study reported first, I treat facial action units as representing more or less autonomous responses (e.g., the eye-blink response) that are contingent upon the occurrence of a specific or "critical" event; this event may represent the behavioral outcome, e.g., the opening of a lid on a box. Anticipation of the behavioral outcome or the critical event will be indicated both by facial movements that precede the event after having been highly contingent upon the event and by the decrease in response latency of facial movements that follow the event.

Subjects

The subjects in this study were 44 children (26 girls, 18 boys) ranging in age from 25 to 28 months (mean = 26.4 months).

155

Material and Procedure

Each child came together with his or her mother to the laboratory about 1 week after home visits had been made. The observation room was equipped with two movable remote control video cameras and a one-way screen. The child was seated at a table, the mother sitting to the side and slightly behind the child. The child was exposed to a "jack-in-the-box"-like toy, a 32.5 × 16 × 8 cm plastic box purchased in the United States from Gabriel. It contains five jack-in-the-box figures (Walt Disney characters) in a line. The mechanisms for springing the figures from the box differed from each other; that is, different manipulations were necessary (twisting a knob, pulling a lever, and twisting a dialing disk, for example) in order to produce the effect.

With the split-screen video technique, facial movements of the child manipulating the play material were recorded (larger part of the screen), together with the hands showing the manipulations at the play box (insert display). (See Fig. 8.1.) Observations started after a blanket covering the play box had been removed. Observation time was about 10 minutes.

Data Analysis and Categories

Microanalysis of the recordings was conducted by means of a slow-motion, frame-by-frame technique. Each step in the sequence (frame) represented a time interval of 0.04 seconds.

Facial movements were coded according to the Facial Action Coding System (FACS) by Ekman and Friesen (1978). This system has been widely used in order to register movements or action units (AU) in different regions of the face (upper and lower face). Because our main concern is for specific action units that are more closely related to the special kind of activity associated with the manipulation of the play object, results reported here are restricted to a limited array of action units. Thus, in Table 8.1, only those AUs are entered that represent a cumulative 90% or more of all action units that occurred in this situation and therefore represent the most frequent facial responses associated with the jack-in-the-box effect.

Results

Data analysis centered on the critical event (CE), that is, the moment at which the lid of the box begins to open, no matter which one of the five possibilities has been realized. Figure 8.1a to 8.1d illustrate a sequence of facial action units exhibited before, during (Fig. 8.1c), and after the CE. Usually, the eye-blink response (AU 45) was observed in these sequences. Figure 8.2 demonstrates that the latency of the lid reflex changed with the number of the CE's occurrences. All 44 subjects exhibited this response, and there were very few instances in

FIG. 8.1 A sample item of a sequence of facial movements (critical event occurring in Fig. 8.1c).

157

TABLE 8.1
Action Units (AU) Used in Study I

AU	*Description*
1	Inner brow raise
2	Outer brow raise
5X	Upper lid raise
5Y	Upper lid raise (more pronounced)
6	Cheek raise
12	Lip corner pull
25	Lips part
26	Jaw drop
45	Eye blink (<1 sec.)

Note: Taken from Ekman and Friesen (1978).

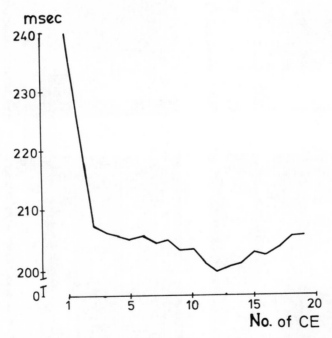

FIG. 8.2 Latency of eye-blink response (AU 45) as a function of number of critical events (CE).

which the eye-blink response failed to occur because of distractions. Latency of response as represented in Fig. 8.2 is equal to the time interval from the beginning of movement opening the box's lid till the full reflex action (eyes closed). As can be seen from Fig. 8.2, there is a sharp decline in latency from the first to the second occurrence of the CE, and a slight increase after the 13th occurrence.

One interpretation would be that after a short period during which the readiness for exhibiting this response is reinforced (which might signal anticipation of the CE), latency increases because of habituation to or familiarization with the jack-in-the-box effect.

The next step in the analysis was to check the proportion of subjects exhibiting one or several facial movements that can be assigned to one of the following categories: The action unit is exhibited (a) both before and after the CE, (b) before but not after the CE, and (c) only after the CE; a fourth category was (d) no response at all. "Before" was defined as the time interval of 1 second before the beginning of the box lid's opening; that is, the first registration that can be made within a time interval of 0.04 seconds, which equals one frame of film. "After" was defined as the time interval of 1.12 after the beginning of the lid's movement; that is, 1 second plus three times the frame length of 0.04 sec, which represents the mean time interval necessary for springing the figure in the box.

Figure 8.3 through 8.7 present the proportion of subjects falling into one of the aforementioned categories. The main results can be summarized as follows:(1) There is a relatively high proportion of subjects exhibiting facial action units before and after the CE (category *a*). This is most pronounced for the cases

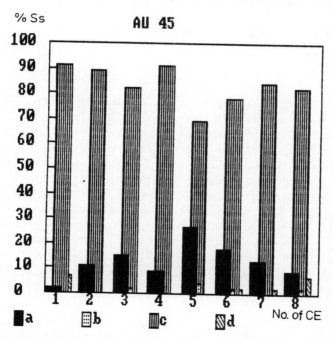

FIG. 8.3 Percentage of subjects exhibiting the eye-blink response both before and after the CE (a), only before the CE (b), only after the CE (c), or exhibiting "no response at all" (d).

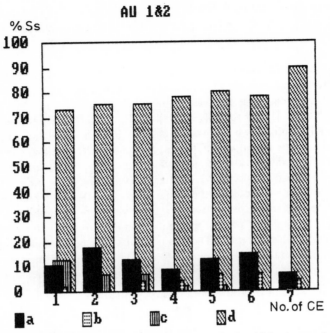

FIG. 8.4 Percentage of subjects exhibiting action units 1 and 2 (eyebrows raised). Categories a, b, c, and d as in Fig. 8.3.

of AU 5X/Y and AU 25/26. Proportions increase most from the first to the second occurrence of the CE; (2) with the exception of AU 45, the number of subjects to be assigned to category (d) increases as the number of times the lid is opened increases, and the proportion of subjects in category (c) decreases; (3) the distribution of subjects in category (b) (before CE only) is similar to the distribution in category (a): There is no instance of a response exhibited before the CE's first occurrence (one exception), and there is an increase in the number of subjects exhibiting pre-event facial movements in later segments of the behavioral sequence. Again, the eye-lid response is an exception. Only very few subjects exhibit this action unit in category (b), a fact that might be due to the "normal" rate of the eye-lid reflex; (4) there is bimodality in the distributions of anticipatory responses (most pronounced in category a), which fact may be a result of a heterogeneity of subsamples, thus calling for a further analysis in terms of individual differences.[2]

---

[2]Proceeding on theoretical assumptions about the relationships between behavioral styles and exploratory behavior (Voss, 1984b), we chose temperament dimensions and inspected them for discriminative power. Step-by-step discriminant analysis with "early" and "late" responders representing the dependent or group factor revealed significant discriminant functions, with temperament dimensions "threshold," "persistence," and "distractibility" being the most powerful predictors. This

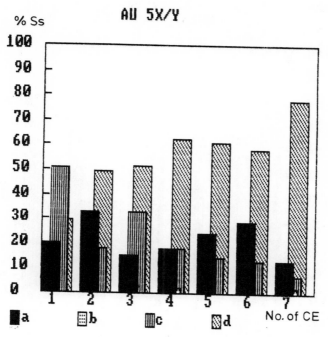

FIG. 8.5 Percentage of subjects exhibiting action unit 5 X/Y (eye-lids raised). Categories a, b, c, and d as in Fig. 8.3.

Discussion

The general assumption was that facial movements, indicating "internal" affective and cognitive states of the individual, can be used for describing qualitative changes in a behavioral sequence of exploration–play. On a microanalytical level, we have focused on action units that may occur before and/or after an event that is the behavioral outcome in a given situation. It was shown that typical changes occur in both the latency of a subject's eye-blink response and the occurrence of action units over several successive trials as that subject manipulates a problem box of the jack-in-the-box type. Exploratory action has been regarded as an attempt of the individual to reduce the uncertainty associated with the object while establishing a preferred goal, which in the present study was the opening of the lid or the production of the jack-in-the-box effect. From a motivational point of view, exploratory manipulation will be accompanied by heightened

analysis was based on a subsample of 12 children (from the original sample of 44 children) for whom temperament scores were available and for whom at least one pre-CE action unit had been observed. Temperament dimensions were assessed by means of the Toddler Temperament Scale developed by Fullard, McDevitt, and Carey (1978).

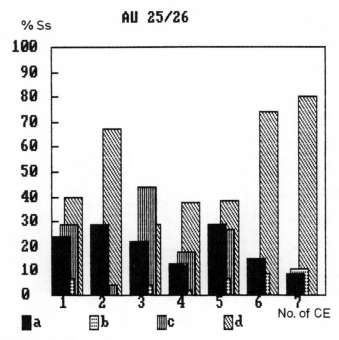

FIG. 8.6 Percentage of subjects exhibiting action units 25 or 26 (mouth opened). Categories a, b, c, and d as in Fig. 8.3.

states of arousal or tension that may be indicative of an unspecified expectation about the forthcoming event. After the occurrence of that event, that is, after the lid has opened and the figure has popped out, the usual affective response would be joy or excitement as when tension is suddenly reduced. Following the eye-blink response, which is prompt, universal, and only slowly habituating, the main affective pattern in this phase of the more advanced exploration–play sequence is composed of the facial action units AU 1 and 2, AU 5X/Y, AU 6, AU 12, and AU 25/26. According to Izard (1977), this pattern signals joy and/ or interest. Our data simply reflect the common observation that children some-times show a specific affective pattern (first of all joy and excitement) while awaiting or expecting a forthcoming, positively evaluated event or a self-monitored result of action. The data also demonstrate that joy cannot be inferred from facial movements as long as there is still a "problem" in handling the object, which is the case in the first trial, at least. Affective patterns as described thus indicate anticipation of a forthcoming event in a problem-solving-like situation. The same interpretation is offered for the decreasing latency of the eye-blink response (shortly after the CE's first occurrence) as well as for its occurrence before the CE.

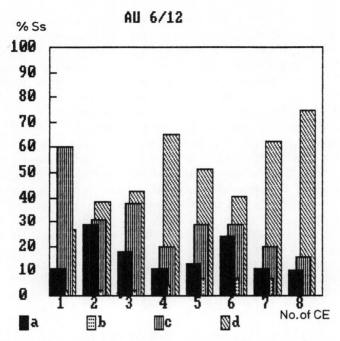

FIG. 8.7 Percentage of subjects exhibiting action units 6 and 12 (cheeks raised). Categories a, b, c, and d as in Fig. 8.3.

Our results also show that the subjects' readiness to exhibit affective patterns decreases (categories c and d) as manipulation of the object continues. This might indicate a process of familiarization with the object and thus describe a change in motivational processes resulting in monotony and boredom during later stages (Nunnally & Lemond, 1973). There might also be a serial effect; that is, affective responses vanish more quickly when already exhibited before the critical event. At the same time, this would make the critical event less and less "critical" in ongoing exploration–play in the sense that the child has mastered the "resistance of the object" and that integration of action-induced effects into the corresponding cognitive schemes has become more advanced.

Anticipatory responses have been defined in terms of facial movements that are exhibited in a pre-event segment of the behavioral sequence. Bimodality of distributions not only points to the fact that individual differences in personality dimensions (temperament dimensions, for instance) account for both intensity and quality of affective patterns that accompany exploration–play but also point to the limited range of anticipatory responses in terms of number of consecutive events: The highest proportions of subjects exhibiting anticipatory responses can be observed not only after the second or third occurrence of the CE (for early responders) but also after its fifth and sixth occurrence (for late responders). I interpret this as the beginning of the formation of a behavioral intent, a beginning that might also be considered as a transitional stage in exploration–play sequences, a stage linking late exploration and early play (e.g., the child has gained knowledge of the object's properties by exploring it and now wants to manipulate it in order to verify the expected behavioral outcome). Thus, the formation of a behavioral goal and its preference might be accompanied by a brief acting-out of internal affective and cognitive states of the individual.

One general conclusion from Study I would be that exploration and play represent intimately related stages in the formation of a behavioral goal and intention. Whereas exploratory action serves the function of altering the "field of external events" in such a way that a specific response becomes more prominent than others—that is, expected and preferred (referred to as "specific curiosity" in Berlyne, 1960)—or that new experiences will result (referred to as "diversive curiosity" in Berlyne, 1960), play might be considered to represent more an instance of "autotelic" activity (Klinger, 1971). In other words, the behavioral goal is intimately related to the performed act itself; it is *endogenic*, to use a term suggested by Kruglanski (1975).

STUDY II: EXPLORATION, PLAY, AND SYMBOLIC BEHAVIOR FROM 13 TO 19 MONTHS

In this section, I report a study on the relationships between exploration–play sequences and some aspects of communicative behavior such as gazing at the mother, vocalizing, and speaking. This investigation is part of the longitudinal study mentioned earlier.

More explicitly, the research reported here concerns the question of how symbolic acts are embedded in sequences of exploration–play in ongoing behavior. Informal observations from Study I concerning the child's vocal/verbal exchange with the mother have led to the assumption that there is "social referencing," e.g., gazing at the mother and vocalizing at the very beginning and end of exploratory action sequences as defined by the manipulation of the novel object.

Whereas in Study I the focus had been on affective concomitants of different segments of the "behavioral stream," I now look for correlates of exploration–play actions in terms of social cognition and symbolic behavior in a developmental framework.

There also is reference to the theoretical position of pragmatism in research on language acquisition, a position that emphasizes "language in use," or the realistic communicational context (Bates, Benigni, Bretherton, Camaioni, &

Volterra, 1977; Carter, 1974). One question concerns the way social and non-social schemes are combined in novel means–end sequences. Lock (1972, quoted in Bates et al., 1977) presented informal observations of one child from his sixth through eleventh month of life, documenting a continuum ranging from the child's actions with objects to his first tentative efforts to involve adults in those actions by making eye contact, reaching, vocalizing, and so on. This is consistent with our conceptualization of exploration–play sequences, which is that they represent a kind of behavioral unit in which communicative acts are embedded. From a methodological point of view the investigation of exploration and play may thus offer a research framework for the study of symbolic behavior under natural conditions.

In this study we look at the pattern of exploration–play and symbolic activities of the child in a situation where the mother is present but does not actively interfere with the child's manipulation of both the novel as well as the familiar object (unless the child wants her to do so). More weight is put on the mother's role of providing a source of "feedback" for the child's actions in a situation that is primarily controlled by the child. The design of the study, therefore, allows the child to be engaged in "social referencing" while exploring a specific object or playing with it. I also show how this pattern changes across age between 13 and 19 months.

Subjects and Material

The subjects were 12 children (6 girls and 6 boys), observed when they were 13 months old and again at 19 months of age. Observations took place at the children's homes in the presence of their mothers and the observer, the latter operating a movable video camera. The mother was told to let her child move around or play with the object situated in the middle of the room. She was not to make any efforts to direct the child's behavior towards the play material but was to remain responsive to the child's communicative behavior.

For the observations made when the children were 13 months old, the object (Fig. 8.8) was a wooden pyramid-like box (50 × 50 cm at its base) that had three openings or lids on each side: One of the lids, located at the top of the box, could be opened by pushing it; the other two, located at the bottom, could be opened by pulling a knob. In each container there was a familiar play object, e.g., a doll, a play car, and a ball.

For the observations made when the children were 19 months, the object (Fig. 8.9) was a wooden box (60 × 50 × 25 cm) with five rows of three drawers on the front side. Each drawer could be opened by putting a finger into a hole and pulling the drawer out. Again, there was a familiar play object in each drawer.

FIG. 8.8 A wooden pyramid serving as novel object for 13-month-olds.

FIG. 8.9 A wooden box of drawers serving as novel object for 19-month-olds.

Procedure and Measures

The child's behavior was videotaped for about 10 minutes. All children moved around, approached the novel object at least once, spent most of the time by sitting in front of the object or changing sides, manipulating details of the object, and playing with the toys.

Video recordings were analyzed by means of an event recorder identical with an on-line microcomputer. This device allowed for a sufficient interobserver reliability (coefficients ranged from .87 to .98) as well as a fine-grained analysis of a frame length down to ⅟₁₀ of a second. An example of the computer printout for one sequence of exploration–play, together with communicative acts of both child and mother, is presented in Fig. 8.10.

According to the "instigation question" of motivational research (Hunt, 1971), investigators of exploration–play have focused on the properties of the object or stimulus that may give rise to exploratory or play behavior, respectively. One of these stimulus characteristics is novelty; as long as an object is judged to be novel, exploratory action will be exhibited. When the object becomes familiar to the actor, exploration is terminated and play begins (Nunnally & Lemond, 1973). In Study I, I have tried to demonstrate how this process can be mirrored in qualitative changes of ongoing behavior, e.g., in facial movements. In Study II, the child is exposed to a novel and complex object that can be explored by manipulating it (e.g., finding out how a drawer is to be opened and what's in it) and that offers, as a possible result, the opportunity to manipulate a familiar toy. Considering molar behavior or larger behavioral units in Study II—as opposed to the microanalytical approach of Study I—qualitative changes in behavior that might indicate transitions from exploration to play can be defined according to different objects manipulated by the child rather than to the same object that is manipulated in several ways (Study I).

Although I am not able to suggest a sharp distinction between exploration and play (in the sense of cutting the behavioral stream into two parts), the special

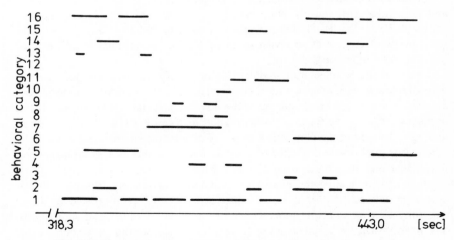

FIG. 8.10 Transcription of a computer printout of 16 behavioral categories activated across a time span of 124.7 seconds. (1) gazing at object, (2) gazing at mother, (3) gazing at other, (4) looking into container/drawer, (5) approaching object, (6) withdrawal, (7) manipulation of novel object, (8) lid/drawer opened, (9) lid/drawer closed, (10) toy removed, (11) toy manipulated, (12) bringing toy to mother, (13) exclamation, (14) unintelligible verbalization, (15) intelligible verbalization, (16) verbalization of mother.

arrangement of novel and familiar objects in Study II does offer an approach for empirically investigating exploration and play as parts of a larger sequence of behavior. Defining exploration and play a priori, that is, in terms of collative variables such as novelty and complexity (Berlyne, 1960), allows for an inspection of the larger, sociocommunicative context.

Thus, exploratory action was operationalized by the amount of time the child manipulated the novel object (e.g., touching, banging on it with the hand) or details of the object (e.g., by turning the lid's knob or opening and closing the drawers several times). *Play* was defined as any manipulation of a familiar object (e.g., placing it in the mouth, touching details, turning the object, moving it on the floor).

Novelty as well as familiarity of the different objects had been checked against the mother's judgment. The two objects we built were declared by all mothers to be novel and the play materials in the boxes to be familiar to the child.

Communicative and symbolic behavior included actions of the child directed to the mother. First of all, gazing at the mother without or in combination with vocal/verbal utterances served as variables. A combination in this sense consisted of both gazing at the mother and vocalizing/verbalizing at the same time, and gazing at the mother in joint succession with vocal/verbal utterances. No other behavioral category such as looking around or moving around occurred in between gazing and vocalizing.

Vocalization and speech acts included the following categories: (a) exclamations and physiological sounds such as "oh," "uuh," and "effort sounds," (b) intelligibles, that is, all words that could be identified as meaningful by two raters making independent observations, and (c) unintelligibles, that is, all speech-like utterances that could not be identified.

To avoid the segmentation problem in observational research, the several parts of one sequence of exploration–play had to be defined a priori. Exploration–play sequences extend from gazing at the novel object, manipulating the object or parts of it, grasping for the familiar object, inspecting it visually, and manipulating it, to putting the play object aside. Action theory implies that a person's behavior is goal oriented or governed by an intent. Withdrawal from a specific object that had attracted a person's attention for a while seems to be a good candidate for indicating the end of an exploration and/or play episode. Withdrawal is defined here as a loss of interest in the object, signalled in these experiments when the child looked away from the novel object and approached any other physical or social object by locomotion. A description of the behavioral sequence represented in Fig. 8.10 may illustrate what is meant by a fully extended exploration–play sequence (numbers in parentheses refer to behavioral categories):

The 13-month-old child gazes at the novel object (1), approaches it by crawling towards it (5), and manipulates one of the lids (7), then opens and closes the lid several times (8 & 9), looks into the container and removes the doll (10) (exploration), then manipulates the doll (11) (play), and brings it to the mother (12), gazing at her at the same time (2) (withdrawal from object, end of play, communicative act); after a while, the child approaches the novel object again (5) (beginning of another exploration episode).

Embedded in this sequence of discrete actions are several vocal and verbal utterances of both child and mother.

Given the plausibility of this "solution" to the segmentation problem, we would now be able to describe exploration–play episodes in terms of their duration or extension as well as their behavioral "makeup," that is, the different patterns of variables that characterize the several parts of a sequence.

Because the main focus in Study II is on an inspection of fully extended sequences of exploration–play, all other segments of the behavioral stream that cannot be characterized by a joint succession of exploratory and play activities— e.g., the child explores, then gazes at other parts of the room or at the mother, and finally continues with exploratory manipulation—are not considered. Thus, sequences of exploration–play are defined by exploration followed by play. The sequence began when the child gazed at the novel object and/or manipulated it and ended with the last manipulatory act performed with the familiar toy.

Results

The results concern two main areas: (a) the distribution of the several kinds of behavior across the time span of exploration–play sequences or parts thereof, and (b) the changing pattern of variables across age levels.

The transcription of a computer printout covering a sequence of 124.7 seconds of observation time is presented in Fig. 8.10. As can be seen, the different behaviors categorized according to the operational definitions given before were closely interwoven. By definition, exploratory behavior and play, gazing at the mother and gazing at the object, approaching the mother, and the different categories of vocalization/verbalization were mutually exclusive behavioral categories.

The next step in the analysis of the data concerns an inspection of the exploration–play sequences (EPS) as defined earlier. The mean number of EPSes at 13 months was 6.8 ($s = 4.2$); at 19 months, 11.7 ($s = 5.3$) (means are based on raw scores corrected for differences in total observation time). At 39.1 seconds, the mean duration of EPSes was longer for the 13-month-old children ($s = 19.7$), than for the 19-month-olds (25.7 sec., $s = 17.6$). Differences between means were not significant. Both age levels were then compared for the number of communicational and symbolic acts the child performed while exploring the novel object and playing with the toys. In Fig. 8.11, the following variables are represented: (a) gazing at the mother without making vocal/verbal utterances; (b) gazing at the mother while making vocal/verbal utterances; (c) gazing at the object while making vocal/verbal utterances; (d) gazing at other parts of the room

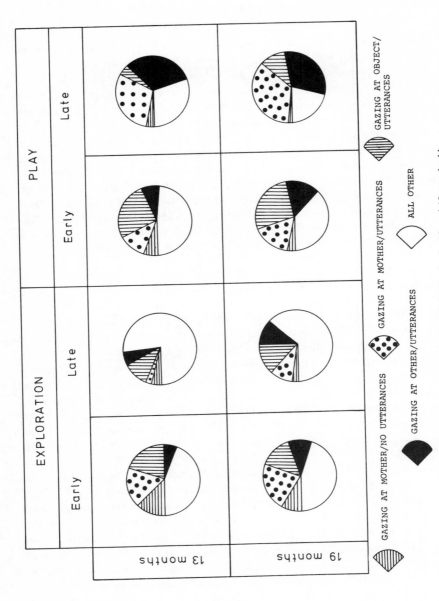

FIG. 8.11 Gazing and vocal/verbal behavior for 13- and 19-month-olds.

and vocalizing at the same time; and (e) all other behavior, including gazing at the object or other parts of the room without making utterances.

In order to demonstrate changes in relative proportions across EPSes, both the time span during which the child explored the novel object as well as the time span of play were divided into halves, referred to as "early" and "late" exploration or play, respectively.

The same was done in Fig. 8.12 and 8.13, which present mean frequencies of the several categories of vocal/verbal utterances. The mean of the mothers' verbal responses (based on the absolute number of sentences spoken) is also shown in these figures.

The main conclusions that can be drawn from Fig. 8.11, 8.12, and 8.13 are:

1. There was an overall similarity between patterns of proportions and frequencies of the several classes of behavior shown by the child. The main differences concern the amount of time spent with noncommunicative activities such as looking around and gazing at the novel or familiar object without vocalizing (higher percentage of time for 13-month-olds), and the amount of both intelligible and unintelligible verbalizations expressed across the several stages of exploration–play (higher for 19-month-olds).

2. In the early phase of exploration, the children at both age levels gazed at both mother and novel object, while making vocal/verbal utterances, whereas

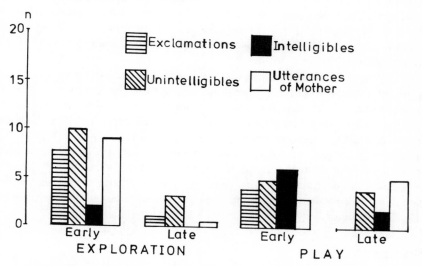

FIG. 8.12 Mean number (n) of utterances in different parts of exploration–play sequences (13-month-olds).

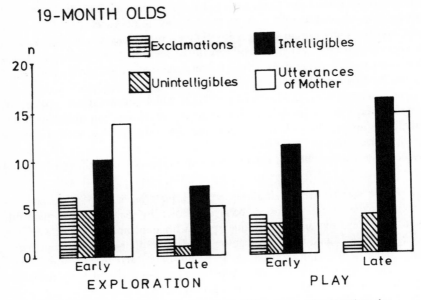

FIG. 8.13 Mean number (*n*) of utterances in different parts of exploration–play sequences (19-month-olds).

in late exploration symbolic and communicative acts diminished. More exclamations were made in early exploration than in either late exploration or play in general. There was also a maximum of noncommunicative gazing behavior in the second part of the exploration episode. This might have been due to the intensified manipulation of the novel object that occurred towards the end of the exploration episode.

3. Vocal and verbal utterances (mainly intelligible ones) that were expressed while the child gazed at the mother or at other parts of the room were the main characteristics of late play. It is also noteworthy that early play can be discriminated from late play by the amount of gazing at the familiar object in combination with vocal/verbal utterances (more pronounced in early play) as well as by the amount of intelligible utterances that the child expressed while looking around (at the mother or at other parts of the room). This would mean that the child's usage of intelligible verbalizations peaks when play is being terminated; at the same time, the mother becomes the main addressee of the child's communicational activities.

Discussion

Study II was devoted to the question of how exploration and play are embedded in the sociocommunicative context and how the pattern of the child's gazing and vocalizing/verbalizing changes across the segments of the exploration–play sequence. The criterion for labelling the child's behavior as communicative and symbolic was limited in this study to the combination of gazing at the mother and speaking—either simultaneously or successively. Noncommunicative behavior comprises the symbolic activity of the child in terms of vocal/verbal utterances not directed to the mother or any other person being present (e.g., the observer). The results demonstrate that the child vocalizes or exhibits communicative efforts to a lesser extent during a period of intensified exploration, that is, during the manipulation of the novel object, than during play or after the play object has become less attractive. The only similar statement I have found in the literature was made by Roberta Collard (1979), who reported the informal observation that the child vocalizes less during a phase of exploration than during play.

At the beginning of exploratory action there is more gazing at the mother together with exclamations. Does this mean that the child is more engaged in "social referencing" in this part of the sequence? And might one consider the child's behavior to be governed by questions such as "May I further approach this object?" or "What is it and what can I do with it?" And does the use of unintelligible as well as intelligible verbalizations starting with the early part of play express the child's wish to communicate the results of his exploratory manipulation?

A sufficient answer to these questions would certainly imply a more detailed analysis of the dyadic mother–child system, taking into account the mother's role of providing a "point of reference" for the child. Because of the instructions given to the mother, her verbal behavior represents a passive response to, rather than an active intervention in, the child's actions. It is not possible, therefore, to give a full account of reciprocal transactions that govern mother–child interaction. The only result that might demonstrate a "matching" of behaviors between mother and child would be the parallel between the two persons' vocal and verbal activities, peaking at both the beginning and the end of exploration–play sequences. There is also a developmental trend towards a higher level of verbal exchange between mother and child from 13 to 19 months.

CONCLUDING REMARKS

Are there qualitative changes in sequences of exploration–play that can be described empirically? This question includes the problem of segmenting the behavioral stream into observable units of behavior and at the same time calls for a specification of the level of analysis to be involved in exploration–play research. As Newtson and his collaborators (e.g., Newtson, 1976; Newtson, Engquist, & Bois, 1977) have demonstrated, observers may come to very different answers when asked to segment or to organize the ongoing activity of a person. This approach, however, puts more weight on the psychological processes of the observer by demonstrating how concepts of behavioral units are formed as one observes another person's behavior; it does not operationalize behavioral entities in terms of the behavior itself. Treating facial movements as indicators of cognitive and affective "events" inside a person involves microanalysis aided by slow-motion video technique, for changes in the behavioral stream would be too fast for an observer to record under natural conditions. In Study I, I have shown how facial movements accompany the several parts of the child's manipulatory actions in a problem-solving-like situation. On a conceptual level, exploration and play have been separated here in terms of action theory: Exploration leads to the formation of a new behavioral goal that is equivalent to producing a behavioral result. Establishing means–end relationships allows the child to structure his surroundings while feeling that forthcoming events are under his own control. One may also call this process *cognitive learning*, or the process by which cognitive schemes are built up; the consolidation and elaboration of these schemes, then, would be governed largely by the child's attempt to make use of a newly learned behavioral sequence by handling the object repeatedly, manipulating parts of it, producing effects, and experiencing pleasure.

In Study II, I have dealt with sequences or episodes of exploration–play on a macroanalytic level. The main point was to demonstrate that there are qualitative changes across segments of ongoing behavior predefined by the stimulus conditions as exploration and play. The consideration of the social context of the child's manipulation of both the novel and the familiar object broadened the perspective of Study I in the sense that the child would now be able to communicate the results of his activity or to use expressions of personal feelings and intentions in an instrumental manner. Results demonstrate that a specific behavior, e.g., gazing at the mother, will serve a different function, depending on its placement on the exploration–play continuum, e.g., ensuring that the exploratory behavior is reinforced by the caregiver, sharing subjective feelings of "efficacy" (White, 1959) with the mother, or using the adult as a source for new stimulation. In Study II, both exploration and play represent object-related activities of the child. Sociocommunicational concepts are not only embedded in the child's object-related activities but also stem from them. Thus, it may be possible that both exploration and play first develop outside communicative contexts—as acts that aid in both the generating of meaning and the experiencing of personal competence. Later on, the same cognitive acts are incorporated into prepared communicative schemes. There is some evidence in Study II that exploration–play episodes become more integrated beween 13 and 19 months of a child's life in the sense that the number of complete sequences increases while their total length decreases. (Tests for significance of differences between means failed to yield positive results, however.) One tentative conclusion would be that there is a process of hierarchization of behavioral segments or sequences; parts of a sequence that are performed by the 13-month-old child independently of each other (e.g., exploration and play being performed separately) may later become integrated into a larger behavioral unit (e.g., an exploration–play sequence).

Although the main concern in Study II was not with the child's linguistic achievements in the first half of the second year, some of the results reported might be interpreted in terms of the "language-in-use" point of view referred to earlier. Nelson (1979) has speculated about the roots of linguistic competence in prelanguage cognitive and social development and has argued that, with the beginning of the second year of life, the child will coordinate social relations and object relations as part of the means–ends differentiation that takes place at that time (Bates, 1976; Sugarman-Bell, 1976). A primary distinction is made between the physical-object world and the sociocommunicative world, the first allowing primarily individual exploration; the latter, social interaction and communication. From the theoretical standpoint of Piaget (1936), the child between 1 and 2 years of age is an active explorer of and experimenter with objects. Exploratory action serves the function of gaining knowledge about the object and thus may be crucial for acquiring the cognitive prerequisites of early language development. As the results have demonstrated, the 13-month-old child will be able to coordinate object-related activities—e.g., gazing and manipulating—and sociocommunicative actions; there are qualitative differences in these coordinations according to the several parts of the exploration–play continuum. Thus, exclaiming and gazing at the novel object, followed by an overall decrease in vocalizing may be indicative of the child's attempt to overcome the "resistance of the object" (Piaget, 1936) or to "pick up the object message" (Nelson, 1973). It seems that this process, at its very beginning, needs to be reinforced by the caregiver because "gazing at the mother" is also obvious in early exploration, and this holds especially true for the younger child of 13 months.

One further interpretation of the results of Study II is that object orientation is going to be replaced by sociocommunicative orientation at two points on the exploration–play continuum: first, when the child starts to play, that is, when exploration has come to an end, resulting in the wish to communicate the results of prior exploration; second, when the play material has become unattractive and loses its incentive value for further manipulation. One general assumption is that exploration–play situations provide a research framework for the study of early language development; amount and quality of vocal/verbal behavior can both be considered as being functionally related to a variety of "tasks" the child is performing while exploring a novel object or playing with a familiar toy, e.g., naming the object, finding out how it works, and expressing subjective feelings of tension and pleasure.

Summary

Two studies are reported in this chapter. The first demonstrated how qualitative changes in the patterning of exploration–play sequences can be empirically tested. Facial movements of 44 children (26 girls, 18 boys) ranging in age from 25 to

28 months were recorded while the children manipulated a problem box (jack-in-the-box type) and were analyzed in terms of the anticipation of the behavioral result. Anticipatory responses were defined in terms of behavioral outlets that signal a forthcoming event and were indicated both by facial movements and action units that precede the event after having been highly contingent upon the event and by the decrease in response latency of facial movements that follow the event. The "critical" event that represents the behavioral outcome was the opening of the lid on the box. The overall assumption tested in this study was that changes in the temporal patterning of action units and in the location of units in the face signify the formation of a behavioral intent and thus represent empirical indicators for qualitative changes in sequences of exploration–play.

Anticipatory responses, in turn, indicate the onset of the formation of a behavioral goal or intent. Results demonstrated that there was a relatively high proportion of subjects exhibiting facial action units before the second or third occurrence of the behavioral outcome. There was also a sharp decline in the response latency of the eye-blink response from the first to the third occurrence of the critical event. The results also showed that the subjects' readiness to exhibit affective patterns decreases as manipulation of the object continues. Results were interpreted in terms of anticipatory responses that are indicative for the beginning of the formation of a behavioral intent, a beginning that might also be considered as a transitional stage in exploration–play sequences.

The second study was on the relationships between exploration–play sequences and some aspects of communicative behavior such as gazing at the mother, vocalizing, and speaking. The question was how symbolic acts are embedded in sequences of exploration–play in ongoing behavior. Twelve children (6 boys and 6 girls) were observed when they were 13 months old and again at 19 months of age. Observations took place in the children's homes in the presence of the mother and the observer. The child was exposed to a novel object (pyramid-like box with openings and lids for the 13-month-olds, a drawer box for the 19-month-olds), and the whole scene was videotaped. There were also several pieces of familiar play material available for the child. Exploratory action was operationalized by the amount of time the child manipulated the novel object, and play was defined as any manipulation of a familiar object. Communicative and symbolic behavior included actions that the child directed to the mother (gazing at the mother with or without vocal/verbal utterances, for example).

Sequences of exploration–play were defined by the joint succession of exploration and play; the sequence began when the child gazed at the novel object and/or manipulated it and ended with the last manipulatory act performed with the familiar toy. Among other things, the results demonstrated that children at both age levels gazed at both mother and novel object in the early phase of exploration while making vocal/verbal utterances, whereas symbolic and communicative acts diminished in late exploration. More exclamations were made in early exploration than in either late exploration or in play in general. Vocal and verbal utterances (mainly intelligible ones) that were expressed while the child gazed at the mother or at other parts of the room were the main characteristics of late play.

Generally, results showed that the child at both age levels vocalizes less and/ or exhibits fewer communicative efforts during the manipulation of the novel object than during play or after the play object has become less attractive.

Both studies dealt with qualitative changes in sequences of exploration–play. On a microanalytical level (Study I) facial movements may be considered to serve the function of indicating cognitive and affective "events" inside a person. Larger segments of the behavioral stream were considered in Study II, and it was shown that exploratory as well as playful activities provide a frame of reference for the child's communicative acts. Thus, one general assumption is that exploration–play situations provide a research framework for the study of early language development.

ACKNOWLEDGMENTS

The author thanks the editors of this volume, Dietmar Görlitz and Joachim F. Wohlwill, for critical comments on an earlier draft.

REFERENCES

Bates, E. (1976). *Language and context: The acquisition of pragmatics*. New York: Academic Press.
Bates, E., Benigni, L., Bretherton, I., Camaioni, L., & Volterra, V. (1977). From gesture to the first word: On cognitive and social prerequisites. In M. Lewis & L. Rosenblum (Eds.), *Interaction, conversation and the development of language* (pp. 102–168). New York: Wiley.
Berlyne, D. E. (1960). *Conflict, arousal, and curiosity*. New York: McGraw-Hill.
Bruner, J. S. (1973). Organization of early skilled action. *Child Development, 44*, 1–11.
Carter, A. (1974). *The development of communication in the sensori-motor period: A case study*. Unpublished doctoral dissertation, University of California, Berkeley.
Collard, R. R. (1979). Exploratory and play responses of eight- to twelve-month-old infants in different environments. Discussion. In B. Sutton-Smith (Ed.), *Play and learning* (pp. 112–121). New York: Gardner Press.
Ekman, P., & Friesen, W. V. (1978). *Manual for the Facial Action Coding System*. Palo Alto, CA: Consulting Psychologists Press.
Fullard, W., McDevitt, S. C., & Carey, W. B. (1978). *The Toddler Temperament Scale*. Unpublished manuscript.
Görlitz, D. (1983). Entwicklungsmuster attributionaler Handlungsanalyse. In D. Görlitz (Ed.), *Kindliche Erklärungsmuster* (pp. 146–179). Weinheim: Beltz.
Heider, F. (1958). *The psychology of interpersonal relations*. New York: Wiley.
Hunt, J. McV. (1971). Toward a history of intrinsic motivation. In H. I. Day, D. E. Berlyne, & D. E. Hunt (Eds.), *Intrinsic motivation: A new direction in education* (pp. 1–32). Toronto: Holt, Rinehart & Winston.
Hutt, C. (1970). Specific and diversive exploration. In H. Reese & L. P. Lipsitt (Eds.), *Advances in child development and behavior* (Vol. 5, pp. 119–180). London: Academic Press.

Irwin, F. W. (1971). *Intentional behavior and motivation: A cognitive theory.* Philadelphia: J. B. Lippincott.

Izard, C. E. (1977). *Human emotions.* New York: Plenum Press.

Klinger, E. (1971). *Structure and functions of fantasy.* New York: Wiley.

Klix, F. (1971). *Information und Verhalten.* Bern: Huber.

Kreitler, H., & Kreitler, S. (1976). *Cognitive orientation and behavior.* New York: Springer.

Kruglanski, A. W. (1975). The endogenous–exogenous partition in attribution theory. *Psychological Review, 82,* 387–406.

McDougall, W. (1908). *An introduction to social psychology.* London: Methuen.

McDougall, W. (1930). Autobiography. In C. Murchison (Ed.), *A history of psychology in autobiography* (pp. 1–24). Worcester, MA: Clark University Press.

Miller, G. A., Galanter, E., & Pribram, K. H. (1960). *Plans and the structure of behavior.* New York: Holt, Rinehart & Winston.

Nelson, K. (1973). Structure and strategy in learning to talk. *Monograph of the Society for Research in Child Development, 38* (Serial No. 149).

Nelson, K. (1979). The role of language in infant development. In M. H. Bornstein & W. Kessen (Eds.), *Psychological development from infancy: Image to intention* (pp. 307–337). New York: Wiley.

Newtson, D. (1976). Foundations of attribution: The perception of ongoing behavior. In J. H. Harvey, W. J. Ickes, & R. F. Kidd (Eds.), *New directions in attribution research* (Vol. 1, pp. 223–248). New York: Wiley.

Newtson, D., Engquist, G., & Bois, J. (1977). The objective basis of behavior units. *Journal of Personality and Social Psychology, 35,* 847–862.

Nunnally, J. C., & Lemond, L. C. (1973). Exploratory behavior and human development. In H. W. Reese (Ed.), *Advances in child development and behavior* (Vol. 8, pp. 59–108). New York: Academic Press.

Pervin, L. A. (1983). The stasis and flow of behavior: Toward a theory of goals. In M. M. Page (Ed.), *Nebraska Symposium on Motivation: Personality—Current Theory and Research* (pp. 1–53). Lincoln: University of Nebraska Press.

Piaget, J. (1936). *La naissance de l'intelligence chez l'enfant.* Neuchâtel: Delachaux & Niestlé.

Piaget, J. (1959). *Imitation, jeu et rêve - Image et représentation.* Neuchâtel: Delachaux & Niestlé.

Sugarman-Bell, S. (1976). Some organizational aspects of preverbal communication. In I. Markova (Ed.), *The social context of language* (pp. 273–296). New York: Wiley.

Tomkins, S. S. (1962). *Affect, imagery, consciousness* (Vol. I & II). New York: Springer.

Voss, H.-G. (1981). Kognition und exploratives Handeln. In H.-G. Voss & H. Keller (Eds.), *Neugierforschung: Grundlagen - Theorien - Anwendungen* (pp. 175–196). Weinheim: Beltz.

Voss, H.-G. (1984a). Curiosity, exploration, and anxiety. In H. M. Van Der Ploeg, R. Schwarzer, & C. D. Spielberger (Eds.), *Advances in test anxiety and research* (Vol. 3, pp. 121–146). Lisse/Hillsdale, NJ: Swets & Zeitlinger/Lawrence Erlbaum Associates.

Voss, H.-G. (1984b, May). *Patterns of temperament in first- and second-born children.* Paper presented at 2nd European Conference on Personality, Bielefeld, FRG.

Weisler, A., & McCall, R. B. (1976). Exploration and play. *American Psychologist, 31,* 492–508.

White, R. W. (1959). Motivation reconsidered: The concept of competence. *Psychological Review, 66,* 297–333.

Young, P. T. (1961). *Motivation and emotion.* New York: Wiley.

CHAPTER NINE

SUBJECTIVE UNCERTAINTY
AND EXPLORATORY BEHAVIOR
IN PRESCHOOL CHILDREN

KLAUS SCHNEIDER
University of Marburg

The motive to explore the environment is presumably an evolved behavioral tendency that enables man and other higher animals to gain information or knowledge about the environment in the interest of survival (see Lorenz, 1969). However, this ultimate goal of exploratory behavior does not explain the instigation of curiosity in a given situation. So the question remains what situational factors instigate curiosity and to what proximal goals curiosity-oriented behavior leads or, in other words, what are the incentives for exploration?

According to Berlyne (1960, 1966, 1978) exploratory behavior is instigated by so-called *collative variables* of physical and mental objects, like novelty, ambiguity, complexity, and the objective uncertainty of coming events. The common denominator of these variables seems to be the state of subjective uncertainty created by such object characteristics in the subject (Berlyne, 1978). Under nonthreatening conditions, subjective uncertainty causes curiosity and exploratory behavior; at other times uncertainty may cause anxiety and retreat. Through the investigation of an object the individual receives information or knowledge about the object; the more the individual investigates, the more uncertain she or he was to begin with. Thus the immediate cause of exploratory behavior is the state of subjective uncertainty, and the proximal goal of exploration is the dissolution of this state.

It follows from this assumption that a person should remain interested in an object as long as the uncertainty created by that object has not been reduced to threshold level and that the motivation to explore should be a positive function of subjective uncertainty.

However, a person might lose all hope that he eventually will understand what it all means, i.e., his expectancy to learn more about an object or to understand it better by further exploration may become very low, and he might give up exploring the object before his subjective uncertainty is completely reduced. Therefore, we have to assume that the rate of uncertainty reduction and thus the rate of information input is a controlling factor as well (see Lanzetta, 1971). Figure 9.1 illustrates these assumptions.

A person encounters a novel object, which she or he cannot assimilate mentally because the necessary cognitive schemata or categories are not existent (McReynolds, 1971). The discrepancy between the percept and the categories at hand instigates the state of subjective uncertainty and, with that, the interest in the object. This motivates the exploration of the object. As a result the person learns the fabric and functions of the object, and through this subjective uncertainty is reduced.

180

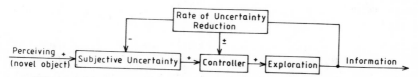

FIG. 9.1 Picture of the control system of specific exploratory behavior instigated by a novel object.

Uncertainty reduction progressively reduces interest in the object and thereby the motivation to explore the object. In the model this is represented by a negative feedback loop. However, the rate of uncertainty reduction, and thus the rate of information input, is monitored as well. As long as the rate of uncertainty reduction is high, this will strengthen the interest in the object and, therefore, the motivation to explore. If the rate has fallen below an optimal value, the motivation will be reduced and the person will finally stop exploring the object altogether, although there is some uncertainty remaining. In this case the payoff of exploring becomes too low compared with the time and the effort spent, and the person will go on to other activities.

The schema proposed is only a first step toward formulating a model of exploratory behavior: Only one internal-state variable, subjective uncertainty, is conceptualized as a behavior-controlling variable. However, other controlling variables, like fear of the novel object, can be easily integrated.

How can such a general model relate to individual differences in exploratory behavior and developmental changes? It is generally accepted (see Dember & Earl, 1957) that the amount of subjective uncertainty and/or complexity of a stimulus configuration that can be processed by an individual depends on the complexity of the cognitive schemata at hand. Therefore, the same object will create different degrees of uncertainty in different subjects or different age groups, and the same amount of exploratory behavior will lead to more or less reduced uncertainty depending on the cognitive capacity of the child. In addition, individuals might prefer and tolerate different amounts of subjective uncertainty (Sorentino, Short, & Raynor, 1984).

Our first concern, then, was to examine to what extent different forms of exploratory behavior can be predicted on the basis of the assumption that curiosity and interest in an object is a function of subjective uncertainty created by that object. A second but related goal was to document the sequence of exploratory behaviors and other activities in the first encounter with a novel object. We present here the main results of four studies pertinent to these questions. The results of the first two studies have been reported in greater detail elsewhere (Schneider, Barthelmey, & Herrmann, 1981; Schneider, Moch, Sandfort, Auerswald, & Walther-Weckman, 1983); the results of the third and fourth study are reported here for the first time.

VISUAL EXPLORATION

Study I

The main goal of the first study was to examine whether subjective uncertainty predicts visual exploratory behavior in preschool children. For that purpose a direct assessment procedure for subjective uncertainty should be used. Although subjective uncertainty is considered as the immediate cause of specific exploration in Berlyne's theory, there are only a few studies in which subjective uncertainty was not only manipulated but measured directly.

In the area of achievement-oriented behavior we had found earlier (see Schneider & Heckhausen, 1981) that decision time was a valid behavioral measure of subjective uncertainty and predicted the choice of task difficulty levels in samples of high school and university students. In such an achievement-oriented situation decision time measured was the time subjects needed to predict a success or failure at a given difficulty level.

The goal of the first study, therefore, was to examine if decision time is a valid indicator of subjective uncertainty in preschool children in a curiosity-oriented situation and if subjective uncertainty predicts visual exploratory behavior at this age.

The subjects were 39 boys and 42 girls between 3½ and 6½ years old. They were shown two series of three slides (animals: horse, cat, and dog; toys: truck, doll, and spinning top) at three exposure times (20 msec, 60 msec, and 120 msec) in three different boxes arranged in a semicircle. These boxes had a 15 × 10 cm transparent screen in the front wall. The slides were projected from behind on this screen. The boxes were placed in a semicircle at a distance of 80 cm from the subject, the subject sitting in the center of the circle. The midpoint of the screen was approximately at the subjects' eye level. The three exposure times were systematically varied over the three boxes following a Latin square schema.

An intermediate time of 60 msec was chosen on the basis of some pilot work in order that approximately 50% of the subjects could recognize the displayed object. Children were asked if they had recognized the displayed object, and the time needed for the answer was measured. Objective recognition probabilities for the three exposure times were in the range of 0, 50, and 100% (on average 94%). Later all subjects were given a chance to inspect all slides again in the three viewing boxes in the order of their choice. For this, subjects chose a box for the first viewing, inspected the slide by pressing a button, and then went on to the second and the third and last box. We took the rank order of this choice, the subjects' preference function, as the indicator of the amount of curiosity for the three sets of slides presented at different lengths of exposure. For the data analysis subjects were divided into three age groups: 1 (from 3:6–4:5 years); 2 (from 4:6–5:5 years); and 3 (from 5:6–6:5 years). There were 13 boys and 14 girls in each age group.

Figure 9.2a presents the recognition frequencies (in %) for the two picture series in the three age groups as a function of three predetermined exposure times. The percentages of recognition are highly similar for the two series, toys and animals, and for the three age groups. On the basis of the relative frequencies of recognition, objective uncertainty values for the three age groups and the two series could be calculated (Fig. 9.2b) by using Shannon's formula (Shannon & Weaver, 1949).

Averaged decision times, the behavioral measure of subjective uncertainty, reflect the objective uncertainty values of the exposure times perfectly in the middle and oldest group—but not in the youngest group of children, those between 3:6 and 4:5 years old (Fig. 9.2c).

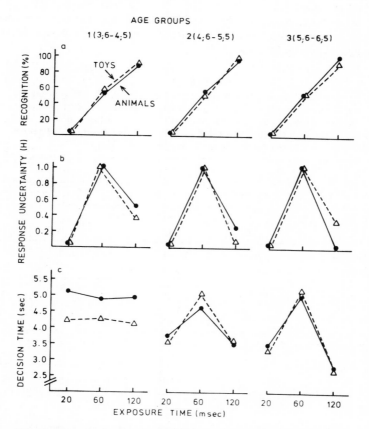

FIG. 9.2 Mean recognition percentages of the figures at each exposure time (Fig. 9.2a), corresponding mean objective uncertainty values, and decision times (Fig. 9.2b and 9.2c) of the three age groups for the two series of slides (toys and animals). There are 13 boys and 14 girls in each age group.

An analysis of variance of the decision times not only demonstrated the highly significant main effect for exposure time (F (2, 243) = 28.8, $p <$ .001) but also a significant interaction age $\times$ exposure time (F (4, 243) = 9.49, $p <$ .001). Exposure time has apparently no effect on the decision time of the youngest children but influences decision time in the way predicted by the information theory model for children from 4½ years on. The computation of simple main effects for each group confirms this. The effect of objective uncertainty (exposure time) is significant ($p <$ .001) in the second and third age groups, not in the first.

The sequences in which the viewing boxes (exposure times) were chosen for further inspection were related to subjective uncertainty only in the group of oldest children, ages 5½ to 6½. In Table 9.1 the frequencies in which the different boxes were chosen as the first, the second, and the third for further viewing are presented as a function of subjective uncertainty (decision time) for the three age groups and the two slide series.

TABLE 9.1
Frequencies of Choosing Boxes Associated with Long (l), Intermediate (i), and Short (s) Decision Times (Subjective Uncertainty) as the First, the Second, and the Third for Further Viewing (Preference Order) for the Three Age Groups and the Two Slide Series (Animals and Toys). There are 27 Children in Each Age Group

	Age groups								
	1(3:6–4:5)			2(4:6–5:5)			3(5:6–6:5)		
	Preference Order								
	1	2	3	1	2	3	1	2	3
Decision Time					Animals				
l	6	10	11	6	8	13	19	7	1
i	8	11	8	8	11	8	5	15	7
s	13	6	8	13	6	8	3	5	19
			n.s.			n.s.			z = 6.16 p < .001
					Toys				
l	6	9	10	3	12	12	15	7	5
i	8	12	7	15	6	6	2	13	12
s	11	6	10	9	9	9	10	6	11
			n.s.			n.s.			z = 1.73 p < .05

Note: Each child's preference order for a second inspection of the three slides is related in this table to the rank order of the three decision times of each child, regardless what the exposure times and the objective uncertainties of the three presentations were.

The relationship between subjective uncertainty (decision time) and preference for a second inspection of the different slides is only significant in the oldest children, aged 5:6 to 6:5 years (Page-test; see Lienert, 1973).

MANIPULATORY EXPLORATION

The operational definition for the construct of curiosity in the first study was the preference order for a second viewing of the exposed figures. Viewing or visual inspection is only one way to investigate a new object. There are others of equal importance like manipulation and asking questions.

In addition, the dynamics of uncertainty increase and reduction is not manifested in such preference data which do not document the stream of exploratory behavior. Therefore, we planned studies in which the sequences of exploratory and other behaviors should be assessed and related to assumed changes in subjective uncertainty. In the first of the following studies, subjective uncertainty was inferred from behavioral signs shown spontaneously by the children; in the second and third study subjective uncertainty was manipulated experimentally.

Nearly 20 years ago Corinne Hutt (1966) described a typical sequence of specific, object-instigated, and diversive exploratory behaviors in preschool children in a situation where the children were confronted with a new play object in combination with well-known toys. When entering the room the children "looked at the novel object immediately, or approached it, often asking the observer what it was. They would then examine the object manually or inspect it visually . . . and finally engage in active manipulation of the lever" (p. 67).

In subsequent sessions investigatory behaviors became more seldom and gave way to play activities like incorporating the object into games or transposing its function (see also Hughes, 1978, 1979; Hutt, 1970). At this point the children may have learned enough about the novel object. They no longer experience uncertainty about what the object is all about and go on to play with that object or even get bored and look for new activities (see Hughes, 1983; Nunnally & Lemond, 1973).

In some pilot work with an adaptation of Hutt's novel object, we observed among preschool children that specific exploration gave way to forms of diversive exploration and play even within a 15-minute observation period. We assumed that subjective uncertainty instigated by such a novel object in children of this age group is reduced already in 10 minutes or so, i.e., that by the end of that time children know the main functions of the object and go ahead to other activities. The goal of the second and third studies, therefore, was to examine if the transition between different forms of specific exploration and play in a short observation period of 15 minutes is caused by a decrease of subjective uncertainty instigated by that novel object.

Study II

The first study of this series tried to answer this question indirectly through an examination of the differences between different age groups in a cross-sectional comparison and by a correlational approach. Our main concern in this study, however, was, as mentioned before, to document the temporal sequence of exploratory behavior and play in an initial brief encounter with a novel object.

The object was a wooden box (20 × 30 × 30 cm) with a metal lever on top movable in all directions. Movements in the four main directions triggered either the flashing of a red or green lamp, inserted into the top of the box at both sides of the lever, or a high or deep sound from inside the box. The position of the lever at which these effects could be produced changed irregularly after 1 to 5 minutes. We assumed that those children who recognized the changing function of the lever movements and indicated this in spontaneous verbal and nonverbal signs would become more uncertain again and explore the object longer.

The novel object was offered to the child in the observation room together with three well-known toys: a puzzle, a doll, and a truck. At the outset we adapted not only Hutt's novel object but also her observation system. Our final checklist had 12 categories, 5 of which represented specific exploration; 3, play; and 4, nonobject-related activities (see Table 9.2). Because we were interested especially in question asking as one form of specific curiosity, all verbal reactions were recorded with a tape recorder and later categorized (see Moch, this volume).

Children were observed for 15 minutes using an instantaneous time sampling method. Every 10 seconds the observer sitting in the back of the room marked on the checklist the behavior that had just occurred. If two or more exploratory behaviors had been observed at the same point, the one highest in the list from 1 to 8 (Table 9.2) was scored. All observation was done in the different institutions attended by the children.

Two of the 87 boys and girls between 3 and 7:5 years confronted with the novel object did not explore at all. In more than half of all recorded events (54%), the remaining 85 children explored the novel object in one way or other or used the object in different kinds of play.

Only a quarter (24%) of the 4- to 7-year-old children gave verbal and nonverbal signs indicating that they had recognized the change in the relationship between lever movement and light and sound effects, whereas none of the 3-year-old subjects had apparently recognized this. The recognition of the change in the functions of the apparatus correlated significantly (point biserial correlation) with observed manipulation of the lever (.51, $p < .001$) and also with the number of electronically counted lever movements (.34, $p < .001$), indicating that those subjects who had recognized the change and became, as we think, uncertain again continued to explore the novel object with manipulative behavior.

There were also differences between age groups during the period of object manipulation, which might be the expression of different rates of uncertainty reduction in the four age groups.

TABLE 9.2
Behavioral Categories Used to Observe the Exploratory and Other Behaviors Instigated by a Novel Object

Categories

A. Specific exploration

1. Looking ("orienting behavior": looking at the novel object from a distance)
2. Visual inspection (inspection of single parts of the object, subject is sitting or kneeling in front of the object)
3. Touching (touching of the box or single parts of it, touching without moving it)
4. Verbal reaction (questions and remarks about the novel object)
5. Manipulation (manipulating the lever)

B. Playing

6. Unconventional manipulation (manipulating the lever with parts of the body other than the hands, e.g., elbows, or from unusual positions, e.g., lying down)
7. Incorporation (including other toys in play with the new object)
8. Transposition of function (the novel object is used in a different play context, e.g., as a bridge, or it is used with a pretended function, e.g., as a telephone)

C. Nonobject related activities

9. Play (with the three familiar toys)
10. Locomotion (running, jumping, crawling, not associated with the object)
11. Observer reactions (looking, touching, and verbal communications not related to the object)
12. Room reactions (e.g., manipulating parts of the furniture, looking out of the window)

In Fig. 9.3 the curves over time of manipulation as well as of the two aggregated categories of perceptual investigation (categories 1–4, see Table 9.2) and play (categories 6–8) are presented. As numbers of observations were low for perceptual investigation and play, observed events were grouped into blocks of 3 minutes. Subjects were divided into four age groups: (1) 3-year-olds (3:1–4:0; $n = 15$); (2) 4-year-olds (4:0–5:0; $n = 20$); (3) 5-year-olds (5:1–6:0; $n = 27$), and (4) 6-year-olds (6:0–7:5; $n = 25$). The numbers of boys and girls were approximately equal in the four age groups. Children of the oldest age group were attending a grade school; all other children were attending two different nursery schools.

Perceptual investigation declined over the observation period ($F (4, 316) = 4.82, p < .001$), only the linear trend being significant ($p < .01$). The frequency of manipulation, however, increased for the whole sample first to the midpoint of the period and then decreased ($F (4, 316) = 3.82, p < .01$). This quadratic trend ($F (1, 79) = 15.17, p < .01$) was different for the four age groups ($F (3, 79) = 6.31, p < .001$) and for the two sexes ($F (11, 179) = 8.18, p < .01$): Unlike the preschool children, the oldest subjects, the 6-year-old grade school children, reached their maximum of manipulation in the first 3 minutes (exactly in the third minute); girls reached their maximum earlier than boys. Besides that,

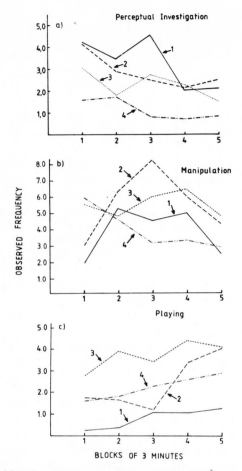

FIG. 9.3 Mean frequencies of perceptual investigation (9.3a), manipulation (9.3b), and playing (9.3c) in the four age groups (1 to 4) as a function of the observation time (blocks of 3 minutes).

a general effect for sex was found in this variable (F (1, 79) = 20.12, $p <$ .001): Boys manipulated significantly more than girls.

Finding out what the functions of the lever movements are—the lever and the optical and acoustical effects are the main features of the object—is only possible by manipulating the lever. Therefore, the increase of manipulatory behavior in the first half of the observation period might indicate an increase in subjective uncertainty because only at that point do the children realize the functions of lever movements are not stable. Alternatively, this effect could be explained by a sensory reinforcement hypothesis (see Rheingold, Stanley, & Doyle, 1964). The observation that older children reach their maximum of manipulation earlier was predicted on the assumption that older children understand the functions of the lever movements sooner. Probably the sex differences—girls reached their maximum of manipulation earlier than boys—could be explained in the same way. This is examined in a further study.

Playing with the new object (categories 6–8) was observed as predicted with increasing frequency towards the end of the period (F (14, 316 = 3.97, $p <$ .01).

Figure 9.4 presents the first-order transition among the different categories of specific exploratory behavior, playing, and nonrelated activities. The assumed sequence from visual inspection to manipulation and then to playing with the novel object was observed, although children shifted back and forth between categories of exploratory behavior and playing with the novel object (categories 6 and 7). Perhaps subjects found new aspects of functions of the novel object during play and went back to some further exploratory behavior. Thus there is a considerable amount of vacillation between exploring and playing even within a 15-minute observation period (see Weisler & McCall, 1976).

A hierarchical cluster analysis (single linkage analysis), using the transition probabilities between the 11 categories of Table 9.2 as indices of similarity, groups the forms of specific exploration together as well as two forms of playing with the new object, "unconventional manipulation" and "transposition of function" (Fig. 9.5). "Incorporation," the third form of playing, is grouped together with playing with the other toys, proving that this behavior is a transition state between dealing with a new object and playing with the familiar toys. "Looking," however, is grouped together with "locomotion/room" and "observer-reactions." Although looking is one form of exploration, it also marks a point of decision.

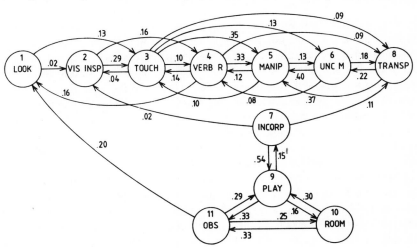

FIG. 9.4 Significant transition probabilities ($p < 0.05$; see Goodman, 1968) between the categories of behavior related to the novel object and the categories of other activities not related to the object (cat. 9, 10, and 11). Categories 10 and 12 were combined as one category.

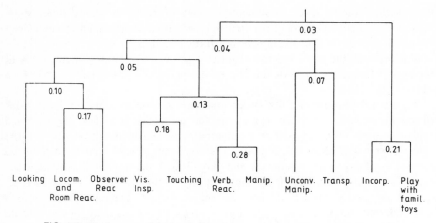

FIG. 9.5 Dendrogram of the results of a cluster analysis (single linkage analysis) using the transition probabilities between the behavioral categories of exploratory behavior, playing, and nonrelated activities (Table 9.2) in ascending order.

From here the child might either go on exploring the novel object or shift to other activities not related to the object. In the two following studies, subjective uncertainty was manipulated experimentally in order to examine our assumption that exploration is instigated and maintained by subjective uncertainty.

Study III

In this study an attempt was made to manipulate subjective uncertainty by keeping the function of the lever movements fixed for the whole observation period in one condition and changing it every second in an unpredictable way in the second half of the observation period in another condition. In both conditions the effects, which could be released by moving the lever in one of the four main directions, were fixed in the first 8 minutes of the observation period (15 minutes). After 8½ minutes the light and sound effects became random in the uncertain condition (UC) and remained the same in the certain condition (CC). We assumed that children would explore the novel object longer in the uncertain condition, especially in the last third of the observation period.

The novel object was presented again together with three familiar toys—a puzzle, a truck, and a teddy bear. Children were observed during the morning hours in a separate room in their nursery school. The behavior of 38 children ranging in age from 3:6 to 6:2 years was recorded on videotape during the whole observation period. Behavioral categories (see Table 9.2) were coded from the video screen with the help of slow motion and a timer. Beginning and ending times of all behaviors were recorded to the nearest 0.1 sec. In order to form an aggregated index of exploratory behavior, the amount of time that children were engaged in "looking" (No. 1), "visual inspection" (No. 2), "touching" (No. 3), or "manipulation" (No. 5) in each minute of the observation period was summed. Similarly, the amount of time children spent playing with the new object in the way of "unconventional" manipulation (No. 6), of transposing the function of the object (No. 8), and of incorporating other toys in a game with the novel object (No. 7) was summed for an index of playing.

Figure 9.6 demonstrates that the children spent more time exploring the novel object in the last third of the observation period in the uncertain condition, in which the light and sound effects of the box had become unpredictable, than in the certain condition. In the certain condition they spent more time playing with the novel object in the last part of the observation period than exploring it.

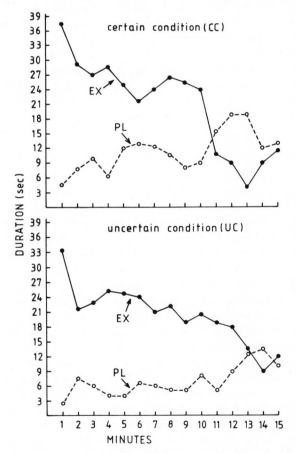

FIG. 9.6 Average time per minute spent in specific exploratory behavior of the novel object (EX) and playing with the novel object (PL) in the certain condition (CC) and uncertain condition (UC).

However, the differences between both conditions are not significant. An analysis of variance of the time spent in specific exploration for which the seconds per minute were summed for the first, the second, and the last third of the observation period (minutes 1–5, 6–10, and 11–15) proved only the main effect of time to be significant ($F(2, 68) = 18.16, p < .01$) not the interaction group $\times$ time ($F(2, 68) = 1.68$ n.s.). The increase in playing with the novel object is, roughly the same for both groups.

The main hypothesis that exploratory behavior is instigated and maintained by subjective uncertainty is thus not convincingly supported by the results of this study. Although some children in the uncertain condition explored the novel object to the very end of the observation period, others quit soon. Perhaps the ever-changing lever function in the last third of the observation period posed too big a problem for the children, causing them to give up exploring the object altogether because they lost hope that they could ever find out what effect the lever movements were supposed to have. For other children the manipulation of uncertainty was not effective. Some had already given up manipulating the lever in the first 10 minutes and therefore could not recognize the change; others apparently did not notice the change of the lever function because of their inadequate attention or information processing.

Experiment IV

In the following experiment the lever function changed in the uncertain condition after only 5 minutes and again after 10 minutes but remained stable in the interim. Thus the first change was at a time when most children were engaged in manipulating the lever, and the problem was such that they *could* find out what sound and lights were triggered by the lever movements. After the experiment the children were also asked whether they had recognized the change of the lever function. Other than that, the same general procedure was followed as in experiment III. Children were observed again, however, with an instantenous time sampling method (interval 10 sec) based on the checklist from experiment II. The subjects were 47 preschool children (24 girls and 23 boys) between 3:5 and 6:5 years old. Boys and girls were randomly divided into the two conditions of the study, the certain condition with the stable lever function and the uncertain condition with the lever function changing every 5 minutes. The frequencies of the behavioral categories "looking" (No. 1), "visual inspection" (No. 2), and "touching" (No. 3) were summed for an index of perceptual investigation, as were the frequencies of "unconventional manipulation" (No. 6), "incorporation" (No. 7), and "transposition of function" (No. 8) for an index of playing with the novel object. In Fig. 9.7 the mean frequencies for 3-minute blocks of these two aggregated indices and for manipulation are shown. For all three variables the effect of time is significant: (perceptual investigation: $F(4/80) = 13,95$, $p < .05$; manipulation: $F(4/180) = 2,69, p < .05$; playing: $F(4/180) = 3,57$,

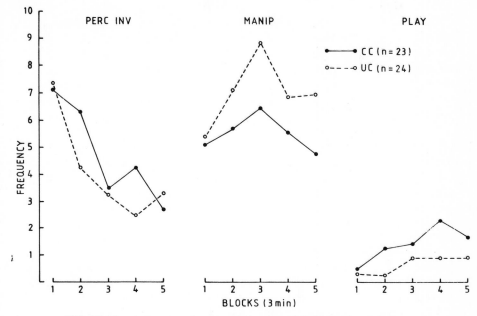

FIG. 9.7 Mean frequencies of perceptual investigation (PERC INV), manipulation (MANIP), and playing with the novel object (PLAY) for the uncertain (UC) and certain condition (CC) as a function of the observation time (blocks of 3 minutes).

$p < .01$). The main effects of the uncertainty manipulation were not significant in any case, nor were any of the interactions "condition $\times$ time" significant. However, as predicted, children manipulated more in the uncertain condition (F (1/45) = 1.43, (n.s.) and played more with the object in the certain condition (F (1/45) = 3.47, $p < .10$).

On the basis of the postexperimental questioning, children in the uncertain condition were divided into those who became aware of the changes of the lever function and those who did not. In Fig. 9.8 the average frequencies for manipulation in blocks of 3 minutes are presented for these two groups.

From the third 3-minute block, aware children manipulated on average twice as much as unaware children. Besides significant main effects for the conditions (F (1/22) = 5.13, $p < .05$) and the time (F (4/88) = 2.84, $p < .05$), there is a significant interaction "condition $\times$ time" (F (4/88) = 2.25, $p < .05$). Only those children who became aware of the change of the lever function continued manipulating the lever, presumably to find out what effects are caused by these movements.

In summarizing, we can conclude that the amount of subjective uncertainty created by a novel object determined the time spent exploring that object. The only way to find out what function the lever of our novel box had was to

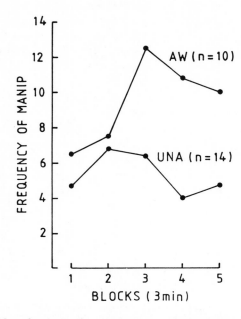

FIG. 9.8 Mean frequency of manipulation by those children in the uncertain condition who became aware of the changing lever function (AW) and by those who remained unaware (UNA) as a function of the time of the observation period (blocks of 3 minutes).

manipulate it. The children who recognized the change of the function kept manipulating the lever and thus could find out what the change of function was.

CONCLUSIONS

Therefore, we can conclude that subjective uncertainty seems to be an important variable controlling the switch from exploring a novel object to playing with it. However, this conclusion needs to be supported by more experimental evidence. In addition, the assumption proposed in the scheme presented in Fig. 9.1, that individuals will give up exploring an object if the payoff in uncertainty reduction or information intake has become too low, needs to be tested separately.

To be sure, the model proposed has to be expanded. Perceiving a novel object instigates subjective uncertainty as well as fear of the unknown. In the short, 15-minute observation period of our investigations, we were seldom able to observe diversive exploratory behavior—the child looking for something else to do (see Hughes, 1983)—at the end of the observation period. However, we did observe such behavior at the beginning. After looking at the novel object, some children did not explore but walked around and inspected the room, which was well known to them, addressed the experimenter or played with the familiar toys (see Fig. 9.4 and 9.5). However, the motivational state behind this behavior did not seem to be boredom but anxiety.

The antagonistic relationship between curiosity and anxiety was already noticed by students of emotions at the turn of the century (see Voss, 1984). In our model we may conceptualize this assumption in different ways: Either it could be assumed that one and the same object instigates two qualitatively different emotional states—subjective uncertainty and at the same time anxiety—leading to different behavioral tendencies competing for the final common path. Or we could follow McCall and McGhee (1977) in assuming that higher states of uncertainty are experienced less positively than intermediate states and that they finally become aversive. At the moment I prefer the conflict hypothesis of these two affective states and their related behavioral tendencies. We are planning studies in which exploratory behavior in preschool children will be examined as a function of both subjective uncertainty and fear of the novel object. We hope that this will help us to reconceptualize the model proposed.

SUMMARY

The usefulness of the concept of subjective uncertainty in predicting exploratory behavior in preschool children was examined in four studies. Perceptual investigation, i.e., the preference for a second inspection of briefly presented slides, was studied in the first experiment, perceptual and manipulatory exploration in the second, third, and fourth. In these experiments children were confronted with a novel object, Hutt's box, in which the movement of a lever on top of the box released sounds and light effects.

Subjective uncertainty was experimentally manipulated in the first study by the length of the exposure times of the slides and, with the novel object used in experiments II, III, and IV, through a varying relation between lever movements and light and sound effects. In both situations subjective uncertainty seemed to be an important cause for exploratory behavior. However, only those children who realized the varying relation between movements of the lever and effects on the novel object increased the frequency of their manipulation of the lever.

In addition, we found cross-sectional age differences for both situations. Only for children between 5:6 and 6:5 years of age could the rank order for a second inspection of the slides be predicted on the basis of their assessed subjective uncertainty values for the different presentations (Experiment I). On the other hand, manipulation of the lever atop the novel object used in Experiments II through IV peaked earlier among grade school children than among the younger children, presumably because subjective uncertainty was reduced earlier in the older children.

ACKNOWLEDGMENTS

I thank M. Friedemann for conducting the third experiment and F. Schneider for her help in coding the behavioral observations of this study. I thank also P. Hanses and C. Schrimpf for their help in conducting experiment IV.

REFERENCES

Berlyne, D. E. (1960). *Conflict, arousal, and curiosity.* New York: McGraw-Hill.
Berlyne, D. E. (1966). Curiosity and exploration. *Science, 153,* 25–33.
Berlyne, D. E.. (1978). Curiosity and learning. *Motivation and Emotion, 2,* 97–175.
Dember, W. N. & Earl, R. W. (1957). Analysis of exploratory, manipulatory and curiosity behavior. *Psychological Review, 64,* 91–96.
Goodman, L. A. (1968). The analysis of cross-classified data: Independence, quasi-independence and interactions in contingency tables with or without missing entries. *Journal of the American Statistical Association, 63,* 1091–1131.
Hughes, M. (1978). Sequential analysis of exploration and play. *International Journal of Behavioral Development, 1,* 83–97.
Hughes, M. (1979). Exploration and play re-visited: A hierarchical analysis. *International Journal of Behavioral Development, 2,* 215–224.
Hughes, M. (1983). Exploration and play in young children. In J. Archer & L. J. A. Birke (Eds.), *Exploration in animals and humans* (pp. 230–244). Wokingham: Van Nostrand Reinhold.
Hutt, C. (1966). Exploration and play in children. *Symposia of the Zoological Society,* London, *18,* 61–81.
Hutt, C. (1970). Specific and diversive exploration. In H. W. Reese & L. P. Lipsitt (Eds.), *Advances in child development and behavior* (Vol. 5, pp. 119–180). New York: Academic Press.
Lanzetta, J. T. (1971). The motivational properties of uncertainty. In H. I. Day, D. E. Berlyne, & D. E. Hunt (Eds.), *Intrinsic motivation: A new direction in education* (pp. 134–147). Toronto: Holt, Rinehart & Winston.
Lienert, G. A. (1973). *Verteilungsfreie Methoden in der Biostatistik* (Vol. 1, 2nd ed.). Meisenheim: Anton Hain.
Lorenz, K. (1969). Innate bases of learning. In K. H. Pribram (Ed.), *On the biology of learning* (pp. 13–93). New York: Harcourt.
McCall, R. B., McGhee, P. E. (1977). The discrepancy hypothesis of attention and affect in children. In F. Weizmann & I. Č. Užgiris (Eds.), *The structuring of experience* (pp. 179–210). New York: Plenum.
McReynolds, P. (1971). The three faces of cognitive motivation. In H. I. Day, D. E. Berlyne, & D. E. Hunt (Eds.), *Intrinsic motivation: A new direction in education* (pp. 33–45). Toronto: Holt, Rinehart & Winston.
Nunnally, J. C., & Lemond, L. C. (1973). Exploratory behavior and human development. In H. W. Reese (Ed.), *Advances in child development and behavior* (Vol. 8, pp. 59–109). New York: Academic Press.

Rheingold, H. L., Stanley, W. C., & Doyle, G. A. (1964). Visual and auditory reinforcement of a manipulatory response in the young child. *Journal of Experimental Child Psychology, 1,* 316–326.

Schneider, K., Barthelmey, E., & Herrmann, P. (1981). Subjektive Unsicherheit and visuelle Exploration bei Kindern im Vorschulalter. *Zeitschrift für Entwicklungspsychologie and Pädagogische Psychologie, 13,* 106–115.

Schneider, K., & Heckhausen, H. (1981). Subjective uncertainty and task preference. In H. I. Day (Ed.), *Advances in intrinsic motivation and aesthetics* (pp. 149–167). New York: Plenum.

Schneider, K., Moch, M., Sandfort, R., Auerswald, M., & Walther-Weckman, K. (1983). Exploring a novel object by preschool children: A sequential analysis of perceptual, manipulating and verbal exploration. *International Journal of Behavioral Development, 6,* 477–496.

Shannon, C. E., & Weaver, W. (1949). *The mathematical theory of communication.* Urbana: University of Illinois Press.

Sorentino, R. M., Short, J.-A. C., & Raynor, J. O. (1984). Uncertainty orientation: Implications for affective and cognitive views of achievement behavior. *Journal of Personality and Social Psychology, 46,* 189–206.

Voss, H.-G. (1984). Curiosity, exploration, and anxiety. In H. van der Ploeg, R. Schwarzer, & C. D. Spielberger (Eds.), Advances in test anxiety research (Vol. 3, pp. 121–146). Lisse: Swets.

Weisler, A., & McCall, R. B. (1976). Exploration and play. *American Psychologist, 31,* 492–508.

CHAPTER TEN

ASKING QUESTIONS:
AN EXPRESSION
OF EPISTEMOLOGICAL
CURIOSITY IN CHILDREN

MATTHIAS MOCH
Verein für Sozialtherapie, Tübingen

Among the different modalities of exploratory behavior, epistemological curiosity (from *episteme* [Greek]: knowledge) takes a position of its own. Berlyne (1954) defined it as an exploration of symbolically representable contents aimed at increasing one's knowledge. This clearly separates it from purely perceptive curiosity. According to Berlyne (1960), knowledge allows "stimuli that belong to the past or the future, or even stimuli that will never be part of the stimulus field, to make their influence felt through their internal representatives" (p. 266). Asking questions is one of the main expressions of epistemological curiosity, in addition to observation and directed thinking. Isaacs (1930) stressed the function of asking questions as an expression of children's attempt to test the adequacy and applicability of their own schemes of thinking. Such questions will mostly be stimulated by their widening field of perception or by contradictions in their scheme of thinking.

Along with the cognitive development of a child, the questions will shift both in grammatical form (Davis, 1932) and in the aspects of reality considered. Until the end of the third year, the different question types concerning name, place, time, and reason will be acquired in this order (Savic, 1975). There remains a close connection between the cognitive development in the child and the degree of abstraction in the questions asked (Arlin, 1977).

So far, relatively few experimental studies have been conducted on the question-asking behavior of children in specific situations of curiosity. It usually proved difficult to investigate spontaneous questioning under concretely circumscribed and comparable conditions. Therefore, the reports cited often are limited to observations of particular cases in daily life. Other, rather experimentally oriented investigations (Berlyne & Frommer, 1966; Ross & Balzer, 1975) do actually focus on the situative instigators of questioning and, therefore, their curiosity-satisfying character. Pictures or objects with strange properties eliciting uncertainty instigate the greatest amount of epistemological curiosity. But in the experiments referred to here, the children were requested to ask questions according to the presented stimuli. This prevented questions from being asked spontaneously within the context of a sudden conceptual conflict (Berlyne, 1960; Isaacs, 1930) and from being linked with the perceptive and manipulative aspects of behavior from which questions often arise only during the process of activity.

This shortcoming was eliminated by Henderson (1981), who examined the ways in which children's question asking was influenced by peers present in a free-exploration situation and the special properties of objects. He found that high-exploratory children could be expected to ask the most questions when they were alone with the experimenter and when the objects had movable parts and high perceptual attractiveness rather than conventional or bizarre properties.

199

Whereas the purely informative aspect of questioning was shown through several studies (Endsley & Clarey, 1975; Robinson & Arnold, 1977), the social aspect of questioning to which Lewis (1938) referred in his study on the development of children's questions has been neglected in most of the more recent investigations. Lewis discovered that the first questions children ask adults when acquiring language have the character of testing language as an instrument of social interaction.

Thus children use questions in a social sense very early on to induce grown-ups to engage in some activity ("Can't we go for a walk?"), to express a want ("Where is my ball?"), or to invent a game (Piaget, 1959), for instance. Therefore, the adults are actually the ones who interpret such expressions of desire as questions, and they answer accordingly. According to Lewis, this is how the children learn to ask questions. The informational function develops from the need for social feedback. The actual, epistemological character of questioning becomes significant only when the child recognizes the opportunity to replace his physical means of satisfying curiosity with the instrument of questioning.

Such different pragmatic functions and the substance of children's questions have only rarely been investigated. Paying particular attention to such relevant aspects as accompanying activity, motivation, and the questioner's topic of conversation at home and at school, Tizard, Hughes, Carmichael, and Pinkerton (1983) examined the context in which 4-year-old girls asked questions. They also pointed out that many questions do not have the function of satisfying curiosity but rather express other needs like planning an activity or challenging an adult's admonition.

A brilliant study that emphasized different pragmatic functions of children's questions was reported by James and Seebach (1982). These authors observed children in various situations in their day-care center and discriminated informational, conversational, and directive functions. They found that the number of informational questions in their early acquired form decreased as the children grew older, whereas the number of questions with directive and conversational functions became more frequent.

The latter two investigations also were carried out in a great variety of everyday life situations. Because of this it is difficult to compare the different findings about the development and accompanying conditions of the epistemological function of questions.

In our investigation of the development and significance of childlike questioning, we thus tried to consider the aforementioned aspects of question asking, i.e., situation, spontaneity, and function, in a more experimental way. In this respect the present study goes beyond investigations so far available. The main goals of this study are (a) to investigate the spontaneous question asking of children in a circumscribed curiosity situation in connection with other explorative modalities of behavior, (b) to record the changes in question frequency over time during the course of observation, and (c) to clarify the function of different classes of questions asked during the exploration of a new object. Additionally, the frequency of questions in different age classes and different types of informational questions, as observed by Piaget (1923), are to be recorded.

THE STUDY

Method

The data used in this study stem from the experiments also reported on by Schneider (this volume). For a closer description of the subjects, apparatus, and procedure, refer to Chapter 9 (see also Schneider, Moch, Sandfort, Auerswald, & Walther-Weckman, 1983).

Subjects. There were 87 boys and girls between 3 and 7:5 years of age who took part. They were divided into four age groups: 3- to 4-year-olds (15), 4- to 5-year-olds (20), 5- to 6-year-olds (27), and 6- to 7-year-olds (25). The three younger groups all attended kindergarten. The oldest group consisted of primary school children.

Procedure. After the two experimenters (one male, one female) had taken part for 3 days in the daily kindergarten program or the school class and had become familiar with the children, the actual experiment started. The children were led individually into a familiar room that bordered directly on their play-rooms. In the middle of the room, four toys lay on the floor. Three of them came from the play material of the institution and were quite well known to the children. The fourth toy was absolutely new for the children. It was a green wooden box modelled after a toy described by Hutt (1966). Moving a lever on the top of the box produced different sound and light effects. To induce conceptual conflict, the relationship between lever movements and effects was randomly changed every 1 to 5 minutes.

Upon entering the room, the child was instructed by the male experimenter with the following words:

> Look here (name) ! We have put here something to play with. You can play with all the things and do what you like. We will watch for a little while, and if you want to ask something, just ask. You can sit there and I shall sit there. Everything clear? Well then, let's start!

Then the male experimenter sat near the child on the floor. The female experimenter sat in the background. The observation period lasted 15 minutes. All questions were answered in a standardized way by the experimenter, who was sitting near the child. During the whole observation phase, all verbal reactions were recorded by a tape recorder, and the transcribed questions were categorized afterwards as follows:

Informational questions were questions whose main function consists in demanding information about a happening, an incident, or an object. This information equips the child with knowledge about the conditions of his environment. These questions were differentiated from the socioemotional questions, whose main function consists in demanding feedback about one's own social behavior, giving expression to an emotional sensation, or requesting an action or reaction from the partner.

The main category of informational questions was subdivided according to a scheme developed by Piaget (1923) that distinguishes among questions concerning explanations, facts, classifications, and motivations and actions. Additionally, expressions of surprise and perplexity such as "oh" and "ah" were registered. With the socioemotional questions we distinguished all functions of asking permission, seeking social contact, and maintaining a conversation or play activity in a rhetorical manner. Examples of the various types of questions are listed in Table 10.3. Two judges had to assign each question to one of these categories. Additionally, we distinguished questions about the new object and about other things.

The coefficient of inter-rater agreement in the classification of the questions was .82 (in 949 observations). The frequencies of informational and socioemotional questions were subjected to a $4 \times 2 \times 5$ analysis of variance using the variables of age, sex, and time.

Results

There were 15 of the 87 children who asked no question at all. Of these, 7 were boys, and 8 were girls. In this group there were four 3-year-olds, four 5-year-olds, two 3-year-olds, and five 6-year-olds. Furthermore, 3 girls did actually ask socioemotional questions, but no informational questions.

A total of 949 questions were asked during the 15-minute exploration phase, yielding an average of 10.9 questions per child. Of the questions posed, 80% were informational ($M = 8.8$, $SD = 10.5$) and 20% socioemotional ($M = 2.1$, $SD = 4.6$). This difference was significant ($z = 6.7$, $p < .001$, using the Wilcoxon-test for matched pairs).

The informational questions mainly concerned the new toy (67%, $M = 5.9$, $SD = 6.6$) rather than other things (33%, $M = 2.9$, $SD = 6.1$). This difference was also significant ($z = 4.8$, $p < .001$). Only 24% of the children gave a verbal or nonverbal expression of having noticed the changes in the coupling of lever movements and sound and light effects. The mean number of informational and socioemotional questions in the experimental groups is shown in Table 10.1. The results of the analysis of variance are stated in Table 10.2.

TABLE 10.1
Mean Number and Type of Questions Asked by Children During a 15-Minute Period of Play with a Novel Object

Age	n^a	Informational Questions		Socioemotional Questions	
		Boys	Girls	Boys	Girls
3:1–4:0	7/8	6.7	10.5	0.4	8.5
4:1–5:0	8/12	15.8	12.0	1.5	2.5
5:1–6:0	15/12	6.9	4.0	0.8	1.7
6:1–7:5	11/14	9.5	8.3	1.4	1.9

^{a}Number of boys/number of girls.

TABLE 10.2
Analysis of Variance of Number of Questions Asked by Children During a 15-Minute Period of Play with a Novel Object

Source	df	MS	F	P
		Informational Questions		
Age (A)	3	53.27	2.46	N.S.
Sex (S)	1	5.98	0.28	N.S.
A × S	3	9.06	0.42	N.S.
Error	79	21.70		
Time (T)	4	14.20	3.81	< 0.01
T × A	12	3.17	0.85	N.S.
T × S	4	2.33	0.63	N.S.
T × A × S	12	1.14	0.31	N.S.
Error	316	3.73		
		Socioemotional Questions		
Age (A)	3	7.30	2.02	N.S.
Sex (S)	1	27.60	7.65	< 0.01
A × S	3	10.99	3.05	< 0.05
Error	79	3.61		
Time (T)	4	3.05	3.98	< 0.01
T × A	12	1.94	2.53	< 0.01
T × S	4	3.75	4.89	< 0.01
T × A × S	12	2.76	3.61	< 0.001
Error	316	0.77		

There was no significant difference between the number of informational questions in boys and girls. The age function showed a peak at ages 4 to 5, and there was a distinct difference between the children in this "question-asking age" (Bühler, 1930) on one hand and older and younger children on the other. Still, the overall effect of age was not statistically significant.

Now we turn to the time development of the frequency of the informational questions (see Fig. 10.1). For the analysis, the observation time of 15 minutes was divided into five blocks of 3 minutes. After the first 3 minutes informational questions decreased on average to a fixed value of about one question per 3 minutes. The time effect was significant.

Unlike the other age groups, the 4- to 5-year-olds showed a more or less constant question frequency over the entire observation time. This effect was not significant, though, and neither was the sex × time interaction.

The distribution of the socioemotional questions showed a completely different pattern: The average frequency increased significantly with time. Additionally, the difference between boys and girls was significant, the girls using questions rhetorically or to establish social contact more often than boys. This effect requires closer investigation because the interactions age × time and age × sex × time were also significant.

Separate ANOVAs for boys and girls proved the general effect of time and time × age to be significant only for girls, F (2, 84) = 5.55, $p < .01$ and F (6, 84) = 3.09; $p < .01$, respectively. These results are shown in Fig. 10.2a and 10.2b.

Additionally, separate single comparisons for the four age groups of girls showed a significant time effect only for the 3- to 4-year-olds, F (2, 84) = 9.19, $p < .001$.

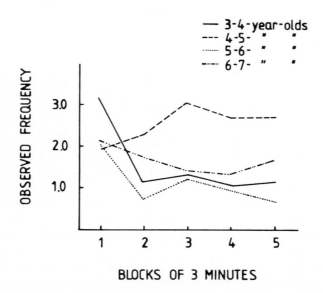

FIG. 10.1 Mean frequencies of informational questions in the four age groups as a function of the observation time (blocks of 3 minutes).

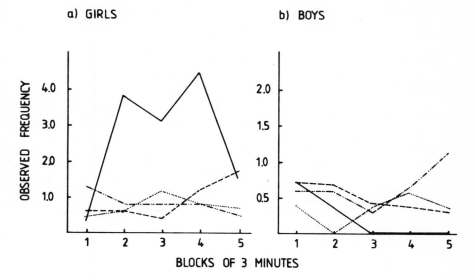

FIG. 10.2 Mean frequencies of socioemotional questions for girls ($n = 46$) and boys ($n = 41$) in the four age groups as a function of the observation time (blocks of 3 minutes).

More detailed information about the different functions of the questions is given by the consideration of the various question types, for which some examples are listed in Table 10.3.

The distributions of the question types inside the two main categories (informational and socioemotional) over sex and age groups differed greatly. Because of the many zero-values, analyses across subjects were not conducted. Examples of the different informational question types were observed in only about half the children, and the different socioemotional types in only a third. Therefore, age and sex differences were tested with the median test. The only significant age effect occurred in the questions about facts ($\chi^2 = 10.3$, $df = 3$, $p < .05$). Fact questions were more frequent in the two younger groups than in the two older groups.

Table 10.4 shows the percentages of the different question types summed up for each age group. More than half the informational questions asked by the youngest children were questions about facts. Desires for explanation made up

TABLE 10.3
Examples of Different Types of Informational and Socioemotional Questions

Question Type	Examples
Informational	
Explanation	Why is the red light flashing now?
	How can I make the sound ringing?
Facts	Is there electricity in here?
	Where is the switch?
Classification	What is this?
	Is this a fire-fighter's care?
Motivation and action	Why did you bring this here?
	Do you hear the sound?
Expression of perplexity	Hm? (astonished)
	How? (while exploring)
Socioemotional	
Permission	May I sit on the box here?
	Shall I tilt it on this side?
Rhetorical	(while playing with the sounds:)
	Did someone ring the bell?
Social contact	Shall we play this game together?

TABLE 10.4
Percentage of Questions of Different Types for Each Age Group

Question Type	Age			
	3:1–4:0	4:1–5:0	5:1–6:0	6:1–7:5
Informational questions				
Explanation	21	33	36	16
Facts	52	37	24	34
Classification	16	10	19	19
Motivation	9	18	14	24
Perplexity	2	2	7	7
Total number of questions	132	270	151	210
Socioemotional questions				
Permission	10	33	22	22
Rhetorical	79	60	72	44
Contact	11	7	6	34
Total number of questions	71	42	32	41

206

about one fifth of the informational questions. In the 4- to 5-year-olds, each of these two types of questions accounted for about one third of all questions asked. In the older age groups the proportion of all questions accounted for by classification questions and expressions of perplexity increased, and the 5- to 6-year-olds asked more explanation questions than other informational types. The children of the oldest age group expressed a higher number of demands for social contact in question form, whereas the younger groups particularly asked rhetorical questions during their play.

There were two remarkable sex differences in the percentual distribution of the question types. Although the total number of informational questions was nearly equal for girls and boys (382 and 381, respectively), boys asked more explanation questions than girls (33 and 20%, respectively). In the category of socioemotional questions, girls asked more rhetorical questions than boys (75% of 144 questions and 33% of 42 questions, respectively).

Obviously, the strong decrease in informational questions after the first 3 minutes of the observation time is mainly due to the decrease of classification and explanation questions. Thirty-five percent of the explanation and 41% of the classification questions were asked in the first 3 minutes. This portion decreased with time; during the last 3 minutes it was only 12% in both cases. Fig. 10.3 depicts the time development of the different question types in more detail. The fact and motivational questions increased toward the end of the observation period, and the rare expressions of perplexity increased slightly during the exploration as well.

The correlation of the two main question categories and the different types of informational questions with nonverbal expressions of curiosity (see Schneider et al., 1983) was analyzed. Significant correlation was found between the number of informational questions and the complete time used for exploration of the novel toy ($r = .28, p < .01$), the number of lever manipulations ($r = .18, p < .05$), time used for perceptual investigation as visual inspection and touching ($r = .21, p < .05$), and time used for manipulating the toy ($r = .19, p < .05$).

The socioemotional questions correlated only with the variable of "play" and not with the explorative variables mentioned previously. The portion of observation time used for exploration of the novel toy correlated with the following informational question types: explanation ($r = .40, p < .01$) and fact ($r = .29, p < .01$). Expressions of perplexity showed significant correspondence with the variable of "manipulative exploration" ($r = .42, p < .01$) and with the variable of noticing the varying lever functions ($r = .47, p < .01$).

Discussion

Spontaneous questioning as a form of epistemological activity of curiosity in connection with other kinds of exploratory behavior was investigated in this study. It has become apparent that the questions children ask in a circumscribed

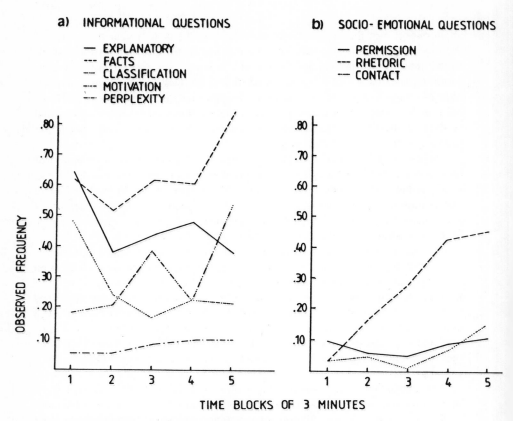

FIG. 10.3 Mean frequencies of different question types of (a) informational and (b) socioemotional questions as a function of the observation time (n = 87).

situation of curiosity in which they are confronted with a new item mainly have the function of reducing as quickly and as effectively as possible great subjective uncertainty present in the beginning. The informational questions refer largely to that object that was new and unfamiliar to the children. Decisive information is obtained in the very first minutes in order to reduce uncertainty, whereby the new object, its attributes, its origin, and its functions are classified accordingly. This search for information precedes an intensive manipulative investigation and, perhaps foremost, constitutes a secure basis for this.

Questions of classification notwithstanding, questions about the explanation of the physical surroundings seems to have the highest informational value in new situations. On the other hand, questions about motivation and action reflect rather desires for security in the social field and become important only after the orientation in the physical environment. Thus motivational questions have functions that are informative as well as socially orienting.

After the first few minutes of the encounter with the new object, during which the children asked the bulk of the informational questions, remarkably less verbal information was demanded, except by the 4- to 5-year-olds, who showed a more persistent manner of inquiry. Children of this age group, which Bühler (1930) described already as a questioning age, asked most of the questions. In children older than 5 years, the activity of questioning clearly declines. Two considerations might help explain these observations. First, the 4-year-olds are in a stage of development that enables them to exploit fully the informational function of their language competence. They thus feel it to be a challenge to construct and keep retesting new hypotheses based on the answers they receive. The incentive to ask questions arises for them especially through the newly experienced discrepancy between available and possible information that is quickly mediated through speech. This interpretation would partly correspond to the finding of Tizard et al. (1983), who also worked with 4-year-olds, that passages of persistent questioning occur in the majority of cases when children are chatting to an adult who is occupied with some activity and that this questioning refers to topics outside the present context.

The second consideration concerns the interaction between the specific character of the situation (such as the degree of novelty or complexity of the stimulus field) and the cognitive state of development. As earlier studies (Davis, 1932; Smith, 1933) have already suggested, only certain aspects of situations or contents are conflict inducing and therefore "interesting" for certain age groups. This would signify that the new toy we used carried attributes that induced epistemological curiosity, especially for the 4-year-olds.

Our main result is the sharp distinction drawn between informational and socioemotional questions. The epistemological character of informational questions is evident in the typical development in time, known to be valid for other explorational activities over longer periods of time, too (see Hutt, 1966), as well as in the correlation with specific curiosity variables such as visual inspection, touching, and manipulation. This correlation was not shown in the socioemotional questions as defined here. As the play aspect starts dominating over pure exploration and as the contact with adult playmates increases, the nonepistemological questions become more frequent in girls.

When we compare our results with the findings of James and Seebach (1982), the proportion of informational questions among all questions asked by the children we studied are much higher in all age groups, a fact due to the specific situation of curiosity in our study. On the other hand the case is very similar with questions having clear social functions like asking for permission or requesting contact with the listener or some activity. Questions about motivation of behavior (such as "Why don't we read this book?"), which in our study are counted under the epistemological functions, also serve the function of social directives. The older the children, the higher the proportion of their questions expressing social requests and invitations.

Our results can even clarify partly conflicting earlier opinions about sexual differences. Girls do not ask more questions to obtain information but rather to seek contact this way in a playful, social manner. Furthermore, young children seem more interested in static information such as existence, description, location, and other statistical attributes than older children are, as one can see from the greater number of fact questions that young children ask. It is possible that the logical structure of these questions is easiest to handle for the younger children.

Signs of perplexity and astonishment often are expressions of internal conflict (Berlyne, 1960) and are more closely linked to manipulative than verbal exploration. They cannot be considered to be questions directed toward another person but rather as requests of oneself to engage in further exploration.

Two aspects seem to be important to consider in further investigations. Our conjecture is that the content and complexity of the specific situation interact with the cognitive development of children as expressed through the questions they ask to increase their knowledge. This interaction needs closer exploration. Furthermore, it might be fruitful to pay more attention to the substance of the questions and their relation to the special elicitors, which might correspond to adventures in everyday life as well as to influences of certain stages of development.

SUMMARY

The epistemological function of children's questions are examined in an experimental study. Seventy-eight children who were between 3 and 7:5 years old played for 15 minutes with three familiar toys and one novel toy: a green wooden box fitted with wheels and a movable lever to produce different sound and light effects. All questions of the children were tape recorded and then classified according to their different communicative functions. The frequencies of the questions by sex, age, and time were observed. Most questions were asked by the 4-year-olds. A clear distinction between informational and social functions of questioning was found for all age groups, which is shown particularly by a different development of frequencies during the exploration time and also by various correlations to other behaviors of curiosity. Separate informational functions indicate different informational values of special types of questions. The discrimination between the epistemological and social nature of children's questions was discussed in comparison with results of earlier studies.

ACKNOWLEDGMENTS

I am grateful to Klaus Schneider for much helpful advice. Monika Auerswald deserves special recognition for her productive cooperation and critique during the execution of this study.

REFERENCES

Arlin, P. K. (1977). Piagetian operations in problem finding. *Developmental Psychology, 13,* 297–298.

Berlyne, D. E. (1954). A theory of human curiosity. *British Journal of Psychology, 45,* 180–191.

Berlyne, D. E. (1960). *Conflict, arousal, and curiosity.* New York: McGraw-Hill.

Berlyne, D. E., & Frommer, F. D. (1966). Some determinants of the incidence and content of children's questions. *Child Development, 37,* 177–189.

Bühler, K. (1930). *Die geistige Entwicklung des Kindes* (6th ed.). Jena: Fischer.

Davis, E. A. (1932). The form and function of children's questions. *Child Development, 3,* 57–74.

Endsley, R. C., & Clarey, S. A. (1975). Answering young children's questions as a determinant of their subsequent question-asking behavior. *Developmental Psychology, 11,* 863.

Henderson, B. B. (1981). Exploration by preschool children: Peer interaction and individual differences. *Merrill–Palmer Quarterly, 27,* 241–255.

Hutt, C. (1966). Exploration and play in children. *Symposia of the Zoological Society,* London, *18,* 61–81.

Isaacs, N. (1930). Children's "Why"-questions. In S. Isaacs (Ed.), *Intellectual growth in young children* (pp. 291–349). London: Routledge.

James, L. S., & Seebach, M. A. (1982). The pragmatic function of children's questions. *Journal of Speech and Hearing Research, 25,* 2–11.

Lewis, M. M. (1938). The beginning and early function of questions in child's speech. *British Journal of Educational Psychology, 8,* 150–171.

Piaget, J. (1923). *Le langage et la pensée chez l'enfant.* Neuchâtel: Delachaux et Niestlé.

Piaget, J. (1959). *La formation du symbole chez l'enfant.* Neuchâtel: Delachaux et Niestlé.

Robinson, W. P., & Arnold, J. (1977). The question–answer exchange between mother and young children. *European Journal of Social Psychology, 7,* 151–164.

Ross, H. S., & Balzer, R. H. (1975). Determinants and consequences of children's questions. *Child Development, 46,* 536–539.

Savic, S. (1975). Aspects of adult–child communication: The acquisition of questions. *Psychologia Wychowawcza, 18,* 629–640.

Schneider, K., Moch, M., Sandfort, R., Auerswald, A., & Walther-Weckman, K. (1983). Exploring a novel object by preschool children: A sequential analysis of perceptual, manipulating and verbal exploration. *International Journal of Behavioral Development, 6,* 477–496.

Smith, M. S. (1933). The influence of age, sex and situation on the frequency, form and function of questions asked by preschool children. *Child Development, 4,* 201–213.

Tizard, B., Hughes, M., Carmichael, H., & Pinkerton, G. (1983). Children's questions and adults' answers. *Journal of Child Psychology and Psychiatry, 24,* 269–281.

PART THREE

EMPIRICAL RESEARCH AND METHODOLOGICAL ISSUES: PLAY AND IMAGINATION

CHAPTER ELEVEN

THE EMERGENCE OF PLAY
IN PARENT–INFANT
INTERACTIONS

MECHTHILD PAPOUŠEK, HANUŠ PAPOUŠEK, and BETTY J. HARRIS
Max-Planck-Institut für Psychiatrie, München

Denn, um es endlich auf einmal herauszusagen, der Mensch spielt nur, wo er in voller Bedeutung des Worts Mensch ist, und er ist nur da ganz Mensch, wo er spielt.[1]

—Friedrich von Schiller in the fifteenth letter on the Aesthetic Education of Man to the patron Friedrich Christian, Duke of Schleswig-Holstein-Augustenburg.

THE WAY TO THE ORIGINS OF PLAY

To play seems to be the easiest thing to do; to define play, however, is quite the opposite. The word *play* itself is a deceptively simple symbol masking a conglomerate of meanings, a rich kaleidoscopic picture of many facets and colors. Such a picture can hardly be captured in a single definition or concept. This difficulty has been acknowledged by the many students of play, who, coming from different fields of science, have attempted to operationalize the term. We believe it to be more advisable to modestly concentrate attention upon individual, partial aspects of play and, additionally, to follow a general developmentalistic recommendation and look more closely at the very origins of play. Elucidating the *status nascendi*—both phylogenetic and ontogenetic—of a difficult phenomenon may provide a clue for understanding the complexity of its later form.

In the case of play, unfortunately, the question of origins still escapes elucidation. Anthropologists lack the evidence of precultural products of playful activities; only comparative primatology and cross-cultural studies in surviving populations of hunter-gatherers allow a careful reconstruction of the history of play in human evolution. Infancy researchers have not yet paid enough experimental attention to the ontogenetic beginnings of play in order to establish whether there are parallels between the roles of play in the development of an individual and in the evolution of the entire species. And yet the interrelations between play, the evolution of culture, and the cognitive development of individuals represent a most interesting problem.

The idea that children acquire knowledge most easily in a playful way is not new and can be dated back to the founding of the academies of science prominent during the Enlightenment. Comenius was the first to consistently apply the principle of playfulness to educational systems in a book, *Schola Ludus* (1657). He also wrote *Orbis Pictus*, a didactically revolutionary picture book for learning languages. A similar view of education can be seen in the writings of such outstanding educational theorists as Rousseau, Pestalozzi, Froebel, and Montessori.

---

[1]For, in order to tell it bluntly at last, man plays only where he is a man in the proper sense of this word, and he is every inch a man where he plays.

Progress in cognitive psychology in the 20th century has repeatedly brought the problems of play to the center of attention. Developmental psychologists have recognized the participation of a number of cognitive processes in children's play. Vygotsky, for instance, emphasized the role of rule detection, symbolic transformation, and exploration in various forms of play (Vygotsky, 1962). From the field of epistemology, Piaget (1951) examined the relative involvement of accommodation and assimilation, i.e., the two fundamental processes underlying cognitive development according to his concepts. In addition, child psychiatrists have drawn attention to the relation between play and emotionality as another aspect that is particularly relevant not only for interpretative but also for diagnostic and therapeutic approaches to behavioral and mental disorders in children (Erikson, 1963; Winnicott, 1971). The recent revival of interest in play as an educational tool has been reviewed carefully by Flitner (1973), who also stressed the favorable effect of play on learning and cognition.

The approaches exemplified by the aforementioned authors have concerned mainly the play of preschool and school-aged children. They have defined play within given situational contexts, focusing on the availability of toys and play-mates and leaving speculation on the early developmental stages of play aside. Other authors have considered much more general aspects of play; for instance the role of play in human culture was stressed in an interesting manner by Huizinga (1962). Examining artists' contributions to civilizing tendencies in the history of mankind, Huizinga argued that play has been the major determinant of human culture and suggested that humans should be classified as Homo ludens rather than Homo sapiens. With the widespread dissemination of Darwin's theory, increasing attention has been drawn to the evolutionary significance of play and also comparative research on play.

The growing amount of field observations of primate behavior, including various categories of play activities, social interactions, and cognitive capabilities, encouraged Bruner (1974) to combine evidence from comparative research with his own expertise in early human cognition and to suggest a detailed conceptualization of the evolutionary significance and functional characteristic of play. According to his concepts, the role of play has increased during evolution with the loosening of tight primate bonds in all three of the great apes species: the gorilla, the orangutan, and the chimpanzee. They all are virtually free of predators and have no need to defend a territory. Consequently, they are also less rigid in the rules of social hierarchy and reproductive behavior and show greater reciprocal exchange and altruism within groups as well as among groups. Infants depend on their mothers for a prolonged period of time during which more time is spent in play, and play is more frequently initiated by mothers. In considering the crucial functions of play, Bruner (1974, 1983) stressed that (a) play results in a reduction in the seriousness of the consequences of errors and setbacks; (b) it is characterized by a very loose linkage between means and ends, allowing frequent opportunities to try combinations of skills that would hardly be tried under functional pressure; (c) there is present in play an underlying scenario in which children create a rich and idealized imitation of life; (d) children use play to transform the external world according to their own perceptions; and, (e) play can function as a problem-solving situation that then serves as a source of pleasure when solutions are successfully discovered.

Thus in congruence with comparative and cross-cultural literature, Bruner depicts human childhood as an outcome of evolutionary adaptations that, to a certain degree, are similar in man and great apes. Selection has favored pressure-free periods of time in childhood during which the subroutines of adult skills can be acquired through observational learning and imitation. These activities are incorporated in playful combinations and varied ad libidum without much risk under the challenging guidance of an attentive, altruistic environment in small and relatively stable social groups. Comparative research (reviewed, for instance, by Bekoff, 1972; Hinde, 1971; Lorenz, 1970, 1971) has pointed out some universal prerequisites: the "babyishness" of the young and those various behavioral patterns signaling the intention to play that allow the organism to try out behaviors that, outside of play, would be considered threatening by the other individual and that would then lead to aggression. In human infants, too, "babyishness" elicits attention and readiness to help in adults (Hess, 1970), cues signals for play, such as the play–smile (van Hooff, 1962), and reduces the seriousness of rough-and-tumble play among children (Blurton Jones, 1972).

Conversely, some ethologists question the benefits brought about with the evolution of play, arguing that even among the great apes only a very small amount of play can be observed in gorillas (Schaller, 1963) and orangutans (MacKinnon, 1971) and, additionally, that increased exploratory and playful behaviors can increase the danger of predation and mortality as it has been reported in olive baboons (Berger, 1972) and chimpanzees (Teleki, 1973). However, the majority of researchers (Bekoff, 1972; Loizos, 1967; Poirier, 1972; Suomi & Harlow, 1971) have viewed play as an important factor in evolutionary adaptations. The fact that play characterizes only the higher vertebrates—there is, for instance, no evidence of play in reptiles—raises the question of whether and how play may be interrelated with the evolution of a larger brain.

Considering the evidence on tool use in the play of primates, Bruner (1974) made a rather unorthodox suggestion (p. 21) that, in order for tool use to develop, it was essential to have a long period of optional, pressure-free opportunities for combinatorial activities. Although Bruner does not go into detail, it is easy to imagine that this postulation may concern both the ontogenetic and phylogenetic emergence of tool use. In evolutionary terms it would then require the assumption of a long period of bipedalism that freed the hands and allowed a wide variation of subroutines upon which the selection of tool using could operate. The earlier, post-Darwinian interpretation, however, assumed a reverse order between bipedalism and tool use in which bipedalism evolved as a consequence of tool use. Interestingly, the recent discovery of fossil relics of the *Australopithecus afarensis* has dated the evidence for bipedalism in hominids almost 2 million years prior to the first paleontological evidence of tools. Some anthropologists (Lovejoy, 1981) have, therefore, suggested another interpretation. Lovejoy has suggested that bipedalism appeared perhaps merely as an incidental, genetic variation, disadvantageous due to slow locomotion but influential in the selection of compensatory social cooperation, communication, and cerebralization before tool use could emerge.

Lovejoy's interpretation stresses yet another interesting aspect of the natural selection process, namely, the potential of faster reproductive propagation in hominids as compared to other primates, and hence the necessity for hominid parents to care for several dependent offspring simultaneously. One could speculate, and it is only speculation, whether the coexistence of several siblings close in age might have favored the selection of play in hominids.

The evolution of human play has obviously been influenced by several circumstances that contribute to its species-specific features. The highly developed symbolic capacity of human speech, enculturation, the fine-grain division of professional tasks within social systems, and the separation of sexual activities from reproductive cycles do not only mark the departure points along the evolutionary path of differentiation between hominids and other primates, but they may also have much in common with the differential evolution of human play. Undoubtedly, humans also experience play as something particularly pleasurable; however, in this respect, it is rather difficult to compare human and animal feelings without anthropomorphizing. Using a preference selection paradigm, animal play has been shown to belong to the category of preferred activities (Mason, 1967). The mechanisms causing such preferences or expressions of joyful emotionality in humans still require further neurophysiological research, and understanding these mechanisms is crucial to the interpretation of both intrinsic motivation and evolutionary selection for play. As Bertrand (1969) stressed, linking a behavioral pattern with the internal experience of pleasure may be one of the best evolutionary tricks to ensure that the given pattern becomes part of the behavioral repertoire.

Most of the evidence that allows us to draw parallels between comparative animal research and human studies on play, as well as to conceptualize the evolution of play, have come from studies on preschool children (for instance, Hughes, 1978; Hutt, 1966; Sylva, Bruner, & Genova, 1976). Such studies can utilize children's capacities to communicate verbally, to understand instructions adequately, and to report, at least with some competence, on the course of their engagement in play. Observers can thus concentrate upon selected processes—physiological and psychological—involved in play and can modify experimental designs correspondingly. It would be superfluous to discuss the achievements of this approach in the presence of more competent contributors to this volume (see chapters by Fein and Hughes).

Rather, we are going to introduce some concepts about, and several pieces of evidence of, related problems in human infants as we have elaborated on them in our own studies. Understandably, the age peculiarities of infancy dictate restrictions and detours in experimental approaches, and instructions must give way to patient observations. The higher costs of research investment may, however, be counterbalanced by certain benefits, such as the lower degree of diversity in the behavioral repertoire of infants prior to the onset of verbal communication, which opens the door for effective cultural intervention. Although we have not primarily designed our studies to examine the problems of play, we have repeatedly been confronted with them while studying the early postpartum development of integrative capacities (i.e., the processes of exploration, learning, and cognition), the infant's emotionality, and the social interactions between infants and parents. During these recurring confrontations, it has become increasingly evident how intimate the ties are between integrative processes, play, emotionality, and social communication. In the next two sections of this presentation, we discuss these ties in greater detail, first outside the context of social interactions, then in relation to parental caregiving.

PLAY AND THE ACQUISITION OF KNOWLEDGE

As long as we have no direct approaches to observing the processes of thought in human infants, we have to focus our attention upon their responses to controlled environmental situations and attempt to infer some fundamental principles about the integrative processes in which these responses might have been rooted. This is easier to do in nonsocial laboratory settings with traditional stimulus–response types of experimental designs as they have been applied in studies on infant conditioning. During the last 2 decades, however, research on infants has moved away from designs based on behavioral learning theories towards more cognitively oriented approaches that require other, perhaps more difficult and thus more appealing, types of experimental designs. One component of exploratory mechanisms in infants—visual scanning—has been successfully utilized as a relatively easy methodology in intricate studies of cognitive operations involved in the processing of informational input (Haith, 1980). Unexpected cognitive competence has been evidenced, however, only on the perceptual side of behavioral regulation. If at this point we want to consider the other side of infant competence, namely, the integration of adaptive behaviors, in order to look there for the potential origins of playfulness, we must ask for the reader's patience as we make an excursion back to the earlier studies that one of the authors carried out on the learning competence of young infants. It was in these studies that H. Papoušek was first confronted with behaviors in learning situations that suggested playfulness.

Ludic Elements in Developing Integrative Processes

In studies described in detail elsewhere (H. Papoušek, 1961, 1967, 1977), long-term learning designs were modified so as to have a model in which a simple adaptive response—head turning—might be observed during its development from a fundamental reflexive response up to an intentional, purposeful act. For this reason, H. Papoušek's designs deviated from the traditional conditioning designs in the following ways: (a) As in Konorski's type of learning, an instrumental conditioning paradigm was combined with the application of conditioning signals. In other words, the presence of an acoustic stimulus signaled an opportunity to learn through trial and error how to achieve a relevant extrinsic reward (for instance, the delivery of milk or a visual display of blinking colored lights). This type of learning seemed to simulate naturalistic learning sets more adequately. Moreover, it allowed better utilization of the response latency as a parameter of adaptation; (b) the learning process was followed not only until the moment of significant evidence on learning but up to the level of stable performance of learned responses; (c) together with the substantial response in question, changes in general motility, breathing, heart rate, and vocal and facial expressions were recorded as well and provided additional information about ongoing behavioral integration; (d) the designs were modifiable so as to evoke integrative processes in varying degrees of complexity. They started with testing the forms of orienting to and exploring the novel acoustic stimulus, and in the advanced stages of the experiments they tested the achievement of extrinsic rewards requiring the detection of and adaptation to a rule of reinforcement in the absence of any instructions. The rules included simple numerical concepts that were not usually included in contemporary research with infants.

In relation to the topic of this chapter, two sets of conclusions derived from our studies on head turning can serve as points of departure for further considerations on the emergence of playfulness during early infancy.

First, in contrast to altricial development in neuromotor coordination, the development of central integrative processes in infants is obviously very rapid. From the first postpartum days on, the infant is capable of detecting the contingency of extrinsic events in relation to its own behavior and begins learning how to utilize such contingencies. During the first trimester, the infant's learning capacity is constantly improving. Learning capacities increase rapidly during the first 8 weeks, partly due to the infant's learning how to learn. It is during this period that the infant also masters discriminative learning. At age 4 months (no studies have been done at an earlier age), the infant can detect and conceptualize various rules introduced by observers as requirements for the achievement of a given reward. The rules used in our studies were, for instance, that turns of the head, learned in order to switch on a visual reward, elicited the desired effect only if carried out alternatively once to the left and once to the right, twice to the left and twice to the right, or grouped in homolateral triads, tetrads, etc. The infant was able to retain such learned concepts for over 72 hours, or to discard them and learn new ones. Rule detection, concept formation, and symbolic capacities that we mention in the next section thus develop early enough as prerequisites for the use of first words around the end of the first year. Such advances in central integration are unparalleled in other primates.

Second, the course of the aforementioned integrative processes appeared to be interrelated in interesting ways to the expression of emotionality and social communication. Relative to the age of the individuals, and particularly to their still immature motor coordination, the learning situations just described may represent problematic situations for young infants. As the changes in general motility, physiological functions, and facial and vocal behaviors indicated, the infant sometimes mobilized enormous efforts to solve the problem to which it had been exposed, although the physical quality of, for example, a visual reward had little to do with the infant's physiological needs. We can interpret *per exclusionem* that only some internal changes resulting from the perceptual-cognitive processing of the environmental situation are intrinsically motivating. Facial and vocal expressions signaling unpleasant feelings were indicative of the strenuousness of the effort involved in the learning process. With further progress in learning, the infant's responses became smoother, better coordinated, and reduced to only those movements crucial for the achievement of goals. The percentage of correct responses increased and, concurrently, signs of pleasant feelings, which sometimes escalated into signs of joy, prevailed in facial and vocal expressions. At this time, the infant's attention to extrinsic rewards decreased, making it even more obvious that some intrinsic motivation caused the infant to continue performing instrumental acts correctly and rapidly and to accompany these acts with signs of pleasure.

In order to verify the hypothesis on intrinsic motivation, H. Papoušek modified the learning experiments with appetitive reinforcement and prolonged experimental sessions in 4-month-old infants while offering milk as many times as necessary to satiate the infants. Even then, infants continued responding to the conditioning signals with fast, correct turns of the head and signs of pleasure although they refused more milk with slight signs of displeasure. Here was experimental evidence that 4-month-old infants could enjoy learning activities as such, independent of external rewards (H. Papoušek, 1967). The pleasure associated with their performance and the separation of means and goals correspond to the features of play described by Bruner (1974, 1983) as mentioned in the first section of this chapter. Thus the verification of the hypothesis on intrinsic motivation also served as a model of playful activities developing from simple, instrumental acts in conjunction with increased levels of integration.

Fundamental System of Adaptive Responses

In spite of a social vacuum in the laboratory setting, the central integrative processes in question appeared to be closely connected with expressions of emotionality and with features of playfulness. In the same vein, this process was accompanied by physiological changes in breathing, blood circulation, and motility, indicating a differential activation of mechanisms supportive of problem solving. It is possible for the observed expressions of emotionality to be interpreted as communicative signals indicating a need for social help or announcing the solution to a problem with a readiness to share the pleasure of success (Scheflen, 1969).

Such close ties between the observed phenomena, often treated as rather independent objects of interest by different subdisciplines of behavioral research, understandably raised the question whether these phenomena did not have some common roots in a fundamental system of adaptive responses that might be quite homogeneous and more easily detectable in the beginning of postpartum life. We have attempted to conceptualize and verify the existence of such a fundamental system (H. Papoušek & M. Papoušek, 1979), combining our observations with information available in neurosciences and believing that synthesis in relation to analysis of data and interpretation of meaning in addition to mere description should be attempted for the sake of future research strategies. Briefly, our concept is based upon several rather common assumptions. However, it may stress some of these aspects in uncommon contexts.

First, the set of central nervous processes involved in the perception and evaluation of any given situation and for the choice and organization of responses in any behavioral category is assumed to be the most general. Thus, it is the fundamental response system and is adaptive in an evolutionary sense.

Second, in accordance with the structure of a given situation (here emphasizing structure as opposed to physical qualities) and with its internal evaluation (with emphasis on the assessment of meaning), the fundamental system can mobilize or demobilize a broad repertoire of functions (the bidirectional and active regulation is stressed as opposed to unidirectional and on–off regulations). This repertoire may be much more unified than an observer of overt behavior is able to recognize and record, for he or she is inclined to observe categorically and to divide each complex unit into categories for the sake of easier description. In general, however, the fundamental system regulates the access to necessary information and processes of information (with respect to the individual's and the species' past experience). It operates in conjunction with the availability of energy reserves, the choice of behavioral patterns from the existing repertoire (or the construction of internal plans for novel patterns), and the evaluation of feedback information on the course and consequences of chosen responses.

Third, the fundamental system of adaptive responses includes a powerful mechanism of intrinsic motivation. Although neuroscientists cannot yet give sufficient details on the substrate and neurochemical or neurohormonal agents of this mechanism, most observers of overt behaviors would agree that there is a "need" to acquire knowledge, to solve problems, to be in active, mental rapport with the environment and with one's self. Thus, in relation to this need to acquire knowledge, the individual experiences distress when confronted with discrepancies and novelties, and, conversely, experiences "pleasure" when he or she is successfully adaptive or involved in playful activities. Clearly, overt expressions of motivational functioning have been generally categorized by observers as expressions of emotionality. Without the slightest intention of demystifying emotions in the eyes of those who consider them as the primary *agens movens* of human behavior and almost taboo for cold experimentation, we want to stress that, in infants, the changes in emotionality along the pleasure–displeasure continuum are closely interrelated with the course of fundamental integrative processes as discussed in detail by H. Papoušek, M. Papoušek, and Koester (1986).

Fourth, to the extent that humans are social beings, all observable behaviors bear the potential of communicative significance. They can be specifically and intentionally used as communicative signals, but they can also be perceived and interpreted as communicative merely by the observer, independent of their original nonsocial, perhaps physiological meaning. Vocal sounds, for instance, may be secondarily altered while respiration is adjusting to changing blood oxygenation levels, and yet the new sound quality will give the conspecifics relevant information or may even be learned for future, primarily communicative purposes. In this area, any descriptive categorization runs an increased risk of being too artificial. Nevertheless, we assume that evolutionary selection has been influenced by the social significance of certain patterns, for instance, those signaling the presence, the difficulty, or the solution of a problematic situation, and that this selection has involved patterns of vocal and facial behaviors in particular.

The Concept of Play in Relation to the Acquisition of Knowledge

In H. Papoušek's earlier experiments, infants used head movements for various purposes such as scanning, orienting toward sources of stimulation, reaching for food, switching on visual stimulations, and avoiding unwanted events. In the same vein, head movements were expressions of various integrative processes: orientational or preferential attention, habituation, exploration, various forms of learning, and cognitive processes (H. Papoušek, 1977, 1979). Simple modifications in experimental designs (in the structure rather than the physical parameters of stimuli) initiated adequate integrative processes in the absence of any instructions.

Within the period of observation covering the first 6 to 8 months of life, the heterogenity of integrative processes increased. However, a great part of the repertoire often was displayed during a single session in a sequence of escalation if the experimental situation appeared to be a difficult problem for the infant. When the problem had been solved, the scene changed strikingly and ludic elements appeared, as already mentioned. The observer was left with the impression that the costly search for a solution was followed with refinements in the detected solution. For example, the rather crude, generalized, and exaggerated initial correct head movements visible in polygraphic records (H. Papoušek & Bernstein, 1969) became distinctly smooth, exact, and concise. Was this the path to playfulness? Although the preceding observations had not been designed for the study of play, they provided enough incentives for a hypothetical conceptualization of the interrelation between play and the acquisition of-knowledge—the central aspect of our interest. We suggested such a concept, and in the flowchart in Fig. 11.1, used already in H. Papoušek and M. Papoušek (1978) and H. Papoušek (1979), we extrapolated the direction of its essential operations far beyond the scope of infancy and into the perspective of evolution.

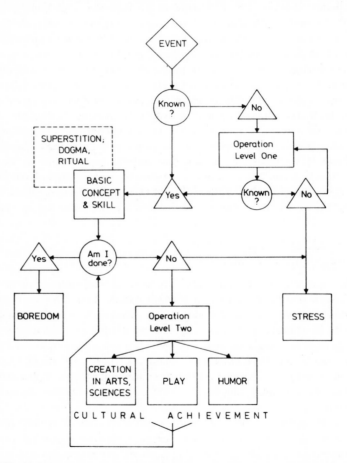

FIG. 11.1 Flowchart showing a hypothetical progression of the acquisition and integration of knowledge. Integrative processes protect against stress from the unknown or against boredom from trivial knowledge. Operational Level One includes learning basic concepts, rules, or skills and tends to create closed concepts. Operational Level Two tends to reopen basic concepts, view events from innovative or humorous standpoints, and create and solve new problems (H. Papoušek & M. Papoušek, 1978).

According to the Papoušeks' conceptualization, the accumulation of knowledge is viewed as a movement from "unknown" to "known" that requires the functioning of various integrative operations such as exploration, various forms of learning, imitation, rule detection, concept formation, and other cognitive operations. The motivational factors mobilizing or demobilizing such operations are, on one hand, connected with unpleasant feelings resulting from exposures to either too much novelty or too little novelty, i.e., feelings known as the fear of the unknown and the insufferability of boredom, respectively. On the other hand, other authors have reported that successful coping with the unknown and with boredom may be connected with motivational factors eliciting internal feelings of pleasure—pleasure of success, familiarity, and knowing how, for instance (see Chapter 16 by Heckhausen). Thus, an individual may be motivated for further progress in the accumulation of knowledge by a kind of push–pull effect of displeasure and pleasure, or indirectly by the expectancy of these feelings. What is true of an individual may also be valid for culture, albeit in much more complex analogies. Although assumptions concerning motivational factors are primarily based upon the empirical evidence of unpleasant feelings in the observed infants, they will certainly remind the reader of earlier theories on the role of novelty, discrepancy, and incongruity in motivation (Berlyne, 1964; Hebb, 1949; Hunt, 1966). As to pleasant feelings, the present concept approaches those theories that have emphasized "pleasure seeking" (as postulated by Brown, 1961) and takes into consideration the neurophysiological evidence of positively reinforcing centers in the rat brain as stressed in self-stimulation experiments (Olds & Milner, 1954). The reader may refer to Berlyne and Madsen (1973) for more detailed discussions.

In the present model, however, the central integrative operations are assumed to function differently in the process of moving from the unknown to the known. The initial confrontations with a novel event compel the system to accumulate enough information to integrate a concept on the unknown and make the event known enough to avoid excessive distress or fear (Operation Level One). The initial concepts may be only crude, "black and white" assumptions based on false premises or superstitions, and yet the system may adhere to them as long as a closer look at the event might re-elicit too much distress. With time the initial concept may become boring and/or the risks of distress may decrease, thus allowing a revision. The temporary concepts may then be reopened for further exploration and integration under pressure-free conditions (Operation Level Two). This step may repeat itself many times and lead to conceptual improvements that move away from triviality towards innovation, creativity, or humorous surprises. With increasing enculturation after infancy, this progress may also be arrested by cultural taboos, dogmatic interventions, etc. Level Two operations bring about an increased probability of pleasant motivators and new features that are homogeneous during infancy but that can be attributable later in life to playfulness, inventiveness, creativity, or humor.

Playful Monologues in Infancy

In a search for infant capacities that might be integrated at a very early age at a pressure-free level of execution and with ludic elements, we have focused our attention on noncry vocalizations. The universality of vocal communication, its precocity, and the presence of innate predispositions for vocalization doubtlessly prove its significance for human evolution and make its postpartum adaptation particularly interesting. Like head movements, vocal sounds, too, can be adaptively integrated as a means serving various goals. For example, they can mediate messages to caregivers; they can be used as an omnipresent toy (H. Papoušek & M. Papoušek, 1983) or as a musical expression (Görlitz, 1972; Lewis, 1975; M. Papoušek & H. Papoušek, 1981); and they can express empathetic attunement. Of course, infant vocalization should be studied in the context of parent–infant interchanges, which we discuss in the next section. Here, we first want to comment on infant monologues and explicitly probe whether they may provide parallels in the infant's naturalistic ecology to the experimental learning situations described earlier.

Using audiovisual recording, auditory evaluation of phonological and musicological parameters, and computer-aided and sonagraphic evaluation of acoustic parameters (M. Papoušek & H. Papoušek, 1981), we have found that at the age of about 8 weeks there are substantial changes in vocalization—together with some other qualitative transitions in behavioral development (H. Papoušek & M. Papoušek, 1984)—indicating changes analogous to the transitions from Level-One to Level-Two operations as suggested in Fig. 11.1. Prior to 8 weeks, the initial, quiet vocal sounds merely are made as isolated utterances lacking the differentiated spectrographic qualities and patterning seen in later vocalizations. The newborn is unable to prolong expiration for the sake of noncry vocalizations; pattern-like vocalizations are caused by the rhythm of respiration, which changes with the infant's behavioral state and ongoing activities (such as sucking, adjusting body position, defecation) to which the undifferentiated voicing is passively subordinated.

After 8 weeks of age, better control of breathing and the vocal tract allows for an increase in the frequency of quiet vocalization and an increase in the heterogeneity of its spectrographic parameters. Prolonged sounds are indicative of the first variations, and facial expressions indicate signs of interest and/or pleasure that have been noted by most observers as features of vocal play (Lewis, 1975; Stark, 1980; Wolff, 1969). We see an analogy in these qualitative changes to Level-Two operations in our hypothetical model of playful features in the acquisition of knowledge.

The variations appearing at this age are of two main types. The first variations concern merely the quality and intensity of prolonged sounds, whereas the similarity of consecutive sounds is minimal. The infant seems to utilize the potential variability without evident concepts in patterning. Such exercises do, of course, improve the quality of vowel-like sounds, and every new sound feature caused by the participation of fingers or objects brought to the mouth or by the development of articulatory prerequisites is immediately embedded into this type of variation. Two examples are shown in Fig. 11.2 (a, b).

Whereas the first type of variation continues to develop during later ages, a new type of variation appears during the second trimester with the infant's new capacity to produce consonants and syllables, and to segment expiration so as to repeat a syllable several times during a single expiration. From this time on, discrete patterns become evident in repetitive babbling, and variations are superimposed upon these patterns as shown in Fig. 11.2 (c). The infant seems to retain every concept temporarily with a new syllable and sticks to it in the repetitive patterns while trying out fine-grain modifications. These variations may often be interrupted or may end with laughter or with joyful squeals. The significant increase in the frequency of similar expressions has been shown in a detailed analysis of the development of emotionality by H. Papoušek, M. Papoušek, and Koester (1986).

Thus, we have found it possible to detect and study certain parallelisms between learning how to use vocalizations and the appearance of the features of playfulness in pressure-free situations. In the same vein, we hope to have demonstrated another, perhaps still groping step in the given hypothetical concept operational in the sphere of the infant's naturalistic ecology. This ecology is inconceivable without the caregiver, whom we have omitted in this section for good reasons. As we are going to show in the next section, the more the caregiver may facilitate the infant's developmental progress, the more difficult it is for the infancy researcher to apply those neat, simple techniques and theoretical concepts that were elaborated upon during the era of S–R approaches.

PLAYFULNESS IN INTERACTIONS
BETWEEN YOUNG INFANTS AND PARENTS

The difficulties connected with analyses of playfulness multiply considerably when play is observed during the infant's interactions with the social environment. All our experience has shown that dyadic interactions are the interactions that young infants tolerate best and cognitively benefit most from. However, dyadic interaction alone brings about serious problems in attempting to assess who stimulates whom or in what proportions the course of play is affected either by the infant, by the social partner, or by the interactional context. Social interactions are processes that are highly dynamic in relation to time and dialectic as to the bidirectional effects between interacting agents. Thus, there is an increased danger that the observer, when confronted with these problems, may end up with a vague category of play and with mere time parameters to compute,

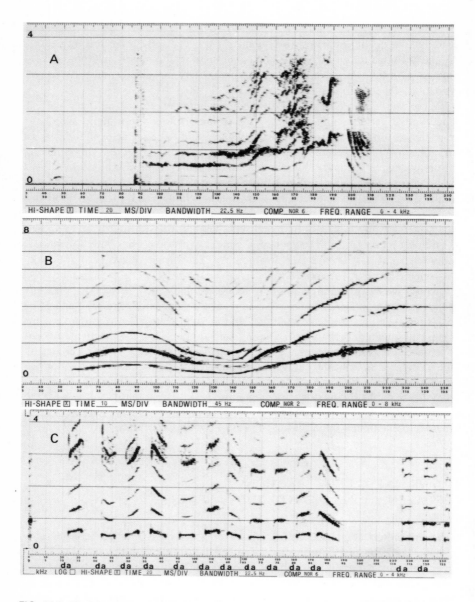

FIG. 11.2 Playful variations of vocal sounds in the infant's monologues: (A) exploration of pitch range and pitch contouring at four months. A sonagram shows a range of 28 semitones between 293 and 1500 Hz, a discontinuous contour with rapid up-and-down shifts and vibration, duration 2.46 s, and a high signal-to-noise ratio; (B) expertise in pitch contouring at 13 months. A sonagram shows a range of 28 semitones between 400 and 2000 Hz, smooth continuous pitch transitions from normal to high pitch register, duration 1.88 s, and a low signal-to-noise ratio; (C) play with melodic and rhythmic patterns, superimposed upon a highly regular, repetitive syllabic pattern at 10 months. A sonagram shows a range of 5 semitones between 520 and 700 Hz, pitch accents upon syllables 1, 3, 6, and 10, the rhythm freely moving between 2-, 3-, and 4-beat rhythms, duration 3.28 s.

an approach that, taken alone, provides for only limited insight into the distribution of this troublesome category but not into its functional meaning.

Contemporary audiovisual recording techniques make it possible for researchers to see the same interactional episode repeatedly and to analyze it using *microanalytic techniques.* These techniques also make it quite apparent how much courage or ignorance—or both—is necessary in order to put the highly dissimilar response patterns that are observed in highly dissimilar contexts into one pot labeled as *play,* and then to analyze its quantitative parameters with sophisticated, computer-aided statistics. Yet ways of filtering out qualitatively more homogeneous subcategories are still being sought, and none of them seem easy.

Didactic Aspects of Parental Engagement

Attempts to elucidate the significance of play for adaptive processes and, hence, for human evolution also require a discriminating look at individual, narrow aspects of play. Conversely, they may also provide helpful criteria for differential analyses, particularly of playful interchanges between infants and caregivers. One of the fundamental questions concerns a potential didactic lead with which the caregiver can help the infant detect and better utilize elements of playfulness in the acquisition of knowledge. In previous reports (H. Papoušek & M. Papoušek, 1978, 1982, 1983), parental caregiving has been discussed from a similar perspective and has been shown to include behavioral adjustments interpretable as supportive of the earliest forms of infant learning and thinking.

Although some of the parental behaviors in question might be superficially categorized as play with the infant, a more detailed analysis of the context in which they regularly appear has indicated some other specific meanings. For instance, one form of "play with the infant's hands" can appear regularly during the infant's transition from waking state to sleep state and be followed with soothing and preparing the infant for sleep without any other attempts to initiate play. This form is interpretable as one of the means allowing the parent to test muscle tone as a state parameter and make a correct decision on further caregiving (H. Papoušek & M. Papoušek, 1982). Similarly, other behavioral patterns have been identified as parts of parental interventions facilitating the infant's transition between sleep and waking or helping to establish direct visual contact and a face-to-face position between parent and infant. Whereas these patterns can only indirectly improve the infant's cognitive gain from interactions with the environment, there are other interactions that seem to be directly intended as support for cognition and that can be delivered with an astonishing degree of synchronization with the infant's real progress in integrative capacities. For more details and the first evidence of effectance, we refer to M. Papoušek, H. Papoušek, and Bornstein (1985).

Although parents seem to follow a didactic script with a certain universality and consistency, they are unaware of the existence of any such script and are unable to report on what they are doing in this respect. Present scientific knowledge has helped in the construction of a hypothetical script as the best fitting model for what has become apparent from evidence of both infant cognitive competence and parental behaviors. Assuming that universality (across sex, age, and culture) together with minimal conscious awareness indicate a deeper biological rather than cultural determination of a behavioral tendency, we see parental support of the earliest integrative development in the progeny as an outcome of the evolutionary selection process. An investigation of the specific role of communicative and symbolic capacities in human evolution requires careful attention to expressions of such support in vocal interchanges between parents and infants.

Evidence of Playfulness in Early Interactions

Using a set of data that had already been analyzed in a study on emotionality in mother–infant interactions (H. Papoušek, M. Papoušek, & Koester, 1986), we first attempted to discover to what extent and in what ways mothers may influence the appearance of ludic elements in the infant's behavioral repertoire. For this purpose, we preferred considering elements of playfulness in any behavioral patterns rather than a problematic differentiation of particular forms of play.

The behavior of interacting partners was recorded audiovisually so that the picture included a visual oscillographic display of voice and a digital display of the time base from a quartz clock in 0.01 sec intervals. The presence of undifferentiated play situations was evaluated in 20 dyads at the ages 2, 7, and 12 months. Specifically, we asked three students to find and demarcate in time all periods of interactions that they would consider as playful. The students were skilled in demarcating other events in films or videotapes, but they were not yet influenced by our particular concepts of playfulness.The comparison of their findings with ours is representative of the recent shift in infancy research from less differentiated classifications of play to attempted objective verifications of partial aspects of play such as imitation, emotionality, or vocal interchange. Not surprisingly, all three students used relatively broad concepts of playfulness. In spite of the limited possibilities for generalizing their findings, we discuss some of the interesting features that these had in common.

First, the frequency of those behaviors broadly conceptualized as *play* was found to increase strikingly with age. Whereas up to half of the sessions with 2-month-old infants included no periods of play, all sessions with 12-month-old infants included periods of playfulness during a majority of the observation sessions.

Second, the type of *play* changed with the age of the infants as well. At the age of 2 months, play was seen in vocal interchanges, repetitive or rhythmical activities (particularly touching), the matching of different expressions, displays of fingers or pacifiers in the infant's visual field, and tickling. Parents were found to be the more frequent initiators of play and to have no particular difficulties in gaining the infant's attention. Evidence from other data has shown that this is also true about interactions with 4-month-olds. In the older age groups, the roles in the interactions dramatically changed. The older infants showed not only more initiation but also more interest in the laboratory environment while rejecting parental invitations to play. Parents obviously had increasing difficulties with controlling the locomotor impulsiveness of the infants for the sake of the observation and often had to incorporate toys into their activities in order to gain the infant's attention. Next to play with toys, ritualized games combined with nursery rhymes or songs appeared as the new and dominant type of play eliciting the most striking expressions of emotionality in 7-month-old infants.

Third, the aforementioned age-related qualitative changes confirmed how problematic it would be to attempt quantitative comparisons across such different behavioral repertoires, integrative capacities, and situational contexts. One of the common qualitative features involved in the detection of playfulness was obviously vocal interchange. Vocal interchange as a means for repetitive, matching, or imitative actions, for variations in various modalities, and at other times as an expression of pleasure also helped to determine the assignment of playfulness to observed interactions. However, it is more difficult to make an objective analytical assessment of the similarity between two sounds, the mode of variations, or the acoustic parameters of emotionality than to make an intuitive one. To examine more precisely and reliably to what degree analyses of vocal interchanges may help in solving the given problems appears to be a challenging task rather than a tried-and-true procedure.

Playful Elements in Vocal Interchanges

Concentrating on the earliest evidence of interactional playfulness in vocal interchanges, we reanalyzed in more detail data on 2-to-4-month-old infants interacting with both parents successively. These data have already been used for a detailed analysis of vocal interchanges irrespective of playful situations (M. Papoušek, H. Papoušek, & Bornstein, 1985). Analyses of vocalizations were performed by the use of a Digital Sona-Graph TM 7800 (Kay Elemetrics), which allowed narrow band (45 Hz) and broad band (500 Hz) sonagrams, sound wave displays, analyses of power spectrum at selectable points, measurement of duration, and qualitative evaluations of musical elements. A computer-aided, real-time analysis of the fundamental frequency was used for the categorization of the types of melodic contours. Additional auditory analyses included voice quality, pitch, and five degrees of loudness as assessed by a musically trained person. Observable behaviors of interacting partners were synchronically filmed with Super-8 mm cameras in a laboratory setting on three occasions, at the ages

2, 3, and 4 months, during spontaneous, 6-minute interactions. In this presentation we are going to discuss only the parts of these rather extensive materials that are directly related to the topic of this chapter.

The stress upon early evidence and interactional evidence of vocal play differentiates our approach from that of researchers who pay more attention to fully developed vocal play in infants older than 4 months of age (Stark, 1980), or of those who prefer S–R type of testing situations. Sroufe (1979), for instance, used standard social stimulations (including games) in systematic studies of emotionality but viewed expressions of emotionality as noninteractional responses. Although Sroufe stressed the interrelations between emotionality and cognition, he did not attempt to outline the position of play in these interrelations.

With respect to our concepts on the significance of play, analyses of vocal interchanges across parental sex promised additional possibilities to judge the universality of parental tendencies in playful interactions. We consider this analysis a first step that could be followed by further comparisons across ages and cultures, for the universality in these tendencies may be considered as evidence for preadaptedness and evolutionary significance as discussed earlier in this chapter. We have already shown that both parents use the same repertoire of prosodic contours in didactic ways when sharing experiences with young, preverbal infants, or when supporting their categorical processing of vocal communication (M. Papoušek, H. Papoušek, & Bornstein, 1985). Similarly, when analyzing the significance of emotionality in parent–infant interactions, we had demonstrated parallel changes in melodic contours in both parents under the influence of two different emotional states in the infant—pleasant excitement and fussiness (H. Papoušek, M. Papoušek, & Koester, 1986).

Our pilot approaches to episodes of playfulness and our previous experience with vocal interchanges directed our attention to the following vocal sequences, variously associated with observable features of playfulness in overt behaviors: (a) infant vocalization accompanying facial expressions of pleasure; (b) any vocalization repeatedly following some aspect of the partner's behavior and thus becoming potentially contingent on it; (c) reciprocal matching of vocal sounds or some partial parameters of vocal sounds; (d) repetitive strings of reciprocal sounds belonging to the repertoire of infant sounds; and, (e) prosodic features in parental baby talk in various types of play with infants.

Vocal Expressions of Pleasure.   Vocal sounds of the first type may accompany playful situations as expressions of pleasure, although vocal expressions of pleasure occur in other, nonplayful contexts. As such, they have been analyzed by H. Papoušek, M. Papoušek, and Koester (1986) and differentiated as to the degree of expressiveness. Until now, however, no specific parameters have been found that allow one to distinguish pleasure experienced by infants in play situations from the pleasure they experience in nonplay situations. One of these sounds—laughter—occasionally appears during interactions at the age of 2 months

(Stark, 1980). At first it is most reliably elicited by parental tickling (Wolff, 1969), and its increasing frequency is, interestingly, associated with the parental use of ritualized games, including tickling. However, because laboratory observations represent only a minimal sample of everyday interactions, it is impossible to find out whether the independently developing laughter functions as a cue signal eliciting the introduction of ritualized games as a new tendency in parental interventions or, vice versa, whether laughter is to some degree also determined by the use of this new parental tendency.

An example of ritualized games including parental tickling and infant laughter is shown in a seriogram in Fig. 11.3. The reconstruction of such seriograms is one of the techniques for detecting and documenting the interrelations between play and integrative processes in infants. In this example, the mother uses a nursery rhyme while marching her fingers through the air above the lying infant, moving them upwards from the legs towards the armpits. At the culminating point in the rhyme, dramatized in the prosody of the maternal voice, she tickles the infant's armpits. The seriogram in Fig. 11.3 shows the infant's luring sound, which is understood as a request for another repetition of this game, then the initial part of the game, and finally a burst of laughter from the infant prior to the real climax, the actual tickling. Although this form of analysis still includes interpretative descriptions and attributions of intentionality—the presence of a game concept and anticipation of the demonstrated expressions—it at least makes the interpretations controllable by other observers. The early occurrence of tickling and displays of simple, repetitive contours in the prosody of maternal baby talk indicate that adaptive subroutines are integrated in a didactic way. The universality of this maternal intervention across the observed sample and its intuitive character may support arguments for the evolutionary selection of similar interventions. The microanalytic evidence of anticipatory shifts in timing of laughter in the infant indicates one form of transition from operant learning to playfulness as expressed in the pleasure of mastering relevant events.

Vocal Contingencies. Vocal sequences of the second type characterize frequent situations in which the parent introduces and/or reinforces ludic elements and thus facilitates the infant's mastery of environmental control. The parent may regularly answer some infant behaviors with certain utterances or with certain melodic contours in the prosody of utterances. While doing so, the parent offers contingencies that the infant may detect and learn so successfully that the operant control becomes playful and pleasurable. A similar process may, of course, take place in the opposite direction during the interactions, and the parent may be affected by emotional signs of the infant's integrative success.

Reciprocal Vocal Matching. Reciprocal matching in vocal sequences of the third type is a very frequent introduction to playful vocal interchanges. Matching has become a matter of more general interest (and controversial discussion) in

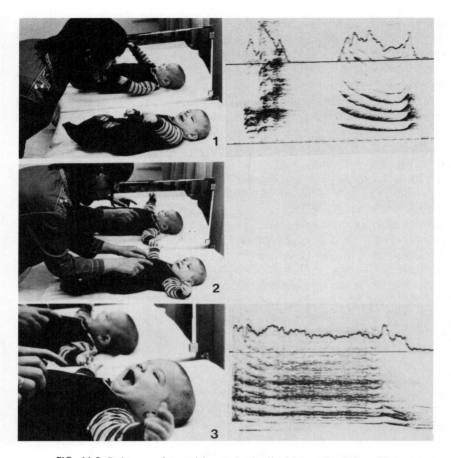

FIG. 11.3 Seriogram of essential parts in ritualized interactional play: (1) the infant's request for another repetition of a game in which the mother makes walking motions with her fingers above the infant, singing an accompanying nursery rhyme until she approaches the child's armpits and surprises it with tickling; (2) the infant's attentive state of expectation; (3) a burst of anticipatory laughter from the infant precedes the climax of the game. (Vocal expressions shown in sonagrams to the right of pictures.)

infancy research due to discrepant findings concerning the early functioning of imitation, which is considered indicative of important cognitive processes (Meltzoff, 1981; Meltzoff & Moore, 1983) and of cross-modal perception (Born, Spelke, & Prather, 1982; Kuhl & Meltzoff, 1982). As reviewed previously (M. Papoušek, H. Papoušek, & Bornstein, 1985; Pawlby, 1977; Užgiris, 1983), parents hold a didactic lead inasmuch as they are the first to imitate in interactions with newborns. Matching in pitch appeared in the present data in infants as young as 2 months and occurred in one-shot trials rather than in a process of gradual tuning or successive steps. The ability of infants to match pitch is far more acute than is the ability to match more complex phonological structures. Vocal matching is a particularly interesting aspect of the integrative processes, for it supplies the infant with immediate feedback and the opportunity to make perceptual comparisons. A detailed analysis of the present data on 3-month-old infants revealed that matching occurred more frequently in the infant–parent sequences than in parent–infant sequences (23.2 vs. 15.8% of all recorded sequences, respectively) and that no differences in matching could be related to the sex of the parent (M. Papoušek, H. Papoušek, & Bornstein, 1985).

Repetition and Variation in Vocal Interchanges. The repetitive strings of reciprocal sounds (vocal sequences of the fourth type) are another frequent step towards vocal play that can develop from reciprocal matching or from repetitive applications of contingencies. Frequently, however, it occurs in the infant's monologues mentioned in the preceding section of this chapter. As soon as the new elements of vocal interchanges can be repeated in smooth forms without any difficulties, the infant's attention seems to be freed to attend to minor differences caused by some uneveness in coordination that can be tried out by trial and error and, eventually, brought under control. Repetitions may thus not only make improvements possible but, according to most theoreticians of play, also open an important avenue of variations assumed to be essential to play.

Didactically speaking, variations in parental speech directed to infants can help parents contribute to the infant's vocal development in several meaningful ways. Variations allow parents to alter the proportion of familiarity and novelty so as to maintain the infant's attention at an adequate level. They may also instruct the infant on the very possibility of variation or on new modes of variability. Needless to say, they also prepare the way for later artistic uses of variations and point out hedonic aspects of relevant stimulations. Thus, variations of prosody in the parental part of interchanges—vocal sequences of the fifth type—deserve particular attention.

The Role of Prosodic Features in Vocal Play. The mere presence of a newborn elicits in adults a tendency to talk to the infant (Rheingold & Adams, 1980), and mothers tend to increase their average pitch and to modify melodic contours in their voices strikingly, but only in the physical presence of the newborn (Fernald & Simon, 1977). These are some of the changes that are universal features of so-called baby talk in adults (Ferguson, 1978; Snow, 1977). Together with other prosodic features, one of the first relevant functions of such modified melodic contours seems to be to differentiate messages addressed to the infant as opposed to others. Another function is to direct the infant's attention to the categorical messages in those prosodic contours that in themselves mediate universally important messages prior to the further development of speech and that the infant is going to be able to modify first (M. Papoušek & H. Papoušek, 1981). The repertoire of melodic contours in parental baby talk is limited and equal in both parents and is significantly less variable than the lexical content in corresponding utterances. This repertoire is dependent on two factors: the behavioral–emotional state of the infant and the categories of messages to be mediated (M. Papoušek, H. Papoušek, & Bornstein, 1985).

In general, the categories of messages characterized by prosodic contours and other prosodic features concern relevant general social situations; they differentiate statements from questions or requests; they signal danger, threats, or aggression; or conversely, they signal friendliness and readiness to help. Melodic contours in the prosody of parental baby talk and, in the same vein, their analogies in music also affect infants' behavioral–emotional states, mobilizing their attention, increasing their tendency to vocalize, or soothing them. Not enough is known about the mechanisms of similar effects to decide whether the infant learns to understand such nonspecific messages or is preadapted to answer them adequately. In general, however, various integrative processes have time to occur before repetition and variation appear in the infant's monologues and interactional vocal interchanges, giving them a playful character.

Occurrence of Vocal Play during Early Interactions.   Thus, we realized that all five of the preceding types of sequences contributed in one way or another to the development of vocal interchanges, which may be considered as features of play inasmuch as they typically occur in pressure-free situations, consist of freely combined and varied subroutines with no direct connections between means and goals, at least temporarily follow a scenario, and elicit pleasure. Therefore, we attempted to define a prototype of such episodes of vocal play in order to operationalize them for further studies. Accordingly, a vocal play episode is a repetitive string of at least two vocal sounds from the infant's repertoire, produced by either of the two interacting partners in any sequence for no other apparent specific purpose than to play. The following circumstances seemed to deserve further attention: (a) who initiated the string; (b) whether the sound of one partner was answered by the other one with either a rewarding or a matching turn, if rewarded at all; (c) the incidence of duetting or of vocal expressions of pleasure (including laughter); (d) the length of a vocal play episode as expressed by the number of sounds in the string (not interrupted by more than one unrelated utterance); and, (e) the relative contributions of parents and infants to the length of an episode of vocal play in dyadic interchanges.

The present data on 2-, 3-, and 4-month-old infants was collected during a total number of 64 sessions. The percentage of infants engaged in vocal play was high (91.7%), with only one infant exhibiting no engagement at all. The percentage of sessions including vocal play episodes increased with age from 38.1 to 47.8 and to 70.0, respectively (averaging 51.6 of the sessions). The total number of vocal play episodes per age group also increased with age from 21 to 41 and finally to 66, reaching a total of 128 episodes. In none of these parameters were there noticeable differences between the mothers and fathers involved.

Of the total of 128 vocal play episodes, 82.0% were initiated by the infants and 18.0% by the parents, with no significant differences between mothers and fathers and no significant dependence on the age of the infants. In the episodes initiated by the infants, parents answered the infant's sounds with matching turns in 61.9% of the cases (with no sex differences). In 32.4% of the cases they used other rewarding turns, and in 5.7% of the cases there was no turn-taking response. In contrast, infants answered only 17.4% of parental sounds with matching turns in episodes initiated by the adult partner. Only maternal sounds were effective in the present sample, no paternal sounds in vocal play were followed by matching turns in infants, although by definition—a fact we stress—parental sounds in vocal play episodes belonged to the infant's repertoire. Other differences between parents being negligible, this one seems to indicate that the use of similar behaviors was counterbalanced with some factor in fathers, perhaps by the infant's insufficient everyday experience with the fathers as an interactional partner. In 17.4% of the cases, infants answered parental sounds with expressions of pleasure; in 65.2% of the cases, with no vocal turns.

Audible expressions of pleasure were recorded in 63.3% of the episodes of vocal play (see example in Fig. 11.4). Laughter, which in test situations can be regularly elicited from infants by the age of 10 months (Sroufe, 1979), was recorded in 31.3% of the episodes independent of tickling, age, and parental sex. Obviously, once vocal play occurs, it is relatively reliable in leading to audible expressions of pleasure, including laughter, in infants as young as 2 months. Some authors consider vocal duetting as a particular form of expressing pleasure in parent–infant interactions (Stern, Jaffe, Beebe, & Bennett, 1975). In the present data, duetting appeared in 30.5% of all episodes of vocal play. As in all audible expressions of pleasure, no significant relation to either age or parental sex was found.

The average length of vocal play episodes as measured by the number of repetitive sounds per episode appeared to be influenced by the infant's age and by the sex of the parent in different ways. The average number (2.62) of the parents' repetitive sounds per episode did not change with the infant's age and was not significantly different between mothers and fathers. By contrast, the average number of the infant's repetitive sounds per episode significantly increased with age from 2.43 to 4.55 ($p < 0.01$). Moreover, it was also significantly larger in mother–infant interactions than in father–infant interactions at 2 months (3.00 vs. 1.50, $p < 0.05$) and at 3 months (6.20 vs. 2.76, $p < 0.05$). A similar difference between mothers and fathers continued to affect vocal play in 4-month-old infants but did not reach the level of statistical significance. Such an environmental effect upon the infant's capability of carrying out more repetitive sounds within playful strings indicates that this capability is not merely a product of maturation

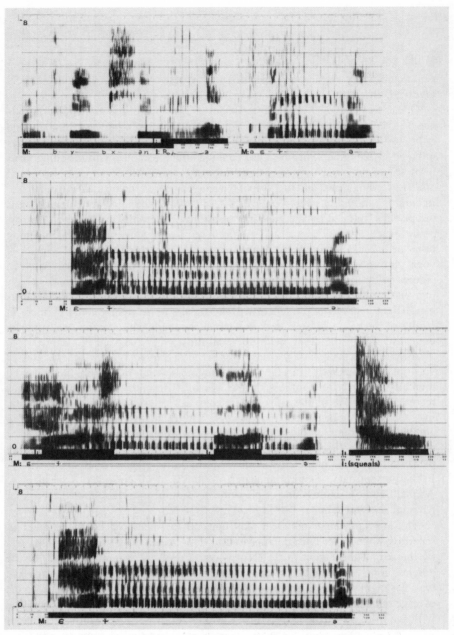

FIG. 11.4 Episode of dyadic vocal play between a mother and her 2½-month-old son. Black bars below sonagrams show the sequence and the duration of maternal (M) and infant (I) sounds. The infant's favorite "r"-like sound (a velo-pharyngeal friction noise) in line 1 is followed by the mother's repetitive matching turns of "r" (an alveolar trill) with expanded duration, pitch range, and pitch contours in lines 1 to 4. The infant joins the mother with two cheerful, vowel-like sounds and a joyful squeal in line 3.

238

but is also a product of an adaptive integration of experience. Moreover, the parent seems to contribute to this capability not only because of the set of displayed behaviors. The contribution also seems to depend on the extent of the infant's previous experience with these behaviors during parent–infant interactions. The families in our observations represented the traditional German pattern in which fathers spend most of the day in professional activities while mothers care for the infants.

A typical example of an episode of vocal play—and an illustration of its objective analysis—is demonstrated with the help of sonagrams in Fig. 11.4. A 2½-month-old boy initiates the episode with his favorite sound, a velopharyngeal friction noise, which is similar to a German "r." The mother imitates this sound in her turn and executes it repeatedly in a perfect, prolonged alveolar trill ("ř"). After listening to two such demonstrations quietly, the infant joins the mother with two cheerful vowel-like sounds and then a joyful squeal.

Insights as to the Roots of Play

On the whole, the attempt to define a prototype of vocal play has helped us to study—under comparable conditions and in rather objective ways—a form of play that is universal enough and develops early enough to give us a better insight into the ontogenetic origins of playfulness. Developmental changes occurring in vocal play between 2 and 4 months of age indicate a gradual integration of predispositions such as the ability to carry out repetitive strings of sounds. Within interactions, this ability seems to depend not only on the presence of certain necessary behaviors in both partners but also on the extent of the infant's interactional experience with a given partner. In the culture in question, fathers appeared to be less successful than mothers in contributing to the infant's capability to produce matching turns and as many repetitive sounds consecutively, but no other differences could be found between mothers and fathers in playful interactions with infants.

The reported analyses of vocal play confirmed again that parents as caregivers support the occurrence of play in various indirect and direct ways. In our interpretation, some of their supportive tendencies, such as vocal matching or a differential use of melodic contours in baby talk, function from the moment of the infant's birth and probably fulfill some other more fundamental didactic tasks before they become regular parts of playful interchanges accompanied by expressions of pleasure.

The developmental progress in vocal play, evident at 4 months, opens further avenues towards more complex forms of play and simultaneously towards a more differentiated utilization of potentials included in vocal plays. One concerns the increasing opportunity for variations resulting from the development of integrative processes and the growing repertoire of vocal sounds. The illustration in Fig. 11.5 demonstrates a typical German nursery game as one of the new forms

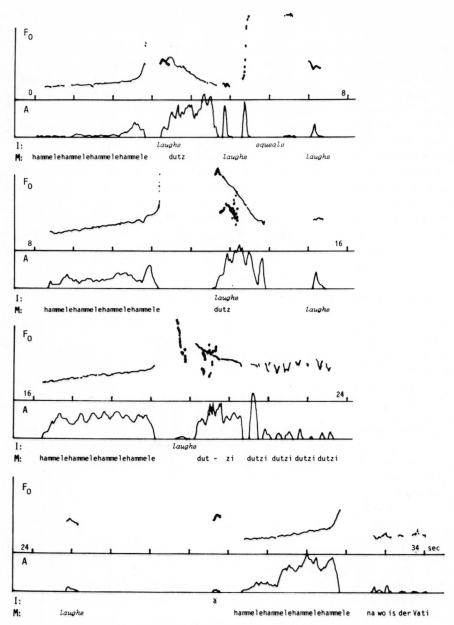

FIG. 11.5 Ritualized German play between a mother and her 4-month-old daughter.

The figure represents computer-drawn, real-time contours of fundamental frequency F_0 and intensity (A) in four repetitions of the game with increasing excitement in both partners, as evident in steeper slopes of corresponding pitch contours, higher pitch, and increased ranges of pitch and intensity. See text for a description of the game.

240

of ritualized games appearing with increasing frequency around the age of 4 months. Imitating playful head butting in young lambs, the parent slowly approaches the infant's face and says "hammele, hammele, hammele." Then, after a short pause, the parent gently butts the infant's head saying "dutz" and finishes the episode with a display of pleasure. Thus the phase of escalated tension is separated from the release by a dramatic pause. The course of this game can be read from the computer-aided construction of melodic contours in the fundamental frequency of maternal voice during four repetitions of the game. Melodic contours together with the intensity of the voice are modified in rather general patterns proven to escalate attention and anticipation to a climax and then, with a surprising reversal of escalation, to elicit sounds of joy. These patterns are additionally varied from one repetition to the other until an intervening person distracts the infant's attention and the partner no longer attempts to regain the infant's attention. Joyful squeals and anticipatory laughter evidence the effect of this game upon the infant's emotionality.

Other directions in the further development of vocal plays may concern the introduction of musical pieces, toys, further ritualized games, and speech exercises, among other things. The complexity quickly exceeds limits within which it is still possible to verify interpretative concepts objectively. Needless to say, it would be far beyond the frame of this presentation to describe the many-sided consequences of the onset of speech and walking in the variability of playful situations.

A CAVEAT

This attempt to explain one's theoretical approach, including its justification, without boring the reader with a myriad of descriptive details and sophisticated analyses of data may end by depicting a problematic puzzle as a question with simple explanations or as an enjoyable little piece of logical gymnastics. We started this chapter with a statement on how easy it is to play, a naive statement reflecting a common underestimation of play rather than our own impression of the complexity and value of playfulness. We hope, though, that we have demonstrated, both in terms of our concepts and the evidence presented, that play should be viewed as an achievement not only in an ontogenetic but also in a phylogenetic sense. In the same vein we also hope that the reader is not left with the impression that we believe we have solved the problems of play in general.

Our attempts to approach the most fundamental roots of play has brought us to the basic problems of behavioral regulation and development where one usually starts thinking of the adaptive meaning of observed phenomena. We believe that raising such questions is relevant to further progress in the study of play. No matter how simple behavioral phenomena may seem when observed in the form of precursors or initial expressions, the problem of play is an open one and has to be kept open. What we should like to stress is the importance of this problem. Among others, we believe that play is a significant process of adaptation. The potential risk of an increased exposure to the danger of predation or other dangers during play, which is pointed out in some primatological studies, appears in quite another light in relation to human evolution. If play has contributed to the evolution of culture, then the price of increased mortality due to predation and other dangers has been counterbalanced many times with the benefits inherent in the development of culture. Among other dangers, predation has been virtually eliminated, to the point of making extremely rare zoo specimens out of dangerous, predatory carnivores.

Whether play might threaten humans because of its involvement in the evolution of culture is another question, for culture has also brought about some very dangerous, self-destructive tendencies. Even war games may be playful, after all. What can infancy researchers say to this argument? Perhaps we can return to Friedrich Schiller's fifteenth letter on the Aesthetic Education of Man and add one more quotation to the motto of this chapter:

> *Der Mensch soll mit der Schönheit nur spielen, und er soll nur mit der Schönheit spielen.*[2]

SUMMARY

The emergence of playfulness in young infants during the course of early learning situations and in vocal interchanges between parents and infants was examined in relation to both the phylogenetic and ontogenetic significance of play in humans. Central integrative processes related to learning and the acquisition of knowledge has been previously shown to be closely connected to expressions of emotionality and features of playfulness in infants. Vocal play in infant monologues as well as in vocal interchanges between infants and parents is a form of play that can be rather objectively analyzed, and because of its universality and early emergence it can provide insights into the ontogenetic origins of play. Analyses of vocal play confirmed that parents support the occurrence of play in both direct and indirect ways. Some of their supportive tendencies, such as the contingent use of vocalizations, vocal matching, repetition and variation in vocal interchanges, and the differential use of melodic contours in baby talk, function from the moment of the infant's birth and probably fulfill some other more fundamental didactic tasks before they become regular parts of pleasurable, playful interactions between parents and infants. Developmental changes in vocal play indicate a gradual integration of fundamental adaptive responses

---

[2]Man should only play with beauty and play only with what is beautiful.

in the infant; in parents they indicate very sensitive matching of parental behavior to the developmental changes and needs in the infant. The developmental progress seen in vocal play opens further avenues towards more complex forms of play and simultaneously towards a more differentiated utilization of potentials included in vocal play. Previous interactional experience with a given partner seems to affect vocal matching and repetition in infant–parent interchanges, but no other differences could be found between mothers and fathers in playful interactions with their infants.

ACKNOWLEDGMENTS

Our research has been kindly supported by *Die Deutsche Forschungsgemeinschaft*. We owe special thanks to Evi Bleicher, Lucia Harzenetter, Monika Haekel, Steffen Pöhlmann, and Michael Theile for their devoted help in the evaluation of data and assistance in the preparation of this chapter.

REFERENCES

Bekoff, M. (1972). The development of social interaction, play, and metacommunication in mammals: An anthropological perspective. *Quarterly Review of Biology, 47,* 412–434.

Berger, M. (1972). Population structure of olive baboons (Papio anubius, J. P. Fischer) in the Laikipia districts of Kenya. *East African Wildlife, 10,* 159–164.

Berlyne, D. E. (1964). *Structure and direction in thinking.* New York: Wiley.

Berlyne, D. E., & Madsen, K. B. (Eds.). (1973). *Pleasure, reward, preference: Their nature, determinants, and role in behavior.* New York: Academic Press.

Bertrand, M. (1969). The behavioral repertoire of the stumptail macaque: A descriptive and comparative study. *Bibliotheca primatologica* (No. 11). Basel: Karger.

Blurton Jones, N. (1972). Categories of child–child interaction. In N. Blurton Jones (Ed.), *Ethological studies of child behavior* (pp. 97–127). Cambridge: Cambridge University Press.

Born, W., Spelke, E., & Prather, P. (1982). Detection of auditory-visual relationships by newborn infants. *Infant Behavior and Development (Special ICIS Issue), 5,* 27.

Brown, J. S. (1961). *The motivation of behavior.* New York: McGraw-Hill.

Bruner, J. S. (1974). Nature and uses of immaturity. In K. Conolly & J. Bruner (Eds.), *The growth of competence* (pp. 11–48). New York: Academic Press.

Bruner, J. S. (1983). The legacy of Nicholas Hobbs: Research on education and human development in the public interest: Part 1. *Peabody Journal of Education, 60* (3), 60–69.

Comenius, J. A. (1968). *Orbis pictus.* New York: Bardeen. (Originally in Comenius, J. A. *Opera didactica omnia.* Amsterdam, 1657.)

Erikson, E. H. (1963). *Children and society.* New York: Norton.

Ferguson, C. A. (1978). Talking to children: A search for universals. In J. Greenberg (Ed.), *Universals of human language* (Vol. 1, pp. 203–225). Stanford, CA: Stanford University Press.

Fernald, A., & Simon, T. (1977). Analyse von Grundfrequenz und Sprachsegmentlänge bei der Kommunikation von Müttern mit Neugeborenen. *Forschungsberichte: Institut für Phonetik und sprachliche Kommunikation der Universität München, 7,* 19–37.

Flitner, A. (1973). *Spielen–Lernen.* München: Piper.

Görlitz, D. (1972). *Ergebnisse und Probleme der ausdrucks-psychologischen Sprechstimmforschung.* Meisenheim: Hain.

Haith, M. M. (1980). *Rules that babies look by.* Hillsdale, NJ: Lawrence Erlbaum Associates.

Hebb, D. O. (1949). *The organization of behavior.* New York: Wiley.

Hess, E. H. (1970). Ethology and developmental psychology. In P. H Mussen (Ed.), *Carmichael's manual of child psychology* (3rd ed., Vol. 1, pp. 1–38). New York: Wiley.

Hinde, R. A. (1971). Development of social behavior. In A. M. Schrier & F. Stollnitz (Eds.), *Behavior of nonhuman primates* (pp. 1–68). New York: Academic Press.

Hughes, M. (1978). Sequential analysis of exploration and play. *International Journal of Behavioral Development, 1,* 83–87.

Huizinga, J. (1962). *Homo ludens. Vom Ursprung der Kultur im Spiel.* Reinbek: Rowohlt.

Hunt, J. McV. (1966). The epigenesis of motivation and early cognitive learning. In R. N. Haber (Ed.), *Current research in motivation* (pp. 335–370). New York: Holt, Rinehart & Winston.

Hutt, C. (1966). Exploration and play in children. In Play, exploration, and territory in mammals. *Symposia of the Royal Zoological Society,* London, *18,* 61–68.

Kuhl, P. K., & Meltzoff, A. N. (1982). The bimodal perception of speech in infancy. *Science, 218,* 1138–1140.

Lewis, M. M. (1975). *Infant speech: A study of the beginnings of language.* New York: Arno Press.

Loizos, C. (1967). Play behavior in higher primates: A review. In D. Morris (Ed.), *Primate ethology: Essays on the socio-sexual behavior of apes and monkeys* (pp. 226–282). London: Weidenfeld & Nicholson.

Lorenz, K. (1970). *Studies in animal and human behavior* (Vol. 1). Cambridge, MA: Harvard University Press.

Lorenz, K. (1971). *Studies in animal and human behavior* (Vol. 2). Cambridge, MA: Harvard University Press.

Lovejoy, C. O. (1981). The origin of man. *Science, 211,* 341–350.

MacKinnon, J. (1971). The orangutan in Sabah today. *Oryx, 11,* 141–191.

Mason, W. A. (1967). Motivational aspects of social responsiveness in young chimpanzees. In H. W. Stevenson, E. H. Hess, & H. L. Rheingold (Eds.), *Early behavior: Comparative and developmental approaches* (pp. 103–126). New York: Wiley.

Meltzoff, A. N. (1981). Imitation, intermodal co-ordination, and representation in early infancy. In G. Butterworth (Ed.), *Infancy and epistemology* (pp. 85–114). Brighton, England: Harvester Press.

Meltzoff, A. N., & Moore, M. K. (1983). Newborn infants imitate adult facial gestures. *Child Development, 54,* 702–709.

Olds, J., & Milner, P. (1954). Positive reinforcement produced by electrical stimulation of septal area and other regions of rat brain. *Journal of Comparative and Physiological Psychology, 47,* 419–427.

Papoušek, H. (1961). Conditioned alimentary motor responses in infants. *Thomayerova Sbírka Přednášek, 409,* (in Czech). Praha: Státní zdravotnické nakladatelství.

Papoušek, H. (1967). Experimental studies of appetitional behavior in human newborns and infants. In H. W. Stevenson, E. H. Hess, & H. L. Rheingold (Eds.), *Early behavior: Comparative and developmental approaches* (pp. 249–277). New York: Wiley.

Papoušek, H. (1977). Entwicklung der Lernfähigkeit im Säuglingsalter. In G. Nissen (Ed.), *Intelligenz, Lernen und Lernstörungen* (pp. 75–93). Berlin: Springer.

Papoušek, H. (1979). From adaptive responses to social cognition: The learning view of development. In M. H. Bornstein & W. Kessen (Eds.), *Psychological development from infancy: Image to intention* (pp. 251–267). Hillsdale, NJ: Lawrence Erlbaum Associates.

Papoušek, H., & Bernstein, P. (1969). The functions of conditioning stimulation in human neonates and infants. In A. Ambrose (Ed.), *Stimulation in early infancy* (pp. 229–252). New York: Academic Press.

Papoušek, H., & Papoušek, M. (1978). Interdisciplinary parallels in studies of early human behavior: From physical to cognitive needs, from attachment to dyadic education. *International Journal of Behavioral Development, 1,* 37–49.

Papoušek, H., & Papoušek, M. (1979). The infant's fundamental adaptive response system in social interaction. In E. B. Thoman (Ed.), *Origins of the infant's social responsiveness* (pp. 175–208). Hillsdale, NJ: Lawrence Erlbaum Associates.

Papoušek, H., & Papoušek, M. (1982). Integration into the social world: Survey of research. In P. Stratton (Ed.), *Psychobiology of the human newborn* (pp. 367–390). Chichester: Wiley.

Papoušek, H., & Papoušek, M. (1983). The psychobiology of the first didactic programs and toys in human infants. In A. Oliverio & M. Zappella (Eds.), *The behavior of human infants* (pp. 219–240). New York: Plenum.

Papoušek, H., & Papoušek, M. (1984). Qualitative transitions in intergrative processes during the first trimenon of human postpartum life. In H. F. R. Prechtl (Ed.), *Continuity of neural functions from prenatal to postnatal life* (pp. 220–244). Spastics International Medical Publications. Oxford: Blackwell Scientific Publications Ltd./Philadelphia: Lippincott.

Papoušek, H., Papoušek, M., & Koester, L. S. (1986). Sharing emotionality and sharing knowledge: A microanalytic approach to parent–infant communication. In C. E. Izard & P. B. Read (Eds.), *Measuring emotions in infants and children* (Vol. 2, pp. 93–123). New York: Cambridge University Press.

Papoušek, M., & Papoušek, H. (1981). Musical elements in the infant's vocalization: Their significance for communication, cognition, and creativity. In L. P. Lipsitt & C. K. Rovee-Collier (Eds.), *Advances in infancy research* (Vol. 1, pp. 163–224). Norwood, NJ: Ablex.

Papoušek, M., Papoušek, H., & Bornstein, M. H. (1985). The naturalistic vocal environment of young infants: On the significance of homogeneity and variability in parental speech. In T. M. Field & N. Fox (Eds.), *Social perception in infants* (pp. 269–297). Norwood, NJ: Ablex.

Pawlby, S. J. (1977). Imitative interaction. In H. R. Schaffer (Ed.), *Studies in mother–infant interaction* (pp. 203–224). London: Academic Press.

Piaget, J. (1951). *Play, dreams, and imitation in childhood.* London: Heinemann.

Poirier, F. E. (1972). Introduction. In F. E. Poirier (Ed.), *Primate socialization* (pp. 1–39). New York: Random House.

Rheingold, H. L., & Adams, J. L. (1980). The significance of speech to newborns. *Developmental Psychology, 16,* 379–403.

Schaller, G. B. (1963). *The mountain gorilla: Ecology and behavior.* Chicago: University of Chicago Press.

Scheflen, A. E. (1969). Behavioral programs in human communication. In W. Gray, F. J. Duhl, & N. D. Rizzo (Eds.), *General systems theory and psychiatry* (pp. 209–228). Boston: Little Brown.

Snow, C. E. (1977). The development of conversation between mothers and babies. *Journal of Child Language, 4,* 1–22.

Sroufe, A. L. (1979). Socioemotional development. In J. D. Osofsky (Ed.), *Handbook of infant development* (pp. 462–516). New York: Wiley.

Stark, R. E. (1980). Stages of speech development in the first year of life. In G. H. Yeni-Komshian, J. F. Kavangh, & C. A. Ferguson (Eds.), *Child phonology: Vol. 1. Production* (pp. 73–92). New York: Academic Press.

Stern, D. N., Jaffe, J., Beebe, B., & Bennett, S. L. (1975). Vocalizing in unison and in alternation: Two modes of communication within the mother–infant dyad. *Annals of the New York Academy of Sciences, 263,* 89–100.

Suomi, S. J., & Harlow, H. F. (1971). Monkeys at play. *Natural History, Special Supplement,* 72–75.

Sylva, K., Bruner, J. S., & Genova, P. (1976). The role of play in the problem-solving of children 3–5 years old. In J. S. Bruner, A. Jolly, & K. Sylva (Eds.), *Play—Its role in development and evolution* (pp. 244–257). Harmondsworth: Penguin.

Teleki, G. (1973). *The predatory behavior of wild chimpanzees*. Lewisberg, PA: Bucknell University Press.

Užgiris, I. (1983, July–August). *Mother–infant communication during the first year of life*. Paper presented at the 7th Biennial Meeting of the International Society for the Study of Behavioral Development, Munich.

van Hooff, J. A. R. A. M. (1962). Facial expressions in higher primates. In Evolutionary aspects of animal communication. *Symposium of the Royal Zoological Society*, London, *8*, 97–125.

Vygotsky, L. (1962). *Thought and language*. Cambridge, MA: M. I. T. Press.

Winnicott, D. W. (1971). *Play and reality*. New York: Basic Books.

Wolff, P. H. (1969). The natural history of crying and other vocalizations in early infancy. In B. Foss (Ed.), *Determinants of infant behavior* (pp. 81–109). London: Methuen.

CHAPTER TWELVE

THE RELATIONSHIP
BETWEEN SYMBOLIC
AND MANIPULATIVE
(OBJECT) PLAY

MIRANDA HUGHES
formerly University of Leeds

In this chapter I consider symbolic play in relation to manipulative play and develop a theoretical position which both facilitates the interpretation of existing data and the formulation of clear hypotheses concerning the functions of different types of play. That term *play* is used to subsume both ludic and exploratory behavior, thereby reflecting the theoretical position that these behaviors can be considered usefully within the same conceptual framework. In a series of experiments on manipulative play, Hutt (1966, 1967, 1970) described the qualitative characteristics of exploratory and ludic behaviors and argued that they bore a specific temporal relationship to one another; I argue that symbolic play can be classified in a similar manner and intend to draw analogies between (a) exploration and imitation and (b) ludic behavior and fantasy play.

THE CLASSIFICATION OF MANIPULATIVE PLAY

During exploration, a child's activity is focused on a particular object (or set of objects); during ludic behavior, however, a child's attention to an object will be less vigilant, and familiar toys are likely to be incorporated in sequences of behavior that are relatively idiosyncratic. It is possible to quantify and illustrate the differences between exploratory and ludic behavior using hierarchical analysis of relevant sequences of behavioral elements (Hughes, 1979).

Hutt (1970) argued that a child learned the properties of an object during exploration, whereas ludic activity is more a reflection of a child's ability to be creative (Hutt & Bhavnani, 1972). Subsequent experiments by Sylva, Bruner, and Genova (1976) and Smith and Dutton (1979) have suggested that children who engage in some manipulative play with objects are better able to use those materials in a problem-solving task than children who do not have play experience. However, these experiments did not clearly distinguish the exploratory and ludic components of the manipulative play. I recently conducted an experiment to clarify and extend the findings of Sylva et al. (1976) and Smith and Dutton (1979) and, more specifically, to test the hypothesis that exploratory behavior was associated with learning in a manner that distinguished it from ludic behavior.

EXPERIMENT I: EXPLORATION VERSUS PLAY
AS MEDIATORS OF PROBLEM SOLVING

In order to examine the significance of the way in which children played with the materials during the pretask period, two distinctive sets of materials were designed, both of which were equally appropriate to the eventual task. Set A comprised three brightly colored sticks (each 18″ in length) and three strips (keys) of copper tubing (2 mm diameter, 6.35 cm long with rounded ends); each stick had a small slot at one end and a rounded section of copper tubing (insert) at the other. Two sticks could therefore be joined by placing the insert from one stick into the slot of another and sliding a key through the insert to secure the join. Set B comprised a similar set of materials except that the "sticks" were designed to look like dolls: There was a policeman, a red Indian, and a woman holding a baby; and the "keys" were designed to look like a small truncheon, a tomahawk, and a baby's rattle. It was hypothesized that set B would elicit more ludic behavior from the children than set A because set B could be more readily incorporated into representational play. Set A was expected to elicit more exploratory behavior because of the ostensibly more unusual features of the materials.

Method

Subjects.   The subjects were 40 children aged 4–5 years drawn from preschool playgroups with a predominantly white, middle-class (professional parents) background.

Procedure.   The experiment took place in a small room within the preschool. Children came into the room with the experimenter (E) and were shown either set A or set B of the task materials. E explained that these were some toys she had brought with her and that she wanted to see what sort of things children could do with them. The children were invited to play with the toys for a bit and were told that after a few minutes E would want to know whether they thought the toys would be useful to have in the playgroup. During a 5-minute pretask period the children were observed, and data were collected on a checklist that recorded the occurrence of behavior that would be used in the subsequent problem-solving task: These behaviors included "inspection of slots or inserts," "putting a key through the insert," "appropriate matching of slot and insert," and "inappropriate matching of slot and insert" (for example, placing two sticks on top of one another rather than joining them lengthwise). Any occurrence of clearly ludic behavior was also noted (for example, one child built a wigwam and then a road with the colored sticks; another child enacted a complex sequence of events including the mutilation of the policeman by the Indian). Children who were inactive or expressed boredom were positively encouraged by E to "try and think of an interesting game you could play" until the full 5-minute period was completed.

Task.   After each child had spent 5 minutes familiarizing himself with the materials, E explained the task: A strip of white tape had been placed down the center of the room before the experiment began, and the child was told that he could not now cross this white line. A jelly baby was placed in a paper cup, which had a large handle attached, on the side of the line opposite the child. The child's problem was to obtain the jelly baby without crossing the white line. He was told he could use the toys to help him if he wished.

Hints. A series of hints, arranged so that each succeeding hint revealed more information about how to solve the task, was developed. These were offered if the child remained inactive for 30 seconds or indicated that he or she wanted help. The particular hint that was given depended on the child's performance and was always one level above the strategy already attempted. For example, if the child attempted to reach the object with a stick and then gave up, he or she was then given the hint that suggested using a longer stick.

Level 1. (Child stymied at outset): "You would be able to reach it if you had very long arms, wouldn't you? Could you use the toys to make your arms long?"
Level 2. (Child tries to reach using one stick): "Could you make a longer stick that would help you reach?"
Level 3. (Child unable to make longer stick): "Could you join two of the toys/sticks together somehow?"
Level 4. (Child makes no progress joining sticks): "Look, you can join them like this." (Slot and insert joined but not keyed together.)
Level 5. (Child has joined sticks but can't make them stay together): "Could you use one of those little toys to help join them?"
Level 6. (Child unable to use keys): "Look, if you put this in here, the sticks/toys will stay together when you pick them up."

Scoring. Scores on the task were developed so that a child who only had a low-level hint scored lower than a child who had only a high-level hint (see Table 12.1). It was assumed that for the first five hints the successive increments of information revealed were equal, and children were assigned 1 to 5 points, respectively, for each of the first 5 hints that were needed. Because the last hint

TABLE 12.1
Scoring on Problem-Solving Task

Level of Hint	Points Assigned for Needing Hint
1	1
2	2
3	3
4	4
5	5
6	9
Total	24

revealed the entire solution, a weighting of 9 was given if it was needed (so that solving the task with the 4th and 5th hints was equivalent to solving the task with the final hint).

An exploration score 0–5 was devised based on the observational measures in the pretask period. A zero score indicated that the child had paid no attention at all to the slots, inserts, or keys, whereas a score of 5 would have indicated that the sticks had been joined lengthwise using the keys (see Table 12.2).

Results

As predicted, the children who spent the pretask period with set A were more likely to spend time exploring the materials than children who played with set B; children with set B were more likely to engage in at least some clearly ludic behavior. The median exploration score in Group A was 3.2, and in Group B was 2.1 (Mann–Whitney $U = 135.5, p < .05$ (1-tailed), $N_1 = N_2 = 20$). Only 3 children in Group A displayed any ludic behavior, compared to 11 children in Group B ($\chi^2 = 7.03$, 1 df, $p < .01$). No children from either group made a full construction appropriate to the task. The higher exploration scores of Group A showed that children in this group were engaging in more task-related activity than the children in Group B.

Table 12.3 shows the mean task scores (a function of the number of hints needed) and the mean times taken to complete the task by the two groups. No child was able to solve the problem without being shown how to join the sticks by using the keys, so the lowest score was 9 (one child from each group). There was no significant difference between the two groups on the time taken to solve the problem ($t = .31$, 38 df, n.s.), but Group A had a lower mean task score,

TABLE 12.2
Exploration Scores

0	No attention to slots, keys, or inserts
1	Visual inspection and manipulation
2	Key through slot
3	Key through insert
4	Sticks joined without key
5	Full construction appropriate to task

TABLE 12.3
Task Scores and Times to Completion

	Mean Task Score	Time Taken (secs.)
Group A	16.1 ± 3.2	334.5 ± 77.1
Group B	18.049 ± 3.3	327.7 ± 57.6

showing that they needed fewer hints, and this difference approached significance ($t = 1.90$, 38 df, $p = .062$ 2-tailed).

Discussion

One surprising aspect of this study was the degree of application that children showed in trying to solve the problem. It is in marked contrast to the Smith and Dutton (1979) study where more than one third of their subjects in a "training" and three quarters of their subjects in the control condition (which consisted of 3 minutes of familiarization time with the materials) were unwilling to concentrate on the task presented to them. In effect, the present study distinguished the effects of "epistemic" and "ludic" play behavior, and they were equally potent in maintaining the children's interest in the problem; but it is not clear exactly why the children in this study did not lose interest in the same way as the children in the Smith and Dutton experiment. One possible reason is the lack of constraint on the children's behavior in the present study: Smith and Dutton required their subjects to sit formally at a table, whereas the subjects in the present study were permitted a good deal more freedom of activity during the pretask period. They may therefore have felt less constraint by the adult presence. As Loizos (1967) and Bruner (1972) have both pointed out, a child will not play in surroundings that create a feeling of insecurity. The children in the Smith and Dutton study may well have found the experimental conditions so aversive that they engaged in displacement activities that distracted them from the task ahead.

The present study does indicate that when children respond to objects as having a familiar use (the dolls in set B), they do not examine the less familiar features that may be present. Their behavior is "ludic" in that it is relaxed and in that it incorporates the objects into a variety of activities. Children who are confronted with materials that are relatively unfamiliar and have no obvious use "explore" the properties of those materials. It is exploration that gives children an ultimate advantage in using the materials in a problem-solving situation.

The finding that exploration facilitates the type of "convergent thinking" necessary for the problem-solving task described previously cannot necessarily be generalized to the proposition that exploration facilitates *all* problem-solving activities. For example, because it is during ludic behavior that children typically use materials in different ways ("What can *I* do with this object?"; see Hutt, 1970) it may be that ludic behavior facilitates divergent thinking, whereas exploratory behavior facilitates convergent thinking.

EXPERIMENT II: THE ROLE OF PLAY IN DIVERGENT THINKING

In an experiment to test the hypothesis just stated, two groups of children spent 6 minutes with a set of familiar objects. In the Play (P) condition the children were left to their own devices, and in the Imitation (I) condition they copied the experimenter's activities with the objects. A control group (C) did some coloring. At the end of the 6 minutes, all the children were tested on standard creativity tests. They were asked for alternative uses of a paper towel (one of the set of familiar objects), and they also did a pattern-meanings test. The results are shown in Table 12.4.

The results of experiment II provide support for the view that spontaneous manipulative play does facilitate the expression of creative ideas—both with materials that have been incorporated in play and with independent test material. The concurrent observations during the pretest periods identified occasions when children were using combinations of the materials and found a significant relationship between play richness and subsequent creativity scores, thus confirming the view that the flexible, combinatorial sequences of behavior during play are precursors of creativity. The finding that there was no difference between the experimental conditions in the number of standard uses they were able to suggest for the paper towel is actually inconsistent with the Dansky and Silverman (1975) results; however, the results for the nonstandard uses show that the pretest play facilitates novel ideas rather than orthodox ones.

The classification of the spontaneous play as ludic rather than exploratory was not as clear in experiment II as it had been in experiment I. Nevertheless, the children clearly were familiar with the materials despite the fact that some of them were a little baffled when confronted with such a motley collection of objects. Clearly, any experimental situation is not entirely conducive to relaxed, ludic behavior, but the children in the Play condition approached this state more closely than those in the Imitation or Control conditions. The behavior of the children in the I group was certainly more epistemic in that this condition required the child to attend to the experimenter and to reproduce her actions; it therefore did not permit the child to engage in behavior of the type "What can I do with this object?"

The improved performance of the P group children relative to the I and C groups on the pattern-meanings test does lend support to the view of Bruner

TABLE 12.4
Creativity Test Scores

Groups	Standard Uses	Non-standard Uses	Pattern-Meanings
P[a]	4.3 ± 1.9	6.4 ± 2.4	6.8 ± 1.6
I[b]	3.8 ± 1.7	4.3 ± 1.6	4.4 ± 2.5
C[c]	4.1 ± 2.4	3.2 ± 1.5	2.7 ± 2.6
Difference between groups	n.s.	$p < .01$	$p < .01$

[a]Play condition
[b]Imitation condition
[c]Control group

(1972), Lieberman (1977), and Wallach and Kogan (1965) that the state of mind associated with playfulness is related to divergent thinking.

The functional distinction which can be made between exploratory and ludic behavior confirms the hypotheses that were derived from earlier observational studies. The validity of the distinction is further confirmed by physiological indices that reflect an attentive state during exploration and a relaxed state during play (Hughes & Hutt, 1979).

CLASSIFICATION OF SYMBOLIC PLAY

Much of the play that children engage in is symbolic—that is, the child enacts adult (or other) roles, and uses materials to represent a variety of objects (rather than being interested in the materials for their own sake). Whereas manipulative play is common to all primates, symbolic play is uniquely human, and many play theorists have regarded it as an essential precursor of adult conceptual abilities (Groos, 1898; Piaget, 1951; Smilansky, 1968; Sutton-Smith, 1973). What I argue here is that, in the same way that manipulative play with objects enables children first to learn the properties of those objects (exploration) and subsequently to consolidate them (ludic behavior), symbolic play enables the learning and consolidation of ideas to take place. Representational play, during which a child repeats behavior he has seen enacted by others (for example, washing-up or driving) and focuses on the salient aspects of those events, could be regarded as analogous to exploration. In contrast, fantasy (imaginative) play, during which a child integrates these events into a creative theme (for example, the acting out of doctor and nurse roles, or the pretense of an expedition to an imaginary land) would be analogous to ludic behavior.

The potential usefulness of drawing a parallel between manipulative and symbolic play and of distinguishing exploratory and ludic behavior within these categories is exemplified in a study by Dansky (1980). He examined the comparative effects of sociodramatic play training (S), exploration training (E), and free play (P) over a 3-week period with 1½ intervention hours per week. In the S condition an adult played with groups of four children, enacting specific themes and using props. In the P condition children were given similar access to the props, but the adult did not guide them in any way. In the E condition the emphasis was on the examination of objects; children were encouraged to note similarities and differences between objects, and to play games whereby one child described an object (without naming it) and the other children had to guess its identity. During posttesting children in the S condition scored significantly higher than the other two groups on "imaginativeness" and "verbal comprehension, production and organization"; children in the E condition were able to give more detailed and accurate descriptions of a "curiosity box" than the children in the other two groups. Dansky (1980) argues that sociodramatic play training has important consequences for children's performance on a range of cognitive-type tasks, whereas the results of exploration training are more specific: "there are important differences in these two kinds of activity and in the impact which each can have on a child's development" (p. 54). This conclusion is a little premature in the absence of any evidence that the superior performance of the S group in cognitive skills could be maintained, and it is obscured by the absence of any theoretical framework. A conceptualization of play that permits the separation of symbolic and manipulative play would predict different functions for each and permit the formulation of more relevant test procedures.

We are currently undertaking some observational studies that consider the analogy between exploration and representational play. At a behavioral level, one similarity is immediately obvious: Both exploration and representation are severely constrained behaviors in the sense that the sequences of behavior are highly predictable. If one considers "training" children in exploratory behavior or representational play, a further analogy emerges in that neither activity is inherently creative. Much as teachers can show a child how to ask questions about an object (as in Dansky's study), they can also show how to ask questions about an activity such as driving a fire engine. On the other hand, both fantasy play and ludic manipulative play are behaviors in which children restructure existing knowledge in an idiosyncratic manner. The temporal sequence between representational play and fantasy is the same as that between exploratory and ludic behavior with a novel toy. Many authors (Elder & Petersen, 1978; Fein, 1975; Feitelson, 1975) have documented that early symbolic play is greatly facilitated by the presence of "literal" props and adult role models, and this is further support for the view that children "explore" a behavior through imitation and representation, whereas the ludic model is more evident in fantasy-play themes. To plagiarize Hutt's (1970) phraseology: During imitation a child asks "can I imitate this behavior?"; during fantasy s/he asks "what can I create using this behavior?"

IMPLICATIONS FOR A GENERAL CLASSIFICATION OF PLAY

I have argued that exploration and imitation are essentially epistemic in nature and that they are usefully distinguished from ludic behaviors. Imaginative play lies firmly within the ludic classification, and, as such, hypotheses concerned with its function are probably best formulated in terms of implications for creativity rather than learning and what might be termed *convergent* intellectual development. General questions concerned with the role of play in psychological development can be more precisely formulated if play is not regarded as a unitary concept that has some functional homogeneity. Symbolic and manipulative play are concerned with behavior and with objects, respectively, and within each type of play epistemic and ludic models can be identified and ascribed different functions.

SUMMARY

Exploratory and ludic aspects of object play can be distinguished in terms of motivation, behavior, and function. Two experiments on object play are described that demonstrate the learning inherent in exploratory behavior, in contrast to the creativity that is associated with ludic behavior. It is suggested that the types of distinctions that can be made between the exploratory and ludic aspects of object play are mirrored in symbolic play. Symbolic play that is merely imitative and uses "literal" representation is analogous to exploration, whereas creative, fantasy play is ludic. Analogies can be made both in terms of the structure of behavior and functional outcomes. At a theoretical level these distinctions are important to the formulation of more concise hypotheses concerning the role of play in psychological development.

REFERENCES

Bruner, J. (1972). Nature and uses of immaturity. *American Psychologist, 27*, 1–28.
Dansky, J. (1980). Cognitive consequences of sociodramatic play and exploration training for economically disadvantaged preschoolers. *Journal of Child Psychology and Psychiatry, 21*, 47–58.
Dansky, J., & Silverman, I. (1975). Play: A general facilitator of associative fluency. *Developmental Psychology, 11*, 104.
Elder, J., & Petersen, D. (1978). Preschool children's use of objects in symbolic play. *Child Development, 49*, 500–504.
Fein, G. (1975). A transformational analysis of pretending. *Developmental Psychology, 11*, 291–296.
Feitelson, D. (1975). *Representational play: Its developmental role and prerequisites.* Paper presented at "The Biology of Play" conference, Moor Park College.
Groos, K. (1901). *The play of man* (Elizabeth Baldwin, Trans.). London: Heinemann. (Original work published 1898)
Hughes, M. (1979). Exploration and play re-visited: A hierarchical analysis. *International Journal of Behavioral Development, 2*, 215–224.
Hughes, M., & Hutt, C. (1979). Heart-rate correlates of childhood activities: Play, exploration, problem-solving and day-dreaming. *Biological Psychology, 8*, 253–263.
Hutt, C. (1966). Exploration and play in children. *Symposia of the Zoological Society of London, 18*, 61–81.
Hutt, C. (1967). Temporal effects on response decrement and stimulus satiation in exploration. *British Journal of Psychology, 58*, 365–373.
Hutt, C. (1970). Specific and diversive exploration. *Advances in Child Development and Behavior, 5*, 119–180.
Hutt, C., & Bhavnani, R. (1972). Predictions from play. *Nature, 237*, 171–172.

Lieberman, J. N. (1977). *Playfulness: Its relationship to imagination and creativity*. New York: Academic Press.

Loizos, C. (1967). Play behaviour in higher primates: A review. In D. Morris (Ed.), *Primate ethology* (pp. 176–218). London: Weidenfeld & Nicholson.

Piaget, J. (1951). *Play, dreams and imitation in childhood* (C. Gattegno & F. Hodgson, Trans.). London: Heinemann. (Original work published 1945)

Smilansky, S. (1968). *The effects of sociodramatic play on disadvantaged preschool children*. New York: Wiley.

Smith, P. K., & Dutton, S. (1979). Play and training in direct and innovative problem solving. *Child Development, 50*, 830–836.

Sutton-Smith, B. (1973). Spiel als Mittler des Neuen. In A. Flitner (Ed.), *Das Kinderspiel* (pp. 32–37). München: Piper.

Sylva, K., Bruner, J., & Genova, P. (1976). The role of play in the problem-solving of children 3–5 years old. In J. Bruner, A. Jolly, & K. Sylva (Eds.), *Play: Its role in development and evolution* (pp. 244–257). New York: Penguin.

Wallach, M., & Kogan, N. (1965). *Modes of thinking in young children*. New York: Holt, Rinehart & Winston.

CHAPTER THIRTEEN

ANALYSIS OF SPONTANEOUS
PLAY ACTIVITIES
IN EVERYDAY SITUATIONS
WITHIN MIXED AGE GROUPS

IRENE BURTCHEN
University of München

Play is one of the most fascinating topics of research, but it is full of ambiguities and contradictions. In almost every textbook on child development, there is a chapter dedicated to *play*, but its value as a scientific term has repeatedly been questioned (Oerter, 1980; Schlosberg, 1947). Although research on play has a long tradition and the number of studies is immense, a generally accepted definition of the concept is still missing.

In psychology, there are three main lines of interpreting the play process: the psychoanalytic approach, the perspective of motivation theory, and cognitive theories. All of them show a form of tension, a duality, in viewing the function of the play in terms of personal expression versus social adaptation (Christie & Johnsen, 1983).

Because play as a generic concept does not seem to lend itself to an integrative definition, most recent authors have been willing to take seriously Berlyne's (1969) advice to use either narrower or broader categories. Thus, several subcategories of play have been identified for research purposes such as pretend play, social play, and solitary play.

Nevertheless, attempts to find a comprehensive definition have continued. Some writers have tried to summarize the common elements of various definitions as the core of an encompassing concept. Vandenberg (1980) and Krasnor and Pepler (1980), for example, have defined play as behavior that is intrinsically motivated, pleasurable, flexible, and not literal in nature. However, many experimental studies of play treatments do not fulfill these conditions. Others are confounded with variables such as exploration and social interaction.

In addition, there are direct objections to this definition. Vygotsky (1966) argues that play is not always pleasurable and that the flexibility of play is quite limited by certain rules. Csikszentmihalyi (1979) has his doubts about the condition of nonliterality. He describes several instances of playfulness where this condition is not found. His concept of "flow" is an interesting alternative definition, but it is so broad that it overlooks some important aspects of play; for example, it gives no information about developmental processes.

The list of controversies may be continued; indeed, the richness of the play concept seems to place it outside the scope of a universal definition. There is, however, another theoretical approach that could be used as an integrative perspective; that is the concept of action. In recent years, this concept has been favored for the review of psychological research in general, and its advantages have already been proven in other fields of developmental psychology (Oerter, 1981). Could this concept also be fruitful for the study of play?

THE CONCEPT OF ACTION

The basic assumption of this concept is that action is the primary reality of human beings (see Oerter, 1982). In all psychological research that concerns itself with the interaction between the individual and environment, a certain dualism of realities is inherent. The individual is, on the one hand, an experiencing, planning, and acting subject who, on the other hand, is confronted with entities outside the self. Thus, the problem of transfer from material to psychic entities, and vice versa, arises—the old dispute of materialism versus idealism.

If one considers the reality of action to be the primary one, then the action is neither materialistic, as postulated by the representatives of Soviet psychology (Leontjev, 1977; Rubinstein, 1977), nor is it idealistic, as these authors characterize the western point of view. Materialism and idealism are already results of human action; i.e., philosophical systems are secondary realities, only produced by action.

Oerter (1982) cites the directedness of action towards objects as one of its characteristic criteria. Human acting is always directed to the environment; i.e., to specific objects within the environment. This has been called the *object relation* (Burtchen, 1983). This object relation not only includes material objects, but also immaterial or personal objects (such as an object of discussion, another person). If two or more individuals are interacting, they have to find a common object relation. Otherwise, the interaction process will be full of conflicts or will stop.

During socialization, individuals have to learn the "object concepts" (Boesch, 1982) of their society. Many actions are culturally determined. On the other hand, individuals have varying facilities to manipulate objects, to act differently, or to create new object relations.

The object relation itself was classified by Oerter (1981) into three levels. These levels deal with the relationship of subject and object and the different valences of objects.

At the first level, the subject and the object are not yet separate. The action has certain results, but these results are inseparable from the action. As soon as the action is finished, the results lose their meaning. During the action, the object has a subjective valence; it obtains its value and meaning only from the acting individual. An example for this level of object relation is the child's use of a stick as a horse. This meaning is only important during the action and will be neglected afterwards.

At the second level, the subject and the object are separate. The results of the action are "frozen" in the object; the object has its meaning independent of the individual action. The object now possesses objective value. This valence is attributed whenever several persons relate to an object in the same or in a similar way. Objects of this kind are not only material goods (for example: tools or utensils), but also social roles, rules of interaction, etc. (e.g., the role of a leader, greeting rituals).

The third level is characterized by abstraction and formalization. The object becomes independent of its concrete attributes. Abstract value arises when the object receives a general structure. The first example for this level is taken from commercial trade. There goods are only evaluated by their commercial value and no longer by their special use. Producer and seller must disregard the subjective and objective valence of their products; the price is determined by supply and demand, an index of the abstract valence. Another example is the individual as a citizen of a democratic society. His/her valence is irrespective of external and internal features such as sex, race, and talent. Although these features may vary, all individuals must be equally evaluated within the democratic system.

As already mentioned, subjects have to learn the object concepts of their society. The reality generated by societal acting (conventions, generally accepted actions) has to be taken into consideration if the individual is to survive in the surrounding culture. This reality has been called the *objective structure*, whereas the action potentials of the individual (knowledge, strategies, habits, etc.) are called *subjective structure* (Oerter, 1982).

The two structures are systematically connected. Although the development of the subjective structure is strongly influenced by the objective structure, the individual also produces different and perhaps new object relations. Thus, there is a dynamic process on both sides.

On the Developmental Process

Applying the concept of action to developmental psychology, Oerter (1981) has differentiated five stages of development. He stresses that abstract value is the most important one in modern society. Thus, his classification concentrates on this level of object relation.

In the beginning of the developmental process, children do not experience themselves as separate from the environment. As soon as they conceive events in their environment as the results of their own action, the first stage has been reached. The structure of action is dominated by the object itself. This stage can be designated by the following formula:

$$S - O,$$

where S = subject and O = object.

At the next stage, the structure of action is differentiated by specific forms of activity. The child understands the relation between activity and result. For example, diligent activity leads to a good result, lackadaisical activity to a poorer result. Thus, activity (A) becomes a connecting link between subject and object:

$$S - A - O.$$

At the third stage, the concept of capability (C) arises. The child realizes that talent can compensate for the expenditure of energy. The structure of action is accordingly extended to:

$$S - C - A - O.$$

The next step of development is characterized by the child's change in evaluating capability and activity. With increasing age, capability is evaluated more highly than effort and diligence. The corresponding formula is:
$C > A$.

At the last stage, the subject is able to handle the entire chain of action flexibly. If necessary, tasks can be delegated to others, and the individual becomes free to act as a "pure" subject (Oerter, 1981).

Formula: $S - \boxed{C - A - O}$.

This classification of stages is similar to Heckhausen's ontogenetic model of action (see Görlitz, 1983). Although the theoretical framework of the action concept was only briefly summarized here, the basic assumptions are used now for the concept of play.

APPLICATION OF ACTION THEORY TO THE CONCEPT OF PLAY

The concept of action could help to avoid the shortcomings of previous definitions and to systematize the results of previous empirical findings. In terms of action theory, play can be defined by means of different object relations and a specific connection between the subjective and the objective structure. A preliminary definition is derived in the following paragraphs.

To begin with the object relation, this central category can be applied to all the main definitions of play. Whether one approaches play as a means of socially acceptable expression of one's inner emotional experience (Elkind, 1981), as a means of arousal control in the child's response to the environment (Hutt, 1979), or as an expression of the child's subjective cognitive view of the world (Sutton-Smith, 1979), the subject–object relation is always in question. Thus, the traditions of the psychoanalytic (Freud, 1941), the motivational (Berlyne, 1960), and the cognitive points of view (Piaget, 1975; Vygotsky, 1966) can be integrated in this concept.

Previous studies of play that use the term *object relation* have unfortunately been restricted to material objects. The broader concept of object relation, including personal objects, connects the different aspects of recent work on play (see Kreuzer, 1983; Rubin, 1980) and seems to be useful with regard to the discussion of the early interaction process, for instance. In that discussion, the question has arisen whether interaction with the mother comes first (Lewis, 1979), or whether social interaction is a by-product of interaction with material objects (see Jacobson, 1981). From the perspective of action theory, the crucial point is the variability, the flexibility, and the individual "reactibility" (a literal translation of "Reagibilität"; Lehr, 1978) of the object, and not whether it is material or personal.

In research, play and social interaction have not always been differentiated. Both processes can be described by means of common object relations, but in the case of play some further conditions must be fulfilled. For social interaction, the object relation can be prescribed or even extorted, whereas one undisputed characteristic of play is that it is voluntary. The subject establishes and maintains an individual object relation. This object relation is dominated by subjective valence. The dominance of subjective valence does not mean that the individual is unable to consider the objective and abstract valence of an object, but the object relation obtains a subjective meaning in play. (In Piaget's terminology it is the dominance of assimilation.) Thus, play is a self-centered activity.

Another criterion for play actions is the voluntary acceptance of parts of the objective structure. During play the subject may observe a certain frame (e.g., rules of the game, sections of the objective structure like roles and conventions), but this frame is accepted by the subject's own will. Vygotsky (1966) illustrates this with the example of two sisters "playing sisters." Some obligations of daily life as stressed in the objective structure were easily fulfilled by the children in play because they independently decided to act "as if" they were sisters. The voluntary acceptance of the action frame makes the related activities playful. Accordingly, play can be described as a self-centered object relation combined with the voluntary acceptance of parts of the objective structure. Such a definition is, of course, only a first step toward an integrative concept of play and should be improved through further research.

In addition to this basic characterization of play, information is required about the developmental process of play activities. As already mentioned, Oerter (1981) has postulated a classification system of developmental stages. Because this classification is restricted to the level of abstract valence of object relations and has been confirmed empirically for only one type of action structure—activities in the field of work—it should also be examined in relation to play. For this purpose, a number of studies were undertaken. Two of them are presented later. They concentrate on one facet of play activities, that is, play within "symmetrical relations" (Youniss, 1982). On the basis of the proposed definition of play, these interactions were analyzed by means of common object relations in order to identify the structures of action that appeared. Following Bronfenbrenner's (1981) advice about ecological validity, the subjects were observed in everyday situations.

STUDY 1

Method

Subjects.   The subjects were 117 children (59 boys and 58 girls) aged 4 to 10 years (51 preschool and 66 school age). They were randomly drawn from all children who played during the observation period at 10 selected places in two German cities (Bonn and Munich).

Procedure.   The children were observed in natural settings (at home, in their yards, on the street, on the playground). The observations were videotaped. In order to avoid the effects of artificial behavior created by the realization that one is being filmed (Field & Ignatoff, 1981), the camera was present for 2 hours in each case, but taping was only done in the case of natural situations, i.e., if the children no longer noticed the apparatus and no longer let it disturb them. (This was quite easy if no adult interrupted the play or no new children arrived.)

A total of 46 interaction sequences were recorded. Of these, 27 were sequences with 2 children, 14 with 3 children, and in 5 sequences with more than 3 children. The ages of the children in the individual sequences are shown in Table 13.1.

Reduction of the data contained in the videotapes was accomplished in two steps: (a) Detailed descriptions were written of each sequence, including body and hand movement, line of sight, and vocalization of the children involved; (b) the sequences were coded in terms of the establishment, the development, and the completion of interaction with the help of the symbols: $S_l - S_n$ (interacting subjects), O (object), A (activity), and C (capability). The coded data were analyzed according to the play process and related action structures.

For the coding of the sequences the following conventions were applied: The children involved in the interaction were described by the order of their participation in the action as S_1, S_2, etc. The direction of each action was shown by an arrow. The goal of the action was symbolized by O. If a certain order of activity was necessary for the maintainance of the common object relation, this was signified by A. If a certain developed capability became apparent in the activities (prior learning), the symbol C was used.

The sequences were described and coded by three independent observers, who reached an interrater reliability of $r_{cc} = 0.89$. The analysis of the common object relation was undertaken by a group of psychology master's candidates who were thoroughly acquainted with the theoretical concept. The rate of agreement on the analysis was 83%.

Results

The interaction process is described in the following paragraphs. The establishment of contact was accomplished in one of two ways: In the majority of the

TABLE 13.1
Frequency Distribution of Age Groups in the Interaction Sequences
(In Percentages)

Number of Children Involved	Frequency of Sequences	Preschool Group	School-Age Group	Mixed Age Group
2	60	24	23	13
3	30	10	9	11
> 3	10	2	4	4

cases (88%), a common object relation was proposed (verbally and/or nonver-bally) by one subject and accepted by the other(s). In the remaining cases (12%), two or more proposals were made and the interaction could only be maintained if an agreement was reached about one of the proposals (8%), or a new choice of a common object relation was made (4%). During dyadic interactions, the partners were always willing to establish a common object relation, whereas in group play some children insisted on their counterproposals, and finally left the group. Because the other children continued playing together, the basic inter-action process was not stopped. Within sequences involving more than two children there were also examples (4%) where intermediate interactions (with two children) interrupted the original object relation. After the interruption, this object relation was, however, continued.

The termination of the individual interaction sequences was either caused by a one-sided change of the common object relation (57%) or by mutual consent (43%). In the latter, a continuation of the interaction was possible through the choice of a new common object relation. This occurred in 13% of the cases. In these cases, a new sequence was coded.

The action pattern through which the common object relation was maintained became clear during the course of the interaction. In the beginning of the inter-action and during the maintenance of play, the following three forms were identified:

1. The interaction focused on a toy. The object relation was determined by the characteristic of the object without an exactly determined activity and without well-developed capabilities being necessary. Examples: digging together in the sandbox, playing with bricks. The formula for this structure is: $S \rightarrow O \leftarrow S$, with the converging arrows indicating agreement between two subjects on a common object relation.

2. The common object relation was started and maintained by following roles or rules. This was begun less with objects in the immediate field of view, but rather with play "ideas." For the maintenance of the common object relation, a common activity was necessary. Examples: playing "store" (buying and selling wares), playing "mother and child." For this structure the formula is: $S \rightarrow A \rightarrow O \leftarrow A \leftarrow S$.

3. The common object relation was planned and maintained by the use of capability and related activities. In these cases, the evaluation of capability became important for the play process; adroit children were preferred as partners. Examples: playing tennis, games of dexterity like "Taking off the thread." This structure is shown by the formula: $S \rightarrow C \rightarrow A \rightarrow O \leftarrow A \leftarrow C \leftarrow S$.

The frequency distribution of these three forms from the observed sequences is shown in Table 13.2.

In 20% of the play sequences, conflict situations appeared. They were caused by the children's following rules at different levels. Such differences could lead

TABLE 13.2
Frequency Distribution of Action Structures (In Percentages)

Form of Common Object Relation	Preschool Group	School-Age Group	Mixed Age Group	Total
1 (determined by the characteristics of the object)	38	4	4	46
2 (common activity)	6	35	9	50
3 (use of capability)	0	2	2	4

to the termination of the common object relation or to further cooperation (each 10%). The following of rules can be divided into three levels:

1. The following of rules is oriented to a rough framework, which is characterized by the use of the object, i.e., the features inherent in the object determine its use. For example: A doll's cup was used for pretend drinking, for digging in the sandbox, or as a hat, all uses being appropriate to its shape.

2. A particular schema determines the following of rules. This means that adherence to the rule is compulsory, and these rules cannot be changed. An example may illustrate this, too. A game of dice was played. The usual rules of this game require of the players that they successively throw the die and that the spots are counted for each of them. If a "six" is rolled, the player is allowed to throw again. In a new variant of this game, some children proposed that 5 spots become necessary for repeating and 6 spots be counted as 12. This variant was rejected by children of level two. They argued that it is not allowed or even not possible to repeat throwing the die in the case of 5 spots because 6 is the crucial number.

3. The rules are flexible and based on the situation; they are interpreted as an agreement and can, after discussion, be changed during the play process; i.e., the principle of action maintenance is dominant. For example, the children played "Chinese jumprope." In this game, two players stretch an elastic band while the other players twist different figures by jumping on the band and connecting both sides of it with their legs. Although there are fixed rules for playing "Chinese jumprope," children of level three simplified them for some less skillful players, and they also allowed children to create new figures if they had a knack for this activity. The frequency distribution of these levels is shown in Table 13.3.

Different understandings of the rules resulted in conflict if the participants with the higher level tried to continue the object relation at that level. This caused a change in the object relation by the other subject so that the interaction was broken off. If the children at the higher level operated at the lowest level present, then the interaction could be continued without friction.

With regard to the different age groups, the following similarities and differences were found: During their spontaneous play activities, the children most frequently interacted in the same age groups; less than one-third of the interactions were mixed age ones. In play sequences of the same age groups, the interaction with only one partner was dominant, whereas in the mixed age group more than one partner was equally preferred ($\chi^2 = 19.736$, $p < .001$).

The preschool group substantially showed more object relations of form 1 (determined by the characteristics of the object) than the school-age group ($\chi^2 = 28.785$, $p < .001$) and than the mixed age group ($\chi^2 = 49.090$, $p < .001$). The common activity dominated in the school-age group (as compared to the preschool group: $\chi^2 = 20.031$, $p < .001$; compared to the mixed age group: $\chi^2 = 34.289$, $p < .001$). The frequency of form 3 (use of capability) did not significantly differ between the three groups.

The differences in the following of rules is shown in Table 13.4.

There, the first level (rough framework) dominated in the preschool group, whereas level 2 (strict rules) was prevalent in the school-age group. In this group, however, level 3 (flexible rules; not present in the preschool group) was also represented slightly more than in the mixed age group. Nevertheless, the positive

TABLE 13.3
Frequency Distribution of the Following of Rules (In Percentages)

Form of Following of Rules	Preschool Group	School-Age Group	Mixed Age Group	Total
1 (rough framework)	38	4	4	46
2 (strict rules)	6	16	3	25
3 (flexible rules)	0	20	9	29

TABLE 13.4
Group Differences in the Following of Rules (Tested by χ^2)

Form of Following Rules	Preschool/ School-Age Group	Preschool/ Mixed Age Group	School-Age/ Mixed Age Group
1 (rough framework)	28.785^{+++}	49.090^{+++}	0
2 (strict rules)	4.031^{++}	1.111	9.431^{++}
3 (flexible rules)	12.647^{+++}	5.769^{++}	3.333^{+}

$^{+}p < .05.$
$^{++}p < .01.$
$^{+++}p < .001.$

267

resolution of conflicts (adaptation of the individual level to the lowest level present; see earlier) dominated in the mixed age group (6%).

In summary, one can deduce the following from the observations:

• The beginning of interaction is characterized by the choice of a common object relation. This object relation includes a specific form of action structure (prevalence of object features, activity, or capability). These forms are ordered hierarchically, and in children's play the preference of the forms varies with age.

• For the maintenance of the interaction, a common structural level of action is necessary. This level is not only dependent on the chosen form of object relation but is also related to the following of rules. This following of rules can be divided into three developmental levels (rough framework, strict rules, and flexible rules); these levels also vary with age in children's play.

• The termination of a common object relation is either reached by mutual consent, or it is a consequence of conflict situations. Conflicts can be caused by: lack of agreement on a common object relation; appearance of different structural levels of action; one-sided change in common object relation. Strategies used for resolution of conflicts include: proposal of another common object relation; adaptation of the individual structural level to that of the partner; the joint change of a common object relation.

These summary statements about the process of interaction can be graphically represented (see Fig. 13.1). The model illustrates the critical points of the interaction process and the strategies used for resolution of conflicts.

Discussion

First, some findings that can be coordinated with findings of other research are discussed. During their spontaneous play activities, the children most frequently interacted with only one partner; this is consistent with the research on the development of peer relations (Mussen, Conger, & Kagan, 1976). On the other hand, the results of the mixed age group (nearly as many interactions with more than one partner; prevalence of positive conflict resolution) supports Beller's (1982) finding regarding the developmental stimulation in mixed age groups. The relatively low number of play activities in mixed age groups, as compared with the total number of interaction sequences, might be caused by the socialization practices in our culture. Because the predominant educational system of our society is based on the organization of homogeneous age groups (e.g., nursery school, preparatory school, and age-related classes in the school, and children are rarely accustomed to growing up and interacting within mixed age, nonfamily groups.

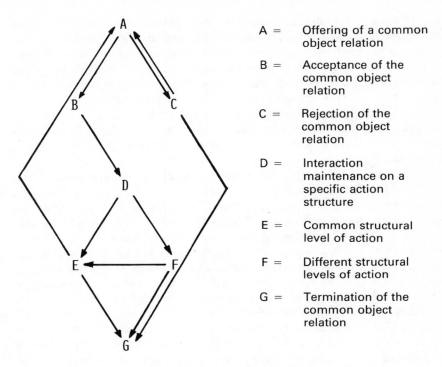

A =   Offering of a common
      object relation

B =   Acceptance of the
      common object
      relation

C =   Rejection of the
      common object
      relation

D =   Interaction
      maintenance on a
      specific action
      structure

E =   Common structural
      level of action

F =   Different structural
      levels of action

G =   Termination of the
      common object
      relation

FIG. 13.1 Model of the interaction process.

The observations of strategies children used for resolution of conflicts brings to mind recent research in social cognition (see Butterworth & Light, 1982; Damon, 1982). The ability to adapt one's individual structure of action to that of the partner seems to be stimulated by interactions with children at different developmental levels (Mugny & Doise, 1978). Previous studies in this field, however, have mostly been done by means of interview methods. The observational method used in this study broadens the possibilities to the analysis of developmental processes at a period when verbal skills are not yet well developed.

The observed forms of action structure related to the choice of a common object relation have shown that the postulated classification could be applied to play. Form 1 and form 2 are similarly described by Vygotsky (1966). He characterizes the first structure as inversion of the object/meaning quotient; i.e., the subject gives an individual meaning to the object in consideration of its basic features. The second form is, in Vygotsky's terms, the inversion of the activity/meaning quotient. In both forms, the subjective valence of the object relation is stressed.

The evaluation of effort, diligence, and talent (as empirically found in the field of work) applied, however, to only one aspect of the play sequences. It was especially taken into consideration by the children within specific games and sports. In those games, parts of the objective structure that dominate the modern structure of work (see Oerter, 1981) are crystallized so that the children can lose their sense of voluntary participation in play. In that case, play can easily be transformed into work-like activities. Thus, form 3 of the action structure seems to be a critical stage in the development of play. As long as spontaneity is maintained, the use of capability remains playful and can be subordinate to the principle of play action maintenance. Otherwise, the game itself becomes a part of the objective structure (e.g., in adulthood "playing" chess or football as a profession).

The adherence to rules is another important aspect of play with partners. The occurrence of different levels in the following of rules brings to mind Piaget's (1932) early work in this area. The results are also similar to Oerter's (1983) classification of peer relationships. Within this system, development is characterized by different regulations of the common object relation. The principle of interaction maintenance represents the highest level. At this level, capability in the form of adroitness becomes subordinate to capability in the field of social interaction. From this point of view, the postulated general classification of developmental stages can be applied to social interaction, too.

The results of the study as a whole show that the action theory approach not only supplies an integrative perspective for the study of play, but it also leads to an insight into the interaction process that might be helpful in the planning of future intervention studies. The encouragement of spontaneous play activities within mixed age groups could be used as a means of promoting cognitive and social development.

EXTENSION OF THE CLASSIFICATION SYSTEM

After having completed the first study, there was discussion among the raters about the different aspects of the action structure. Whereas the differentiation of O, A, and C is already obvious at the beginning of the play, i.e., through the choice of a specific object relation, the following of rules gives additional information about the maintenance of play action during the play process. The question arose whether both aspects could be integrated in one classification system. Based on the empirical findings of Study 1, an extension of the "O, A, C" classification was proposed. Accordingly, Oerter's (1981) model of development was specified for play, and the following levels were postulated:

1. The object relation is determined by the characteristics of the object. The following of rules is oriented toward features inherent in the object itself. The formula for this structure is: $S - O_R$, where R = rules. Example: As already

mentioned, a doll's cup can be used for several actions related to its special shape, but it would never be used outside this frame, for instance, as a comb.

2. The object relation is determined by different forms of activity. The action frame is oriented toward specific rules that regulate the play process. If the rules are strict and immutable the formula is $S - A_R - O$; if the rules are flexible and based on the situation, this is shown by R in parentheses: $S - A_{(R)} - O$. Examples: role play, round games.

3. The object relation is determined by the use of capability and related activities. Accordingly, rules become more distinctive and complex. In the case of strict rule adherence, the formula is $S - C - A_R - O$; in the case of flexible rule adherence, it is $S - C - A_{(R)} - O$. Examples: games of skill, sports.

4. The object relation is determined by the principle of play action maintenance (represented by P). Capability and activity can be handled flexibly; both are equally subordinate (C,A) to this principle. Neither adroitness nor a specific activity dominate the object relation. The formula for this structure is $S - P (C, A) - O$. Example: On this level, the game "Master Mind" can be played either in the usual manner (finding out the arrangement for four hidden pieces of different color) or in an advanced variant (using more than four colors, doubling the pieces of the same color), or it can simply be used for placing all available pieces on the board into different patterns. The choice of the action frame is, in each case, adapted to the individual situation; i.e., the game is only used as a means to the goal of play action maintenance.

If two or more subjects are playing together, the individual action patterns must be accommodated. This begins with the choice of a common object relation, continues with the interaction maintenance on a common level of action structure, and ends with the abandonment of a common object relation (as shown in the model presented previously). In the case of structural differences between the action patterns of the partners, conflicts may arise that can lead to the termination of interaction.

With the help of the extended classification system and the interaction model, the course of play and related conflicts can be analyzed. This procedure was used in a training program for educators to improve their observational skills and to teach them intervention strategies for conflict situations in children's play. Because that program and its results are reviewed elsewhere (Burtchen, 1985), they are not discussed in this chapter. During the preparations for the program, however, a second study was undertaken to complement the results of Study 1.

The special aim of Study 2 was to examine conflict situations during children's play in a setting where adults are also available as partners. Because the children in the first study preferred playing in the same age groups, but because developmental stimulation was higher in mixed age interactions, the broadening of the age range was interesting; i.e., the influence of an adult's presence on children's play and their resolution of conflicts was examined. For this purpose, the adults were asked to act as a potential play partner who—in the case of conflict—could help the children in finding a positive resolution (i.e., not to give up the interaction).

STUDY 2

Method

Subjects. The subjects were 36 students (8 males and 28 females) and 113 children (55 boys and 58 girls) aged 3 to 10 years. The students participated in an advanced tutorial class in the University of Munich's education department. In addition, they all completed a course of practical work in kindergartens and play centers from which the children's sample was drawn.

Procedure. First, the students became acquainted with the theoretical framework and were introduced to the analysis of spontaneous play activities. They were also informed about their role in the subsequent play sessions; i.e., three basic strategies were agreed upon: (1) Do not compel the children to play but let them act spontaneously; (2) in conflict situations, do not intervene immediately but first let the children find a resolution themselves; (3) if the children do not find a resolution other than fighting or giving up the interaction, try to demonstrate a positive resolution.

After this introduction, the students went in pairs into the kindergartens and play centers. One member of each pair played with the children while the other observed the interactions. This combination was changed at every meeting. The "observers" made a protocol of each interaction sequence and discussed it with the "players" when the play session was over.

A total of 144 interaction sequences were recorded. Of these, 96 were sequences with 1 child and the student "player," 22 with 2 partners, and 26 sequences with more than 2 partners. The ages of the children in the individual sequences are shown in Table 13.5.

TABLE 13.5
Frequency Distribution of Age Groups in the Interaction Sequences
(In Percentages)

Number of Children Involved	Frequency of Sequences	Preschool Group	School-Age Group	Mixed Age Group
1	67	34	33	—
2	15	6	4	5
> 2	18	3	11	4

The evaluation was accomplished in three steps. The protocols were coded and all interaction sequences including conflict situations were selected. Then, these protocols were analyzed by means of the extended classification system of the action structure (pp. 270) and the model of the interaction process (p. 269). Finally, the strategies used for resolution of the conflict were classified and assigned to the individual actor (child or adult), and the consequences for the maintenance of the play were described. The analysis was completed by two independent observers, who reached a rate of agreement of 88%.

Results

Because the prerequisite for the play interactions was the spontaneity of the children, the adult players never started proposing an object relation but waited for the children's initiative. In most of the cases, the children preferred playing in dyads. Thus, in two-thirds of the sequences only one child was involved (there was no significant difference between the preschool and the school-age group). No conflict arose in these sequences because the adult subjects always accepted the common object relation proposed by the child and adapted their individual action structure to that of the partner. Thus, the termination of the interaction was caused by mutual consent.

During the interactions in which two or more children were involved, a total of 25 conflict situations were recorded. Of these, 11 were caused by the lack of agreement on a common object relation, and 14 by the appearance of different structural levels of action. In 12 of the cases, the differences appeared on level 2 (common activity), or between levels 2 and 3 (use of capability). These differences were found in all age groups. Two differences appeared in the preschool group between level 1 (characteristics of the object) and level 2. The frequency distribution of all conflict situations is shown in Table 13.6. There were neither significant differences between the age groups with regard to the number of children involved in the interaction nor with regard to the frequency of conflict situations.

The strategies used for resolutions of conflicts are described in the following. In the case of lack of agreement on a common object relation, an alternative

TABLE 13.6
Frequency Distribution of Conflict Situations (In Percentages)

Number of Children Involved	Frequency of Conflicts	Preschool Group	School-Age Group	Mixed Age Group
1	—	—	—	—
2	8	4	2	2
> 2	9	2	5	2

was proposed either by the children (4 times) or by the adult (7 times). If the children did not find a resolution themselves, the adult encouraged them to find their own resolution by proposing different alternatives. Finally, with the exception of one sequence, an agreement on a common object relation was reached in each case.

Conflicts caused by the appearance of different structural levels of action were resolved in 13 interaction sequences; here, too, one conflict was not resolved. In six cases, the children found the resolution without intervention. The strategy used in five cases was the adaptation of the higher action structure to the lower level. Once (conflict between levels 1 and 2), the "inferior" child adapted his action structure by imitating the activities of the "superior" children. They played "baker's shop" in the sandbox. The roles were: bakers, sales persons, cashiers, and buyers. The child of level 1 was a baker, but he unsystematically filled the cake tins with sand and piled up the sand on the border of the sandbox. The other players protested because the border was the counter and the "cakes" had to be arranged in a line for sale. The price of the ware was determined by its size and perfection. Some of the children wanted to exclude the "intruder" from playing and, for a while, he only watched the game. Then, he imitated the activities of the other players, and the play was continued without friction.

In seven cases, the resolution was reached by intervention of the adult player, who encouraged the children to find a common action structure. The conflict was discussed and the possibility of adapting the rules to the individual situation stressed. Only once did three of the preschool children persist in a strict adherence to the given rules. In this sequence, the game "my aunt from America" was played. The rules are: The players successively name a present brought by the aunt, and each of the players has to repeat all previously mentioned presents. Besides repeating verbally, the players must mime the typical activity related to the presents (e.g., riding a bicycle, sewing with a sewing machine). One child proposed to repeat the names of the presents only by miming, but this was rejected by the other children. Because they were the majority in the group, the fourth child was willing to forego the change of the rules.

In the other cases, the children of the lower level first wanted to continue the game in their way, but, after discussion, they agreed to a modification of their particular play schema, and the interaction was maintained on a higher level of action structure. The frequency distribution of all conflict resolutions is shown in Table 13.7.

There was neither a significant difference between the total number of children's own conflict resolutions and that intiated by the adults nor between the children's and the adult's proposing another common object relation. The type of adapting the individual action structure to that of the partner(s), however, was different in both groups: In the children's own resolutions, adapting to a lower level was prevalent ($\chi^2 = 4.888$, $p < .05$); whereas in the resolutions

TABLE 13.7
Frequency Distribution of Conflict Resolutions (In Percentages)

Type of Resolution	Children's Own Resolutions	Intervention by the Adult
Offering another common object relation	16	24
Adapting the action structure to a lower level	20	4
Adapting the action structure to a higher level	4	24
Other (negative)	8	

intiated by the adults, adapting to a higher level dominated ($\chi^2 = 6.632$, $p <$ .01).

As already mentioned, two of the conflict situations could not be resolved. In the first case, there was a difference between two children acting at the structural level 1 and 2. A "Lotto" game was played whereby different small pictures must be coordinated with a picture card including the same details. The first child simply put the pictures on the card as he liked, whereas the second child followed the given rules of the game. Both children continued playing on their different levels, and the adult player became the link connecting the interaction. The children clung to the adult, but they did not stop quarreling with one another.

The second conflict situation was caused by lack of agreement on a common object relation. Some of the children wanted to play "policeman," the others preferred playing "hospital." The adult offered an integrative alternative (playing "accident"), but the leaders of both groups rejected this alternative. Although most of the children agreed to the adult's proposal, the opponents tried to convince one another that their proposal was the best. Because the adult wanted to demonstrate a resolution, he continued the interaction with those children who were willing to accept a common object relation.

In these two sequences, all the play activities were determined by ambivalent actions. The children wanted to play, but they seemed to dislike their partners. This was obvious from their facial expressions and verbalization while playing. Thus, the interaction process was influenced by a negative valence. Unable to overcome their differences, they discontinued playing together.

Discussion

In contrast to the first study, the second study offered some additional information about conflict and cooperation in children's play when an adult was involved in the interaction process. Although dyads were preferred in both studies, in the second study only adults were chosen as partners in dyadic play. This might have been caused by the adult's concentration on the individual interests of each child, something that does not usually occur in play centers.

The number of conflict situations was relatively low during the second study in comparison with Study 1. The presence of the adults might have been the reason for this. Above and beyond that, the adults set an example by their cooperative behavior. In sequences where only one child was involved, the adult's adaptation to the child's level of action may, however, also hinder his/her development. Because the resolution of conflicts in the other sequences showed that the children were able to adapt their action structure to an even higher level, a systematic introduction of moderate discrepancies in the child's experience should perhaps be considered in future studies.

In about half the sequences where several children were involved, "natural" conflicts arose. Here the encouragement of the children to find their own resolutions and the offering of different alternatives was a successful intervention strategy. This "stimulation task" of the adults is stressed by Bryant (1974). He argues that a conflict per se does not lead to further development; only the directed intervention of an adult can promote this. The results of this study showed, however, that the children were also able to find their own solutions without adult intervention. Similar findings are presented by Morrison and Kuhn (1983).

Although there was no significant difference in the frequency of conflicts between the preschool group and school-age group, most of the conflicts were observed in sequences where children advocating strict rule adherence were present. This compulsory adherence to given rules restricts the action potentialities of the child and increases the conflict potential in social interactions during a period when common activities are becoming prevalent. On the other hand, the strict regulation of actions seems to be a necessary step in the developmental process because the extension of the action field has to be clearly arranged. Children make following the rules a part of the objective structure by restricting themselves within play activities. This process was described by Vygotsky (1966).

As mentioned earlier, the children were usually able to resolve their own conflicts. A significant difference in the frequency of solutions was not found when adults intervened as compared with the children's own resolutions. Significant differences were, however, found in the type of solutions. Without intervention, the children more often adapted their individual action structure to a lower level; the adult intervention enabled a more frequent adaptation to a higher level. Thus, flexible rules were already present in the preschool group, which was not the case in Study 1.

Although Study 2 showed that the adult could play an important role in conflict resolution, the valence of the partner should also be considered. Two conflicts resulted from the valence of the partners themselves. In addition to differences between structural levels, negative valence of the play partner can lead to the termination of interaction. In this situation, the influence of the adult is minimized. The conflict can only be resolved if the children are willing to grapple with the resistance of the partner (see Gugler, 1976). The analysis of these conflict sequences showed that the maintenance of the common object relation not only depends on the homogeneity of action structures, but also on the positive valence of the interaction partners.

In summary, the results of the second study confirm the advantage of children's spontaneous play activities within mixed age groups as a means of experiencing and exercising cooperation. Play with partners of different structural levels of action can stimulate children's cognitive development and social competence. Thus, the promotion of mixed age group interactions should be emphasized.

CONCLUDING REMARKS

The application of the action theory framework to the concept of play began with a general definition. This definition was used in two empirical studies for analyzing children's play activities in everyday situations. Because these studies were restricted to specific age groups and to play within social interactions, further studies need to be done to prove the advantage of this integrative approach in other contexts.

The central category of the action concept is the object relation, and in the case of play the object relation is dominated by subjective valence. This prerequisite was a clearly distinctive criterion for the analysis of children's activities. During the action, the object relation is maintained at a specific level of action structure. It was shown that the classification of structural levels in play is similar to that in work but that there are also some differences. These differences are mainly based on the different value of the objective structure. In play, only parts of the objective structure are accepted, and this acceptance is voluntary. Otherwise, play can easily be transformed into work-like activities.

Play with partners is much more complicated than solitary play because not only does a common object relation (accepted by both sides) have to be established and maintained during the interaction process, but differing structural levels of the partners must sometimes be accommodated as well. This complex task was already managed well by preschool children, especially within mixed age group interactions. The children adapted their individual structural level of action to that of the partner(s), i.e., in most of the cases to a lower level, whereas adult intervention also enabled the children to adapt their action structure to an even higher level. The adults promoted cooperation by encouraging the children to find their own resolutions in conflict situations and by demonstrating a positive resolution when the children were unable to resolve a conflict themselves.

In the case of the partner's negative valence, however, the influence of the adult was minimized and the conflicts of the children were not resolved. This might have been caused by a shift in the subject–object relation, whereby the partner himself seemed to become the object of the relation. Because the second study only touched upon this problem, further studies need to be done to examine it in detail.

Another problem is generated by the connection of play and social interaction in both studies. The question arises whether the classification of structural levels could also be applied to other contexts of play. Thus, related studies are necessary to test the general applicability of the action-theory concept of play, and the concept itself must be elaborated.

SUMMARY

An approach based on action theory is proposed as an integrative perspective for research on play activities. The central category of this concept, the object relation, was used in two empirical studies to analyze 190 spontaneous play interactions of 230 preschool and school-age children and 36 adults. Common object relations were identified as the interactions commenced, proceeded, and ended. Three types of action structure significantly distinguishing between the age groups are described. Additionally, levels of competence in dealing with rules differ, accounting for conflict behavior and cooperation. The action structures and levels of competence in dealing with rules were integrated into an expanded classification system and a related interaction model. The analysis of play activities revealed the children's strategies for resolving their own conflicts and showed opportunities for stimulation by adult intervention.

The advantage of a perspective based on action theory is that it integrates previously disparate concepts of play.

REFERENCES

Beller, E. K. (1982). Die Förderung frühkindlicher Entwicklung im Alter von 0-3 Jahren. In R. Oerter & L. Montada (Eds.), *Entwicklungspsychologie* (pp. 704–728). München: Urban & Schwarzenberg.
Berlyne, D. E. (1960). *Conflict, arousal, and curiosity*. New York: McGraw-Hill.
Berlyne, D. E. (1969). Laughter, humor and play. In I. Lindzey & E. Aronson (Eds.), *The handbook of social psychology* (Vol. 3, pp. 795–852). Reading, MA: Addison-Wesley.
Boesch, E. E. (1982). Das persönliche Objekt. In E. D. Lantermann (Ed.), *Wechselwirkungen* (pp. 29–41). Göttingen: Hogrefe.
Bronfenbrenner, U. (1981). *Die Ökologie der menschlichen Entwicklung*. Stuttgart: Klett-Cotta.
Bryant, P. (1974). *Perception and understanding in young children. An experimental approach*. London: Methuen.
Burtchen, I. (1983). Analyse von Spielverhalten im Vor- und Grundschulalter unter dem Aspekt des gemeinsamen Objektbezugs. *Zeitschrift für Entwicklungspsychologie und Pädagogische Psychologie, 15*, 139–148.
Burtchen, I. (1985). *Psychologie der Gesundheit*. Donauwörth: Auer.

Butterworth, G., & Light, P. (1982). *Social cognition: Studies of the development of understanding.* Chicago: University of Chicago Press.

Christie, J. F., & Johnsen, E. P. (1983). The role of play in social–intellectual development. *Review of Educational Research, 53,* 93–115.

Csikszentmihalyi, M. (1979). The concept of flow. In B. Sutton–Smith (Ed.), *Play and learning* (pp. 257–274). New York: Gardner Press.

Damon, W. (1982). Zur Entwicklung der sozialen Kognition des Kindes. Zwei Vorgänge zum Verständnis von sozialer Kognition. In W. Edelstein & M. Keller (Eds.), *Perspektivität und Interpretation* (pp. 110–145). Frankfurt/M.: Suhrkamp.

Elkind, D. (1981). *Children and adolescents.* New York: Oxford University Press.

Field, T. M., & Ignatoff, E. (1981). Videotaping effects on the behaviors of low income mothers and their infants during floorplay interactions. *Journal of Applied Developmental Psychology, 2,* 227–235.

Freud, S. (1941). Analyse der Phobie eines fünfjährigen Knaben. *Gesammelte Werke* (Vol. 7, pp. 239–377). Frankfurt/M.: Fischer.

Görlitz, D. (Ed.). (1983). *Kindliche Erklärungsmuster. Beiträge zur Attributionsforschung* (Vol. 1). Weinheim: Beltz.

Gugler, B. (1976). *Zur Erfassung und sequentiellen Analyse des Streitgeschehens bei Vorschulkindern.* Unpublished doctoral dissertation, University of Bern, Swiss.

Hutt, C. (1979). Exploration and play. In B. Sutton-Smith (Ed.), *Play and learning* (pp. 175–194). New York: Gardner Press.

Jacobson, J. L. (1981). The role of inanimate objects in early peer interactions. *Child Development, 52,* 618–626.

Krasnor, L., & Pepler, D. (1980). The study of children's play: Some suggested future directions. *New Directions for Child Development, 9,* 85–94.

Kreuzer, K. J. (1983). *Handbuch der Spielpädagogik* (Vol. 1). Düsseldorf: Schwann.

Lehr, U. (1978). *Die Rolle der Mutter in der Sozialisation des Kindes* (2nd ed.). Darmstadt: Steinkopff.

Leontjev, A. N. (1977). *Tätigkeit, Bewußtsein, Persönlichkeit.* Stuttgart: Klett.

Lewis, M. (1979). The social determination of play. In B. Sutton-Smith (Ed.), *Play and learning* (pp. 23–33). New York: Gardner Press.

Morrison, H., & Kuhn, D. (1983). Cognitive aspects of preschooler's peer imitation in a play situation. *Child Development, 54,* 1041–1053.

Mugny, G., & Doise, W. (1978). Socio-cognitive conflict and structure of individual and collective performance. *European Journal of Social Psychology, 8,* 181–192.

Mussen, P. H., Conger, J. J., & Kagan, J. (1976). *Lehrbuch der Kinderpsychologie.* Stuttgart: Klett.

Oerter, R. (1980). *Moderne Entwicklungspsychologie* (18th ed.). Donauwörth: Auer.

Oerter, R. (1981). Cognitive socialization during adolescence. *International Journal of Behavioral Development, 4,* 61–76.

Oerter, R. (1982). Interaktion als Individuum-Umwelt-Bezug. In E. D. Lantermann (Ed.), *Wechselwirkungen* (pp. 101–127). Göttingen: Hogrefe.

Oerter, R. (1983). Peers. In R. K. Silbereisen & L. Montada (Eds.), *Entwicklungspsychologie. Ein Handbuch in Schlüsselbegriffen* (pp. 145–155). München: Urban & Schwarzenberg.

Piaget, J. (1932). *The moral judgment of the child.* New York: Harcourt Brace.

Piaget, J. (1975). *Nachahmung, Spiel und Traum.* Stuttgart: Klett.

Rubin, K. H. (1980). *Children's play.* San Francisco: Jossey-Bass.

Rubinstein, S. L. (1977). *Sein und Bewußtsein.* Berlin: Akademie Verlag.

Schlosberg, H. (1947). The concept of play. *Psychological Review, 54,* 229–231.

Sutton-Smith, B. (1979). *Play and learning.* New York: Gardner Press.

Vandenberg, B. (1980). Play, problem-solving and creativity. *New Directions for Child Development, 9,* 49–68.

Vygotsky, L. S. (1966). Das Spiel und seine Rolle für die psychische Entwicklung des Kindes. *Voprosy psichologii, 6*, 62–76.

Youniss, J. (1982). Die Entwicklung und Funktion von Freundschaftsbeziehungen. In W. Edelstein & M. Keller (Eds.), *Perspektivität und Interpretation* (pp. 78–109). Frankfurt/M.: Suhrkamp.

CHAPTER FOURTEEN

PRETEND PLAY:
CREATIVITY AND
CONSCIOUSNESS

GRETA G. FEIN
University of Maryland

Over a decade of research has deepened our appreciation of pretense, a behavior in which one thing is playfully treated as if it were something else. For many of us, this behavior marks a basic developmental phenomenon, as basic as language or attachment. Like these other behavioral phenomena, pretense displays distinctive structures that change over time and serve consequential developmental functions. Like attachment behavior, pretend play is sensitive to environmental conditions, but unlike attachment behavior, pretend play is suppressed by stress and facilitated in secure and comfortable settings. Like language, pretend play is a symbolic behavior, one that may even use words and vocal gestures; but unlike language, the semantic structures of pretend behavior are personal, its syntax is informal, and its pragmatic orientation essentially is impractical. Despite these important differences, pretense is charged with feelings as intense as those characteristic of attachment, and it expresses thoughts as intricate as those conveyed in language. Perhaps the claim that pretense is a distinctive form of behavior rests largely on this unique confluence of emotional intensity and conceptual depth.

The events represented in pretend play also have a special relationship to events in the real world. On the one hand, pretend representations seem to float free of real-world conventions; on the other, these conventions seems to be embedded in these representations. A child in the role of mother might be imitating what at first glance appears to be a highly stereotyped sequence of maternal actions. A second glance, however, reveals a maternal caricature, recognizable as what it represents but not a copy of what it represents. People and things in the immediate environment are given nonconventional meanings (child as mother, doll as baby); but the relation between pretend signifiers and that which is signified can best be described as representation in the service of exaggeration, embellishment, and ulterior signification. It is this embedding of the nonliteral in the literal with unexpected, unlikely elaborations that gives pretend play the appearance of a creative endeavor.

Recent research supports the usefulness of a contrast between divergent and convergent thinking and between divergent problems and convergent problems (Guilford, 1950; Kogan, 1983; Pepler & Ross, 1981). Although several correlational and experimental studies report a relation between play and measures of divergent thinking (see Fein, 1981; Rubin, Fein, & Vandenberg, 1983 for reviews of this literature), research most germane to pretend play was reported by Dansky (1980a, 1980b). In one study (Dansky, 1980a), preschool children were divided into "players" and "nonplayers" based on classroom observations of make-believe play. These children were then randomly assigned to three experimental situations. In one, children could play freely with a set of materials; in the other conditions they either observed an adult's novel actions or attempted to solve problems using the same materials. On an alternative uses test, the highest scores were obtained by pretend players in the free-play condition. In another study, Dansky (1980b) provided pretend play training to disadvantaged children. Controlled for adult involvement and for props, the findings indicate that play training facilitated sociodramatic play and higher scores on tests of divergent thinking. At least in preschool children, pretend play seems to involve processes similar to those presumably measured on tests of divergent thinking. It should be noted, however, that these tests grew out of the view that creative thought is characterized by the fluency, originality, and flexibility of an individual's approach to problems that permit alternative solutions and diverse answers. If pretend play is viewed as a natural form of creativity, Dansky's findings validate these assumptions. By the same token, a closer analysis of pretend behavior might yield a model of creative thinking that goes beyond tests of ideational fluency. What kind of a system must be conceptualized in order to comprehend the creative structures of pretend play?

The following analysis is based on pretend play episodes produced by children whose observed behavior confirmed the judgment of their teachers that they were highly skilled pretend players. I chose master players for this analysis because they provide glimpses of what pretend play is like when its potential is realized. Some of these children come from affluent families, whereas others come from working-class families or single-parent households. Some of the children attended classrooms in which pretend play was encouraged, but others were in settings that provided little inducement beyond the traditional "housekeeping" area. The material used in the following discussion was collected by my students as part of in-depth case studies of the play of individual children. All in all, 15 master players from 15 classrooms were studied.

Theoretical considerations suggest that when master players produce pretend episodes, the play is marked by referential freedom, denotative license, affective relationships, sequential uncertainty, and self-mirroring. One purpose of the present chapter is to illustrate these characteristics of pretend play and to examine their implications for a theoretical model of pretense as a creative activity. A second purpose is to describe aspects of a cognitive-affective system capable of generating these characteristics.

REFERENTIAL FREEDOM

In pretend play, one object is used as if it were another, one person behaves as if she were another, and an immediate time and place are treated as if they were otherwise and elsewhere. Referential freedom extends beyond persons and objects in the immediate environment; children will talk to imaginary persons and use imaginary things. Of all the numerous possibilities, object substitutions have been the most extensively studied.

Children's ability to substitute one object for another shows striking changes between 12 and 24 months (Watson & Fischer, 1977). With age, the need for physical or functional similarity between a substitute object and its referent diminishes (Elder & Pederson, 1978; Jackowitz & Watson, 1980; Watson & Fischer, 1977). By 36 months, children can inhibit actions toward structured objects likely to elicit a conventional manipulative response (Pederson, Rook-Green, & Elder, 1981). These studies trace a developmental shift from a form of mental organization in which objects in the immediate external environment structure pretend behavior to a form in which pretend behavior can be structured by an internal, mentally represented environment. These data support the idea that referential freedom grows between 1 and 6 years of age (see Fein, 1981 for a review of this research).

It is a mistake, however, even for experimental simplicity, to treat pretend substitutions or creations as single isolated acts, a particular idea in relation to a particular object. Rather, this activity is sensitive to relationships between objects (Fein, 1975). The meaning of one object (cup) influences the meaning of another (horse) when the two are related in an action (drinking). These influences most likely reflect interrelated networks of ideas and understanding (cups are for drinking and horses are able to drink). A novel relationship between horse and cup is thinkable even though the referent activity (a horse drinking from a cup) is not likely to ever be observed. In experimental studies it is necessary to seek a simplified and even static expression of what are often intricate, dynamic, and more elaborate relationships. Although my 1975 study indicated that novelties emerge when previously disparate concepts are related, the types of relationships occurring in spontaneous pretend play are far more diverse and multilayered than this. One curative for the limitations of experimental designs is to examine spontaneous behavior for evidence of more subtle transformational patterns. The following episode was produced by 4-year-olds who were master players for their age:

Ellen, Alison, and Sally are on the rug. Charles is hovering nearby. Paul joins the group later.)

Ellen (To Alison): My daughter's at school.

Sally: I'll go check. O. K., Mom?

(Charles takes a bean bag out of a bucket on the shelf.)

Ellen: Hey, no, that's for my daughter. She's at school.

(Alison walks over to Ellen.)

Ellen (cheerfully to Alison): Hi, daughter. Oh, you're a good girl. You're home now. (To Sally) I think they're having a fire out there.

Sally: Yes, they are. We better go out there.

Ellen carries the bean bags to a nearby table and begins pounding them.)

Ellen (still pounding): These are nice steaks, eh? (To Alison) Baby, you go to your room and get ready for bed, eh?

Sally (loudly): Supper's done! (To Charles, who has been watching) Baby, you go to your room.
Charles: Well, I'm hungry and I want to help you.
Ellen: No, you're not going to help us.
Alison (trying to use baby talk): Me tryin' to help.
Ellen (to Alison, who has not done anything): Thanks, honey, for helping me to make supper.
(The girls cover each bean bag with a small piece of cloth representing slices of cheese.)
Sally: I'm putting this in the oven.

* * * * *

Paul: Here's two sandwiches. I got two more sandwiches. (He picks up the wastebasket.) I need this trash can.
Sally (pointing to the basket): Hey, Mom, look!
Ellen (alarm in her voice): Something happened to our basket!
Paul (to Ellen): Hey, Mom, can you make more burger?
(Ellen screeches like a baby.)
Paul (to no one in particular): I wonder what's wrong with her? (He turns the basket upside-down.) This is gonna be a grill. Let's put these on.
Ellen: Hey, I'm the one who works here.
Paul: Well, we're making these burgers.

The preceding episode is rich in transformational complexity. First, there are person transformations that yield a mother (Ellen), an elder daughter (Sally), and a young daughter (Alison). Note, however, that these three roles embody doubly differentiated relationships in a triadic structure; "mother–elder daughter" is differentiated from "mother–young daughter," "elder daughter–mother," and "elder daughter–young daughter." The role of "mother" is further differentiated as she reluctantly acquires two sons. Each generic role thus implies several subroles according to who is participating in the relationship at any given moment (Fein, 1983). There also are secondary person transformations in which "daughter" changes in age from school girl to baby.

In addition, this sequence contains object transformations in which bean bags are gifts for children, until the action of pounding them with fists turns them into steaks. The action of pounding functions as a double-layered transformation: Mother is rendered as a forceful figure as bean bags are converted into steaks. "Cloth-on-top-of-bean bags" yields their further conversion into hamburgers. Cookout fires and an oven are ideational transformations, until Paul proposes a material transformation whereby a waste basket becomes a grill (Matthews, 1977).

A transformational mechanism has been posited to account for the referential freedom of pretense (Fein, 1975). In this account, the term *transformation* refers to the mental process whereby a representational template is mapped onto persons and objects in the immediate environment. This process is presumed to be operating when objects, persons, or places are treated as if they were other than they are. But there needs to be a way in which these templates become activated. Piaget's (1962) notion of play as assimilation introduces the idea that, in play, behavior is detached from accommodative pressures. Because this decontextualizing of behavior from the immediate environment disrupts the adaptive balance between behavior and its practical consequences, convergent problems are converted into divergent problems. In infant play, sensorimotor schemes are detached from their practical outcomes. In early childhood, the emergence of a generalized semiotic function brings with it the ability to manipulate representations of decontextualized behavior. Piagetian theory thus implies a mechanism for decontextualizing behavior and activating the representational templates responsible for pretend transformations. This mechanism, which first appears during the second year of life, accounts for the rapid growth of referential freedom in this period.

Initially, the notion of transformation served as a heuristic device to guide research on the substitutional aspects of pretense. The results of these efforts are impressive enough to warrant an effort to attempt the transition from heuristic device to theoretical construct. Studies of the development of referential freedom suggest that the decontextualization of behavior is essentially an affective-motivational phenomenon. The baby who pretends to sleep is not actually tired and has no intention of falling asleep. The neural and physiological mechanisms responsible for sleep are not operating. Rather, the infant simulates a need state that is not being experienced directly. At first, the simulation is suggested by a pillow or a bed; later, a soft fabric will do. Eventually, the simulation is activated by predominantly ideational processes. With development, the affective-motivational range of these simulations expand as representational vehicles or template structures of diverse experiences become organized. When activated, these affective-motivational structures alter the child's relationship to the immediate surroundings. But, they may also alter the child's relationship to her own actual affective experience.

DENOTATIVE LICENSE

Referential freedom refers to the pretending child's divergent relation to the immediate environment. By denotative license, I mean to suggest that the playing child also adopts a divergent stance with respect to actual experience. The pretend events generated by master players are inventions rather than documentaries of real-world occurrences; a readout of what the child feels might be (some of which may have been) rather than an accurate account of the child's knowledge of what is.

About 4 decades ago, Sears and his colleagues launched an extensive research program based on a correspondence theory of pretense (Sears, 1947). These investigators pursued the notion that because the content of pretense presumably reflected children's real-life experiences, one domain could be used to predict the other. It soon became clear, however, that the relation between play content and children's real experience was far from simple (Levin & Wardwell, 1962). Children who engaged in aggressive sibling doll play had every manner of real sibling experiences. In some cases, play aggression appeared to reflect real aggression directed toward the child; in other cases it reflected fantasized experiences; and in still other cases, play aggression appeared to reveal the child's own inhibited aggressive impulses. This first version of correspondence theory was abandoned when an empirical relationship between observable real-world events and the events rendered in play could not be demonstrated.

A new version of correspondence theory has recently surfaced. This new version holds that pretense represents children's knowledge of everyday events organized as "scripts" (Bretherton, 1984). Although children's practical declarative knowledge might well be organized in script-like structures similar to those proposed by Schank and Abelson (1977), the question is whether pretense makes use of a system designed to store practical, veridical representations of routine, real-world experiences. This question has two parts. One part concerns whether pretend scenarios necessarily represent events children have actually experienced or whether pretend scenarios can represent fabricated events. The second part concerns the conceptual status of these pretend scenarios. Early pretend theorists held that pretense reflects the child's confusion about the real world, a way of thinking in which imagined events are confused with real events (Fein & Apfel, 1979). When children pretend, do they distinguish between scripts of real events and scripts of pretend events? Are pretended events likely to be stored as if they were real events?

A script-theory approach implies that a pretend statement about a restaurant, for example, would be understood by the players as meaning "This is a restaurant, and everything we know of restaurants applies to the actions we are about to perform." In the previous example, Ellen's opening statements would be understood to mean, "This is a mother whose daughter has just returned from school, and everything we know of mothers and daughters under these circumstances applies here." According to script theorists, pretend statements can be understood as statements "of" real-world events based on children's everyday experiencing of these real-world events. Thus pretend scenarios can illuminate children's real-world knowledge.

Consider, however, the relationship between the symbolic signifiers produced in the preceding episode and that which these signifiers might signify. At first glance, we seem to have a rendering of family life in the suburbs, represented as a backyard cookout with children returning from school and being nagged to bed. At second glance, however, the rendering becomes considerably different from a veridical representation of mundane family activities. What initially appear to be simple person transformations imply secondary transformations in which "mom" acquires several sons and daughters of different ages and ability. Mom rejects Charles's offer of help, and accepts Alison's; Sally structures her own relationships with mom and the younger children, while Paul makes it clear that he, too, is mom's helper. What kind of family is being represented? At the very least it is a family in which children may be freely added, their ages may change, a father is not present, and helping relations are arbitrarily or self-determined. The family is constructed by the children as they interact with one another; it is at best a changing composite of assorted family-like features.

The scene does not make a great deal of physical or social sense; it does not matter very much to the children whether the bean bags are steaks or hamburgers, or whether the cooking appliance is an oven or a grill. For all the effort put into food preparation, there is no move toward serving or eating it. The knowledge represented within this pretend episode is fluid and unstable. At one level, these pretend relationships permit social accommodations to the needs of individual players. At another level, the children tolerate transformational sequences producing combinations that are unlikely to occur in real life. Because of the apparent arbitrariness of these relationships, the representational templates used in this episode cannot be viewed as literal representations of a particular family or family activity. The powerful illusion created by these children rests on highly selective snatches from diverse sources blended into a representational potpourri. Contrary to expectations of script theory, the children appear to exercise considerable denotative license in the meanings expressed in these pretend episodes.

Consider the following sequence, which occurred during the episode described earlier.

Sally (to Alison): Why don't you go and do your homework? You got any homework? You want to play with your teddy bear?
Ellen: No, she's being a bad girl today.
Alison: No I didn't.
Sally (to Ellen): What did she do?
Ellen: She picked up a knife. Was trying to kill her dad.
Alison (with a sad frown on her face): No, I didn't. I just maked a play one.
Ellen (warmly hugging and kissing Alison): That's O. K., then?

What slice of routine, everyday knowledge is represented in this sequence? Are we to assume that the real Ellen was punished by her mother for killing her dad? Or, are we to assume that Ellen saw someone kill her dad or wished someone would kill her dad? We know that Ellen's mother and father are divorced; we also know that Ellen's visits to her father, who lives in a distant city, are unhappy occasions. However, her real father is very much alive, and her mother recently remarried. Was Ellen's contribution to this event based on an overheard adult conversation, a TV show, a dream? Alison's response is equally provocative.

She apparently understood Ellen's accusation. What kind of script did she use to reach this understanding? Where would Alison have encountered an event in which a child attacked dad with a pretend knife? Are we to assume that this is a common form of father–daughter play that simply has not been reported? Even more astounding, Ellen joyously accepted Alison's explanation, thereby subtly revising the meaning of the word "kill" in her earlier statement.

A distinction between real-world experience and real-world knowledge might help script-theory account for pretend sequences such as these. We might use this distinction to argue that scripts reflect children's knowledge, not their actual experience. Children might very well know things that they have never experienced directly. Whereas a qualification such as this might bring pretend events into better harmony with scripted knowledge, it also raises an enormous number of new problems. Where does this nonexperiential knowledge come from? Do children "know" that daughters kill fathers, or do they simply think that daughters might kill fathers? A theoretical distinction between "knowing that" and "thinking about knowing that" is needed, because otherwise our theory leaves the normal child unable to separate the real world from an invented world.

Children in the preceding episode used vivid gestures and dialogue to create a play canvas of considerable force. Whereas the canvas was recognizable, its basic elements were conveyed in quick schematic strokes exaggerating some lines and ignoring others. The relationship between pretend signifiers and that which is signified cannot be viewed as a straightforward readout of the child's social and physical knowledge although elements of this knowledge are present. The representational system used in pretend play must contain something other than the declarative or procedural knowledge used in practical nonplay activity.

Bateson (1955) commented on the denotative peculiarity of pretend play when he noted that "The playful nip denotes the bite, but it does not denote what would be denoted by the bite." Consider the statement "This sentence is false," or the two-part sequence "The following sentence is false. The preceding sentence is true." Something in these statements jumps out and acts on itself. The meaning keeps recycling: If true, then false; if false, then true," on and on without stopping. In Bateson's example, the self-referencing statement is placed within a frame: "All statements within this frame are untrue. I love you. I hate you." The first statement seems to point to the second two until one realizes that it also points to itself. The opening statements of Ellen and Sally illustrate this recycling of meaning: "My daughter's at school," followed by "I'll go check. O. K., Mom?" Remember that the children are really in school. That reality is declared false, except for one daughter for whom it is true, yet not true because school itself is sucked into the pretend frame. The scene and the roles established in this frame are untrue even as the players announce their intention to behave as if they were true, but untrue. Expressions of love and expressions of hate are also untrue, or are they?

The play frame proposed by Bateson represents a kind of understanding in which "statements about statements of" inform the player that behavior within the frame are statements about behavior, not statements of behavior. The engaging paradox is that these metacommunicative "statements about statements of" actually convey the message that play statements are themselves to be understood as "statements about statements of."

Bateson's analysis suggests that the cognitive mechanisms responsible for pretense differ from those that guide children's practical encounters with the world. Pretend behavior seems to reflect cognitive mechanisms that permit children to engage in an intuitive form of suppositional thinking capable of manipulating quasireal or imagined events. This system is recursive in the sense that suppositions can be repeated as transformed suppositions preserving kernels of the original, which in turn preserves crucial kernels of knowledge. As supposition, pretense functions as an interpretive–expressive system designed to manipulate representations without regard for the veridicality or plausibility of the represented outcome. As supposition, it can use exaggeration, absurdity, and distortion of original kernels of truth. Ellen, Alison, and Sally are representing constructions of supposed events—relationships that might exist someplace and sometime even as they indeed exist in the pretense itself.

The collective suppositions illustrated in the foregoing examples are possible because these master players know that the real world is not being represented in the play. They do not make literal demands on the play; they do not quibble about whether the bean bags are steaks or hamburgers, whether Alison is a baby or a school-age child, or who is related to whom. One testable implication of the aforementioned is that play will terminate if children insist upon reality criteria, i.e., if the suppositional atmosphere is disrupted by the insertion of an external standard for evaluating the appropriateness of pretend enactments. Although several investigators have noted that children occasionally negate one another's pretend proposals (Goncu & Kessel, 1986), there is no evidence concerning the impact of these negations on the maintenance of play. In the view offered here, play will be disrupted if these negations involve an insistence upon adherence to real-world standards (e.g., babies don't go to school). Along with Piaget, I argue that overt sociodramatic play is undermined during the early school years by the social literalness of children's interpersonal relations. If this play survives, it survives between trusted friends and in private, secluded places.

A theory of pretense must therefore include a mechanism for uncoupling that which is represented in the play from script-like knowledge as well as a mechanism for decontextualizing the behavior from the immediate situation. Because the representational system exercised in pretense is detached from the system of representation used in practical affairs, children must be assumed to know they are pretending. Metacommunicative statements such as those described by Giffin (1984), statements that monitor the boundary between pretend events and real events, offer one type of evidence that children are conscious of pretending.

Chaille (1978), in an interview study, found that 5-year-olds had little difficulty discussing the role and object transformations of pretend play. Because this issue is a consequential one for a theory of pretense, other techniques, for example, asking children to comment on video recordings of their own play, might be used to map the fine details of what children actually know about this behavior (Fein, 1981).

So far, I have suggested that a theory of pretense needs to posit a system able to manipulate certain kinds of representations separated in some way from those used in practical affairs. Whatever the representational form, the system yields thoughts about thoughts, suppositions about what might have been or what might be experienced. Children are able to activate this system. When they do so, they are able to generate behavior marked by both referential freedom and denotative license.

AFFECTIVE RELATIONS

Although divergent thinking is characterized by novel and original associations, most theorists exclude bizarre or inappropriate associations from their definitions of novelty and originality. In pretend play, however, there is often ludicrous distortion, exaggeration, and extravagance, at times bordering on the bizarre. At the same time, the distortion, exaggeration, and extravagance reveal a considerable degree of affective force. Although psychoanalytic theory offers the only extant affective interpretation of pretense (e.g., Erikson, 1977; Peller, 1954), research within this perspective has been limited to the notion of catharsis (Gilmore, 1966). In contrast, cognitive theorists have all but ignored the affective side of pretense.

Consider the affective force of the exchange described in the previous episode. Suddenly, Alison finds herself transformed from a good girl into an awesomely bad girl. Sally, wanting to support this new transformation, asks why? Ellen answers Sally's question. Alison responds to Ellen's answer with a remarkable twist, embedding pretense within pretense. Ellen, satisfied because the slaughter was only pretend, proposes a transformation back to good girl. This interesting sequence draws our attention first to the affective meaning of pretend transformations and second to the affective coherence of the symbolic relationships that unfold (anger may be expressed in violent behavior, but real violence and pretend violence are different things). In this example, coherence comes also from the deontic logic of punishment, justification, atonement, and forgiveness. The transformations involve affective attributes associated with life's do's and don'ts.

These sequences convey vivid experiences, whether real or imagined. To think about killing dad with a knife certainly is bizarre from the perspective of a 4-year-old's real-life experiences. A pretend episode such as that just related probably does not reveal declarative knowledge about patricide as much as it reveals affective experiences of anger towards an arbitrary parental figure (mother) who forgives the child's anger towards a second parental figure (father). Punishment, atonement, and forgiveness, or the arbitrariness and lability of adult authority, may well be common childhood experiences shared by all three players. A somewhat different kind of affective understanding appears in the following sequence, which occurred a few minutes later:

Ellen (to Alison): Here, honey. Go to school.
Alison: I can't go to school. I'm just a little girl.
(Ellen hands her a pile of books. Alison takes them and skips along singing, "La, la, la, la.")
Ellen (to Alison): Suzie's over. You better get up to bed. (With a smile, she gives Alison a push.)
Alison: Don't push me.
Ellen: You wanna go to school like her, right? Be a nice girl. See that girl? She's being in a good mood. (Ellen picks up a purse.)
Alison: I'll be a big girl. I'll go to school anytime when I wake up in the morning. Why do you have that purse?
Ellen: 'Cause I'm gonna drive you to school, honey.

Good girl, bad girl; big girl, little girl; come home, go away; obey, resist. Throughout this lengthy episode the children express ambivalent and polar feelings, momentary mood shifts that fold endlessly back on themselves. The episode begins with reunion and ends with separation, a sequence anchored to a diurnal cycle marked by coming home and going to school. Smaller separations occur in between, but these events are frought with tension between mother and daughter. Even though several children share in the play, Ellen, Alison, and to some extent Sally participate in one set of affective relationships, while Paul and Charles participate in another.

The vividness and coherence of this episode comes largely from a series of affective transformations around which role and object transformations are organized. From a theoretical perspective, it may be useful to view these affective transformations as derived from symbolic units representing affective relationships such as "anger at," "fear of," "love for," "approval of," or more subtle feelings about power and helplessness, safety and danger. These affective representational units differ qualitatively from those associated with declarative and procedural knowledge because they respond selectively to vivid, deeply felt experiences. Our first look at the previous episode conveys a sense of emotional chaos. Our second look conveys a remarkable point-and-counterpoint among diverse emotional elements. The bad news is that daughter must leave; the good news is that she will return to a welcoming mother. The bad news is that daughters resist parental authority; the good news is that they will eventually comply. In pretense, affective symbolic units are manipulated, interpreted, coordinated, and elaborated in a way that makes affective sense to the players.

Because this affective symbol system represents real or imagined experiences at a fairly general level, it permits the child to recreate emotional moments by adding the particulars of persons, things, or occasions. Although play partners may have had little real experience with one set of particulars, they are able to understand general affective meanings and improvise the details as they go along. In fact, the details do not matter so long as they fit reasonably well with the affective meaning being expressed. These affective units, which constitute affect-binding representational templates, yield the "motivated" symbols of Piagetian theory. These motivated symbols are always present in pretense, from the infant's rendering of a physiological state in pretending to sleep, to the older child's rendering of intricate emotional overtones in pretending about being sent to bed.

Although symbolic templates store the child's affective experience, this experience is not necessarily derived from real-life events. It is not necessary for Alison and Ellen to have seen a child chasing her father with a knife so long as the symbolic content is compatible with the affective meaning of bad girl or bad father. Nor is it necessary for Sally to have witnessed steaks being pounded in order to understand that a forceful mother is being cryptically rendered. The preceding episode preserves to a remarkable degree feelings about being home and feelings about leaving, feelings familiar to each child but expressed by each in somewhat different ways.

These affective templates are built around vivid experiences rather than mundane, familiar, automated routines. The children's representation of food preparation in the earlier episode is based on a selective sampling of events not translatable into culinary expertise. The affective symbol system plays no direct role in the acquisition or application of convergent knowledge. Quite the contrary, affective templates store salient information about especially intriguing, troublesome, or celebrative encounters: gestures, statements, postural adjustments, tonal qualities, facial expressions, and patterned sequences that preserve the vividness of these encounters. These templates may become elaborated when children introduce new saliencies to one another; the assimilation rule seems to be: If the affect fits, take it in. Affective templates permit children to think about emotionally important things, about pleasant things and nasty things, satisfying things and confusing things. In pretend play, children are thinking out loud and sometimes together about experiences that have emotional meaning for them.

This affective symbol system can be inhibited or evoked depending on circumstance. This symbol system is more appropriate in some situations than in others. In convergent problem solving, it is better put on hold; in divergent activities such as daydreaming, pretend play, or drawing the system can be activated. Thus the system must be linked to an evaluative component that monitors deontic features of the immediate environment. When evoked, the system alters the balance between the inner world and the outer world, giving an inward tilt to the thinking. When tilted inward, thinking tends to be convergent with respect to the inner world and divergent with respect to actual experience and with respect to the immediate physical and social surroundings. In pretense, affective symbolic templates are the source of ideas and actions that dominate the immediate stimulus field.

SEQUENTIAL UNCERTAINTY

Affective symbolic templates can be viewed as distinctive representational structures. When behavior is decontextualized and these templates are uncoupled and activated, the resulting behavior acquires the characteristics of referential freedom and denotative license. However, these phenomena do not exhaust the transformational scope of pretend activities. In pretense, the sequences that emerge have a nonlinear recursive quality. New affective themes appear and old ones return. Pretense is divergent in its sequential organization as well as in its rendering of the immediate stimulus field and in its relation to accurate representations of reality.

Consider the following pretend episode generated by two highly skilled players. These two children generated the most literal, script-like behavior of any children in our sample. In this episode, Terry (6:4) plays the role of mother, Cara (5:10) is the housekeeper, and an E. T. doll is the baby. Terry has just acted out an elaborate sequence in which she prepared E. T.'s imaginary cereal and began feeding him, all the while chattering in motherese. Suddenly, her tone and expression changes:

> *Terry* (in a querulous motherly tone): Why are you spitting it out? It tastes good with salt and butter. I like it. What's the matter, E. T.? Hmmmm?
> (Terry frowns at E. T., then smiles and wipes his mouth. She tastes the cereal and begins feeding him again.)
> *Cara*: Don't make him eat any more, Mrs. Can't you see he's not looking well. His eyes are swollen and his nose is running.
> (Cara bends down, tilts her head to one side, and places her hand on E. T.'s forehead.)
> *Terry*: What disease has he got, Cara? Chicken pox? Oh, yes. E. T., you have red rashes all over your face and arms. I must take you to Dr. Busybee right away. Cara, please iron E. T.'s clothes.

Terry began with a perfectly calm, maternal feeding sequence in keeping with an affective relational theme, "Mother Tends Child." This theme originated from a template we might call "loving mother feeds good baby" made up of lower order units representing "preparing food," "talking to baby," "bringing food-to-mouth," and so forth. Each of these units in turn embed representations of substance (cereal), utensils, baby behavior, motherese, and other elements used to render events portrayed in the episode.

Then, without apparent warning, Terry changed the intially compliant baby into a "food-spitting-baby" and the loving, gentle mother into an irritated, annoyed mother. The scene is so vividly rendered that the observer easily imagines cereal oozing from a baby's mouth. This sequential transformation altered the affective tone of the initial sequence while at the same time generating a new set of referential transformations. No sooner did Terry announce this shift than Cara stepped in with a second sequential transformation.

In the previous example, Cara recognized a transforming moment when Terry changed the affective tone of her motherly portrayal. Cara answered an unasked, though implicit, question: "WHY would a nice child behave like this?" Terry caught the novel possibilities inherent in Cara's answer, and together they shifted from an upset mother–bad child module to a solicitous mother–sick child module. Specifications of the sick child's disease involved further referential transformations of the doll: state transformations dealing with the baby's physical condition, and appearance transformations dealing with the baby's facial color and pox. Having posed the problem of a sick baby, the children made preparations to see the doctor, as if another question—"WHAT WILL FIX the sick child?"— had been posed. At this point, however, different symbolic units were operating for each of these children. Terry is eager to "fix it," while Cara dwells on specific manifestations of the disease:

> *Cara*: E. T., don't keep scratching your arms. Ooooh, you've got big and dirty nails! Shall I cut them for you?
> *Terry*: Cara, could you please bring the nail scissors? You can fold up some of the laundry. (To E. T.) E. T., your shirt will be soft and smooth in a minute and then no more scratch, scratch, scratch.

This sequence is interesting in the context of sociodramatic play. Terry and Cara are remarkable in their ability to coordinate these fairly intricate constructions. At this point, however, different symbolic templates surface. Cara connects chicken pox and scratching with long nails needing to be cut. Terry, on a different tac, assimilates the scratching problem into a symbolic structure representing the clean clothes needed for the doctor's visit. For a brief time, these private symbol systems move in a parallel manner. Terry and Cara seem not to view their different preoccupations as conflicting, so the play can continue. The next sequence in this episode ends less happily:

> (Terry changes into a blue and white play dress, combs her hair, and slings a purse over her shoulder.)
> *Terry*: Cara, I'll call for Dr. Busybee. Dick has taken the car to his office.
> *Cara*: Don't wait for Dr. Busybee, Mrs. Just take the bus. E. T. is dressed up now and his cheeks are red and hot.
> *Terry*: No, I won't take him by bus . . . there'll be too many people and they'll get infection. E. T. must sleep now. He's my son, and I'll do what I want.

Reading Terry's dressing routine and E. T.'s clean clothes to mean that Terry planned to take the sick baby to the doctor, Cara suggested the bus. However, she misread Terry's "What Next?" question. For Cara, a mother with a sick child and no car did not include a doctor who makes house calls. Terry rejects Cara's elaboration, but, more serious, rejects the affective relationship among mother, child, and housekeeper established earlier. Cara, seemingly stymied, withdrew from the play, and Terry carried on without her. As I indicated earlier, the mechanism responsible for uncoupling the affective symbol system from the system of practical representations cannot easily tolerate demands for real-world considerations. Terry, by rejecting Cara's established play role, disrupted the illusion under which both were operating and thereby terminated the cooperative play.

In spite of this lapse, Cara and Terry are superb pretend players. Skill is evident in their use of a rich array of role and object transformations. Skill also is evident in the way they build on one another's transformational shifts, easily integrating lower order state, substance, action, and object transformations into higher order affective units. These sequential shifts add another divergent dimension to this pretend episode. The first shift, from positive to negative affect, seemed sudden. The second shift seemed less so. Although shifts are timed to occur when "What Next," "Why," and "How to Fix It" questions emerge naturally in the course of events, these questions may differ in the variety of answers they attract. Because "What Next" questions lack specific grounding in particular events, these questions may encourage more diverse answers than the other two.

When pretense is viewed as an expressive vehicle motored by a system of affective symbols, several interesting issues emerge. Sequential fluctuations can be viewed as sequentially organized affective transformations of previously formed transformations, that is, as transformations of transformations. On the one hand, central relationships are preserved; on the other, these relationships are given new meaning. The notion of sequential uncertainty as transformations of transformations implies a bottom-up processing of pretend scenarios, a view markedly different from the top-down model of action plans proposed by Garvey (1977). Rather than a general action plan such as "treating–healing," the previous episode was characterized by moment-to-moment improvisations; one circumstance gave rise to another and the play meandered leisurely through loosely connected notions about concerned adults and sick babies.

SELF-MIRRORING

The affective symbol system described previously implies that children do not experience pretense as an activity that simply occurs. Considerable observational evidence indicates that children are aware of emerging affective forms and use an intricate system of metacommunication to sustain an unfolding pretend illusion

(Giffin, 1984; Goncu & Kessel, 1984). There appears to be a consciousness of pretending in at least two respects. First, children seem to be aware that pretense deals with thoughts about reality, not reality itself; that pretense is a metarepresentational system, not a system of primary representations.

A second aspect of consciousness that merits attention is the special stance adopted by a pretending child toward the self. When children assume play roles, the events that unfold are essentially self-mirroring. In pretense, the individual looks at herself as a transformed self while retaining the core structure of a nontransformed self. At one level, children retain their customary identities, while at another level they respect one another's chosen identities. If G. H. Mead (1934) is correct, pretend play provides a vehicle in which the self, slipping outside the self, looks at the self. Mead believed that a self-mirroring system of this type implies the beginnings of conscious self-awareness.

Self-mirroring systems tend to produce what Hofstadter (1979) calls "strange loops." Escher, for example, drew a picture of a hand drawing a second hand drawing the first hand, a two-level loop in Hofstadter's system. Alison, pretending to be a child who pretends to attack her father, illustrates a three-level loop in the same system. Interestingly, one-level loops in which children pretend to be themselves (e.g., sisters pretending to be sisters) are also possible (but rare). Also possible is G. H. Mead's (1934) example of a solitary child alternating in the roles of mother and baby, a relationship in which the child in the role of mother talks to the baby and then responds as the baby to what the mother has said. Even in simpler loops, a representation of "I" is tied to a representation of "not I" that can only be understood in reference to "I."

In conceptualizing a symbolic system capable of generating pretend behavior, it seems necessary to make provisions for a symbol of the self (Hofstadter, 1979). The self-symbol stores knowledge of the self as perceived by the self. Because the self-symbol is embedded in a larger affective system, the knowledge is primarily affective. Ellen's rendering of a mother–daughter relationship is necessarily influenced by a view of herself in relation to her own mother; but it is also influenced by a view of herself in relation to her rendering of mother. Terry, too, brings to her maternal play role a double self-mirror, as do all pretend renderings that involve reciprocal relationships. These examples provide a glimpse of the self-symbol embedded in children's role enactments.

The recursive self-mirroring aspect of pretense adds another source of divergent power to pretend behavior. Affective statements about behavioral relationships can be repeated in new and varied forms. Each role transformation engages a powerful reflection of the self that can be repeated with countless variations while preserving all the information in the original symbol of the self. Recursion thus gives the affective symbolic system another transformational tool, whereas the self-symbol gives it an awareness of its own internal representational activity.

A THEORETICAL OVERVIEW

This attempt to move from heuristic guides to better specified theoretical notions owes much to Piaget (1962) and psychoanalytic thinkers (Erikson, 1977; Peller, 1954). It is consistent with these positions to view pretense as a symbolic behavior organized around emotional and motivational issues. Pretense is insulated in some way from a need to behave according to the conventional meanings of persons, things, or locations in the immediate environment; it is protected from pressures to solve convergent problems. The symbols used in pretense are personal even though they may bear upon the grand emotional themes experienced by most children as a normal part of growing up. Although language (certainly) and images (probably) occur when children pretend, the representational system responsible for pretend symbols is separated in some fashion from the system used in practical activities.

In this chapter, I described five characteristics of pretense that are (a) in keeping with these theoretical notions, (b) observable in the play of master players, and (c) definable as contributing factors to the divergent productivity of the behavior. I called these characteristics referential freedom, denotative license, affective relations, sequential uncertainty, and self-mirroring. The remaining task is to describe the kind of mechanisms and representational system needed to account for behavior displaying these characteristics.

In the account offered here, the playing child was endowed with a representational system keyed to detect, pick up, and hold vivid life experiences. These experiences may be real in the sense that they are derived from the circumstances in which appetitive or neural needs are satisfied. These affective experiences may also be imagined or derived from fantasies found on television or in books. Whatever the source or content, the experiences are marked by intense feeling. The storage system is economical insofar as only striking features of a particular experience need to be included. But these striking features hold the affective meaning. The action image of a mother pounding steaks may hold the meaning of determined and controlled maternal force; a child skipping merrily to school may hold the meaning of separation anxiety resolved. Affect is bound to the quality of the motions, sounds, tempo, and linguistic utterance. The affective force is held whether or not the child's real mother ever pounded steaks and whether or not the real child ever skipped to school singing "La, la, la, la." These dynamic features are organized as relationships in a representational system that, insulated from practical problem-solving pressures, is able to concern itself with affective sense rather that cognitive or social sense. A separate template is reserved as a symbol of the self. This symbol, which mirrors the self as a pretend participant, conveys a consciousness of pretending.

These affective templates record subjective, rather than objective, information about people, objects, or events in a real or imagined world. They record affective information about the emotionally consequential aspects of living, rather than declarative information about the real world, or procedural information about how to solve problems in the management of encounters with peers or adults. A reading of this record will provide clues about the child's inner world; it will not reveal what the child's actual, observable world is like, what the child knows about this world, or what the child can do in it.

The characteristics of referential freedom, denotative license, sequential uncertainty, and self-mirroring reflect in different ways the system's independence from the immediate environment, actual experience, or the need to cast one's experiencing of life or self into a tidy story. These affective representations are not "scripts" in the sense meant by Schank and Abelson (1977), and they do not serve immediate practical ends. Thus the system in which they are embedded is not likely to be effective in convergent problem-solving (Pepler & Ross, 1981), as literal representations are not likely to be effective in divergent problem solving. These symbolic structures define the content and sequences of play, and they also may contribute to other divergent efforts.

When children use these representations in play, they are, in effect, playing with representations of their own affective knowledge. In play, the child's inner life imposes itself on the immediate environment; when more than one child is playing, the themes that create cohesiveness are those archetypical themes that each child can recognize. Although sociodramatic play requires some acknowledgment of others' affective preoccupations, the dramatic play of expert children reflects an amazing tolerance for personal variations in the expression of these affective themes.

The system of affective templates is associated with two mechanisms. One mechanism decontextualizes behavior from the immediate physical and social surrounding. Once decontextualization occurs, affective templates may be mapped onto features of the immediate environment, thereby yielding the referential freedom of pretense. This mechanism is responsible for developmental changes in pretense during the second year of life. Self-oriented pretense with realistic objects, the first sign of decontextualized behavior, precedes other-oriented pretense with substitute objects.

The second mechanism uncouples pretend signifiers from the representational system used to store practical real-world knowledge, thereby yielding the characteristic of denotative license. Once stored in an affective template, decontextualized from the immediate environment, and uncoupled from the system representing real-world events, an experience is represented in a system that permits it to be manipulated. Decontextualizing alters the playing child's relation to the immediate environment; uncoupling alters the child's relation to actual experience. Uncoupling yields the play frame in which the nip denotes the bite but does not denote what would be denoted by the bite. In this frame, affective templates are manipulated in a form of suppositional thinking about what the bite might indeed denote. As this process unfolds, new affective features are added, old features are deleted; new templates can be constructed by the expansion, deletion, and combination of old ones.

In effect, I am proposing a double-layered system of representation, one for practical knowledge and another for affective knowledge. This double-layered system emerges during the third year of life as pretend sequences become increasingly marked by nonstereotyped, personal inventions. I am also suggesting that this affective system is essential for an individual to become conscious of an inner life and to gain control over its expression.

One developmental implication of this view is that pretense develops in a two-stage sequence. In the second year of life, affective and mundane knowledge is not differentiated. Children represent their affective knowledge of mundane routines such as eating, sleeping, and grooming. By the third year of life, the affective symbol system is differentiated from the system of practical representations. Pretend representations now acquire the property of denotative license; the thoughts and feelings represented in pretense are uncoupled from real-world knowledge and no longer come exclusively from experienced events. Stereotyped routines are reorganized into new combinations, and pretend sequences become less predictable and less lifelike (see Fein, 1981; Fein & Apfel, 1979 for evidence supporting this developmental sequence).

Gradually, the sequential uncertainty of pretense increases. The behavior begins to demonstrate planning-in-action in which the children look only one sequence beyond the one they are producing; as children explore the potentials of denotative license, pretend sequences become more varied, fluent, and original. This expectation is consistent with evidence that children in the third year of life have less difficulty than younger children in modeling pretend sequences of unrelated or reversed elements (O'Connell, Gerard, & Leong, 1983). Other investigators have reported that the pretense of preschool children lacks attention to literal detail even though more details are represented (Genishi, 1983).

As I indicated earlier, the episode played by Terry and Cara was the most literal episode generated by the master players in our sample. It is of considerable theoretical importance that the play disintegrated when Terry insisted on a literal interpretation of the play roles. In effect, the notion of uncoupled knowledge implies that collective symbolism is possible because children no longer operate in terms of their own practical personal experience. If this uncoupling is central to the pretense of advanced players, we would expect this play to deteriorate when literalness is imposed upon it. For example, a child comments to a nearby adult, "I'm feeding my baby coffee." The adult responds, "Babies don't drink coffee." The teacher is rejecting uncoupled knowledge in favor of declarative knowledge. Because of the theoretical importance of denotative license, I would expect such rejections, whether from adults or peers, to put a damper on the play. This expectation is easily put to empirical test.

The theoretical framework just discussed also indicates a need for studies that assess more directly the difference between pretend activities and their real-life counterparts. For example, do children organize their behavior differently when they are asked to really wash dishes, stir cereal, or brush their teeth and when they are asked to pretend to do these things? The present theory would predict that the difference between pretended activities and real activities would increase as children become more skillful pretend players. In addition, there ought to be a difference between the expression of emotion in real-life situations and its expression in pretense. One would expect to find, for example, that emotional extremes of longer duration occur more frequently in nonplay interactions than in pretense. In effect, the suppositional frame of pretense would be expected to contain and discipline the expression of emotion even as it permits emotional meaning to be explored. A related issue concerns the motivational mechanisms that might explain why our master players find this play so appealing and why they sustain it for such lengthy periods. As I suggested elsewhere (Fein, 1979), pretense provides an unusual opportunity for children to control their own emotional arousal and to maintain a level that is both comfortable and stimulating. The intrinsic motivation of pretense resides in its ability to convert external sources of motivation into an internal symbolic form. Pretense would not be expected to occur in settings that promote real conflict, anger, anxiety, or excitement, an expectation needing further investigation although it is supported by currently available data (Fein, 1981; Rubin et al., 1983).

The affective templates used in pretense are not necessarily benign. If inappropriately uncoupled from real-world knowledge, they may invade the system of practical representations and lead to misrepresentations of real-life experiences. If improperly decontextualized, the affective symbol system may disrupt practical activities. Because the affective symbol system may distort real-life experiences, or disrupt practical real-world encounters, it needs to be sequestered from real and consequential life activities. As children acquire these powerful affective forms, they must also learn how and when to use them. Pretense might provide a medium for protecting these affective representations while children learn to control the form of suppositional thinking involved in modulating their expression. One implication of this notion is that children who are skillful pretenders may become reflective responders to real-life stress.

Recursion is another theoretical property of the affective symbolic system. The notion of play as assimilation implies an inward, appreciative, generative stance, first towards the contours of sensorimotor schemes and later towards the affective representations of those schemes. Because behavior is decontextualized, uncoupled, and subordinated to reflective processes, it can be savored through countless repetitions, variations, and recombinations. As children play with their affective representations, these representations are repeated in new and interesting guises. Missing from the research literature are systematic attempts to trace the unfolding of pretend themes in the same players over time. The repetition phenomena described in psychoanalytic theory needs to be documented in the play of normal children.

In the view offered here, pretense reflects an interpretive–expressive system designed to manipulate representations of emotionally consequential aspects of living. This view has several additional implications for future research. For example, our best hunches about the content of these emotional aspects of living have been provided by psychoanalytic theorists such as Peller (1954). We may be able to learn something about the workings of the affective symbol system by studying the expression of these themes in play. The notion that the repetition and elaboration of these themes serves a cathartic function has not fared well under empirical scrutiny (Fein, 1981). More likely, play with affective symbols aides in reshaping the way vivid life experiences are represented to the self (Peller, 1954). If we knew more about changes in the content of these representations over time, it might be possible to design more powerful studies of the contribution of pretend play to self-awareness and emotional maturity.

Finally, the affective system and its associated mechanisms have implications for the study of creativity. A general model of divergent thinking may need to include a dimension of vividness along with more traditional measures. Further, the interpretive–expressive system responsible for pretense may appear in later creative efforts. We have remarkably little evidence about pretense in school-age children or about the relation between pretense and other spheres of creative endeavor. A major implication of the theoretical framework presented in this chapter is that creative processes cannot be studied independently of an affective symbolic system operating to yield referential freedom, denotative license, and sequential uncertainty. To ignore the affective power of pretense is to risk neglect of what may be its most important contribution to early development.

SUMMARY

In this chapter, I consider several theoretical notions about pretend play. First, five characteristics of pretense are proposed and illustrated in pretend episodes produced by master players. These characteristics—referential freedom, denotative license, affective relationships, sequential uncertainty, and self-mirroring—describe different aspects of pretense that need to be addressed in a general theory of this behavior. Second, several elements of a cognitive-affective system capable of generating these characteristics were described. Among these elements was an affective symbol system, detached from the immediate environment, uncoupled from actual past experience, and used to represent vivid life experiences. These affective representational units, one of which is a symbol of the self, generate a type of fluidly organized suppositional thinking. Because this position differs from correspondence or action-plan theories, problems associated with these latter formulations were also discussed.

REFERENCES

Bateson, G. (1955). A theory of play and fantasy. *American Psychiatric Association Research Reports, 2*, 39–51.

Bretherton, I. (1984). Event representation in symbolic play: Reality and fantasy. In I. Bretherton (Ed.), *Symbolic play: The representation of social understanding* (pp. 1–41). New York: Academic Press.

Chaille, C. (1978). The child's conceptions of play, pretending, and toys: Sequences and structural parallels. *Human Development, 21*, 201–210.

Dansky, J. L. (1980a). Make believe: A mediator of the relationship between free play and associative fluency. *Child Development, 51*, 576–579.

Dansky, J. L. (1980b). Cognitive consequences of sociodramatic play and exploration training for economically disadvantaged preschoolers. *Journal of Child Psychology and Psychiatry, 20*, 47–58.

Elder, J. L., & Pederson, D. R. (1978). Preschool children's use of objects in symbolic play. *Child Development, 49*, 500–504.

Erikson, E. H. (1977). *Toys and reasons*. New York: Norton.

Fein, G. G. (1975). A transformational analysis of pretending. *Developmental Psychology, 11*, 291–296.

Fein, G. G. (1979). Play and the acquisition of symbols. In L. Katz (Ed.), *Current topics in early childhood education* (Vol. 2, pp. 195–226). Norwood, NJ: Ablex.

Fein, G. G. (1981). Pretend play: An integrative review. *Child Development, 52*, 1095–1118.

Fein, G. G. (1983). The self-building potential of make-believe play: I got a fish, all by myself. In T. D. Yawkey & A. D. Pellegrini (Eds.), *Child's play: Developmental and applied* (pp. 125–141). Hillsdale, NJ: Lawrence Erlbaum Associates.

Fein, G. G., & Apfel, N. (1979). Some preliminary observations on knowing and pretending. In N. Smith & M. Franklin (Eds.), *Symbolic functioning in childhood* (pp. 87–100). Hillsdale, NJ: Lawrence Erlbaum Associates.

Garvey, C. (1977). *Play*. Cambridge, MA: Harvard University Press.

Genishi, C. (1983, April). *Role initiation in the discourse of Mexican–American children's play.* Paper presented at the American Educational Research Association, Montreal.

Giffin, H. (1984). The coordination of shared meaning in the creation of a shared make-believe reality. In I. Bretherton (Ed.), *Symbolic play: The representation of social understanding* (pp. 73–100). New York: Academic Press.

Gilmore, J. B. (1966). The role of anxiety and cognitive factors in children's play behavior. *Child Development, 37*, 397–416.

Goncu, A., & Kessel, F. (1984). Preschoolers' play communications. In F. S. Kessel & A. Goncu (Eds.), *Text and context in imaginative play: New directions for child development*. San Francisco: Jossey-Bass.

Guilford, J. P. (1950). Creativity. *American Psychologist, 14*, 469–479.

Hofstadter, D. R. (1979). *Godel, Escher, Bach: An eternal golden braid*. New York: Vintage Books.

Jackowitz, E. R., & Watson, M. W. (1980). The development of object transformation in early pretend play. *Developmental Psychology, 16*, 543–549.

Kogan, N. (1983). Stylistic variation in childhood and adolescence: Creativity, metaphor, and cognitive style. In J. Flavell & E. Markman (Eds.), *Handbook of child psychology*, (Vol. 3, pp. 630–706). New York: Wiley.

Levin, H., & Wardwell, E. (1962). The research uses of doll play. *Psychological Bulletin, 59*, 27–56.

Matthews, W. S. (1977). Modes of transformation in the initiation of fantasy play. *Developmental Psychology, 13*, 212–216.

Mead, G. H. (1934). *Mind, self, and society*. Chicago: University of Chicago Press.

O'Connell, B. O., Gerard, A., & Leong, K. (1983, April). *The development of sequential understanding*. Paper presented at the Society for Research in Child Development, Detroit.

Pederson, D. R., Rook-Green, A., & Elder, J. L. (1981). The role of action in the development of pretend play in young children. *Developmental Psychology, 17*, 756–759.

Peller, L. (1954). Libidinal phases, ego development, and play. *Psychoanalytic study of the child, 9*, 178–198.

Pepler, D. J., & Ross, H. S. (1981). The effects of play on convergent and divergent problem solving. *Child Development, 52*, 1203–1210.

Piaget, J. (1962). *Play, dreams, and imitation in childhood*. New York: Norton. (Original work published in 1945, English translation, 1951)

Rubin, K. H., Fein, G. G., & Vandenberg, B. (1983). Play. In P. Mussen (Ed.), *Handbook of child psychology* (Vol. 4, pp. 693–774). New York: Wiley.

Schank, R., & Abelson, R. (1977). Scripts, plans, and knowledge. In P. Johnson-Laird & P. Wason (Eds.), *Thinking: Readings in cognitive science* (pp. 421–432). New York: Cambridge University Press.

Sears, R. R. (1947). Influence of methodological factors on doll play performance. *Child Development, 18*, 190–197.

Watson, M. W., & Fischer, K. W. (1977). A developmental sequence of agent use in late infancy. *Child Development, 48*, 828–836.

CHAPTER FIFTEEN

THE SYMBOLIC
PRODUCTS OF
EARLY CHILDHOOD

HOWARD GARDNER
Harvard Project Zero, Boston Veterans Administration Medical Center,
and Boston University School of Medicine

DENNIS WOLF
Harvard Project Zero,
Center for the Study of Gender, Education, and Human Development

TRADITIONAL VIEWS OF EXPLORATION
AND THE COGNITIVE REVOLUTION

If one could turn back the clock of psychology a few decades, one might behold an "ideal-type" view of play, art, exploration, and other allied expressive activities. At that time psychology was still in awe of a certain model of scientific procedure (based on physics): As a consequence, there was a search for general laws—laws that could apply to all species, all materials, all ages and stages of knowledge. As part of this quest for simple, explanatory laws that extended across the domains of psychology, researchers were avowedly blind to content. Whether dealing with language or logic, art or science, they assumed that the same laws would obtain. Similarly, investigators typically ignored kinds and levels of meaning, forms of representation, indeed the whole realm of symbolization. Instead, there was an almost exclusive preoccupation with general processes, such as learning, perception, memory, and problem solving, each of which was assumed to exist and operate in equivalent fashion across all materials.

Finally, one encountered widespread belief in the importance of a family of variables that relate to arousal: such "collative variables" as novelty, surprise, conflict, and uncertainty. It was often assumed that participation in exploratory activities had as its evolutionary goal the stimulation and maintenance of a certain level of tension or excitement of the sort that accompanied collative factors.

There was, then, what might be called the Hull–Spence synthesis: belief in the existence of a small set of laws that could explain all behavior (Hull, 1943; Spence, 1936). Neo-Hullian work culminated some 20 years ago in the synthesis put forth by Daniel Berlyne (1960). Berlyne attempted to tie together the activities of play, art, and other forms of exploration and to place them within the framework of general psychological processes.

Recent history has not been kind to this "received wisdom." We have entered an antibehaviorist era, one that arose from a set of disappointments. It has turned out to be impossible thus far to set up general laws that cut across all species, or even, for that matter, operate uniformly within a single species. The work of Garcia and his associates (Garcia & Levine, 1976) indicated that members of a species were biologically prepared to make certain associations or carry out certain actions, whereas "counterprepared" to carry out other actions or learn other sets of behaviors. The work of Chomsky (1957, 1959) indicated that

Skinner's attempts to explain language in the same way that he accounted for other forms of behavior were either tautological or erroneous. The recent studies with chimpanzees demonstrated that human beings have capacities that elude even our closest phylogenetic neighbors (Sebeok, 1981; Terrace, 1979). As a result, we have entered a time where specificity is stressed and nativism is taken seriously: For better or worse, few individuals follow Hull or Spence any more. In place of behavior, the governing principles center around cognition.

The cognitive revolution was initiated by the work of such researchers as Jerome Bruner (1957), George Miller (1956), Ulric Neisser (1967), Jean Piaget (1970), and Allen Newell and Herbert Simon (1972). Rejecting the focus on observable actions and embracing mind in its myriad forms, such investigators speak readily of mental representations, symbols, strategies, and other nonobservable processes and capacities. There is a recognition that animals may not be the same as human beings, that children may not be the same as adults. There is a parallel recognition that specific content may make a great difference, that language may differ from music, that both systems contrast with visual perception or motor activity. There is, finally, increasing recognition that culture plays a formative role in human psychology and that it is a mistake to think of the individual (or his mind or his brain) as divorced from such formative influences. (Cole & Means, 1981; Geertz, 1973, 1983). These views are certainly not without controversy, and cognitivists argue vigorously with one another about the details of each. Nor are they completely without precedent: In some ways they hearken back to the Gestalt psychologists and to others (e.g., the Würzburgers) who grappled with the central issues of thinking. Nonetheless, we may speak of the cognitive point of view as an emerging consensus in psychology in the 1980s, one isomorphic with, though wholly different from the consensus that obtained about behaviorism in the 1940s or early 50s, at least in Anglo–American circles (see Estes, 1981; Gardner, 1980a, 1985; Hunt, 1982).

AN APPROACH IN TERMS OF SYMBOL SYSTEMS

Our work at Harvard Project Zero has reflected, and perhaps even contributed in a modest way, to these cognitive trends. We have stressed the use of symbols as a central, perhaps the central, theme in human psychology. In so doing, we have combined insights from the work of the epistemologist Nelson Goodman (1968, 1978) and the developmental psychologist Jean Piaget (1970). Following Goodman, we underscore the importance of the several symbol systems that human beings are capable of using, and we search for various kinds of logical and empirical differentiations among such symbol systems as language, music, visual art, and dance. Following Piaget, we stress the importance of the developmental method, search for qualitative differences among individuals of various ages, and employ the "clinical method" of careful observation, followed by intensive probing, of a small group of subjects.

In view of this Goodman–Piaget perspective, we have focused our work on the development in children of an ability to use various kinds of symbol systems. Like psychologists of an earlier generation, we began with sympathy toward the idea of general rules: rules that would cut across all symbol systems from music to sculpture; rules that cover all media, from books to television; rules that would obtain across all sensory modes from vision to audition to taste.

But, like these earlier psychologists, our hopes have not been fully realized. Our work with children, as well as much other work with many populations, especially brain-damaged adults, has called into question the faith in general rules that obtain across these various materials (Allport, 1980; Fodor, 1983; Gardner, 1979, 1983, 1984, 1985; Geschwind, 1965; Sperry, 1970). We now take far more seriously the particular dictates of specific symbol systems like language in comparison, say, to music, or arithmetic. Running somewhat counter to the current focus on the processing of information, we have also paid special attention to the kinds of products fashioned by individuals of all ages. In fact, we have looked across the spectrum from the first symbols produced (and understood) by young children to the most complex kinds of notations, such as those involved in texts, musical scores, diagrams, and the like. Stated epigrammatically, our survey spans the gamut from decoding (Chall, 1967) to deconstruction (Derrida, 1967).

We believe that this line of study points toward a new key in the study of play, exploration, and artistic activities. The point of view that we, and others, have adopted takes seriously the particular symbol systems involved in these activities, countenances the possibility that these activities may occur differently depending on the symbolic domain in question, and anticipates differences among species, individuals of different ages, the media of transmission, and modes of reception and production. At any rate, we regard these issues as empirical matters, rather than as theoretical points of departure. Finally, more so than most workers in the behaviorist and cognitive traditions, we are attempting to discover the roles played by the surrounding culture with reference to the nature and variety of symbolic products encountered in our study.

A STUDY OF SYMBOLIC DEVELOPMENT

In this chapter we describe a line of research that we have been carrying out over the past decade and mention some of our tentative conclusions. Given the aforementioned interest in symbolic development, as well as the paucity of detailed information on how these processes occur, we spent several years in intensive study of a group of firstborn, middle-class children living in the Boston area. (See Gardner & Wolf, 1983; Wolf, 1979; Wolf & Gardner, 1979, 1981 for further details.) The purpose of this longitudinal study has been to gain detailed information on the course of symbolic development in seven media: language (particularly metaphor and story telling), drawing, three-dimensional depiction (clay and blocks), music, gestural-bodily expression, symbolic (or pretend) play, and, as our single "nonaesthetic" symbol system, numerical understanding. Our broad purpose in this study has been to determine whether there exist general principles that can account for all of symbolic development, thereby validating the claim that children go through a single symbolic stage (cf. Bruner, 1964; Piaget, 1970; Werner & Kaplan, 1963); or, alternatively, to discover whether there are special trajectories of symbolic development for some, or indeed for all, of these symbol systems.

We may characterize our project as focusing on four separate questions: (a) Are there ordinal scales—rigorous sequences of development through which all children pass in a given symbol system?; (b) are there central symbolic skills— core psychological processes that undergird several symbol systems?; (c) is there a general trajectory of symbol use?; and (d) are there instructive individual differences in patterns of symbolic acquisition?

In recapitulating our findings, we may indicate, with respect to the first question, that there indeed do exist genuine ordinal scales in each of the symbol systems that we have been able to study; that is, every young child initially reflects a simple level of understanding and expression and, during the next several years of life, passes through a discrete set of stages in that particular symbol system. Detailed ordinal scales will appear in Wolf and Gardner (in prep.).

Some aspects of symbolic development turn out to be quite specific to the symbol system in question. For example, in the case of music, the child must master the relations among pitches; this is a task that takes several years and that has, so far as we can see, few deep parallels to acquisition in other symbol systems. In the area of drawing, the child must represent the three-dimensional world in two dimensions, finding means to convey perspective, overlapping of objects, and the like, simply by drawing lines on a piece of paper. Again, this turns out to be quite a complex process, one that bears little relationship to progressions encountered in other symbolic media. As a final example, in the area of narrative, the child faces the challenge of recognizing that a story presents some kind of a problem to be solved. Sometimes the problem is physical—a character trapped in a deep well; sometimes the problem is psychological—a character whose ambivalence prevents her from acting. Moreover, the child must solve that problem with the ingredients contained in the story itself and respect the fictive boundary of a story; that is, the child must not intrude himself or invoke other "deus ex machina" factors in order to solve the "problem" posed by the story. Again, in this case, a quite elaborate set of stages is passed through by the child, and these stages do not seem to bear interesting relations to other symbolic domains.

STREAMS AND WAVES OF SYMBOLIZATION

We call these relatively encapsulated or "impenetrable" aspects our "streams" of symbolic development. In doing so, we emphasize that each trajectory occurs in relative independence of the others. According to our analysis, human beings have evolved over the millenia to perform at a high level in at least seven different content areas (reflected, roughly, in our domains of symbolic development). There may well be certain processes that can cut across or be transferred from one domain to another, but in general there is a functional autonomy, which is respected in the different principles by which each of these streams operates and by the lack of concordance between events in one stream and events in another (cf. Gardner, 1983).

In contrast to the streams, we have identified certain psychological processes—which we call "waves" of symbolization—that have their origins in certain early forms of representation but that rather readily spread to others. These capacities provide certain bridges or unifying skills across otherwise disparate symbolic streams. These waves are our candidates for central skills, the underlying processes that may in fact motivate broader aspects of symbolic development. The four waves unfold in order, at approximately year-long intervals, between the ages of 2 and 6.

Our first wave of symbolization, which we call event or role structuring, comes into its own when the child is between the age of 18 months and 2 years. Its central locus is in the symbolic areas of language and pretend play. At this time the child becomes able to capture in words or gestures the understanding that the world consists of agents who can assume various roles and can carry out actions that have consequences upon the world of objects and/or persons; that is, the child is able to draw on his understanding of how persons work, but to do so in symbolic media, rather than purely on the practical, or sensorimotor, plane. At first, this ability may seem to be a stream-like ability, one restricted to a single corner of symbolization. In fact, however, we find that children also employ the same psychological understanding in domains where it is far less appropriate. Consider, for instance, the area of two-dimensional representation, when the child of 1½ or 2 is asked to draw a truck. At such times we have found that a typical child will grab a marker, move it across the paper back and forth rapidly, and then say "Vroommm, vroommm" as if the marker were itself a vehicle (Rubin & Wolf, 1979; Scarlett & Wolf, 1979; Wolf, 1983).

Here, then, is our first example of a wave of symbolization, a capacity that arises initially in one symbol system but that can be used even inappropriately in order to express meaning in other seemingly remote symbol systems. Of course, not every wave spills over into every symbolic domain, nor do waves affect more peripheral domains in the same order or to the same extent in every child. But what is crucial is that the wave—a newly evolving psychological

310

process—is drawn on quite extensively by the child as an organizing principle for symbolic activities of several sorts.

Our second wave is topological or analogical mapping. The core psychological ability here involves the capacity to recognize some kind of topological or analogical relation that obtains between the field or entity to be symbolized and the symbol system being utilized. Initially, a primary locus of topological mapping is two- and three-dimensional depiction. The child of 3 or so is able to make a drawing of a human being, or a clay replica of a snowman, in which the smaller depictive element is placed on top of the larger element, thus capturing a principal topological relationship that also obtains in the referential field. Similarly, when singing a song, the child is now able to "go up" in pitch when the music ascends the scale and proceed faster when the music is faster, once again capturing a topological aspect of the referent (in these cases, pitch, height, and speed).

Topological mapping is used inappropriately when the child assimilates a complex array or referential field into a simpler kind of dichotomy (many/few; more/less; loud/soft); thus we find a child of 3 or so simply drawing "a lot of lines" if he wants to represent fingers or toes rather than counting them out specifically. Or the child sings a cluster rather than the correct number of tones in an effort to convey a certain complex musical pattern. Here again, although specific patterns differ across children, topological mapping has run rampant, even where more precise forms of enumeration are indicated.

A third wave of symbolization is digital mapping. Coalescing around age 4 in our population, digital mapping entails a numerical (or metric) understanding, the appreciation of the difference in meaning amongst numbers like 4, 5, 6, up through 10, as well as some application of the systemic relations that obtain among numbers. Digital mapping has immediate positive influences on the child's symbolic development. Now, rather than giving merely an approximate rendition of the number of notes in a song, fingers on a person, or characters in a story, the child gets the number exactly correct. This would seem to be an entirely beneficent development, but, in fact, digital mapping can deluge other aspects of symbolization. Thus, if a child is trying to capture the mood of a song but becomes too involved in getting the number of tones or the pitch intervals precisely correct, he may lose that ability to express specific moods or tensions (this is bolder, that is more placid) that was earlier captured via topological mapping.

Our final wave of symbolization is notational or second-order symbolization. Around the age of 5 or 6 in our society, children become capable of using "second-order" symbol systems, ones that themselves refer in part to other symbol systems. As primary examples we have written language that refers to oral language, and written numbers that refer to spoken numbers, but there are also musical scores, dance notations, maps, diagrams, and the like. Children become able to "read" these symbol systems and also to express understanding by "writing" in such second-order symbol systems. In so doing, they open up a happy kind of Pandora's box: They can now devise ever more complex symbol systems that themselves refer to more elementary symbol systems. This happens most transparently in the case of mathematics, in which one system can readily be embedded in a more abstract or complex one, and this process can be repeated independently.

We have come to speak of this final wave as entailing channels of symbolization. Rather than the process of symbolization emanating chiefly from the child's own interactions with the world, it is the symbol systems, the literacies, the notational systems of the culture that come increasingly to channel the child's development. We see, here, a fascinating link between the first kinds of notations used by paleolithic man (Marshack, 1972), the simple tally systems spontaneously devised by children at play the world over, and the most complex kinds of mathematical and scientific symbol systems that are at a premium in this technological age (Menninger, 1969). In each case, the society provides the actual channels for symbolic capacities, but it is the individual's potential to be able to employ second-order (and even higher order) symbol systems, the individual's notational capacity that brings such channeling to the fore.

A GENERAL PORTRAIT OF SYMBOLIC DEVELOPMENT

Our longitudinal study, whose results have been briefly summarized, yields a more general picture of symbolic development. We speak of a period of mundane symbolization during the first year or two of life. At this time the child is capable of understanding the simplest forms of representation: that a picture can stand for an object, that a gesture or a word can have a meaning. At the same time, the child develops the core psychological understandings on which subsequent productive forms of symbolization depend. The appreciation that events have consequences, that there exist numerical quantities in the world, and that drawings can depict objects are all present, at least by the end of the first year of life (Bower, 1974; Gelman & Gallistel, 1978; Kagan, Kearsley, & Zelazo, 1978; Starkey, Spelke, & Gelman, 1980); these can subsequently be drawn upon when the capacity to capture these understandings in symbolic form becomes important.

Between the ages of 2 and 5, children enter into a period of basic symbolization. Here, production of symbols begins in earnest. This is the time when the child passes through the principal ordinal stages in each of the symbol systems that we have been studying. Each of the specific streams unfolds over this period, though not generally in synchrony with one another. At the same time, we see knowledge, which previously had existed only in a perceptual form and only in terms of practical daily sequences being encoded in different symbol systems.

FIG. 15.1 A tadpole man, by a 3-year-old.

The four waves of symbolization constitute Nature's developmental sequence for the transition to full-blown use of symbols.

We may designate two points of stasis. At about the age of 3, children attain a general understanding of symbol systems. They exhibit an initial approximation of symbolic products like songs, drawings, stories. They can recognize exemplars of these categories and can produce very simple "outline" forms—for example, a "tadpole" man (see Fig. 15.1), a story containing a good character, and a villain, a song that explores the ambitus of a fourth or a fifth. There is sufficient progress between the ages of 3 and 5 that we may credit older children with a "first draft" knowledge of basic symbolization. At that age, children are able to produce clear examples of drawings, stories, and pictures, even as they under-stand in some detail what is required for more sophisticated productions in each of these areas. And so one encounters drawings that include several objects (see Fig. 15.2), a story with several characters and a song with a recognizable opening theme, development, and final cadence.

FIG. 15.2 A simple scene by a 5-year-old.

Indeed, the ages of 5 to 7 seem to us a very special time, one that deserves to be termed the flowering of symbolization. Children of this age can readily produce stories, songs, drawings, dances, and other symbolic products and do so in an exceptionally expressive, original, inventive, and spontaneous way (Gardner, 1973, 1980a, 1982) (see Fig. 15.3). It is a time of temporary heights of artistic activity, a brief but treasured moment when children gain genuine pleasure from involvement in the arts and fashion products that, at least to our historical epoch, display a special air of charm and inventiveness.

But even as this flowering is at its temporary height, we discern two new facets of symbolization coming into effect in our culture. On the one hand, children become much more literally oriented in their symbolic products (cf. Alland, 1983). No longer as willing to cut across domains of expression to combine, say, music and drawing, to make unusual figures of speech, or countenance unexpected juxtapositions of color, children become intent upon getting

FIG. 15.3 A flavorful drawing by a 6-year-old.

things exactly right, using language in a precise manner, drawing in a photo-graphically realistic manner (see Fig. 15.4). Whereas to some extent this insist-ence on literal precision represents progress, it has an unfortunate dulling effect on the artwork of most children, making it far less interesting to most adults in our culture (and seemingly less interesting to many children as well). And when this literal mindedness is combined, as it often is, with a quantitative decline in the children's artistic productions, one has the feeling that the symbolic flowering is over.

As a companion to this literalness, however, we also witness throughout our culture the advent of literacy, the capacity to produce notations. These notations include the common garden-variety notational systems of the culture, such as

FIG. 15.4 A realistic drawing by an 8-year-old.

written language and numbers, as well as somewhat more specialized and arcane forms, such as maps, musical notation, morse code, dance notation, and various computer languages.

In general, whatever their specific characteristics, all notations carry out at least three functions: (a) reduction of information, that is, the deliberate selection of only certain privileged items to be notated (thus a map does not include everything on the terrain, but just the houses and the roads); (b) systematicity, that is, the use of the same symbols or marks throughout a notation to represent the same thing (all houses are represented in the same way, all two-lane surface roads are represented in the same way); (c) legibility, the fashioning of a notation that can be decoded by other individuals, perhaps with the aid of a key or legend.

The development of notational capacity (which we have recently begun to study) may turn out to be as complex and multifaceted as the steps of mundane and basic symbolization (Davis & Davidson, 1981). Initially, the child does not even understand the purpose of a notation; he simply attempts to create the actual performance, such as the model's dance or the playing of an instrument. Around the age of 5, the child begins to understand the idea of a notation but produces a version that captures only the most gross distinctions (for example, two contrasting speeds in a dance are captured). At the age of 6 or 7, children begin to understand that notations have to be able to recapture a variety of elements in the model; but at this time children tend to be excessively detailed, failing to reduce the information to a more manageable form. Also, there is an absence of system; that is, the child exhibits scattered local forms of organization (all the houses near the lake are notated in a similar fashion); but the notation as a whole is not consistent. And finally, the notations are still quite egocentric. The children can produce marks that may have idiosyncratic meanings but are not, in the absence of explanation, comprehensible to other "naive" individuals. Only between the ages of 7 and 10 do children become able to produce notations that feature genuine reduction, systematicity, and legibility. However, the development of notational capacity continues well beyond that time, and even adults in our society still exhibit plenty of room for improvement in their notational skills.

Symbolic development beyond the age of 10 remains largely uncharted territory, so far as we know. We might mention, however, that in those children with artistic talent, there is often a crisis of creativity in the preadolescent or adolescent years. Children find that they have some talent in symbolic expression; but they also become far more critical of their own work, quite possibly because they are now able to compare it with the work of other, even more highly skilled, individuals. We have found that unless children have acquired considerable symbolic fluency, they are likely to find their own work wanting and to desist from participation in artistic symbolic activity, particularly as a producer of symbols. Instead, they become more like consumer's audience members who can enjoy the symbol systems of others, but who, unlike young children, no longer fashion pictures, stories, drawings on their own.

Finally, a word about individual differences. Although our own study was not originally focused upon individual differences, we found striking contrasts among very young children in how they approach the task of symbolic development. Perhaps the most profound contrast obtains between two groups of children (Shotwell, Wolf, & Gardner, 1979; Wolf & Grollman, 1982). Patterners are individuals who are very interested in the configurational properties of displays. Thus, in creating or recreating a symbolic entity they pay attention to aspects of form, particularly in the visual realm, and use this configurational approach as their basic means for negotiating other symbolic domains. In sharp contrast, we find another group of children, called dramatists, who adopt the story or narrative as their primary modes of symbolic expression. Faced with a new task, these children pay scant attention to configurational properties but instead try to place or even force the symbolic elements into the guise of a narrative (see Fig. 15.5 and 15.6).

We can gain a feeling for the distinction between these kinds of children by considering how such youngsters approach block play. When faced with a set of blocks, young patterns are likely to make a complex architectonic design laying out column upon column, perhaps building several symmetric towers; if asked about what is happening, the child may say, "Oh, I'm making a building."

FIG. 15.5 Effort by a four-year-old patterner to copy a toy car. This child made
a concerted effort to capture the model's characteristic contours.

But it is clear, in fact, that this child is intrigued by the geometric patterns that
he or she can produce. By contrast, the young dramatist will grab two blocks,
call one the mommy and the other the baby, and say, "Oh, they go store now,
they going on walk" and, while scarcely moving the blocks at all, will weave
a complex narrative tapestry. What captivates this child is the potential to tell a
story.

   We believe these individual differences are recognizable as early as the second
year of life and reach a temporary height during the third year of life. Differences
between patterners and dramatists recede somewhat thereafter. Still they may
well remain as a kind of initial stance toward symbolic learning, reemerging
even when a much older individual invades an unfamiliar symbolic realm.

   There may also be some other telltale individual differences. As part of our
work, we have become increasingly sympathetic to the notion that individuals
differ in their intellectual profiles; that is, human beings are capable of a number
of different "intelligences" and, for either genetic, environmental, or interactive
reasons, some individuals may be stronger in one intelligence, say musical or
linguistic, whereas other individuals will be stronger in another intelligence, say
spatial or bodily–gestural or logical–mathematical. (For amplification, see Gardner, 1983, and references cited therein). Finally, we should note the individual
differences that seem to obtain across styles of teaching and learning, in different

FIG. 15.6 Effort by a 4-year-old dramatist to copy a toy car. This child produced a collection of prominent feature—sides, wheels, simply by listing the essential features of the car. There was no attempt to organize them into a unified view.

households, various social groups, and presumably in diverse societies as well (Cole & Means, 1981). Even in the case of identical twins, it is our guess that symbolic development will be different depending on the parents who rear them, the cultural values they encounter, the notational systems dominant in their surroundings, and kindred other factors.

MEDIATING BETWEEN BIOLOGY AND CULTURE

As we have sought to identify the causes of this general picture of symbolic development, we have viewed our findings in terms of broader scientific categories. It has become clear to us that one must take quite seriously both the biological and cultural constraints upon symbolic development. And indeed, it may be a major lesson of social sciences in the last 20 years that both biology

319

and culture, working separately and together, have more importance than had generally been thought.

From the biological perspective it makes sense to think of individuals as possessing from birth a number of "raw" computational devices. These are information-processing systems in the brain that are so constituted as to be particularly sensitive to certain kinds of information (or certain kinds of content); when that content is presented, these computational devices will operate on that content in specific ways, thereby yielding specific outcomes. These computational devices have evolved over many thousands of years, and it is by virtue of their existence in the human nervous system that we can make rapid progress in such domains as language, music, spatial processing, and even the understanding of other people. These raw informational-processing devices lie at the center of the aforementioned multiple intelligences.

Left to their own, these information-processing devices are purely syntactic: Like the ordinary digital computer, they operate without regard to meanings. However, except in abnormal individuals, the processing of these computers soon becomes enveloped with meaning—indeed meaningful interpretation is inescapable. According to our speculations, meanings become associated with the various computations because particular feelings readily accompany the use of, and the reaction to, these information-processing systems; because these information-processing systems (in humans) are readily and regularly marshalled for symbolic purposes; and because the culture will offer certain kinds of interpretations for, or impose them upon, the products of individual intelligences. Therefore, it is impossible to witness these computational devices at work in pure form in normal individuals after the opening weeks of life, for these "intelligences" interact readily with one another and are perennially imbued by meanings. One can, however, examine the computational mechanisms in a relatively pure form in certain kinds of special populations such as idiot savants, prodigies, children with learning disabilities, or adults with brain damage (Werner, 1961). Thus, these populations prove to be of special importance for those seeking to ascertain the biological basis of symbolic expression.

Donning a cultural perspective, we find it useful to think of each human group as featuring certain roles and functions that must be carried out in order for the culture of that particular group to be successfully transmitted to succeeding generations. A study of symbolic development must focus equally, then, on the kinds of symbolic systems that are valued by a society—the religions, the sciences, the arts—and on the particular products—like stories, drawings, songs, and rites: The culture uses these as an index by which to measure the degree to which the behaviors and knowledge it values are indeed being mastered by the younger members of its society.

We encounter, then, a conundrum. The computational devices are simple information-processing systems, and, as such, they cannot be directly sensitive to the demands of society. Society, on the other hand, has no understanding of the human brain and cannot directly monitor organizations and reorganizations that take place within the nervous system.

Here is where symbolic systems and products become vital. They constitute in fact a kind of tertium quid, a level of analysis that can be "understood" or taken into account by both the culture and biology. They can be "understood" by the society because mature individuals can monitor whether, in fact, symbolic systems are being mastered and the requisite symbolic products are forthcoming. They can be "understood" equally well by biology because the human nervous system is apparently so constituted that it can act appropriately on and assimilate information from symbolic products, such as stories, conversations, and written texts (Gardner, 1975; Luria, 1966); that is, specific regions of the brain appear to be "dominant" for the operations of particular intelligences, and the purely informational processing aspects of these neural zones can be destroyed or spared in isolation.

Recognition of the special role played by symbolic systems and products can be of genuine aid to a range of interested parties. For ethnographers, the level of symbolic system provides a privileged entry point into the goals and values of a culture (Geertz, 1973). For educators, a focus on symbolization provides a gauge wherein they can monitor the extent to which children are learning what has been deemed important in their culture (Gardner, 1983). Finally, for the ordinary individual, attention to the symbolic realm makes it possible to monitor one's own development by examining symbolic products in light of the extent to which they resemble, or deviate from, what is expected and rewarded in one's own culture. The heights of civilization may inhere in the most complex, differentiated, and imaginative kinds of symbolic products, but the roots can be discerned in basic biological processes that allow humans to become sensitive to the particular contents and forms of symbolic products.

CONCLUDING COMMENTS

In this chapter, we have described an approach in terms of symbol systems. Such an approach focuses on emerging abilities to recognize and produce instances of a variety of symbolic systems, ranging from ordinary language to the languages of science to the kinds of meaning system embedded in the use of the body or in the capacity to combine elements of pitch and rhythm. Workers in a number of areas, ranging from artificial intelligence (Newell & Simon, 1972) to anthropology (Geertz, 1973) to philosophy (Goodman, 1968) have recognized the power that can be obtained from an analysis in terms of symbol systems and the importance of incorporating the level of representation of symbolic processes.

The full promise—as well as the limitations—of an approach in terms of symbol systems, remains a task for future research. Yet it does not seem premature to conclude that our behaviorist predecessors, such as Hull and Skinner, made poor bets on the appropriate explanatory mode for the psychological sciences. Their models were not even appropriate for the study of rats, for they did not take into account the degree of "preparedness" for certain experiences rather than others, nor the specific contents toward which even lower mammals are particularly oriented. They failed to note the peculiar biological basis and biases of human intellectual capacities, the fact that humans have specific forms of preparedness, for example, to master language, and that members of our species process different kinds of syntactic and semantic content in characteristic ways. Finally, this earlier generation of researchers tended to ignore cultural and historical forces, those contexts within which any kind of human symbolic production necessarily takes place and which come to play increasingly important and ultimately dominant roles in the productions and interpretations of any sophisticated human being (see Gardner, 1984).

By adopting a focus upon symbolic processes and products, we find ourselves dealing with materials that are far more complex than had hitherto been considered desirable in the area of psychology. When one confronts novels, symphonies, or computer languages, it is clear that simple psychological formulae will not suffice and that one needs to analyze a symbolic product in its own terms (for example, through linguistic or musicological analysis) as well as in terms of the processes that are needed to master it. The tools that have been developed in the disciplines devoted to different symbolic streams must be brought to bear on future psychological analyses. Though this will require training in areas that have often been remote from psychologists, the imperative to analyze the product in such specific terms should significantly enhance our ultimate portrait of the relevant psychological processes.

In the end, there may well be common processes that obtain across a range of symbolic products and symbolic systems. For the sake of simplicity and elegance, one would certainly hope so. The waves of symbolization may provide one way of finding parallel processes across diverse symbol systems. Accounts of human intelligences may serve to limit or prescribe the symbolic activities in which human beings can become proficient. Anthropologists and historians may discover that some common principles reduce the dizzying variety of ways in which human cultures have devised and utilized symbolic products. Eventually, there may even emerge some common processes of exploration, or curiosity, at work across diverse symbolic domains.

What is clear, however, is that these general laws cannot be legislated a priori. Our work, and that of others, has demonstrated salient differences across ages, modes of transmission, symbolic systems, and the products that are fashioned in relevant media: Any generalizations must be put forth with extreme tentativeness. The premature positing of laws turns out to be risky and perhaps even especially maladroit in such inherently open and creative areas as play, exploration, and art.

SUMMARY

Behaviorist explanations of past decades have given way in recent years to a cognitive approach to human activity. Reflecting this trend, researchers at Harvard Project Zero have studied the development in young children of the capacities to employ various symbol systems, including those of language, drawing, numbers, and music. The optimal way of describing these developmental trends requires two separate concepts: "streams of symbolization," referring to psychological processes that occur primarily within a single symbol system, and "waves of symbolization," referring to psychological processes that have their origins in a particular symbol system but that are soon manifest across a range of symbol systems.

The development of these streams and waves is paramount during the preschool period. Between 5 and 7 years of age, there is a flowering of symbolic processes, during which children exhibit the capacity to create songs, stories, drawings, and other "first draft" symbolic products. The acquisition of literacy in various notational systems occurs during the early years of school, a time when the imaginative symbol use of earlier years is less evident.

An analysis in terms of various symbolic competences may be a promising way to describe human cognitive capacities. It builds upon information about human biological potentials even as it takes into account the cultural constraints that affect all of development. In the end, some psychological processes may turn out to cut across all human symbol-using abilities, but at present the evidence seems to point to considerable specificity of symbolic competences.

ACKNOWLEDGMENTS

The work described in this chapter was supported in part by grants from the Carnegie Corporation, the Spencer Foundation, and the Bernard van Leer Foundation.

REFERENCES

Alland, A. (1983). *Playing with form*. New York: Columbia University Press.
Allport, D. A. (1980). Attention and performance. In G. Claxton (Ed.), *Cognitive psychology: New directions*, (pp. 112–153). London: Routledge & Kegan Paul.
Berlyne, D. (1960). *Conflict, arousal, and curiosity*. New York: McGraw-Hill.
Bower, T. (1974). *Development in infancy*. San Francisco: Freeman.
Bruner, J. S. (1957). On perceptual readiness. *Psychological Review, 64*, 123–152.
Bruner, J. S. (1964). The course of cognitive growth. *American Psychologist, 19*, 1–15.
Chall, J. S. (1967). *Learning to read: The great debate*. New York: McGraw-Hill.

Chomsky, N. (1957). *Syntactic structures*. The Hague: Mouton.

Chomsky, N. (1959). A review of B. F. Skinner's *Verbal Behavior*. *Language, 35*, 26–58.

Cole, M., & Means, B. (1981). *Comparative studies of how people think*. Cambridge: Harvard University Press.

Davis, M. E., & Davidson, L. (1981, May). *Symbolic development in middle childhood: The acquisition of notational symbol use*. Paper presented at the Jean Piaget Society, Philadelphia.

Derrida, J. (1967). *De la Grammatologie*. Paris: Les Editions de minuit.

Estes, W. K. (1981). The science of cognition. *National Research Council Outlook for Science and Technology* (pp. 157–181). Washington, DC: Government Printing Office.

Fodor, J. A. (1983). *The modularity of mind*. Cambridge, MA: MIT Press.

Garcia, J., & Levine, M. S. (1976). Learning paradigms and the structure of the organism. In M. Rosenzweig & E. L. Bennett (Eds.), *Neural mechanisms of learning and memory* (pp. 193–208). Cambridge: MIT Press.

Gardner, H. (1973). *The arts and human development*. New York: Wiley.

Gardner, H. (1975). *The shattered mind*. New York: Knopf.

Gardner, H. (1979). Developmental psychology after Piaget. *Human Development, 22*, 73–88.

Gardner, H. (1980a). Cognition comes of age. In M. Piatelli-Palmarini (Ed.), *Language and learning* (pp. XIX-XXXVI). Cambridge, MA: Harvard University Press.

Gardner, H. (1980b). *Artful scribbles*. New York: Basic Books.

Gardner, H. (1982). *Art, mind, and brain*. New York: Basic Books.

Gardner, H. (1983). *Frames of mind: The theory of multiple intelligences*. New York: Basic Books.

Gardner, H. (1985). *The mind's new science*. New York: Basic Books.

Gardner, H. (1984). The development of competence in culturally-defined domains. In R. Shweder & R. Levine (Eds.), *The acquisition of culture*. New York: Cambridge University Press.

Gardner, H., & Wolf, D. (1983). Waves and streams of symbolization. In D. Rogers & J. Sloboda (Eds.), *The acquisition of symbolic skills* (pp. 19–42). London: Plenum Press.

Geertz, C. (1973). *The interpretation of cultures*. New York: Basic Books.

Geertz, C. (1983). *Local knowledge*. New York: Basic Books.

Gelman, R., & Gallistel, R. (1978). *The child's understanding of number*. Cambridge, MA: Harvard University Press.

Geschwind, N. (1965). Disconnexion syndromes in animals and man. *Brain, 88*, 585–644.

Goodman, N. (1968). *Languages of art*. Indianapolis: Bobbs-Merrill.

Goodman, N. (1978). *Ways of worldmaking*. Indianapolis: Hackett.

Hull, C. L. (1943). *Principles of behavior*. New York: Appleton-Century.

Hunt, M. (1982). *The universe within*. New York: Simon & Schuster.

Kagan, J., Kearsley, R., & Zelazo, P. (1978). *Infancy: Its place in human development*. Cambridge, MA: Harvard University Press.

Luria, R. (1966). *Higher cortical functions in man*. New York: Basic Books.

Marshack, A. (1972). *The roots of civilization*. New York: McGraw-Hill.

Menninger, K. (1969). *Number words and number symbols*. Cambridge, MA: MIT Press.

Miller, G. A. (1956). The magic number seven plus or minus two: Some limits on our capacity for processing information. *Psychological Review, 63*, 81–97.

Neisser, U. (1967). *Cognitive psychology*. New York: Appleton-Century.

Newell, A., & Simon, H. (1972). *Human problem-solving*. Englewood-Cliffs, NJ: Prentice-Hall.

Piaget, J. (1970). Piaget's theory. In P. Mussen (Ed.), *Carmichael's manual of child psychology* (Vol. 1, pp. 703–732). New York: Wiley.

Rubin, S., & Wolf, D. (1979). The development of maybe: The evolution of social roles into narrative roles. In E. Winner & H. Gardner (Eds.), *Fact, fiction, and fantasy in childhood. New Directions in Child Development, 6*, 15–28.

Scarlett, W. G., & Wolf, D. (1979). When it's only make-believe: The construction of a boundary between fantasy and reality in story-telling. In E. Winner & H. Gardner (Eds.), *Fact, fiction, and fantasy in childhood. New Directions in Child Development, 6,* 29–40.

Sebeok, T. (1981). *The play of musement.* Bloomington: Indiana University Press.

Shotwell, J., Wolf, D., & Gardner, H. (1979). Styles of achievement in early symbolization In M. Foster & S. Brandes (Eds.), *Symbol as sense: New approaches to the analysis of meaning* (pp. 175–202). New York: Academic Press.

Spence, K. W. (1936). The nature of discrimination learning in animals. *Psychological Review, 43,* 427–449.

Sperry, R. W. (1970). Perception in the absence of the neocortical commissures. *Perception and its disorders. Research Publication ARNMD, 48,* 123–128.

Starkey, P., Spelke, E., & Gelman R. (1980, April). *Number competence in infants: Sensitivity to numeric invariance and numeric change.* Paper presented to the International Conference on Infant Studies, New Haven, CT.

Terrace, H. (1979). *Nim.* New York: Knopf.

Werner, H. (1961). *Comparative psychology of mental development.* New York: Science Editors.

Werner, H., & Kaplan, B. (1963). *Symbol formation.* New York: Wiley.

Wolf, D. (Ed.). (1979). *Early symbolization. New Directions in Child Development, 3* (Whole).

Wolf, D. (1983, September). *Representation after picturing: The depiction of visual–spatial information in the drawings of one to three-year-olds.* Paper presented at the International Conference on Psychology and the Arts, Cardiff, Wales.

Wolf, D., & Gardner, H. (1979). Style and sequence in early symbolic play. In N. Smith & M. B. Franklin (Eds.), *Symbolic functioning in children* (pp. 117–138). Hillsdale, NJ: Lawrence Erlbaum Associates.

Wolf, D., & Gardner, H. (1981). On the structure of early symbolization. In R. Schiefelbusch & D. Bricker (Eds.), *Early language: Acquisition and intervention* (pp. 287–328). Baltimore: University Park Press.

Wolf, D., & Gardner, H. (in prep.). *The making of meanings.*

Wolf, D., & Grollman, S. (1982). Ways of playing: Individual differences in imaginative styles. In K. H. Rubin & D. G. Pepler (Eds.), *The play of children: Current theory and research* (pp. 46–63). Basel: Karger.

CHAPTER SIXTEEN

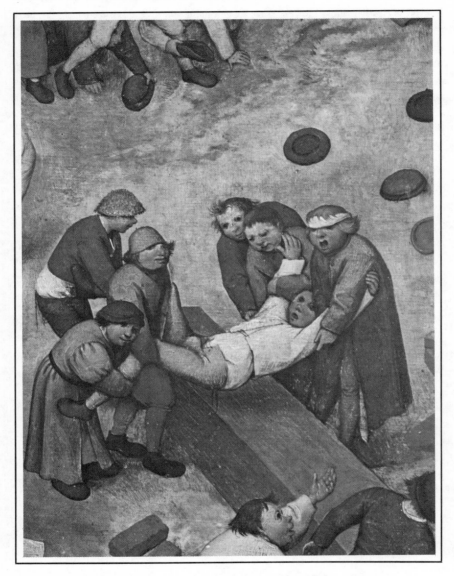

EMOTIONAL COMPONENTS OF ACTION: THEIR ONTOGENY AS REFLECTED IN ACHIEVEMENT BEHAVIOR

HEINZ HECKHAUSEN
Max Planck Institut für psychologische Forschung, München

Plato was the first to partition the human psyche into three functions: cognition, emotion, and conation (motivation). Since then much has been learned in psychology, but this tripartite division of inner life has not changed. The overlapping regions of these functions are a part of psychology's intradisciplinary border areas that remain largely unexplored. Moreover, emotion has been a neglected topic of research and hence remains the "poor relative of motivation." Scherer (1981) gave a number of reasons for this situation, two of them being the methodological difficulties of analyzing the various manifestations of a phenomenon as transitory as emotions and the fact that emotion as an explanatory construct still raises controversy. For example, are emotions simply phenomena concomitant with their Platonic siblings, cognition and conation, or are they superordinate to them? Are they a precondition or a consequence of certain reactions?

THE EMOTIONAL SYSTEM IN A NEW PERSPECTIVE

Research on emotions recently seems to have gained new impetus. I only mention a few approaches. Emotions are a deeply embedded heritage of evolution that can be traced, with amazing similarities, far down the phylogenetic ladder (Plutchik, 1980). What distinguishes man from the other organisms is not only cognition and language but also an excessively well-developed emotionality (Hebb, 1972). That seems to have resulted in two essential evolutionary advantages that favor a flexible adaptation to the changing environmental demands. One of these advantages is the result of a detachment of reaction from information intake. The more an organism is able to experience emotions, the less dependent it becomes on rigid reflex patterns of response (Scherer, 1981). Emotions provide us with a kind of split-second communiqué concerning the immediate environmental situation and our relative position within it. That constitutes a buffer against precipitate, mechanical reaction; it buys time for an appropriate reflection on what is to be done (Lazarus, 1968). Moreover, the concomitant expression phenomena play an important role. They signal our interaction partner how we feel and what we are about to do. Darwin (1872) already pointed to the evolutionary advantage of such a communication function.

The second advantage is the capacity of the emotional system to focus attention on that part of the informational stream that requires priority in cognitive processing. This involves short-term, preevaluative processes, which can only be guaranteed through direct emotional reactions and not through cognitions in the sense of conscious considerations and conclusions.

A number of investigators have broken down the emotional system into individual stages to facilitate the primary evaluation of external and internal stimuli. Scherer (1981) proposed a whole series of processing stages that not only develop phylogenetically but also emerge sequentially during ontogenetic development. The first stage involves an assessment of unfamiliarity and novelty. The emotional reaction is surprise that results in curiosity behavior. Its goal is to make the unfamiliar familiar, which causes the emotion of surprise to disappear. An extreme case of unfamiliarity may result in a fright reaction that can easily lead to escape. The second step distinguishes between pleasant and unpleasant. Zajonc (1980) was able to show that pleasant experiences are not only reliable but apparently also "precognitive" because they are able to function without recognition or inference. From the perspective of motivational psychology, this evaluative step determines the preliminary impulses of approach or avoidance.

The subsequent processing stages are without doubt associated with complex, cognitive information processing. For example, the third stage tests whether the particular situation facilitates or hinders the attainment of an action goal that is being pursued. From the perspective of a psychology of motivation, these are situation outcome expectations, where one ponders what would happen if one did not intervene in the course of events.

The fourth stage provides emotional experiences concerning the extent to which one is able to overcome the obstacles in the path to the goal. Motivational psychology would label these experiences action outcome expectations, which arise from causal attribution that takes into account facilitating or inhibitory, internal or external, but as a rule stable, causal factors. The fifth and last stage leads to self-evaluative emotions once the action outcome has been achieved and has been compared to self-imposed or externally imposed standards or norms.

The last three processing stages that Scherer (1981) postulated for the emotional system are also part of, and fairly extensively studied in, cognitive models of motivation (see Heckhausen, 1980). The third and fourth stages correspond to types of expectations and the fifth to an important motivating incentive, namely, the self-evaluative emotions, the development of which is an evolutionary feat achieved only by humans. A search for self-evaluative emotions in infrahuman organisms, including our closest ancestors, the primates, is not likely to be successful. It is this self-reflectivity in the evaluation of outcomes of one's own action that, in the final analysis, delineates human action from the goal-oriented behavior of animals, which admittedly includes the first four processing steps.

ACHIEVEMENT BEHAVIOR AND ITS MOTIVATION

That brings me to my actual topic, the role of emotions in behavior. I examine it, using achievement motivation as a prototypical example (Heckhausen, 1982a). A review of the research on achievement motivation over the past 30 years reveals that progress in the development of theory can generally be divided into three periods in which the determinants of self-evaluative emotions as motivators were explored, Scherer's fifth motivating process in the emotion system. As a start, achievement motivation was defined as a "concern with a standard of excellence" (McClelland, Atkinson, Clark, & Lowell, 1953). That provides the standard against which one can compare the achieved outcome of action.

Next, the emotions of "pride" and "shame" were conceptualized as the motivating incentives of anticipated success or failure for achievement behavior in an expectancy-times–value model, the so-called risk-taking model. That endowed the two aforementioned emotions with their actual motivating functions, which initiate action or inaction in achievement-oriented situations, i.e., in the face of tasks at which one can meet or fail to meet a standard of excellence.

In this way, the two emotions of pride and shame attained a key role in achievement behavior. Yet, for a long time they remained place holders as postulated constructs in a theoretical net. The model was so cognitively constructed that emotions as such have only recently become the object of empirical research (Weiner, Russell, & Lerman, 1978). By the way, this showed that the identification of pride and shame as mediators of achievement behavior was premature and based largely on commonsense psychology. In reality, there is a broad spectrum of different emotions of success and failure. It appears that these emotions begin to unfold gradually in various directions as feedback about an outcome is received in conjunction with attribution processes and their outcomes (see Heckhausen, 1980; Wong & Weiner, 1981). This involves the fourth processing stage in the emotion system. Here the presence of other persons may lead to an evaluation on their part, and hence the resulting self-evaluating emotion may encompass aspects of social relations. Pride and shame, in particular, are such socially relevant emotions, in contrast to self-satisfaction or self-dissatisfaction.

Finally, a further determinant of self-evaluative emotions was identified, namely, the variable of individual differences. The same success or failure (related to the same standard) can lead different individuals to perceive that success or failure differently, depending on their biases in the attribution of the achieved outcome. For example, individuals who tend to attribute their success to their own ability and their failures to unfavorable situations or lack of effort, optimize their self-evaluative outcomes and remain optimistic in the face of failures. They stand in contrast to those who attribute success to the ease of the task and to luck, and their failure to a lack of ability.

Such individual patterns of attribution are based on the fourth processing stage in the emotional system as postulated by Scherer. Once such stable individual differences in the explanation of identical events are established, it is easy to see why, for example, an individual marked by fear of failure does not become more confident of success even in the face of a whole series of successes and why fear of failure is not experienced by someone who is confident of success, despite a run of failures. That makes the stability of individual differences in

achievement motivation comprehensible. The predominance of positive or negative self-evaluative emotions is stabilized by each individual on the basis of his
or her preconceived causes for success or failure, even in the face of experiences
that are contrary to expectation. Because emotions of self-evaluation involve
self-administered "reinforcement," the individual achievement motive can also
be conceptualized as a "self-reinforcing system" (Heckhausen, 1975, 1980).

Because this volume deals with curiosity, imagination, and play, this introduction should have made it clear that self-evaluative emotions represent a later
product of development than all other emotional prerequisites for curiosity,
imagination, or play. But perhaps this can provide a useful background against
which the subjects of this book can be articulated.

THE ONTOGENESIS OF SELF-EVALUATIVE EMOTIONS

We are less concerned here with individual differences in motives and their
ontogeny than with the ontogeny of self-evaluative emotions in general. In other
words, we want to determine when, in a child's development, we can detect the
first minimal set of features required for the emergence of self-evaluative emotions. For as soon as the latter can be observed, we are justified in attributing
motivated achievement behavior to the child. From the perspective of psychological theories of motivation, there are two spheres of phenomena to be considered. The first sphere relates to the organization of behavior. The particular
action should be discernibly directed toward an outcome that satisfies a standard,
in short, an "outcome-centeredness." The second sphere concerns the "self."
The child should already have some sort of self-concept. He or she should be
able to attribute an achieved outcome to him/herself as originator (author), an
outcome to be attributed to characteristics of one's own self because that is the
minimal requirement for any self-evaluative emotions. Let us label this sphere
self-reference.

THE EARLIEST REACTIONS OF SUCCESS AND FAILURE

We now have two templates—outcome-centeredness and self-reference—with
which to search the findings of developmental psychology. Our first studies of
20 years ago did not explore this ground very systematically. They raised the
more global question: At what age can one observe the earliest self-evaluative
emotions in the form of clearly differentiated expressions after a successful or
unsuccessful action outcome? Our little subjects were made to compete singly
with a female experimenter to see who could be the first to pile a number of
rings around a peg (Heckhausen & Roelofsen, 1962). Each child who could
understand this standard of excellence, namely, to determine who finished first,

entered into the competition and displayed expressive responses that reflected differentiated emotions following success and failure.

Fig. 16.1 illustrates this for a 4 ½-year-old girl. After her success, she triumphantly glances up from her work and looks at the loser. She straightens up and throws up her hands, gestures that expand the self and the psychological field.

(a)

(b)

FIG. 16.1 Typical expressions after (a) success and (b) failure in the tower-building experiment (age 4½ years).

In contrast, after failure the torso is bent forward, she appears crestfallen, her head is tilted to one side, there is an embarrassed grin. She neither moves her eyes nor her hands from her work. The psychological field contracts (examples are shown in the film by Heckhausen, Ertel, & Kiekheben-Roelofsen, 1966). Both reaction patterns already unquestionably reflect fully developed self-evaluative emotions. They were found at age 2½ at the earliest and 3½ at the latest. Similar self-evaluative reactions have been observed in feeble-minded children, but at a later chronological age, when they had reached a mental age of at least 3½ years (Heckhausen & Wasna, 1965).

Children under 3½ years who did not understand the comparative standards of the competitive game (i.e., to finish first) also clearly showed emotional expressions upon completion of the task. The older ones among them expressed joy and amazement at their accomplishments. Here, too, the hands were often raised. But in contrast to the older children, who already reflected a self-reference, these younger children did not immediately free themselves from their task in order to enter into approval-seeking eye contact with the experimenter. Figure 16.2 shows this expressive pattern of a 2¾-year-old boy. Because these expressions are still centered on the accomplished work and not on the self and because they occur not only after the child's own accomplishment but also after someone else's, we labeled this *enjoyment of the effect* and concluded that these children were not yet capable of experiencing self-evaluative emotions. It therefore appeared to us that the significant emotional transition involves the child's ability to experience himself as the originator of an accomplishment, i.e., to refer it back

FIG. 16.2 Delight with the accomplished effect and not with personal success (age 2¾ years).

to the self, to establish a self-reference based on the results of one's own ability. We can also speak here of an early manifestation of internal causal attribution. As we show later, we were recently forced to modify our conceptualizations. Early achievement-oriented emotions presuppose more than just experiencing originatorship. What must be added is that the action outcome is referred to a concept of one's own ability, i.e., an attribute of the self.

THE SEARCH FOR THE SIMPLEST (EARLIEST) STANDARDS OF EXCELLENCE

In retrospect it would appear that a concept of self-competence is already basic to the contrasting expressions following success or failure as aforementioned. But the compelling question is: Can one not elicit such reactions at an earlier age if one makes an even lesser cognitive demand on the child to understand the standard involved in assessing one's own action outcomes? After all, the study involving competition required the child to have already mastered the temporal comparison of finishing before versus finishing after the experimenter. Halisch and Halisch (1980) isolated and tested this latter ability and found that all children who possess it also showed self-evaluative reactions. However, they discovered some younger children who, despite the fact that they had not mastered the temporal comparison and did not enter into competition, nevertheless showed self-evaluative success reactions whenever they finished the tower. These children apparently employed the very simple standard of merely completing the tower by using up all the rings.

Such a task-inherent standard does not permit failure. We invented a number of tricks that nevertheless should give rise to failure experiences. We suddenly let the uncompleted tower drop through a trap door. Following an initial fright reaction this merely elicited curiosity behavior and reduced the child's interest in building the tower. (This experiment employed wooden discs that had to be stacked on top of each other.) Our next trick was a hidden tilt mechanism below the lowest disc whereby the experimenter could cause the collapse of the tower. However, they took this to be a momentary setback and rebuilt the tower. Finally, we let the toppled blocks irretrievably disappear through a hold in the table top. But even that did not elicit a response of defeat or failure from 2-year-olds.

At first we attributed our failure to induce failure in 2-year-olds to our own lack of inventiveness. Or, to be more cautious, success as an anticipated effect of one's activity is probably a more perceptible event than is absence of that effect in spite of one's endeavor. For younger children it could still be too demanding to perceive a non-effect as being caused and, what is even more, caused by one's futile activity. In any case, we now are no longer convinced that the first experiences of success and of failure must necessarily occur at the same time. Self-evaluative awareness of success appears to occur considerably earlier than that of failure. In any case, it would be a nice peculiarity of nature if the ontogenetic course of achievement motivation begins with success, a kind of warm-up period prior to the emergence of an ability to experience failure (as an ever-present alternative to success), a circumstance that then would make all striving for achievement double-edged.

Meanwhile there are others who have confirmed that 3-year-olds show self-evaluative emotions in free-play situations, i.e., they are achievement-motivated, on average perhaps a few months earlier than was shown by our tower-building competition. That was shown by observations of mother–child interactions reported by Lütkenhaus (1984). In that experiment the children were occupied with a picture-matching game while their mothers constantly provided feedback about the correctness of the matches. Persistence in the game was correlated with the frequency of children's spontaneous utterances that they could do the task (e.g., "I can do that!"). The verbal statements can therefore be taken as valid self-evaluations of one's competence.

OUTCOME-CENTERING AS AN ONTOGENETIC TEMPLATE

So far we have explored the first occurrence of self-evaluative emotions after an action outcome in order to determine at what point achievement behavior becomes part of the behavioral repertoire of human life. In this search we employed only the self-reference template because it is obvious that "outcome-centering" (the other template) is a prerequisite for self-evaluative emotions. We now try to press forward into early development to search for precursors. We focus first on precursors of outcome centering and later on precursors of self-reference.

The concept of "outcome of one's activity" can mean many things. For example, if it refers to a finished work that has an existence independent of its author, as in the case of the tower in our study, then it already involves a late developmental form of action outcomes. At a much earlier age the direct effects of a child's own activity is of short duration. An example is Piaget's (1953) observation: "At 0;3 (5) Lucienne shakes her bassinet by moving her legs violently (bending and unbending them, etc.) which makes the cloth dolls swing from the hood. Lucienne looks at them, smiling, and recommences at once" (Observation 94, pp. 157–158).

Piaget speaks here of secondary circular reactions. An activity is repeated because it is apparently associated with a pleasurable expectation that a previously experienced outcome of this activity will recur. Piaget was able to observe such secondary circular reactions, which one could also label as operant learning, starting in the fourth month. But if the infant does not have to produce the contingent effect physically, if it is produced by a caretaker, then one can observe such secondary circular reactions in the first weeks of life. Watson (1966) speaks of "contingency awareness," which is apparently innate. This is exemplified by Papoušek's (1967) conditioning experiments with infants. They quickly learned to move their heads in response to an acoustic signal in order to obtain a small amount of milk. Even after they were satiated and refused to take more milk, they continued the discernibly pleasure-evoking, expressive behavior of turning their heads in the particular direction. Apparently, it is not the effect as such (let alone the need satisfaction) that motivates but rather the expected regularity of the contingency between one's activity and its effect, an earlier stage prior to outcome-centering. In other words, we are dealing with an early precursor of outcome-centering because awareness is not centered on the effect but rather on the association between activity and effect. Such an awareness of contingency appears to be dependent on the first processing stage of the emotional system— the test of familiarity.

Among the later forms of outcome awareness are continuous effects (e.g., when a child pulls a waddling duck). All this occurs before an action outcome in the sense of an enduring work is considered. Hildegard Hetzer (1931), who observed children playing with blocks, noticed this latter action outcome in children not younger than 1½ years old. She writes:

> That it is truly the accomplishment which is the object of this attention is firstly demonstrated by the fact that the child interrupts the playful activity at a moment when he or she has had particular success, e.g., putting away (or arranging) all of the blocks, but secondly also by the fact that the child, from that point in time at which it noticed success, also takes notice of failure, which it had previously totally ignored. (p. 32)

Spangler, Bräutigam, and Stadler (1984) have reported longitudinal observations on the development of outcome-centering. They observed infants aged 14–17 months in everyday activity. Their findings confirm our speculations on the development of centering. For this age group they found an invariant sequence in the following types of behavior: (a) action–effect contingency (simple and short effects of an action); (b) action with continuous effect (effect accompanies action and terminates with it); (c) separation of action and effect (effect is induced only at end of the action and survives it); (d) quasigoal-oriented actions (complexly organized action structures without outcome consideration); (e) action with outcome regard ("respect for one's work" in Hetzer's sense); and (f) action with regard to originatorship (it is clearly discernible that the child is aware of his originator role and wants to be recognized for it).

A quite different phenomenon, which also occurs at about age 1½ years, also dramatically points to the emergence of outcome-centering as part of one's own activity (or, more appropriately, one's own "actions" because there may already be intentionality with respect to the action outcome). These are the so-called temper tantrums with which children rebel when a trusted adult interferes with or disrupts the course of an activity (Goodenough, 1931; Kemmler, 1957). The fully developed reaction to this is a temper tantrum with ranting and raving, dropping to the floor, becoming blue in the face from screaming, and resisting being picked up. Some of this is illustrated in Rembrandt's drawing of the naughty boy, a product of the 17th century (Fig. 16.3).

The apparent reason for all this is the thwarting of an intended action. Even if this does not yet involve the production of a particular action outcome, the intense reaction to the interference bespeaks a higher developmental state of a competence to organize one's activity as goal-oriented actions. However, because children are hardly able to convey their intentions to an adult, let alone to postpone the realization of such intentions, a transitory developmental dilemma ensues that, particularly in the second half of the second year, provokes these temper tantrums (Kemmler, 1957). There is no question about which of the emotional system's processing stages encompasses these temper tantrums. It is the third, in which environmental events that suddenly occur are tested for their goal relevance. It is also clear that an awareness of self has now become inextricably intertwined with the motivation of the action sequence, at least when it becomes blocked.

FIG. 16.3 Temper tantrum (about age 1½ years) as portrayed by Rembrandt's *The Naughty Boy*.

A related phenomenon, which also occurs starting at about the age of 1½ years, is the "wanting-to-do-it-oneself" demand (Klamma, 1957). When confronted with an attractive task, children tend to insist that they want to do it themselves, provided the task is not too difficult and that difficulties occurring do not block the action path. They will refuse all offers of help and will rigorously protest unsolicited intervention. A closer examination of when the "wanting-to-do-it-oneself" demand occurs can reveal something about the development of the child's organization of action.

To this end, Geppert and Küster (1983) involved children between 9 and 78 months of age in attractive play activities (the youngest, for example, were asked to put blocks in a bag). The experimenter intervened in two ways. Sometimes she would insist that it was her turn and took the material from the child's hands. At other times she would intervene in a helpful manner even though the child had not asked for, nor was in need of, such help. There were two further conditions: The experimenter either announced her intention to intervene or proceeded without such announcement. There was not much difference between these latter conditions. Hence we discuss only the two types of intervention.

The youngest children, those up to 1½ years, accepted both types of intervention. Children between the ages of 1½ to 2½ years still tolerated unsolicited help but vehemently protested when the experimenter wanted to take over the very next step in the action sequence. They tried to block the experimenter's access to the materials. In the case of the younger members of this age group, the protests escalated to temper tantrums and aggressive resistance. That was particularly pronounced in the case of the final step in the task sequence. This again represents an early sign of actual outcome-centering beginning at age 1½ years. It is noteworthy that children in this age group also verbalized their demands for doing it themselves by repeatedly calling their own name or "ich, ich" ("me, me"). This clearly reflects a self-reference.

In children 2½ years of age, the behavior reversed. Now they tolerated intervention that removed the materials from their hands, but they would not tolerate unnecessary assistance. It was not the removal of the play material but a questioning of the child's competence through unnecessary help that was seen as threatening. That is also indicated by the fact that, for these 2½-year-olds, the protest response was expanded from "ich" to "Ich kann das!" ("I can do that!"). In other words, the self now literally not only insists on doing a task itself but at the same time says something about its own attribute of competence (to be able to do something). When children reach the age of 4 years, the vehemence of the protest against helpful intervention declined. They proposed rules to transform the adult's intervention into a cooperative taking of turns.

In summary, we can say that in the first 18 months of life, outcome-centering is based on a contingency between one's activity and the resultant effects. The interest in and the repeated initiation of such sequences of activities and effects, as well as the attending expressions, suggest that it is not the effect itself but an awareness of the contingency of the effect on one's action that constitutes the motivating and pleasurably experienced state. Beginning at 18 months contingency awareness is supplemented by a primary and simple form of outcome-centering. The children begin to focus on the accomplished outcome of their activity by interrupting their ongoing behavior for a time. If an adult blocks their activity by trying to take away the material, these children will now insist on carrying out the activity themselves to bring about an action outcome that is clearly in sight.

Intervention in the child's own proposed action, as simple and primitive as its organization may be, elicits vehement protests, possibly even temper tantrums. That means that outcome-centering as a necessary prerequisite for the early emergence of self-evaluative emotion (and hence for achievement behavior) manifests itself in an early and primitive form as early as age 1½ years, i.e., long before one observes the first self-evaluative emotions about a year later. At that point the offer of unnecessary help becomes the threatening event because it challenges the attribution of an achievement outcome to a rudimentary concept of the child's own competence.

SELF-REFERENCE AS AN ONTOGENETIC TEMPLATE

The wanting-to-do-it-oneself demand not only reflects the development of self-centering but also of self-reference. The latter was explored by Geppert and Küster with two further measures of the developmental stages of the self. In one of these tests the child was placed on a blanket and was then asked to give the blanket to his or her mother. If the child stepped off the blanket it was assumed that he or she was able to perceive his or her own body as an external obstacle to an action. This apparently requires an early ability to perceive and to deal with one's own body as an object. The blanket test, according to Piaget (1953), represents a problem that cannot be solved before the developmental phase of tertiary circular reactions (11th to 18th month). At this stage the object of an activity begins to take on a separate identity, distinct from the execution of the act, which means that this execution can lead to alternate ways of reaching for or manipulating the object or can vary the attained effects. To the extent that children are able to isolate the blanket as the object of an activity from the executive schema of picking up, there must be a complementary segregation of their own bodies and an awareness of the obstacle represented by one's body at that moment.

The next (6th) stage of sensorimotor development, which begins at about 18 months, is already marked by new action patterns through "internalized actions."

The next test involved the attempt at self-recognition in a mirror (Gallup, 1970). After the experimenter had surreptitiously applied some rouge to the child's nose, the child was led to a mirror to see whether he would point to the nose in the mirror or touch his own nose (Fig. 16.4).

FIG. 16.4 Experiment on visual self-recognition in a mirror image after the child's nose has been surreptitiously dotted with rouge. This 2:1-year-old child immediately reached for her nose.

Those children (up to 1½ years) who showed no self-reference either in the blanket or the mirror test also accepted all other types of intervention in their activity. Those who passed the blanket test but not the mirror test (at about 1½ years) protested only against interventions in their immediate action sequence. All those who passed both tests (children of about 1½ years of age and up) resisted (up to 2½ years of age) the immediate intervention that took away the object of their activity. This was particularly true when it occurred during the last step in an activity. In that case they loudly proclaimed themselves as creators by shouting "ich" or their first names. At this stage, the determining emotion guiding the behavior is an awareness of one's own originatorship. This emotional awareness is not endangered by help from adults but by the removal of the object of the child's activity.

With children at least 2½ years old, it was no longer the taking away of the activity object (or even the experimenter's demand for a turn) that was the threatening event, but much more the unnecessary help, apparently because it prevented attribution of the outcome of an activity to one's competence ("I can do it"). At this stage, the determining emotion guiding the behavior is an awareness of one's own competence.

Lewis and Brooks-Gunn (1979) carried out a very detailed study of the development of self, using the method of visual self-recognition. These authors distinguish between an existential and a categorical self. The existential self is more primitive and consists of an awareness of one's body as a kind of activity center that evolves during the first 8 months of life. In the categorical self, children perceive themselves not as a subject (as in the existential self), but as an object about which they know something and in which they can detect many of their own features.

Lewis and Brooks-Gunn presented children, starting at 9 months, with four different versions of their own pictures in order to investigate the developmental stages of the categorical self. These four presentational forms represented such ingenious variations that each was able to elicit a distinct reaction reflecting degrees of the existential or categorical self and their relative stage of development. A concurrent portrayal of one's movements either (a) in a mirror or (b) live on a video monitor (so-called contingency) elicits reactions related to the existential self but at the same time also of the categorical self insofar as it is an image of oneself to be recognized by its appearance. By contrast, (c) portraits and (d) video film presentation of oneself or other children do not reflect any temporally parallel sequence of movements (noncontingency). In these cases the reaction elicited by seeing oneself portrayed can only be related to the categorical self. The results of each presentational form can be summarized as follows.

Mirror. If the children had a red dot painted on their noses, one could observe, even among the youngest children (9 months), a more self-referenced activity than in the absence of the dot. Because the "dotted" children laughed more at themselves, touched their own bodies, and pointed to the mirror image, it is clear that they already noticed something different about themselves. It would appear that this reflects the beginnings of a categorical self. But only starting at 15 months did the children direct their behavior toward their own noses, an immediate awareness of a deviation from the categorical self-image.

Live Versus Nonlive Video. Concomitant movements (live contingency) elicited more reaction than noncontiguous movement. For example, the appearance of an unfamiliar adult elicited greater interest in the live than the nonlive condition. The fact that these differences were already present at 9 months of age underlines again the behavioral effects of an earlier appearance of an existential self or self-recognition. But what happens if, in the nonlive condition, one's own person is put opposite that of another child? Here it can only be the recognition of categorical features of the self (i.e., particularly the familiarity with one's facial features) that produces a differential reaction. Such response differences occur only after the age of 15 months. Then the other child elicits more smiling and more motor movement whereas the child's own picture induces more imitation and play activity. That would suggest that the categorical self emerges only after the age of 15 months.

Portraits. The child's own portrait compared to that of another child's elicited more interest between 15 and 18 months of age, which suggests that self-recognition and, hence, the emergence of the categorical self occurs at about 1½ years of age.

The preceding findings convey the following picture of the development of self-reference. Signs of an "existential self" can be observed in children 9 months of age and older in the form of self-recognizing reactions to concomitant contingencies. They apparently do not reflect a subjective experience of self in the sense that children between the ages of 9 and 18 months already experience themselves as acting subjects aware of a self-reliance when carrying out their activities. It is not the awareness of a contingency, as reflected in one's own activity (existential self), but the awareness of self as object, as it first emerges between the 15th and 18th month in the form of visual recognition of external features, that is a direct precursor of the first signs of a relationship between the self and one's activity.

This self-reference manifests itself in various ways starting at 1½ years of age. These include observing the outcomes of one's own activities (outcome-centering), having temper tantrums when one's activities are thwarted by a trusted adult, and wanting to "do it" oneself, which expresses a demand for self-reliance in continuing the self-initiated action if adults intervene in the ongoing activity and take away the object of the child's activity.

When the child is between 1½ and 2½ years old, this action-related self-reference apparently merely relates to the self as the source of an act and only later to attributes of self-competence. Lewis and Brooks-Gunn's discovery of the first signs of a categorical self in the middle of the second year of life leads one to speculate that it initially encompasses only attributes of one's physical (particularly facial) features but does not yet include psychological traits such as competence. A categorical self with self-attributions of competence traits manifests itself only after the age of 2½ years and appears to be a necessary prerequisite for self-evaluative emotions.

THREE STAGES OF ACTIVITY MOTIVATION AND THE ORIGINS OF ACHIEVEMENT BEHAVIOR

We can now try to integrate the developmental findings related to outcome-centering and self-reference and examine the precursors and origins of achievement behavior in this new light. In both cases—outcome-centering and self-reference—we encountered two critical transitions, which one could say represent developmental milestones. They occur at age 1½ and 2½ years, dividing this period into three developmental stages.

In the first stage, up to 1½ years, the children's activity is primarily motivated by an awareness of the contingency between their playful activity and its effects.

This contingency awareness is not yet accompanied by an awareness of self as an "object" but only as a "subject." This "existential" self, as Lewis and Brooks-Gunn call it, consists—at least starting at 9 months—of becoming aware of one's own activity and no more, meaning that there is no subjective awareness that one can initiate activity or produce effects. Contingency-centered activity (as well as the contiguous visual perception of one's own activity) is stimulating and pleasurable. Only the first two phases of Scherer's (1981) processing stages of the emotion system appear to occur in this developmental stage, namely, familiarity and pleasantness. Many action-like activities during this early stage are elicited by moderate surprise and maintained by sensomotoric flow experience as appears to be so prototypical for early play behavior.

In the second stage, between 1½ and 2½ years, activity can already be outcome-centered. Outcome states of one's activity can be isolated from the execution of an activity, i.e., aspired to and conceived as independent entities. The children experience themselves as initiators of their own activity and as causal agents of its effects. The child's activity becomes intentional in nature, and this facilitates product-oriented activity. These are the origins of a categorical self. In other words, the child now becomes aware of himself as an object, but at first this is based only on the features of an external identity, one's own appearance, and not on attributes related to psychological traits.

The protests and resistance occurring when adults impede or thwart the child's activity, or even just their announced intention to do so, are an indication that further processing stages in the emotional system have been reached. First, there is the third stage in Scherer's model, the analysis of environmental events in terms of their goal relevance for one's intentions to act (situation–outcome expectancy). Hence a mother's announced intention to intervene can be anticipated as a threatened impediment or thwarting of one's activity and is to be met with anger and rejected under protest.

During the third phase, starting at 2½ years, the fourth processing stage must be reached. Now children are able to assess their own chances of carrying out particular activities or to reach a desired goal (action–outcome expectancy). This is clearly reflected in their refusal of help on tasks that they can accomplish themselves. When the child is 2½ years old, one finds the first signs of a categorical self that also encompasses attributes in the sense of psychological traits such as competence (to be able to do something oneself), however rudimentary such attributes may be. This is the earliest that one is able to observe self-evaluative emotions in individual children after the successful or unsuccessful performance of an intended action.

Self-evaluative emotions presuppose the last processing stage—a comparison of an action outcome with a standard for reaching a goal. This comparison determines whether an action outcome was successful or not. We have now finally arrived at the phenomenon that—according to the earliest definition of achievement motive—turns goal-oriented behavior into achievement behavior: the concern with a standard of excellence.

THE ONTOGENESIS OF SELF-EVALUATIVE EMOTIONS REVISITED

If we now reexamine the success and failure reactions of our tower-building study, we must admit that our conclusions about the cognitive developmental prerequisites for achievement behavior, which we had based solely on expressive behavior, were inadequate. The mere attribution of an accomplishment to the self as originator is not enough because even children aged 1½ years are capable of such self-reflective attributions, as demonstrated by their temper tantrums and wanting-to-do-it-themselves reactions. What appears to be missing in the second developmental stage, between 1½ and 2½ years, with its "existential" self-reference between one's activity (and its outcome) and the self as originator, are the self-evaluative emotions, the final processing stage in the emotional system. However, self-evaluative emotions of achievement behavior require more than an existential "originating self." They also require a categorical self with rudimentary attributes of one's own competence, an image of oneself as someone who is competent. That became manifest only in the third developmental period—starting at 2½ years—when children refused offers of help and called attention to their ability, or in competitive play when they reacted with joyful pride to winning or with embarrassment to losing.

It could be argued that the outcome-centering of the second developmental stage already reflects achievement behavior. After all, at this stage children already experience themselves as acting subjects who insist on doing something themselves, who display considerable persistence in the pursuit of a goal, and who can focus on an outcome (product) of their activity. It is certainly true that these children's activities frequently have the characteristics of intentional acts, however primitively they may be organized. Intentions that maintain an activity, awareness or means–ends relationship, reduced distractibility, persistence, and outcome-centering all characterize intentional, goal-oriented actions, all of which reflect intentionality of an action. But not everything that relates to such actions at this developmental stage must and can be "achievement-related." Activities encompassing the same action patterns can be directed towards food intake, making social contact, exploration, reduction of uncertainty through exploration, or enjoying the originatorship of one's accomplishments. However, achievement behavior represents a particular context class of action goals that must be restricted to those undertakings whose outcomes are subjected by the actor to comparisons with a standard of excellence and with an attendant self-evaluation.

THE THREE STAGES AS ANALOGS
FOR THREE MOTIVATIONAL GOAL LEVELS

The succession of the three developmental stages surely does not mean that a subsequent period totally replaces and obliterates its predecessor. A more reasonable assumption is that the preceding activity becomes augmented by and integrated into the next stage until, in the third stage, the threshold for achievement behavior is reached. In this way, contingency awareness can become embedded and preserved in outcome-centering just as outcome-centering can become embedded in self-evaluation. Perhaps one could even claim that the particular earlier form of activity-motivating awareness (with its specific emotional components) represents a prerequisite for the succeeding form, analogous to the corresponding sequential processing stages in the emotional system.

This notion is highly speculative. Despite its phenomenological plausibility, it would require a detailed, empirical analysis that is a long way off. In support of this notion there is a conspicuous analogy between the three developmental stages and the three motivational goal levels of achievement behavior as observed in schoolchildren and adults (Heckhausen, 1981).

The third and last developmental stage corresponds to a motivational state centered on self-esteem. Researchers on achievement motivation have categorically insisted that such a state is practically synonymous with achievement motivation. In models of motivation, such as Atkinson's (1957) Risk-Taking Model and Heckhausen's (1977) Self-Evaluation Model, this motive state has also become the necessary and sufficient condition for achievement motivation.

It is the anticipatory, self-evaluative emotions arising from the prospective achievement outcome that motivate. This overemphasis on self-evaluative incentives was primarily encouraged by the methods employed to measure individual differences in motives, specifically "Hope for Success" and "Fear of Failure" (Heckhausen, 1963). Particularly those individuals with an overwhelming Fear of Failure tend to focus, at the slightest provocation, on self-evaluative aspects of their achievement, which makes them in many ways conspicuous and susceptible. They avoid realistic levels of aspiration, manifest self-deprecating attribution patterns for success and failure. In failure situations their performance often deteriorates. They even become helpless because they overemphasize self-centered, task-irrelevant cognitions (see Diener & Dweck, 1978; Heckhausen, 1982b).

It is not just incentives focused on self-esteem but task-centered incentives as well that serve as motivators. The incentive value is inherent in the action outcome itself, as, for example, in a product. Further incentive values may be added, namely, incentives of consequences that are brought about by an intended achievement outcome (such as extrinsic side effects or the advancement toward a superordinate goal). Research on achievement motivation has largely ignored motivation that is predominantly outcome-centered, especially in the sense of task-centered incentives. We label such motivational goal levels as task-centered even if, as a rule, they also encompass self-evaluative components (Heckhausen & Rheinberg, 1980). Such goal levels are likely to arise where one can freely choose one's goals, in a noncompetitive setting, or removed from the critical eyes of others, and most of all when one is not beset by fear of failure (i.e., when "Hope for Success" is the dominant motivation).

A task-centered motivational goal level roughly corresponds to the outcome-centering of the second developmental period. We are not claiming that the two can be equated, let alone that a task-centered motivational goal level represents a developmental regression. But the analogy is suggested by the predominance of the outcome-centering of that motivational goal level, whereas self-evaluative incentives have only peripheral meaning or totally fade away.

Finally, is there a motivational goal level that is not induced by self-evaluative incentives and not even by outcome-centering and their incentives? If so, how could one characterize it? As incredible as it may sound, it exists; in fact, it exists in everyday episodes. It consists of experiences parallel to an action, experiences that are totally devoted to the interactional contingencies of an activity and the retroactive effects from the environment which in turn affect the activity. The individual totally forgets himself and becomes completely absorbed in the immediacy of his actions as well as their effects, which closely follow the continuous and ever-changing demands of the activity. Csikszentmihalyi (1975) studied such motivational states in chess players, surgeons, rock dancers, and mountain climbers. He refers to it as a "flow experience." It consists of a joyful absorption in the activity, a preoccupation with a particular endeavor. The maintaining emotion is "enjoyment." The motivational goal level that is characterized by the flow experience can best be described as "intrinsic" in the truest sense. In other words, the activity is motivated by its own inherent incentives, but it is not directed toward some kind of outcome or in aid of some distant purpose. Episodes and habits in everyday experiences such as whistling to oneself represent "microflow" experiences. Csikszentmihalyi asked his subjects to suppress such microflow experiences for one day. They reported that they were more exhausted and irritable, that they suffered headaches and were less able to concentrate following such suppression. Everyday routine activities became cumbersome, and there was a reduction in spontaneous, creative activity.

The close correspondence between the motivational state of flow experience and the first developmental period up to 1½ years is self-evident. Nor, of course, can it be equated with this early developmental stage of contingency awareness. For even if it is true that awareness of outcome-centering is temporarily absent or ignored, one must also consider that flow experiences (except perhaps microflow) are clearly embedded in an overarching action network that, in the final analysis, can become outcome-related and related to self-evaluation.

However, the insularity of motivational states that refer back to the earliest developmental stage, i.e., contingency awareness, is remarkable. It requires special conditions to initiate and maintain a flow experience and to protect it against a "relapse" to developmentally more advanced, motivational goal levels (or states) that are centered on outcome or self-esteem. There are six such conditions: (a) The demand of the activity is not too high but rather lies within the borders of one's competence; (b) there is continuous, direct feedback concerning the effectiveness of one's activity (contingency!); (c) the actor has, or the situation presents, discrete standards of excellence in order to experience immediately the appropriateness of his or her activity sequences; (d) there is a continuous and rapid fluctuation in the demands on one's activity, fluctuations that cannot be precisely predicted; (e) there are further opportunities for enhancing the demands of one's activity, which can be met by an increased level of competence; (f) the immediate activity sphere is protected against external interference.

With that we have covered the entire spectrum of our topic. We started with the basic positions advanced by a psychology of emotions as well as the determinants of a fully developed achievement behavior as specified by a psychology of motivation. We constructed templates to aid us in our search for early and primary, precursory phases in ontogenetic development. From there we returned to those late forms of motivational goal levels of achievement behavior that, in some ways, correspond to these precursory phases.

In this context, achievement behavior has a paradigmatic meaning because it leads to the highest processing stage in the emotional system, namely, the actors' self-reflexivity and their self-evaluative emotions. Other actions, such as curiosity-motivated behavior, can be categorized within the described stage model of the ontogeny of action-related emotions.

Capacities for outcome-centering and self-references of activities, as manifested in early development, proved to be critical thresholds in the ontogeny of emotions and, hence, in the development of a competence for action.

In this exploration we have admittedly bridged some of the gaps in knowledge and observation with some speculations. That was particularly true of our efforts to account for the previously neglected role of emotions in the development of achievement behavior. But the picture that we have painted is not just speculative; it provides hints about areas where new observations and experimental studies might lead to far-reaching insights. Among theses areas, the early transformations from play and curiosity into achievement-related behavior as well as transformations into the reverse direction have been neglected and deserve priority in future research.

SUMMARY

As background for the present chapter, five processing stages of the emotional system, according to Scherer, are delineated first. The same successive order of these stages is assumed to emerge during ontogeny as well. After specifying the determinants of fully developed achievement behavior and after reviewing the earliest reactions of 2- and 3-year-olds to success and failure, the author constructs two templates to aid the search for early and primary precursory phases in ontogenetic development. The first ontogenetic template refers to "outcome-centering," the second to "self-reference." Finally, three stages in the developmental process of being motivated for an ongoing activity are distinguished and considered to be analogues for three different motivational goal levels as they can be specified in adult achievement behavior.

REFERENCES

Atkinson, J. W. (1957). Motivational determinants of risk-taking behavior. *Psychological Review,* *64*, 359–372.

Csikszentmihalyi, M. (1975). *Beyond boredom and anxiety.* San Francisco: Jossey-Bass.

Darwin, C. (1872). *The expression of the emotions in man and animals.* London: John Murray.

Diener, C. I., & Dweck, C. S. (1978). An analysis of learned helplessness: Continuous changes in performance, strategy, and achievement cognitions following failure. *Journal of Personality and Social Psychology, 36*, 451–462.

Gallup, G. G. Jr. (1970). Chimpanzees: Self-recognition. *Science, 167*, 86–87.

Geppert, U., & Küster, U. (1983). The emergence of "Wanting to do it oneself": A precursor of achievement motivation. *International Journal of Behavioral Development, 6*, 355–369.

Goodenough, F. L. (1931). Anger in young children. *University of Minnesota Institute of Child Welfare Monographs*, No. 9.

Halisch, C., & Halisch, F. (1980). Kognitive Voraussetzungen frühkindlicher Selbstbewertungsreaktionen nach Erfolg und Mißerfolg. *Zeitschrift für Entwicklungspsychologie und Pädagogische Psychologie, 12*, 193–212.

Hebb, D. O. (1972). *Textbook of psychology* (3rd ed.). Philadelphia: Saunders.

Heckhausen, H. (1963). *Hoffnung und Furcht in der Leistungsmotivation.* Meisenheim: Hain.

Heckhausen, H. (1975). Fear of failure as a self-reinforcing motive system. In I. G. Sarason & C. Spielberger (Eds.), *Stress and anxiety* (Vol. 2, pp. 117–128). Washington, DC: Hemisphere.

Heckhausen, H. (1977). Achievement motivation and its constructs: A cognitive model. *Motivation and Emotion, 1*, 283–329.

Heckhausen, H. (1980). *Motivation und Handeln.* Berlin: Springer.

Heckhausen, H. (1981). Neuere Entwicklungen in der Motivationsforschung. In W. Michaelis (Ed.), *Bericht über den 32. Kongreß der Deutschen Gesellschaft für Psychologie* (pp. 325–335). Göttingen: Hogrefe.

Heckhausen, H. (1982a). The development of achievement motivation. In W. W. Hartup (Ed.), *Review of child development research* (Vol. 6, pp. 600–668). Chicago: The University of Chicago Press.

Heckhausen, H. (1982b). Task-irrelevant cognitions during an exam. In H. W. Krohne & L. Laux (Eds.), *Achievement, stress, and anxiety* (pp. 247–274). Washington: Hemisphere.

Heckhausen, H., Ertel, S., & Kiekheben-Roelofsen, I. (1966). *Die Anfänge der Leistungsmotivation im Wetteifer des Kleinkindes.*[Tonfilm]. Göttingen: Institut für den Wissenschaftlichen Film.

Heckhausen, H., & Rheinberg, F. (1980). Lernmotivation im Unterricht, erneut betrachtet. *Unterrichtswissenschaft, 8*, 7–47.

Heckhausen, H., & Roelofsen, I. (1962). Anfänge und Entwicklung der Leistungsmotivation, I. Im Wetteifer des Kleinkindes. *Psychologische Forschung, 26*, 313–397.

Heckhausen, H., & Wasna, M. (1965). Erfolg und Mißerfolg im Leistungswetteifer des imbezillen Kindes. *Psychologische Forschung, 28*, 391–421.

Hetzer, H. (1931). *Kind und Schaffen.* Jena: Fischer.

Kemmler, L. (1957). Untersuchungen über den frühkindlichen Trotz. *Psychologische Forschung, 25*, 279–338.

Klamma, M. (1957). *Über das Selbermachenwollen und Ablehnen von Hilfen bei Kleinkindern.* Vordiplomarbeit, Psychologisches Institut der Universität Münster.

Lazarus, R. S. (1968). Emotion and adaptation: Conceptual and empirical relations. In W. J. Arnold (Ed.), *Nebraska Symposium on Motivation* (pp. 175–270). Lincoln: University of Nebraska Press.

Lewis, M., & Brooks-Gunn, J. (1979). *Social cognition and the acquisition of self.* New York: Plenum.

Lütkenhaus, P. (1984). Pleasure derived from mastery in three-year olds: Its function for persistence and the influence of maternal behavior. *International Journal of Behavioral Development, 7*, 343–358.

McClelland, D. C., Atkinson, J. W., Clark, R. A., & Lowell, E. L. (1953). *The achievement motive.* New York: Appleton-Century-Crofts.

Papoušek, H. (1967). Experimental studies of appetitional behavior in human newborns and infants. In H. W. Stevenson, E. H. Hess, & H. L. Rheingold (Eds.), *Early behavior: Comparative and developmental approaches* (pp. 249–277). New York: Wiley.

Piaget, J. (1953). *The origin of intelligence in the child.* London: Routledge & Kegan Paul.

Plutchik, R. (1980). *Emotion: A psychoevolutionary synthesis.* New York: Harper & Row.

Scherer, K. R. (1981). Wider die Vernachlässigung der Emotion in der Psychologie. In W. Michaelis (Ed.), *Bericht über den 32. Kongreß der Deutschen Gesellschaft für Psychologie* (pp. 304–317). Göttingen: Hogrefe.

Spangler, G., Bräutigam, I., & Stadler, R. (1984). Handlungsentwicklung in der frühen Kindheit und ihre Abhängigkeit von der kognitiven Entwicklung und der emotionalen Erregbarkeit des Kindes. *Zeitschrift für Entwicklungspsychologie und Pädagogische Psychologie, 16*, 181–193.

Watson, J. S. (1966). The development and generalization of "contingency awareness" in early infancy: Some hypotheses. *Merrill–Palmer Quarterly, 12*, 123–135.

Weiner, B., Russel, D., & Lerman, D. (1978). Affektive Auswirkungen von Attributionen. In D. Görlitz, W.-U. Meyer, & B. Weiner (Eds.), *Bielefelder Symposium über Attribution* (pp. 139–173). Stuttgart: Klett-Cotta.

Wong, P. T. P., & Weiner, B. (1981). When people ask "why" questions, and the heuristics of attributional search. *Journal of Personality and Social Psychology, 40*, 650–663.

Zajonc, R. B. (1980). Feeling and thinking: Preferences need no inferences. *American Psychologist, 35*, 151–175.

PART FOUR
CONCLUSIONS

CHAPTER SEVENTEEN

CONCLUDING OBSERVATIONS ABOUT CURIOSITY AND PLAY

DIETMAR GÖRLITZ
Technische Universität Berlin (West)

STORIES OF BARBICAN: REAL AND RETOLD[1]

If curiosity and play are special subjects in the realm of spontaneous human and infrahuman activity, then it is almost a contradiction to treat them in concluding remarks. The act of concluding interrupts or prematurely stylizes all inquiring activity in an open and, in many ways, still undefined field of research. Discrepancies whet curiosity. The following observations are, then, intended more as accompanying commentary in order to highlight what it is about curiosity and the play of children that attracts our scientific curiosity as authors of this book and to emphasize the extent to which this attraction favors styles of exploration that the subjects of developmental research use and exhibit on their own. To paraphrase one of Blumenberg's thoughts,[2] if one wants to speak of curiosity as one of the motivations of human, childlike action, "then one cannot avoid getting entangled in the doubt that one is himself being caught up in the stream of that motivation." How much does the scientific curiosity of the older partner, the researcher, become involved in principles or styles of action that young subjects exhibit in their curiosity and play?

What Determines Behavior

In German, one says that books travel. For a book to which authors from Germany, England, and the United States have contributed, it is only natural to recall journeys and their meaning for the topic treated herein, in particular journeys having to do with those countries. For this German-speaking author, these journeys have a history encompassing at least 300 years (Moltmann, 1982). Sitting upon the Mayflower Steps on the historical Barbican in Plymouth, one becomes steeped in thoughts about voyages, conjectures about the souls that once departed from those shores on that special day of September 6 more than 350 years ago, reflections about curiosity research and its ineluctably circular interests. In his *Laokoön*, Lessing wrote that "nothing would be more deceptive than general laws for our sentiments," and he adds that there is "in nature no single pure sentiment." (Even though that work was written in 1766, one can

---

[1] Part of a more extensive discourse entitled "Concluding observations about curiosity and play and temporal change," which also outlines the aspects of cultural history in occidental philosophy as it relates to epistemic curiosity. Lack of space allows only the chapter's review section to be printed here. The author is especially indebted to Joachim Wohlwill for his helpful suggestions.

[2] To keep this little historical text straightforward as concluding remarks despite all the documentation it contains, all text and source references are listed page by page at the end of this chapter in a glossary. Citations from Blumenberg (1980) are quoted according to him, whereas the list of references gives the original sources, if possible in the English translation.

still learn a remarkable amount about the analysis of *fruchtbare Momente* of action as decisions about where to begin the analysis of action, decisions that have determined much of the work in our book.) Yet what moved the Pilgrims, unshakable in their beliefs, to sail from Barbican into an uncertain future? For a small fee today, one can indeed obtain the Mayflower's passenger list but will look in vain through the abundance of biographical data for information to answer this question. With our knowledge from Stonehenge that even stone-age people— for all their devout veneration, the object of which we have never discovered— did not forget to take astronomical bearings and to calculate celestial movement (Postins, 1982), we are drawn increasingly to the conviction that there are many motives behind human, certainly adult, action. And one becomes uncertain about whether curiosity or play as such can be dissected and mounted for inspection in the action context, although the developmental psychologist is better off than the prehistorian when it comes to the sources and methodology that are available (Renfrew, 1982; Wohlwill, 1973).

WHAT INTERESTS PSYCHOLOGISTS

Motivational Questions

The psychologist's interest in curiosity is articulated through questions. Joseph Keller teaches us that. As the scientific discipline that takes up everyday interpretive questions and helps to throw light upon the motives and control mechanisms underlying what humans do and do not do (Heckhausen, 1980), motivational psychology establishes the frame of reference in this field. Motivational psychology trains and encourages one to ask questions. J. Keller's chapter probes exploratory behavior, requiring answers to such equally significant preliminary queries as those about narrow or broad definitions of exploration. Voss, for example, deals with the problem of defining exploration, and Keller illustrates it in his first question. Keller sees his contribution as a necessary prelude to further questions about the ontogenetic development of exploratory behavior— the fifth decisive question in Keller's chapter. That particular sequence of general motivational psychology and developmental psychology is not one with which everybody would agree. Perhaps developmental psychology transects all established topics with its own questions, questions about process and change over a specified period of time.

Keller seeks the *why* of exploratory behavior, asking about its specific or general motivational basis. He asks *who* becomes active and *from what* the activity stems, asks whether and how much dispositional factors manifested in individual differences are a part of curiosity and exploration. He also studies what the emergence of the behavior is associated with and what the behavior can be reliably distinguished from. Within the spectrum of many significant questions about interrelationships, emotion becomes the important *relatum*, the key factor making it possible to illustrate many different types of relationships— emotion as fear and anxiety perhaps accompanying exploration, emotion as a focus of affective exploration, emotion as an obstructive or conducive antecedent condition in special moods. This third version of emotion, at least, shifts attention to J. Keller's fourth question, which deals with the intrinsic and extrinsic character of exploratory behavior—a question that has long been approached too generally in motivational psychology. As developmental psychologists, we could make his summary connected with the fifth self-directed question less discomforting by rephrasing all these questions more precisely and treating them in a developmental context. Despite the fact that J. Keller centers four of his questions on analyzing conditions, he shows an abundance of psychological curiosity in many passages by specifically examining the spectrum of behavior over time, meaning the time of actual situations: What does the actor do in which sequence? Does it make sense to ask about generalizable sequences of action that cut across situations?

Sequences of Action

We thereby heed Voltaire's crucial piece of advice that the study of the human being can make headway only if we employ the procedures followed in astronomy,[3] but we discard the telescope for the slow-motion technologies of modern video equipment. Unlike the wanderings of Odysseus, which for eons have enticed the curious into vain efforts to retrace his route, exploration and play exhibited in the actions of children occur in plain sight on the "map" of delimited situations. Voss raises a traditional question about both phenomena, one whose importance is not agreed upon by all researchers in the field of curiosity and play. He inquires about the distinction between exploration and play and about the connection that might exist between them. Are they the same thing? If not, what is the one and what is the other? Anyone would see in this the need to define and analyze the terms being used to describe the phenomena in question, but by hesitating, Voss quietly gives developmental psychology a new aspect, at least he makes the broad lines of that new aspect recognizable. A threefold discrimination between micro (or actual) genetics, ontogenesis, and phylogenesis— an approach harking back to German holistic psychology and Heinz Werner— is intended to make the problem at hand managable and solvable: Define a phenomenon by studying it in microtemporal processes, by examining it as clearcut action in a given situation. To be sure, reference to some sequence models

---

[3]In the introduction to his *Traité de Métaphysique* (1734), Voltaire expressed the hope that one will some day be able to proceed with studies of human beings in the same way one proceeds in astronomy (Moravia, 1977, pp. 18–19). According to Moravia, however, he is said to have meant the treatment of man as a mere phenomenon of nature.

in exploration research is often so standard as to be almost a reflex. But developmental psychology does have three geneses (it is still difficult to consider historical change as a type in its own right as well). And apart from the contribution that sequence analysis might make to defining exploration and play—the problem of which is perhaps still unsolved because segmentation in the "stream of behavior" makes the solution circular—important questions about parallels, structural homologies, and other such relationships between microgenetic, ontogenetic, and phylogenetic series of changes can be raised. For me as a developmental psychologist, a much more obvious question seems to be whether and how the one genesis is contained in the other. Let us assume that the task of localizing and defining the types of action involved in play and exploration has been solved or can be solved sufficiently at the level of observable behavior and indicators of expression, for example. (This task is a theme that repeatedly arises in the chapter being cited here.) Besides this problem, a new focus of study much more complex than usual has, thanks to Voss, now quite unexpectedly arisen in developmental psychology. For one thing, one would no longer ask only about ontogenetic changes of, say, the effects of exploratory action (such as the frequency with which new alternatives are chosen spontaneously by subjects being observed in curiosity experiments) but would select courses of action thought to have overt and covert features. One would select microgeneses occurring over a specified period of time as the focus of ontogenesis. The developmental functions discussed in such a framework are, in fact, more complex. For another thing, even the action structure of these microgeneses are more complex than usually thought; they are polythematic. And it does not matter at that point how exploratory actions (as one possible topic) change; important is how parts and structural interrelationships of different topics change in a single action sequence (exploring vs. playing) in the course of ontogenesis—in our case, in the course of early childhood. A semilongitudinal study by Voss himself provides convincing data on this. There are considerable individual differences in both of the aforementioned viewpoints on this new focus of developmental investigation.

All well and good, except that there are also still problems of definition and delimitation. Close analysis in the future will enable us to master these problems more easily than we can at present, especially if one relates such analysis to concordant segmentations of naive or trained observers, who break the "stream of behavior" down into sections of play and exploration according to some sort of "general-impression" or more distinct criteria. Analyses of expression look promising again as an important additional resource in such work (Görlitz, 1972).

Unit Formation

Yet action, even those parts of it that are observable, not only takes place over time; it has its own structure. It consists of subsystems arranged in varying hierarchies. Thematically dissimilar parts may overlap, and sequences planned as a whole may break off prematurely or may remain fragmentary right from the very beginning. Structural sequence analyses of observable action and complementary analyses of conditions governing its ecology are fertile ground for unusual and abundant harvests. The results of longitudinal experiments conducted by Heidi Keller's working group and her analyses of synchronic and diachronic correlations give every reason for hope in this regard. That favors a style of research characterized by the patience demanded by minute observation, a style Papoušek has imparted to his German-speaking colleagues doing research on infants. The observations covering one day in the life of a boy once filled a large book. Now, 10 minutes in the life of a curious or playing child can be the core of empirical studies, for nothing is less appropriate to an approach based on action theory than mere talk and confession of one's doings. Fritz Heider's psychology taught us to take the process of unit formation, the segmenting of real action as it occurs, especially seriously (Heider, 1980a, 1980b). And units are formed in action, too. Newtson's pointing technique, which allows one to designate individual frames in video sequences (Newtson, 1973, 1976) has had very stimulating effects in German psychology (von Cranach, Kalbermatten, Indermühle, & Gugler, 1980; Görlitz, 1983). Unit formation occurs also—and probably especially—in eye movement, a subject to which a chapter (by Groner) originally planned for this book would have contributed. But curiosity researchers are not primarily concerned with the uncontrolled "pick-up" activity (Neisser, 1979) of everyday observers, who establish a framework for their activities during the "free-looking time" as long as they choose the length of the observation period themselves. Rather, curiosity researchers are interested in gross units (a distinction made by Newtson). They are interested in units that the scientist forms, especially the action units of exploration and play and their sequence.

Future longitudinal research work, particularly that dealing with child development, will show if one can justify assuming that there are rigid linkages and set sequences, if one can safely say, for example, that a certain type of exploration always precedes play and that other types of exploration follow it. Schneider's analysis of data gathered during his second experiment is based on categories conceived by Hughes, and it documents, among more general trends, a back-and-forth alternation between exploration and play. Because we are still occupied with defining the morpheme of "action," we ought to handle questions of "syntax" very cautiously for the time being. Perhaps development and spontaneity spring precisely from the flexibility of linkages. Moreover, many other sequences in the doings and actions of children are also relevant to the topic area treated in this book. Heckhausen's contribution illuminates the relationship with achievement-motivated action. One of my own chapters focuses on affiliated activities of exploration, which is able to bring about antecedent probing for subsequent attribution and which may even follow certain attributions. Attributions are special types of unit formation involving linkages between events and their causes or reasons and spontaneous, above all, causal explanation. That draws on elements of a theory from the field of social psychology (Heider, 1958), which does not necessarily ignore aspects of developmental psychology. Much of the substance of the arguments developed in earlier chapters of this book is rooted in the theory's heuristic vitality.

Exploring and Playing

At this point it will not be asked for whom this otherwise uninterrupted "stream" of behavior actually exists or who experiences behavior in this manner. Segmentations of the stream of behavior must be accounted for on the basis of reliable criteria, which guide unit formation (or should guide it), and segmentation needs information about what separates phases of action occurring in play from those occurring in exploration. Let us repeat the question introduced in Voss's chapter: What allows playing and exploring to be distinguished from one another? (We will not consider at this point what it would "cost" if one failed to mind the distinction just proffered.) Let it be noted at the start that Hughes poses this question differently, answering it by classifying the exploratory aspects of behavior at the same level as its ludic aspects, which together can constitute play, and seeing a different purpose behind each of these two phases. Otherwise, the authors represented in our book attempt to draw a distinction based on specific categories of observations made of both types of action. One example is Schneider's use of Hughes's earlier categories (1978), which were conceived on the basis of Corinne Hutt's work. Or, as Voss does in his first chapter, our authors recommend the microanalysis of action sequences as they occur, a view that presupposes rather unrefined unit formations, however (obtained, for example, from the concordant designation of video frames by naive observers). Or they place their trust in the dissimilar kinds of stimulation afforded by the things presented or offered in the experimental situation—the toys versus the utilitarian objects (as described in Hughes's chapter, for example). If less general categories of impressions were to be chosen in research on exploration and play, the experiments by Heidi Keller and her colleagues would otherwise be a caution against too molecular a definition of dependent variables. Her work at least demonstrates the limits of examining dependent variables in isolation and the advantages of using compound, more complex categories.

In his second chapter, Voss demonstrates that one can come to these criteria at different levels of observation and provides a methodological study on the development and operationalization of covert characteristics. His contribution focuses on the anticipation of a certain behavioral result in the actor, an anticipation that may discriminate between exploring and playing. Resolute steps are necessary in this direction—and again we note the importance of phenomena of expression (in this context, facial expression and variables of eye movement) in taking those steps. Phenomena of expression seem to differ greatly from one type of exploration to the next (Wohlwill) and from one style of exploration to the next (Heidi Keller et al.), and one should bear in mind that facial expressions that are akin in appearance (such as laughing and smiling) may be different in their functional import.

The path to reliable operationalizations guided by different goals is strenuous. In the course of his four experiments, for instance, Schneider documents the development of children less (because the work was cross-sectional) than he does the development of a testing strategy that puts subjective uncertainty and its reduction through action at the center of a model clearly based upon exploratory action. In experiments designed for the purpose of analyzing conditions, Schneider attempts to operationalize subjective uncertainty by measuring the amount of time the subject takes to decide on a response to a visual display. This at least teaches us that one probably also has age and developmental functional relationships (models) to contend with in developmental psychology, as suggested by the behavior of Schneider's outstanding group of 4-year-olds, who did not conform to his model. Variations of subjective uncertainty are themes of the subsequent experiments, whose purpose was to study how to distinguish exploratory activities—more specifically, activities involving manipulation of some object—from play and irrelevant actions.

Context and Dialogues

Only that kind of research allows one to continue inquiring with more determination, and it could be demonstrated that the inquisitive questions of the developmental psychologist dealing with exploration and play have more elements and dimensions than the facets of occidental thought on curiosity. Voss expands on the pattern of inquiry now familiar to our readers—"what (in action) follows what?"—by asking "what follows what, when/where, in which action context, when who is acting, and under which circumstances? And how does all this change in the course of children's ontogenetic development?" Voss's experiments related in his second chapter highlight one part of the formula in particular: the action context of children engaged in playing and exploring. That gets into relations in the spectrum of exhibited behavior itself—in Voss's case, how play and exploration are related to variables of facial expressions, which are also able to indicate changing affective states—and he shows how moving the eyes, vocalizing, and speaking are means by which curiosity and play are embedded in the social context of communication. The usually silent partners of the developmental psychologist are the mothers accompanying their children during the experiment. Communication takes place first as an "advance payment" made by the older partner, largely through symbolic acts. Gardner teaches us that the person who has once crossed the symbolic river never returns. But currently we are concerned with the child's keeping in mind that other action partners are present. No one has ever made developmental psychologists swear allegiance to the doctrine that the curious person always stands alone and that a person seeks a partner only when at play.

Even if curiosity's historical path in occidental thought has taken it from being a virtue to being a negative personality trait (Tertullian) of the gawkers and gossipers at the market place, researchers can still make profitable use of the same strategy in the initial stages of their own interest. One of my own chapters documents this path, pitted with the dilemmas of approaches to researching curiosity. The expansive, wide-meshed diagrams of situations can turn out to be traps that ensnare research. They can also help researchers keep their eyes peeled for the diversity of significant factors contributing to the course of exploration and play. These are not repeated here. All of them are superimposed on a basic experience stemming from this specific frame of exploration, in which the experiment's chance partners exhibited a wealth of dialogic modulation, control, and inducement, in which the partners exhibited what Voss calls *social referencing*. Of all the means and levels of exploration, this could have been shown best by those symbolic activities from which continental developmental psychologists of the past calculated a specific "age" of the child: children's questioning or the preverbal analogies of that questioning. Questions usually imply the presence of someone to respond. Matthias Moch has devoted a chapter to that topic and has studied the microgeneses of questioning in the exploratory action of children. This emphasizes certain conclusions drawn in our research work: Analyses of microsequences of symbolic speech activities exhibited in curiosity situations show that the social partner with variable locus or significance (not always present, not always significant to the full degree) is important for a child's activity because that partner facilitates, controls, encourages, or whatever. Nonverbal action, too, has the nature of dialogue.

Supporting Cast of Actors

At this point in the argument, researchers are confronted by a puzzling new perspective that invites one to forget about available process models of curiosity and play. The social dimension of this experimental situation is more richly endowed with relationships than one at first admits. Curiosity researchers often introduce oddly shaped or mounted things into situations familiar or unfamiliar to the child—the important problem of the "optimal stimulus" for different levels of development often being solved in our experiments by a Hutt-box (used by H. Keller, Schneider, and Moch)—and set aside their own desire to know while the child is busy with activity they have induced. The child, on the other hand, becomes epistemically active, provided that the reassurance afforded by the mother's presence allows it, without the researcher's desire to know being able to interact or interfere with that of the child or the mother. Presumably not, that is. As an epistemological subject, the child seems to be privileged; the social context, however, seems to be neutralized. This is one step further than in the era of free-looking time, but it still does not get us close enough to the phenomenon in question. Brueghel, whose painting of children at play represented the motto of the conference from which this book stems, cannot be blamed for portraying isolated figures or only small groups; his purpose was not to depict the whole situation. But the picture does reflect our quandry at present. Brueghel's painting consists of simultaneous scenes of highly interrelated dialogic actions, but these are "played" out on an open square. In 1801 the *Société des Observateurs de l'Homme* formulated a prize question. The organization advertised for a study based on daily observation of how "one or more infants develop [their skills] and to what extent this development is promoted or thwarted by the influence of the objects . . . and by the even greater influence of the persons with which [those infants have] contact" (Moravia, 1977). As far as the participation of the other person goes, researchers of curiosity and play are reformulating their models in light of the question. Clinging to monologic models would also mean fading out all historical aspects of our topic, for rarely are social regulations or permissible spontaneous activities revealed more clearly than through the others who are present and who regulate—a fact supported not only by the experience of West Berliners who have crossed the border.[4]

Thus the phrase "under which circumstances" in the expanded formulation of the question especially means "to whom?" and "with whom?" And bear in mind Irene Burtchen's meritorious clarification of "against whom?" The other person is an essential target of expression and feelings.

---

[4]Cotehele, a manor in eastern Cornwall, provides an unsolicited piece of evidence for this. There, for the amusement of the visitor, is a copy of the *servants' rules* "to be strictly observed" from about the year 1840. In 113 lines printed in three columns, it lays down the rules for behavior when working in the kitchen and waiting on the guests, with bonuses to favor the staff member upholding the rules best (The National Trust, 1984).

So the pressure is on the staff. The restrictions on and, later, the decline in every person's spontaneous activity in life is graphically illustrated by the *Staircases of Life*, popular artwork that has served for many centuries in Europe as a favorite type of propagandistic wall decoration abstracting the path of man and woman over the steps of the decades in their lives (see Görlitz, 1985). (Oddly enough, it is a form of representation that has found scant use in the last half century.) A pertinent example to be seen in the Museum of German Ethnology in Berlin decorates the cover of Germany's most widely used textbook in the field of developmental psychology (Oerter & Montada, 1982).

Pictures are not the only things that regulate or depict codes for exemplary behavior. An era's ruling institutions probably also have always had a varied register of guidelines and techniques to influence behavior, a register that changes over the ages, as Imhof (1984, pp. 123–124) has perceptively shown for the Christian Church of the late Middle Ages and of modern times. In matters of faith these strategies of inducement were not restricted only to mortal existence, which is the focus of the developmental psychologist's study.

An as yet totally unexplored source for developmental psychology and its interest in the temporal life-span is the books on etiquette (and not only those from the past) written as manuals for people

The Affective in Exploration

In his second chapter, Wohlwill poses classic questions of curiosity anew and comes to a distinction especially important in connection with the present line of argumentation: Very different types of behavior can be distinguished in exploration according to their focus. As diversive, inspective, and affective exploration, these types can constitute subphases of a larger context of action that ends with affective exploration instead of play (and may also often constitute independent actions). Unlike the gathering of information, which is decisive for both diversive and inspective exploration, the goal of affective exploration lies "in the elicitation of affective arousal." Only a lack of attention to the temporal structure inherent in action, to differences in the style of action (see p. 000 for our distinction between the "means and levels of exploration"), and to the facial expression of the curious child have allowed this difference in types of exploration to be overlooked thus far.

Without desiring to expand on our line of inquiry systematically, we regard these observations as a prepatory note of what we have gained in factual knowledge. Affects could enter into curiosity research for the time being as a goal state, a goal that regulates action.

As far back as Aristotle and his concept of eudaemonia as the fruit of the desire to know, of the possession of knowledge, the product of the quest for knowledge has been stressed more than the quest itself. It is a pleasure to remember that Jean Itard (1801), to whom the field of psychology owes astutely analytical observations of the "wild boy of Aveyron,"[5] saw (according to Moravia) the constant propensity to seek new feelings in new needs as the main dimension, stemming from a unique emotional capacity, that sets humans apart from other beings.

---

of all social classes or for those who had worked their way up to higher strata. Krumrey's thorough and rare sociological process analysis of German books on etiquette and manners from 1870 to 1970 (Krumrey, 1984) provides material for this interest, as does Susanne Ettl's work, which deals with the letter writers of about the same period (Ettl, 1984). One does not often speak or write straightforwardly. In past eras it was considered at least as a value—regardless of how little attention was paid to the idea by the children who actually lived in those times—to bring up "obedient children with whom a flash of the eye, a disapproving shake of the head suffices to nip an incipient transgression in the bud" (Franz Ebhardt, 1878; cited in Krumrey, 1984, p. 326; by 1931 Ebhardt's book was in its 23rd reprint edition).

Lastly, the leeway remaining for one's physical movement is watched not only by the educator's eyes and words. What children wear and how they are dressed at what age and in what epoch—these were especially tangible rules, in this case, rules shaping spontaneous motor activity. For German research into clothing and dress, see Wilhelm Hansen (1980) and his many references, particularly to classical sources like Percy Macquoid (1923); see also the Swiss exhibition entitled "200 Jahre Kinderkleid und Kindermode" (Two-hundred Years of Children's Dress and Children's Fashion), commented on by Mathys (1984).

[5]See Jean Itard, *Mémoires sur les premiers développemens du sauvage de l'Aveyron* (Paris, 1801), cited in Moravia (1977, p. 278).

Affective-emotional content, however, relinks curiosity research—as was done earlier in Berlyne's work (see Day, 1981)—with the fledgling psychology of aesthetic experiences, a field that has not developed beyond rare short summaries in the *Annual Review of Psychology* since G. T. Fechner's initial contribution. Such content helps one to forge new paths in studying phenomena of expression as an especially related medium or makes them relevant again, without "expression" being restricted only to emotional expression in the view of continental psychologists (Kirchhoff, 1965) and, as Voss has already demonstrated, without "expression," as a reliable medium, having to be limited to affective exploration. Affective-emotional content finally establishes the bridge between current research and the social dimensions of new research paradigms, for feelings also refer to the other person, can touch that person and impart to him or her one's own feelings (*Gefühlsansteckung*), for feelings can consist largely of the desire to share one's own feelings with others.[6]

Developmental Models

For his part, Heckhausen has emphasized this neglected side of subjective experience and behavior in his contribution, a point about which more is noted presently. Among the classical issues treated by Wohlwill—if dimensions of temperament are the basis for exploratory behavior, too—is the significance of individual differences in children's curiosity-related action and the doubt whether exploration is really to be understood as a unitary trait (Heidi Keller's findings also seem to reject the idea). For the authors of antiquity, we listed this (not retained in the present version of this chapter) as a question about generality and dimensionality. In whatever way types of exploration are distinguishable, what does it tell us about a developmental model of exploratory activity? For Voss, this was already the expanded question ("And how does all this change . . . ?"), to which Wohlwill responds by logging references to models (Schachtel), by making developmental forecasts that these will be qualitative shifts in exploration rather than quantitative changes, and by recommending certain topics for future research. In this regard Voss referred to late and subsequent genetic types of young children's exploration and play and questioned whether either sphere of phenomena continues to exist throughout one's life-span.

In a correlation analysis well fit into Wohlwill's program (1973), Heidi Keller and her colleagues teach which aspects of exploration itself can become observable—this "window to cognitive development" (Piaget) that has been neglected for so long—if one only takes it seriously enough as a developmental phenomenon. These experiments can lay the foundation for a tradition inviting

---

[6]Romantic movements like the *Wandervogel* in Germany society under Emperor William II made this "desire for shared experience" an established part of their program.

follow-up analyses, especially single-case studies of individuals. In principle, the overall scores compiled in Keller's work still conceal microgenetic patterns of processes that can be illuminated, but it already shows that there seem to be exploration styles specific to development, styles that remain stable to different degrees through the first 4 years of life. Data forthcoming from H. Keller's work show that the still somewhat delimited behaviors that have been isolated and "mounted" for examination in this chapter can easily be embedded in the actual interaction between parent and child.

Developmental psychology both needs and goes beyond such perceptive descriptions of changes. It needs and calls for explication (and then intervention on the secure basis of such findings). This is reflected in the contributions by Wohlwill and Voss when they write of significant contexts for the development of exploration. In descriptive terms, context can refer to those relations to other forms of children's actions that perhaps change ontogenetically (in Kagan's sense of heterotypic continuity). It means that exploration of whatever type can become a dependent, concomitant accent of forms of action concerning other topics. (To get a sense of this, one must only observe people as they walk through a hall to a specific destination. Often their feet "know" the route to take while their heads and eyes are free to explore.) In explicative terms, the inclusion of further cognitive development is under debate (as in Voss's contribution) as is the inhibitory as well as beneficial influence that exploration has on the development of other types of behavior like cognition and creativity (see Wohlwill's chapter).

The two experiments by Miranda Hughes on the effects of exploration are relevant in this vein, too. Hughes examines the short-term effects that precursory exploration, in which learning is said to be inherent, and that play, in which creativity is said to be inherent, have on subsequent convergent thinking (in a problem-solving situation) and on divergent thinking (spurred by a test). Also part of this is the explanation of a model—which is very similar to that given by Hughes—in the chapter by Papoušek and her colleagues. The call for a broad framework of developmental theory in which exploration, play, and other rather internally instigated types of behavior can be classified is meant in both descriptive and explicatory terms. Heckhausen responds to this call. The two key events he notes in the development of achievement behavior could lay the foundation of a complementary strategy for our conception of developmental models: the strategy of seeking out salient periods of discontinuity, regions of transition in the development of children (perhaps extendable to adults as well) in which their situation fundamentally changes. This would make it possible to check for corresponding changes in those activities of exploration and play, too, that have undergone longitudinal study. Changes in the experience of the self, in the structure of action (according to Heckhausen), the emergence of running and speaking ability, and the initial contact with domains outside the home (the nursery, the school) would be potential "candidates" for study as transitionary regions.

Standards of Excellence and Ordered Emotions

Heckhausen's contribution invites one to take up this challenge but focuses on something different. Heckhausen demonstrates that the emotional components of action also have—or can have—an ontogenetic dimension. His treatment of emotions and expression stresses otherwise neglected viewpoints like the conception of action put forward in this book. In dealing with achievement behavior, he illustrates at the same time an established tangential domain that is touched on, for example, by Schneider but that is not the center of attention in this book. There is a lack of findings showing how many parts of achievement-oriented behavior go into exploration and play (and vice versa), although in athletics, for instance, one speaks less of playing than of games, in which standards of excellence are definitely important. But those are more complex forms of action. Standards of excellence and rules in play perhaps have no more in common than the normative factor, which is considered by the actor of the group as binding. The "history" of the competition, the overlap, or the difference between the ontogenetic patterns of development of the three strands of action known as achievement behavior, exploration, and play has not yet been written, with achievement motivation (as the subject matter of developmental psychology) almost itself formulating a kind of standard of excellence for how that "history" should be structured. In that history thematically rich sequences of action may become apparent in which achieving, exploring, and play constitute different, ontogenetically alternating phases in the process of interaction in a situation. Play and exploration functioning as precursors may, for example, contribute to the emergence of standards of excellence. Heckhausen proposes taking a different route for the time being—adherence to the standard of proper or ordered emotions that, as a phylogenetic, ontogenetic, and microgenetic sequence consistent with a model by Scherer, simultaneously prescribe forms of action in a specific order of steps. The emotional valuation of occurrences according to new versus familiar would cause exploration to branch off from the chain of action very early. We note the problem without being able to solve it at this time: Are there emotions, like self-evaluative emotions in achievement behavior, that are specific to certain actions, or are there emotions that specify action without being exclusive to them? According to Heckhausen, the concentration between subject and object poles of action shifts ontogenetically in emotions as well as in action. (Corinne Hutt put it in a similar way when noting the difference between play and exploration.) Moreover, the history of research on achievement motivation teaches us not to underestimate the qualitative richness of emotions (and not just when affective explorations are concerned).

Emotions Once Again

But if affects are to be treated, what do exploration and play researchers do with anxiety, a construct not restricted to dimensions of subjective experience that can be inferred? Heckhausen has written an initial summary of his work to date and has formulated a kind of "wanted poster" for hidden information concerning the ontogenetic precursors of achievement-motivated action. Researchers of achievement motivation are familiar with the mutually complementary constructs of hope for success and fear of failure—both can lead to achievement action. Marvin Zuckerman's summation of biological research on related constructs (Zuckerman, 1983) suggests distinguishing the traits of extraversion, impulsiveness, and sensation-seeking as one dimension from the dimension of neuroticism and anxiety but concedes that both dimensions interact with each other in certain phenomena such as the behavior of humans who find themselves in a new situation.

By contrast, research on exploration and curiosity today sets rather restrictive conditions. The validity of Schneider's model, for example, which has been partially tested and which is a central contribution to the theoretical side of our book, is said to hold only under nonthreatening conditions. Before that point, though, his model allows for different, conflicting emotions and behavioral tendencies within one and the same object until exploration, seen as somewhat neutral in its affective quality, is given a chance to reduce uncertainty. The approach by McCall and McGhee (1977), cited by Schneider, contradicts his model only when considered for a single situation, provided the uncertainty that is provoked is variable when the situation is repeated. Researchers of attribution, who, in keeping with a decidedly cognitive orientation, had emotions to account for as variables of equal rank (see Weiner, 1980), point out that it is no easy task to interpret the relationships stemming from emotions. For that direction in research, emotions are entities tied in various ways to the individual dimensions underlying attributional judgment and causal explanation (as in Weiner's eight-field schema). Just as there are variations in the degree of waking known as frames in research on infants (Papoušek), these emotions could also constitute a frame for distinct kinds of information processing. Emotions have the character of grounds, too, a fact that reminds one of Rubin's differentiation between a figure and its ground in the psychology of the 1920s. Specific moods worth describing in detail are pointed out by J. Keller in his chapter of this book. To pursue Hughes's questions further (What does exploration do? What are the effects of exploration?), why should exploration, to a certain extent, not also be a strategy helping the individual to control, to "ban," emotions that have been provoked?[7]

Wohlwill's identification of affective exploration gave reason to make some room in these concluding remarks for the problem of emotions and affects. As

---

[7]As Aby Warburg adjudged artistic activity (cited in Schade, 1983, p. 131).

evidence from cultural history shows (Grant, 1967; Tuchman, 1978), research on emotions and affects will not be able to completely avoid the gruesome in its search for the miraculous, be these qualities experienced in reality or imagined in video films.

Early Playing

In addition to exploration, the main accent of our contributions was on certain types of children's play without an attempt being made to delimit that subject. Hughes opened discussion of the topic by analyzing the conceptual status of play and criticizing the presumption that the phenomenon is a unitary construct. She offered suggestions for empirically examining the question of the effects the aspects of play and exploratory behavior have, comparing imitative, symbolic play with creative, imaginative play, which, unlike the former, would correspond to ludic aspects of behavior. It is a subject that Greta Fein picks up on, thereby bringing the issue of affects and emotions to the fore again. In the historical references to the value accorded to curiosity, we had juxtaposed Blumenberg's version of the phenomenon's biological substratum with ethological evidence, which was deemphasized as a frame of reference as our line of argumentation continued. In the triad of genetics, the phylogenetic foundation is always included, however (see Voss and Heckhausen, this volume), not necessarily only as "that old and dangerous principle" (Renfrew, 1982) of partial recapitulation. The biological orientation of the Papoušeks and Harris, which is interdisciplinary, puts phylogenesis manifested in play and playing back into the picture. These authors expand the set of questions we had developed for curiosity research by adding two important queries about play (which need not be restricted to play, however). They ask when play begins. When is the phenomenon in question to be observed and in which context? Of course, the when is indeed rooted in phylogenesis, but the empirical answer is found in the earliest days of ontogenesis. The authors set out upon their path with a problem (which has meanwhile become familiar to the reader): In view of difficulties with definitions,[8] they turn again to the phylogenetic and ontogenetic origins of a complex phenomenon. If Hughes asked what is subsequently brought about by distinguishable parts of children's play, Papoušek and his colleagues are interested in when, how, and with what play would begin—and how parents spontaneously guide this development. This brings out two traditions of investigation associated with the Papoušeks' circle, of which only the second actually has to do with playing and which show the road away from stimulus–response paradigms that were used in the early years of such research. It remains for conceptual models to prove their heuristic power. Much of our work is typified by analyses of microgenetic

---

[8]As a kind of genetic version of a program that, in light of similar difficulties, led the phenomenological psychology of the 1920s to the motto *ad fontes*: to go back to the things themselves.

sequences, and these analyses are taking on new dimensions in the Papoušeks' work. According to two previous approaches to localizing play in the infant's desire to learn from contingencies and in the playful monologues of infancy, these new dimensions include sequences of interaction engaged in by very young children—with researchers paying special regard to the exchange of sounds and verbalizations, the playful elements in vocal exchanges in which play is recognizable at an early age.

If you will, a new and very early form of play thereby appears on the "stage" of scientific attention—the vocal play in the interchange between adults and infants. Doing without formal definitions for now—*playfulness* is always a somewhat loose and unoppressive label—the reader finds the concept easy to grasp in the course of their chapter and is able to become familiar with the phenomenon on his own terms. In addition to the didactic scripts of parents who are active in the pedagogical sense very early, at least implicitly, the reader comes to know both self-acting and independent playmates in a richly woven tapestry of longitudinal orientation. Future research will throw light upon the other, visible areas of expression like facial expressions, gestures, and shifts of position—with the hope, dampened by the Papoušeks and Harris, of being able to keep up such a detailed analysis even in late periods of development.

Symbols and Inherent Knowledge of Objects

Playing (and play) can be tied into action theory, can be interpreted as acting and action. Does that appreciably enhance either phenomenon? Does it not seem only to make it more complicated to speak candidly about play? I think it does help; in fact, it helps a great deal. If cultural development takes place particularly through the creation and subsequent independent existence of works and through the repercussions this has on the creators in their society (Renfrew, 1982), exploration and play—whether detailed analysis in the future shows them to be unitary or in need of greater differentiation (Wohlwill, Hughes)—do suffer from the "soap bubble nature" of the effects they produce. This leads one to forget that action, playing and exploring included, is usually centered on an object, that experiences of a culture and a society are manifested in the way that certain objects are conventionally shaped and manipulated.[9] In specific situations these

---

[9]An aspect that soviet Russian psychology and German critical psychology (in the Holzkamp circle; see Holzkamp, 1983) stress as being particularly fruitful. In German psychology, the toy as a subject of research has otherwise been left too much up to the helpful recommendations made by working groups of educational specialists. There has been little, if any, detailed developmental research on the actual role of toys as effective "partners" in the quite specific interaction exhibited by young and old children, (see Hildebrandt, 1904; Junker and Stille, 1984). In the eighty years between those two publications there was the work of Walter Benjamin, unjustly forgotten in Germany but worthy of mention if only because of his theses, with which Ariès's own are so closely allied. A brief retrospect of Benjamin's work was published in 1982.

experiences transmit the knowledge about objects and call upon the actors to enter into processes of forging consensus about what to do with and how to handle those objects—processes that themselves can be guided by rules, as Piaget demonstrated long ago. This is what Burtchen has to teach us when she borrows from Oerter in asking about the target of joint play that occurs as action. She thus acknowledges that there are agreements and conflicts in action that, in turn, invite older persons to intervene as mediators in disputes. Object-directed action— as in the inquisitive manipulation of the Hutt-box—can produce fleeting effects of action (Kirchhoff's terms) such as those found in the vocalization game studied by the Papoušeks, but it can also be manifested in traces of action and surviving works. Gardner has documented this on the basis of the symbolic activity of the child. Effects of action, however, are also inferrable changes of cognitive and, as Greta Fein's contribution shows, affective schemata.

Like the reader, we moved until late in this book in an intact, simple world. Now the realities are changing and "multiplying." The accessibility and, above all, the availability of things and persons becomes questionable, and the world is duplicated through the child's own creative activity. In the game of pretense, one can play that one is playing.[10] And like Philo's man, who grew by dimensions when his curiosity led him to steal a glimpse of the majesty reserved only unto God, our subject matter does not branch out or ramify but rather multiplies its levels of reality and range of applicability without the content conveyed in pretense actually being true. Curiosity has its twin character, too, except that for children of today the box—both its exterior and its contents—usually remains in one reality with no recourse to sorcery. But how do these duplications of reality relate to each other? What relationships are there between domains like the child's everyday world, his practical knowledge of it, and the fluid trans-formation of objects, persons, and events in actual episodes of play, which are often engaged in with partners? The faithfulness of the copy becomes apparent as a problem, or the child's very act of producing a likeness is a challenge for developmental research. There might be correspondence, but correspondence with what? If not with one's own experience, then of knowledge corresponding with the play activity that happens to be taking place? Of situationally isolated novel creations that follow each other in new, creative combinations? The question is not what the child's pretense play is but rather what is reflected in it and what it allows us as researchers to see. The fact that pretense play happens in a particular way is explained in two models developed by Greta Fein. The first pertains to a mechanism of mental transformation, whose activation she explores through its situational and ontogenetic components. The second is the basic

---

[10]This is reflexive mirroring of the type deliberately practiced in the adult pictorial art known as "peinture dans la peinture" (Georgel & Lecoq, 1983) or in photography (Krauss et al., 1983), not to mention using a representation of an object to paint from rather than the object itself (Nemeczek & Paltzer, 1984).

model of a cognitive-affective system with five facets of pretense episodes observable in the activities of playing children. After Schneider, Papoušek, and Heckhausen, that is the fifth time that a model-oriented approach has been brought to bear. It appears that the representational system involved here differs from that in practical nonplay activities, the former having more metalevels—patterned on the analogous Bateson analysis. This mechanism, which makes representations possible and at the same time manipulates them, is complex enough to contain metacognitions, to allow for metacommunication. But it extends beyond the cognitive realm.

For it is particularly the observable action of pretend play that reveals affective and affectively significant transformations stemming from symbolic units (probably ascribable to the mechanism of mental transformation just mentioned), which, for their part, are special types of motivated representational templates that contain or represent affective interpersonal relations. In 1937 G. Kafka formulated something similar, but less complexly, regarding actions and the four possible interpersonal pivots (*Bezugswendungen*) of expression. Fein postulates an affective system of symbols that represents the child's real or imagined experiences on quite a general level, making them easy to spot in pretend play. This does not mean liking shells that one finds on the beach, does not mean holding them to one's ear and listening because it sounds nice (Wohlwill). At this point something else enters into affects, something that goes beyond the issue of having affects or not having them (in the exploratory mood or in the fear that numbs exploration), beyond showing affects (in the expression of feelings), and beyond the search for affects (in affective exploration). This something is the fact that affective relations are symbolically represented in conjunction with often very animated feelings, that these affective relations are creatively, imaginatively linked with a temporal uncertainty about their further progress and set in a deontic logic of emotional sequence that differs from the Scherer sequence cited by Heckhausen.

Let us pass over what such template representations do for children and the interaction between them. Let us also pass over the fact that children engaged in pretend play seem to improvise from moment to moment rather than follow a general plan of action. The spontaneity of action, which frames our book so auspiciously, will thus become tangible. The child's activity of creating and using (as well as understanding) symbols in pretend play does not belong exclusively to playing, even to pretend play. As Fein shows, however, it does typify a greater freedom and wealth of linkage. As early as 1960, Berlyne's motley definition of epistomological behavior and epistemic curiosity was based on symbolic processes. The everyday play of half-concealed showing (of the "guess what . . ." type) involves an abundance of symbols and relations between them. But that fact is not what appears to be specific. Gardner spoke of a symbolic river. What is important is that someone cross it. Heckhausen pointed out that the self originates in the work and in the process of creating it. That being the case, symbols do not stand only for something quite remote and are not conveyed only from a distance. As Gadamer (1979) formulated it for the *Anwesendsein* (being present) in a work of art, intended emotional content and objective knowledge are more than just revealed, even if plain symbols are used. That remote something is itself present and is manifested in symbols. This immediacy of symbols is further documented in a much later use of symbols, the wearing of buttons by adolescents (Boehnke & Noack, 1983, 1984) as an indication of status and rank in the adult world. Where pictures are concerned, there is ethnological evidence for the human being's fear of being painted and, through the picture (the portrait, for example), being handed over to others for them to do with as they please.[11] As Fein explains, pretend play is characterized not only by having something represent something else, but by being present oneself in the doing. Both self-referencing and the creation of reality in the course of pretending open new dimensions in the context of our contributions. These dimensions lead to other perspectives in addition to the process of representation (concerning the relationship between symbols and that which they symbolize), a process that is historically variable. Moreover, self-referencing and creating reality also mean one's own reflected or conscious referencing to another reality without actually being a fiction that regulates cognition (as Hans Vaihinger put it). There are simple questions to be asked at the outset of such research, questions like "Am I 'saying' what I mean?" and "Do I mean what I am 'saying'?" These new dimensions concern and change the sequence analysis of action as well—in our case, the episode structure of play. In this sense the contributions in this book are simultaneously a didactic sequence.

It cannot be discussed here how much and in what way the developing function of symbols helps establish these dimensions. One may doubt the extent to which the developmental psychologist, in searching for an answer to this question, will be able to figure on general, generalizable developmental functions. But what does "generalizable" mean? Generalizable across longitudinal random samples of children? Across the situations in which children evince exploration or play and across the periods over which they are studied? Gardner and Wolf show that there are many different forms of symbolic activity, too. Even expression has a symbolic side in the continental European discussion if one recalls earlier debates of expression versus representation (*Ausdruck* vs. *Darstellung*). Expression through body gestures, along with symbolic or pretend play and drawing, is only one of seven media of action that use and generate symbols, action whose development is being followed by the two authors in longitudinal studies. "If the use of symbols is one of the clearest indicators of the functioning of mind" (Renfrew, 1982), then Gardner and Wolf's data on the development of domain-specific

---

[11]This is shown in a novel relating the experiences of a physician who had been banned in fascist Italy to a remote village in the south of the country (Levi, 1982, quoted from the German translation, p. 138).

streams and cross-media waves of symbolization would lend credence to the hypothesis that there are frames of mind linked to specific symbols, that there are region-specific computational devices that have developed in the course of evolution. Gardner and Wolf's "new key" to the study of play, exploration, and artistic activity reduces the hope of discovering general laws but at the same time opens up far more complex subjects for future research that addresses the formative role of culture, too. That research will show not only to what extent exploration and play determine these symbols and vice versa, but also how much different frames of mind themselves contribute to specific types of action.

If, as current researchers see it, playing and exploring seem to have such little success in creating lasting works (admittedly, inferring the creator's motivation from the work entails the burden of at least some doubt), if playing and exploring thereby lose a significant, tradition-building, developmental factor— toys and the knowledge and "rules of the game" they transmit notwithstanding— does not the use of symbols offer at least some compensation for the loss?

These concluding remarks have pursued aspects of our own curiosity about exploration and play as documented in this book. Exploration and play have not proven to be a unitary concept, not even unitary in themselves. On the contrary, it has been shown in the positive sense that they are indeed distinguishable phenomena admitting of further discrimination. As the preceding text has pointed out, the aspects themselves fall into an orderly set of questions. It would be natural to compare them with trailmarks of historical value judgments of curiosity. Lack of space precludes this. One could foster the impression that work in developmental psychology has raised and studied an abundance of additional questions about exploration and play. In place of other evidence for this impression, may the reader allow a reference to Plutarch's situational—or rather thematic—analysis, passed down to us in his brief work entitled "De curiositate" in the *Moralia*. Because curiosity in that work is "really a passion for finding out whatever is hidden and concealed, and no one conceals a good thing when he has it" (Plutarch), because it is directed at all that is disgraceful, one needs assured means to curb it, if not to liberate oneself from it. Plutarch recommends effective measures for this. In the research commented on here, curiosity—like play, as the Papoušeks reminded us by citing classical works—is on the bright side of human existence, even in its beginnings. Pedagogical measures for encouraging and controlling curiosity were, in contrast to Plutarch's advice, deemphasized in this text, too. Aristotle's eudaemonia, the promised reward for the satisfaction of epistemic curiosity, is supposed to have been taken from us by Kant (Sternberger), but at least the philosopher feels encouraged to ask once again whether bliss is the supreme good of human action, as Pleines's text has it (1984).

According to southern Italian legend (related by Levi), the souls of children who have died without being baptized manifest themselves in evil doing as *monachicchi*. Even if children as living partners have taught us everything—

this book documents our scientific desire to know about their desire to know—they have so far been strangely silent in this concluding commentary. These pages would have to end with information from two nonprofessional partners, end with that which children in essence really ask and want to know and with that which moved the pilgrim fathers to brave a journey into the unknown. And we would have to recall scientific standards of developmental psychology having to do with our topic as proposed, for example, in the developmental analysis of Siegel, Bisanz, and Bisanz (1983). Such a continuation, however, cannot be undertaken here.[12]

GLOSSARY OF QUOTATIONS

pp.

351   H. Blumenberg (1980, p. 7); G. E. Lessing, *Laokoon* (translated from the Reclam edition of 1983, p. 35)

352   Mayflower's passenger list: *The passengers of the Mayflower 1620*. (Plymouth: Plymouth City Museum and Art Gallery, 1982); J. F. Wohlwill (1973, p. 18)

358   Tertullian, quoted in H. Blumenberg (1980, p. 89)

359   P. Brueghel, the elder, *Children's games*. The painting now hangs in the Museum of Art History, Vienna; S. Moravia (1977, p. 87), who quotes from the *Décade Philosophique* 30th Therm. year VIII, Vol. 26, pp. 368–369; we have translated from the German version into English.

360   J. Itard, quoted in S. Moravia (1977, p. 102)

364   M. Zucherman (1983, p. 249)

365   H. Blumenberg (1980, p. 13); C. Renfrew (1982, p. 14)

366   C. Renfrew (1982, pp. 15 and 24)

367   Philo of Alexandria, quoted in H. Blumenberg (1980, pp. 72–73)

368   D. E. Berlyne (1960, pp. 262–282, pp. 283–303)

369   C. Renfrew (1982, p. 13)

370   Plutarch, in the English translation by W. C. Helmbold (1962, p. 489); D. Sternberger, quoted in J.-E. Pleines (1984, p. 8); C. Levi (1982, pp. 131–135)

REFERENCES

Benjamin, W. (1982). *Über Kinder, Jugend und Erziehung. Mit Abbildungen von Kinderbüchern und Spielzeug aus der Sammlung Benjamin* (6th ed.). Frankfurt/M.: Suhrkamp.

Berlyne, D. E. (1960). *Conflict, arousal, and curiosity*. New York: McGraw–Hill.

---

[12]See footnote 1.

Blumenberg, H. (1980). *Der Prozeβ der theoretischen Neugierde* (2nd ed.). Erweiterte und überarbeitete Neuausgabe von: Die Legitimität der Neuzeit, 3. Teil. Frankfurt/M.: Suhrkamp.

Boehnke, K., & Noack, P. (1983). Zum Symbolgebrauch bei Jugendlichen. In R. K. Silbereisen & K. Eyferth (Eds.), *Berichte aus der Arbeitsgruppe TUdrop Jugendforschung, Jugendentwicklung und Drogen, 29*. Technische Universität Berlin, FRG.

Boehnke, K., & Noack, P. (1984). Zum Symbolgebrauch bei Jugendlichen. *Zeitschrift für Semiotik, 6*, 83–93.

Clamp, A. L. (no date). *Plymouth's historic Barbican*. Plymouth: P.D.S. Printers.

Cranach, M. von, Kalbermatten, U., Indermühle, K., & Gugler, B. (1980). *Zielgerichtetes Handeln*. Bern: Huber.

Day, H. I. (1981) *Advances in intrinsic motivation and aesthetics*. New York: Plenum.

Ettl, S. (1984). *Anleitungen zur schriftlichen Kommunikation. Briefsteller von 1880 bis 1980*. Tübingen: Niemeyer.

Gadamer, H.-G. (1979). *Die Aktualität des Schönen. Kunst als Spiel, Symbol und Fest*. Stuttgart: Reclam.

Georgel, P., & Lecoq, A.-M. (1983). *La peinture dans la peinture*. Exposition. Musée des Beaux-Arts de Dijon. 18 décembre 1982/28 février 1983. Dijon–Quetigny, France: Darantiere.

Görlitz, D. (1972). *Ergebnisse und Probleme der ausdruckspsychologischen Sprechstimmforschung*. [Problems and results of vocal communication]. Meisenheim: Hain.

Görlitz, D. (1983). Entwicklungsmuster attributionaler Handlungsanalyse. In D. Görlitz (Ed.), *Kindliche Erklärungsmuster. Entwicklungspsychologische Beiträge zur Attributionsforschung* (Vol. 1, pp. 146–179). Weinheim: Beltz.

Görlitz, D. (1985). "Norming of everyday life, expectancy change, and historical development." Paper delivered at the Free University of Berlin, Department of Education, 5 December.

Grant, M. (1967). *Gladiators*. London: Weidenfeld & Nicolson.

Grant, M. (1969). *The ancient mediterranean*. London: Weidenfeld & Nicolson.

Hansen, W. (1980). Aufgaben der historischen Kleidungsforschen. In G. Wiegelmann (Ed.), *Geschichte der Alltagskultur* (pp. 149–174). Münster: Coppenrath.

Heckhausen, H. (1980). *Motivation und Handeln. Lehrbuch der Motivationspsychologie*. Berlin: Springer.

Heider, F. (1958). *The psychology of interpersonal relations*. New York: Wiley.

Heider, F. (1980a). Perception and attribution. In D. Görlitz (Ed.), *Perspectives on attribution research and theory. The Bielefeld Symposium* (pp. 3–8). Cambridge, MA: Ballinger.

Heider, F. (1980b). On balance and attribution. In D. Görlitz (Ed.), *Perspectives on attribution research and theory. The Bielefeld Symposium* (pp. 9–18). Cambridge, MA: Ballinger.

Hildebrandt, P. (1979). *Das Spielzeug im Leben des Kindes*. Düsseldorf: Diederichs. (Original published 1904, Berlin).

Holzkamp, K. (1983). *Grundlegung der Psychologie*. Frankfurt/M.-New York: Campus.

Hughes, M. (1978). Sequential analysis of exploration and play. *International Journal of Behavioral Development, 1*, 83–97.

Imhof, A. E. (1984). *Die verlorenen Welten. Alltagsbewältigung durch unsere Vorfahren—und weshalb wir uns heute so schwer damit tun* . . . . München: Beck.

Itard, J. (1801). *Mémoires sur les premiers développemens du sauvage de l'Aveyron*. Paris.

Junker, A., & Stille, E. (1984). *Spielen und Lernen. Spielzeug und Kinderleben in Frankfurt 1750–1930*. Frankfurt/M.: Historisches Museum.

Kafka, G. (1937). Grundsätzliches zur Ausdruckspsychologie. *Acta Psychologica, 3*, 273–314.

Kirchhoff, R. (1965). Grundfragen der Ausdruckspsychologie. In R. Kirchhoff (Ed.), *Ausdruckspsychologie. Handbuch der Psychologie* (Vol. 5, pp. 117–219). Göttingen: Hogrefe.

Krauss, R. H., Schmalriede, M., & Schwarz, M. (1983). *Kunst mit Photographie. Die Sammlung Dr. Rolf H. Krauss*. Berlin: Frölich & Kaufmann.

Krumrey, H.-V. (1984) *Entwicklungsstrukturen von Verhaltensstandarden. Eine soziologische Prozeßanalyse auf der Grundlage deutscher Anstands- und Manierenbücher von 1870 bis 1970.* Frankfurt/M.: Suhrkamp.

Lessing, G. E. (1965). *Laocoon.* D. Reich (Ed.). London: Oxford University Press.

Lessing, G. E. (1983). *Laokoon oder über die Grenzen der Malerei und Poesie.* Mit beiläufigen Erläuterungen verschiedener Punkte. Stuttgart: Reclam. (Original published 1766).

Levi, C. (1982). *Christus kam nur bis Eboli.* [Cristo si è fermato a Eboli.] (H. Hohenemser-Steglich, Trans. in German). München: Deutscher Taschenbuch Verlag.

Macquoid, P. (1923). *Four hundred years of children's costume from the great masters 1400–1800.* London.

Mathys, F. K. (1984). *200 Jahre Kinderkleid und Kindermode.* Riehen, Switzerland: Spielzeug- und Dorfmuseum.

McCall, R. B., & McGhee, P. E. (1977). The discrepancy hypothesis of attention and affect in children. In F. Weizman & I. C. Užgiris (Eds.), *The structuring of experience* (pp. 179–210). New York: Plenum.

Moltmann, G. (Ed.) (1982). *Germans to America. 300 years of immigration, 1683 to 1983.* Stuttgart: Institute for Foreign Cultural Relations.

Moravia, S. (1977). *Beobachtende Vernunft. Philosophie und Anthropologie in der Aufklärung.* Frankfurt/M. Ullstein.

The National Trust (Ed.). (1984). *Cotehele House. Cornwall.* Plymouth: Latimer Trend.

Neisser, U. (1979). The control of information pickup in selective looking. In A. D. Pick (Ed.), *Perception and its development: A tribute to Eleanor J. Gibson* (pp. 201–219). Hillsdale, NJ: Lawrence Erlbaum Associates.

Nemeczek, A., & Paltzer, R. A. (1984). Ohne Fotos kein Gemälde. *art. Das Kunstmagazin, 1,* 20–41.

Newtson, D. (1973). Attribution and the unit of perception of ongoing behavior. *Journal of Personality and Social Psychology, 28,* 28–38.

Newtson, D. (1976). Foundations of attribution: The perception of ongoing behavior. In J. H. Harvey, W. J. Ickes, & R. F. Kidd (Eds.), *New directions in attribution research* (Vol. 1, pp. 223–247). Hillsdale, NJ: Lawrence Erlbaum Associates.

Oerter, R., & Montada, L. (Eds.). (1982). *Entwicklungspsychologie. Ein Lehrbuch.* München: Urban & Schwarzenberg.

The passengers of the Mayflower 1620. (1982). Plymouth: Plymouth City Museum and Art Gallery.

Pleines, J.-E. (1984). *Eudaimonia zwischen Kant und Aristoteles. Glückseligkeit als höchstes Gut menschlichen Handelns.* Würzburg: Königshausen & Neumann.

Plutarch. (1899). *About curiosity.* C. Penberton (Ed.). London: Kegan Paul.

Plutarch. (1948). *Von der Ruhe des Gemütes und andere philosophische Schriften. Über Kindererziehung* (pp. 108–128). Übertragen und eingeleitet von B. Snell (Trans.). Zürich: Artemis.

Plutarch. (1962). *Plutarch's Moralia in fifteen volumes. On being a busybody.* [De curiositate]. (Vol. 6, 439A–523B, pp. 471–517). (W. C. Helmbold, Trans.). London: Heinemann, Cambridge, MA: Harvard University Press. (Reprint)

Postins, M. W. (1982). *Stonehenge. Sun, moon, wandering stars.* Kenilworth: B. J. T. Print Services.

Renfrew, C. (1982). *Towards an archeology of mind.* An inaugural lecture delivered before the University of Cambridge on 30 November 1982. Cambridge: Cambridge University Press.

Schade, S. (1983). *Schadenzauber und die Magie des Körpers. Hexenbilder der frühen Neuzeit.* Worms: Werner.

Siegel, A. W., Bisanz, J., & Bisanz, G. L. (1983). Developmental analysis: A strategy for the study of psychological change. In D. Kuhn & J. A. Meacham (Eds.), *On the development of developmental psychology* (pp. 53–80). Basel: Karger.

Tuchman, B. (1978). *A distant mirror—The calamitous 14th century.* New York: Knopf.

Weiner, B. (1980). A theory of motivation for some classroom experiences. In D. Görlitz (Ed.), *Perspectives on attribution research and theory. The Bielefeld Symposium* (pp. 39–74). Cambridge, MA: Ballinger.

Wohlwill, J. F. (1973). *The study of behavioral development.* New York: Academic Press.

Wohlwill, J. F. (1984). Relationships between exploration and play. In T. D. Yawkey & A. D. Pellegrini (Eds.), *Child's play: Development and applied* (pp. 143–170). Hillsdale, NJ: Lawrence Erlbaum Associates.

Zuckerman, M. (Ed.). (1983). *Biological bases of sensation seeking, impulsivity, and anxiety.* Hillsdale, NJ: Lawrence Erlbaum Associates.

ABOUT THE AUTHORS

Irene Burtchen, Ph.D., is an assistant professor in the Department of Developmental and Educational Psychology at the University of Munich. Her fields of work are social interaction in the course of life, development of play behavior, health psychology, and education. Her recent publications include *The Psychology of Health* (Donauwörth: Auer), "Games at the physician's" in the *Handbook of Play Education* (Düsseldorf: Schwann), and "The role of the teacher in health education" in the *Handbook of Preschool Education* (Weinheim: Edition Psychologie).

Greta Fein is professor of education at the University of Maryland. She has been studying the play of toddlers and preschool children since the early 1970s, an interest that began with the publication of *Day Care in Context*, coauthored with Alison Clarke-Stewart. More recently, these interests have turned to problems associated with a theory of pretense and to the play activities children engage in when interacting with microcomputers.

Howard Gardner, is a research psychologist at the Boston Veterans Administration Medical Center, professor of neurology (neuropsychology) at the Boston University School of Medicine, and Co-Director of Harvard Project Zero. His principal research interests are in the development and breakdown of symbol-using capacities. His most recent book is *Frames of Mind: The Theory of Multiple Intelligences*.

Gudrun Gauda, Delia Miranda, and Axel Schölmerich are assistants in the research project on "earliest infancy" under the direction of Professor H. Keller. The project is funded by the German Research Foundation (DFG).

Dietmar Görlitz is professor of developmental psychology at the Technical University of Berlin (West). After researching nonverbal communication and speech, his interests turned to motivation psychology, especially to concepts in attribution theory. He has investigated attributional judgments in the context of sociocognitive development, expanding such study with microanalyses of the development of attributional processes in verbal and nonverbal communication. His present work delves into developmental aspects of curiosity research and methodologies used in historically oriented psychology. Görlitz is author and coeditor of various publications on psychology in the everyday life context and on attribution research, especially in developmental psychology.

Betty Harris is currently a predoctoral research fellow in the Developmental Psychobiology Unit of the Max Planck Institute for Research in Psychiatry, Munich. She received her graduate degree from the University of North Carolina at Greensboro. Her areas of interest include social aspects of child development and parental care-giving, particularly the role of parental care-giving behaviors in social and cognitive development of infants.

Heinz Heckhausen was born in 1926 and studied at Münster. Since 1964 he has been professor of psychology at the recently founded Ruhr University of Bochum, where he established the Institute of Psychology and a research group in motivational psychology. From 1971 to 1972 he was a fellow of the Netherlands Center of Advanced Study. He has been the director of the Max Planck Institute for Psychological Research in Munich since 1983. His main research interests are motivation and the development of motivation, particularly of achievement motivation. His publications include *The Anatomy of Achievement Motivation* and the textbook entitled *Motivation und Handeln*.

Miranda Hughes was a former student and assistant of the late Corinne Hutt in the Psychology Department of the University of Keele, England, where she obtained her Ph.D. She collaborated with Dr. Hutt, researching on children's exploratory behavior and play and their interrelationship. She subsequently was on the faculty of the Psychology Department of the University of Leeds, and is currently employed at Kidds Advertising, Leeds, England.

Heidi Keller is a professor of developmental psychology at the University of Osnabrück in the Federal Republic of Germany. Her main interests are the development of exploratory behavior, clinical aspects of early parent-child interactions, the development of sex roles, and sex differences with a focus on the first years of life.

Josef A. Keller, born in 1944, studied psychology, philosophy, and pedagogy at the universities of Bamberg, Münster, and Würzburg, where he obtained his master's degree in psychology and his doctoral degree (Dr. phil.). He is now assistant professor at the University of Würzburg. One of his main research interests is motivation psychology, primarily affiliation motivation. He is the author of *Grundlagen der Motivation* (München: Urban & Schwarzenberg, 1981) and has published several articles and reviews in professional journals and books.

Delia Miranda, see Gudrun Gauda et al.

Matthias Moch, born in 1954 in Schönau, West Germany, studied psychology and education in Marburg from 1975 to 1981. In 1982 he served in the department of psychology at the University of Marburg as a junior researcher for a project investigating the curiosity of children. Since spring of 1983 he has been an assistant in the *Verein für Sozialtherapie bei Kindern und Jugendlichen* in Tübingen, West Germany. He has published several articles about subjects in developmental and educational psychology.

Hanuš Papoušek has been the Chief of the Developmental Psychobiology Unit at the Max Planck Institute for Research in Psychiatry in Munich since 1972. As a research pediatrician at the Government Research Institute for the Care of Mother and Child in Prague from 1951 to 1970, Papoušek devoted much effort to the organization of research on the influence of care-giving upon children's health and development. As a fellow of the World Health Organization he studied the systems of care-giving in day-care facilities in both Western and Eastern Europe. In Prague, he co-organized the National Research Project on Day Care and founded a rooming-in research unit for mothers and infants enabling long-term observations on early mental development and health. His own research interest concerned the early postnatal development of higher mental functions in infants. Papoušek was promoted to Doctor of Sciences, the highest scientific degree in Czechoslovakia, at the Charles University in Prague in 1969. From 1965 to 1966 Professor Papoušek lectured as a visiting professor in developmental psychology at the University of Denver, Colorado, in 1968, 1970, 1971 and 1972 in developmental psychobiology at Harvard University in Cambridge, Massachusetts, and since 1973 at the Munich University. His research in Munich has focused on the interrelations between parenting behaviors and infant integrative capacities, with particular emphasis on the role of intuitive forms of parental didactics.

Mechthild Papoušek has worked as a research psychiatrist at the Developmental Psychobiology Unit of the Max Planck Institute for Research in Psychiatry in Munich since 1976. She was promoted to Doctor of Medicine at the University of Tübingen, where from 1964 to 1966 she carried out research on the Emotional Sequelae of Abortion. In 1974 she finished her specialization in clinical neurology and Psychiatry at the University of Munich. As a fellow of the Foundation's Fund for Research in Psychiatry, she studied the chronobiological aspects of manic-depressive disorders and of the course of sleep at Harvard University from 1971/72. During that time Mechthild Papoušek also participated in the research training program at Harvard Medical School and in studies on the early development of self-awareness at the Center for Cognitive Studies in cooperation with her husband, Hanuš Papoušek. Her present research interests concern the psychobiological aspects of parent-infant interactions, the development of preverbal social communication, and intuitive forms of parenting.

Klaus Schneider, born in 1941, studied psychology at the universities of Mainz, Münster, and Bochum from 1963 to 1967. He received his Ph.D. in 1971 while an assistant at the Ruhr University of Bochum and in 1975 completed two years of postdoctoral study in physiological psychology at the University of California, Los Angeles. After serving as a lecturer in the field of physiological psychology at the University of Oldenburg for one year, he became professor of general experimental psychology at the University of Marburg, where he has been since 1978.

Axel Schölmerich, see Gudrun Gauda et al.

Hans-Georg Voss is professor of psychology at the Institute of Psychology at the Technische Hochschule in Darmstadt, Federal Republic of Germany. His main fields of research are the psychology of motivation and the development of personality in early childhood. After having completed a four-year longitudinal study of the development of exploratory behavior in children from their first through their fourth year of life (his chapters in this volume are based on results of that study), he is now conducting a longitudinal research project on early mother-child relationships, including a comparison of first and second born children within individual families. Among his more recent publications is a volume (coauthored by Heidi Keller) entitled *Curiosity and Exploration: Theories and Results* (New York: Academic Press, 1983).

Joachim F. Wohlwill is professor of human development at Pennsylvania State University. He received his Ph.D. in psychology from the University of California, Berkeley. He previously served on the faculty at Clark University and has been a fellow at the Center for Advanced Study in the Behavioral Sciences and at the Educational Testing Service. He is the author of *The Study of Behavioral Development*. His current interests concern the role of the physical environment in behavioral development, as well as problems of exploration, play, and creativity in children.

Dennis Palmer Wolf received her doctoral degree in education from Harvard University in 1978. She has published extensively in the field of child education and development, focusing particularly on the early use of language and symbol systems. Since 1980 she has been consulting editor for narrative and writing software design at Intentional Educations, Inc., in Cambridge, Massachusetts.

AUTHOR INDEX

A

Abelson, R., 287, 299, *304*
Acker, M., 29, *38*
Adams, J. L., 235, *245*
Ainsworth, M. D. S., 13, *18*, 127, 128, *149*
Alland, A., 314, *323*
Allport, D. A., 308, *323*
Allport, G. W., 127, *149*
Ames, E. W., 47, *57*
Ames, L. B., 17, *18*
Anderson, J. P., 29, *40*
Apfel, N. H., 32, *39*, 45, *57*, 127, *149*, 287, 300, *303*
Ariès, P., 366
Aristotle, 360, 370
Arkin, R. M., 89, *100*
Arlin, P. K., 199, *211*
Arnold, J., 200, *211*
Atkinson, J. W., 25, *38*, 329, 344, *347*, *348*
Auerswald, M., 25, *41*, 48, *58*, 68, *77*, 181, *197*, 201, 207, *211*

B

Baldwin, A. L., 96, *100*
Baldwin, J. D., 44, 48, 51, *56*
Baldwin, J. I., 44, 48, 51, *56*
Balzer, R. H., 199, *211*
Banta, T. J., 140, 141, *149*

Barnett, S. A., 31, 38, *38*, *39*
Barthelmey, E., 181, *197*
Bashford, M. B., 60, *76*
Bates, E., 164, 165, 175, *177*
Bateson, G., 289, 290, *303*, 368
Beckwith, L., 129, *150*
Beebe, B., 237, *245*
Bekoff, M., 217, *243*
Beller, E. K., 268, *278*
Belsky, J., 7, *18*, 45, 49, 50, *56*, 61, *75*, 127, 134, *149*
Benesh-Weiner, M., 93, 94, 96, 99, *103*
Benigni, L., 164, *177*
Benjamin, W., 366, *371*
Bennett, S. L., 237, *245*
Berger, M., 217, *243*
Berlyne, D. E., 5, 8, 9, 10, 11, 13, 14, 15, 17, *18*, 25, 27, 30, 32, 33, 34, 37, *39*, 44, 46, 47, 53, *56*, 60, 61, 62, 64, 65, *75*, 84, 85, 88, 89, 90, *100*, 109, 110, 111, 112, 117, 118, *124*, 127, 129, *149*, 164, 168, *177*, 180, 182, *196*, 199, 210, *211*, 225, *243*, 259, 262, *278*, 306, *323*, 361, 368, 371, *371*
Bernstein, P., 223, *244*
Bertalanffy, L. von, 53, *56*
Bertrand, M., 218, *243*
Bhavnani, R., 18, *19*, 71, *76*, 248, *256*
Birch, D., 25, *38*
Birkhoff, G., 32, *39*

381

SUBJECT INDEX

A

Ability, 333, 343
  attribution, 329
  concept of one's own, 333
Abnormal individuals, 320
Accommodation, 54, 216
Achievement activity, 112
Achievement behavior, 334, 338, 343, 344,
    346, 363
  see also *Goal(s)*
  development, 362
  exploration, and play, relationship, 363
  motivation, 328–330
  motivational goal levels, 344–346
  origins, 341–343
Achievement effects, 96, 99
Achievement-motivated action, 355
  ontogenetic precursors, 364
Achievement motivation, 16, 328, 329, 330,
    344, 363
  ontogenetic course, 334
  theory development, 329
Achievement motive, definition, 342–343
Achievement-oriented behavior, 182
Achievement tasks, 112
Achieving, exploring, and playing, 363
Acoustic parameters, 226, 231
Acoustic stimulus, 220
Act, 54

Act-outcome expectancy, 154
Action(s),
  ambivalent, 275
  child's organization, 337, 338
  concept, 259, 260–262
    developmental process, 261–262, 270
  context, exploration and play, 357
  with continuous effect, 335
  courses of, overt and covert features, 354
  definition, 122, 152
  dialogic, 359
  different structural levels, 273, 274, 278
  directedness, 260
  –effect contingency, 335
  and effect, separation, 335
  effects, 93
  emotional components, 363
  fleeting effects, 367
  frequency, 138
  general plan, 368
  goal-oriented, 336
  homogeneity, 122
  human, 328
  internalized, 338
  levels, exploration, 119, 122, 123
  levels, exploration, synchronization, 119
  morpheme, 355
  nonverbal, 358
  observable, 307
    ecology, 355

I